# Attribution Theory and Research: Conceptual, Developmental and Social Dimensions

*Felix qui potuit rerum cognoscere causas*
Virgil, *Georgics*, II, 490

This is a volume in
EUROPEAN MONOGRAPHS IN SOCIAL PSYCHOLOGY

Series Editor: Henri Tajfel

EUROPEAN MONOGRAPHS IN SOCIAL PSYCHOLOGY 32
Series Editor: HENRI TAJFEL

# Attribution Theory and Research: Conceptual, Developmental and Social Dimensions

Edited by

JOS JASPARS
Department of Experimental Psychology
University of Oxford, UK

FRANK D. FINCHAM
Department of Psychology
University of Illinois, USA

MILES HEWSTONE
Psychologisches Institut
Universität Tübingen, Germany

 1983

Published in cooperation with
EUROPEAN ASSOCIATION OF EXPERIMENTAL
SOCIAL PSYCHOLOGY
by
ACADEMIC PRESS
A Subsidiary of Harcourt Brace Jovanovich, Publishers
London   New York
Paris   San Diego   San Francisco   São Paulo
Sidney   Tokyo   Toronto

ACADEMIC PRESS INC. (LONDON) LTD.
24/28 Oval Road
London NW1 7DX

*United States Edition published by*
ACADEMIC PRESS INC.
111 Fifth Avenue
New York, New York 10003

*British Library Cataloguing in Publication Data*
Attribution theory and research: Conceptual,
developmental and social dimensions.—(European
monographs in social psychology; no. 32)
1. Social problems     2. Attribution (Social
psychology)
I. Jaspars, J.     II. Fincham, F. D.
III. Hewstone, M.     IV. Series
362'.0425'019     HM132

ISBN 0–12–380980–0

Typeset by Deltatype, Ellesmere Port, UK
Printed in Great Britain by T. J. Press (Padstow) Ltd., Cornwall, UK

H. TAJFEL
Differentiation between Social Groups: Studies in the Social
  Psychology of Intergroup Relations, 1978

M. BILLIG
Fascists: A Social Psychological View of the National Front, 1979

C. P. WILSON
Jokes: Form, Content, Use and Function, 1979

J. P. FORGAS
Social Episodes: The Study of Interaction Routines, 1979

R. A. HINDE
Towards Understanding Relationships, 1979

A-N. PERRET-CLERMONT
Social Interaction and Cognitive Development in Children, 1980

B. A. GEBER and S. P. NEWMAN
Soweto's Children: The Development of Attitudes, 1980

S. H. NG
The Social Psychology of Power, 1980

P. SCHÖNBACH, P. GOLLWITZER, G. STIEPEL and U. WAGNER
Education and Intergroup Attitudes, 1981

C. ANTAKI
The Psychology of Ordinary Explanations of Social Behaviour, 1981

W. P. ROBINSON
Communication in Development, 1981

H. BRANDSTÄTTER, J. H. DAVIS and G. STOCKER-KREICHGAUER
Group Decision Making, 1982

J. P. FORGAS
Social Cognition: Perspectives on Everyday Understanding, 1981

H. T. HIMMELWEIT, P. HUMPHREYS, M. JAEGER and M. KATZ
How Voters Decide: A Longitudinal Study of Political Attitudes extending over
  Fifteen Years, 1981

P. STRINGER
Confronting Social Issues: Applications of Social Psychology, Vol. 1, 1982

P. STRINGER
Confronting Social Issues: Applications of Social Psychology, Vol. 2, 1982

M. VON CRANACH with URS KALBERMATTEN, KATRIN INDERMÜHLE and
BEAT GUGLER
Goal-directed Action, 1982

G. MUGNY
The Power of Minorities, 1982

*In Preparation*
G. R. SEMIN and A. S. R. MANSTEAD
The Accountability of Conduct: A Social Psychological Analysis

PER HELMERSEN
Family Interaction and Communication in Psychopathology: An Evaluation of
  Recent Perspectives

# List of Contributors

ICEK AJZEN: *Department of Psychology, University of Massachusetts, Amherst, Massachusetts 01002, USA*

JEAN-CLAUDE DESCHAMPS: *Département des Sciences Sociales et Politiques, Université de Lausanne, Avenue Vinet 19, Lausanne, Switzerland*

J. RICHARD EISER: *Department of Psychology, University of Exeter, Washington Singer Laboratories, Exeter EX4 4QG, UK*

FRANK D. FINCHAM: *Department of Psychology, University of Illinois at Urbana-Champaign, 603 East Daniel, Champaign, Illinois 61820, USA*

MARTIN FISHBEIN: *Department of Psychology, University of Illinois at Urbana-Champaign, 603 East Daniel, Champaign, Illinois 61820, USA*

ADRIAN FURNHAM: *Department of Psychology, University College, London, Gower Street, London WC1E 6BT, UK*

MILES HEWSTONE: *Psychologisches Institut, Universität Tübingen, Friedrichstrasse 21, 7400 Tübingen 1, Germany*

JOS JASPARS: *Department of Experimental Psychology, University of Oxford, South Parks Road, Oxford OX1 3UD, UK*

HAROLD H. KELLEY: *Department of Psychology, University of California, Los Angeles, California 90024, USA*

MANSUR LALLJEE: *Department of Experimental Psychology, University of Oxford, South Parks Road, Oxford OX1 3UD, UK*

SALLY LLOYD-BOSTOCK: *Centre for Socio-Legal Studies, Wolfson College, University of Oxford, Oxford OX1 3UD, UK*

ELFRIEDE LÖCHEL: *c/o Department of Experimental Psychology, University of Oxford, South Parks Road, Oxford, OX1 3UD, UK*

THOMAS C. MONSON: *Department of Psychology, Room 313, Life Science Building, The University of Texas at Arlington, Texas 75019, USA*

MICHAEL SCHLEIFER: *Département de Psychologie, Université du Québec à Montréal, CP 8888 succursale 'A', Montréal, Québec, Canada H3C 3P8*

THOMAS R. SHULTZ: *Department of Psychology, McGill University, 1205 McGregor Avenue, Montreal, Quebec H3A 181, Canada*

MARGARET WATSON: *King's College Hospital, Medical School, University of London, Denmark Hill, London SE5 8RX, UK*

PETER WHITE: *Department of Psychology, University of Auckland, Private Bag, Auckland, New Zealand*

# Preface

About three to four years ago the editors of the present volume met at the University of Oxford; one of them (Jos Jaspars) as a continental academic in exile, looking for a more favourable research climate and the other two as research students, looking for problems worthy of doctoral research in social psychology. They brought together three diverse interests which have shaped the contents of this book. Frank Fincham had already worked in developmental psychology, but becoming interested in problems of social cognition joined forces with Jos Jaspars; this led to their first research on the developmental nature of Heider's theory of responsibility attribution. A few months later Miles Hewstone imported an interest in language and intergroup relations from Bristol University; this was the beginning of the research on the social dimensions of attribution theory.

For once this 'ménage a trois' appeared to work. Not only because it was productive and led to a fair number of publications on attribution of responsibility and social attribution, but also because we discovered quite rapidly that others in Oxford had long-standing interests in problems addressed by attribution researchers. Mansur Lalljee had for some time been emphasising the importance of non-causal explanations in everyday life and Sally Lloyd-Bostock, as a member of the Centre for Socio-Legal studies, had pointed out the similarities and differences between legal and social psychological notions of causal and responsibility attribution.

At that stage we were very fortunate to have two visitors in the Department of Experimental Psychology with an interest in developmental and conceptual aspects of attribution theory: Thomas Shultz from McGill University and Elfriede Löchel from the University of Heidelberg. Both developed interests along the lines initiated by researchers already present in the Department and from then on ideas and experiments began to emerge from the group, which had apparently reached a 'critical mass'. Others in the social psychology section of the Department, whose main interests lay elswhere in the discipline, began to discover similarities between their own work and ours and have increased the cross-fertilisation of ideas. This resulted in contributions from Adrian Furnham on the personality aspects of attribution theory.

Of course, we were aware of the fact that attribution theory had generated a vast amount of research, mainly in the United States. The contributions in this volume by Ajzen and Fishbein, Eiser, Deschamps, Monson and, last but not least, Kelley are in a way a tribute to their work (whether in America or Europe) which has inspired us in our research to a large extent, even though we may not agree with every single point they make. With so much research already conducted in a particular field it is important to consider whether it is possible to advance knowledge in a substantial way. We do believe that there is indeed scope for further development in attribution theory, notwith-standing a considerable amount of criticism of the theory in recent years. We do not share the view that attribution theory cannot deal satisfactorily with common sense explanations in everyday life, because it has so far emphasised the study of causal attributions in highly restricted situations. Rather than throwing the baby out with the bath water, we have attempted to develop various aspects of attribution theory which until now had received little attention. In the present volume we have only concerned ourselves with some of these issues, for practical reasons, but all of them are problems which we believe are central to a healthy expansion of the theory and our understanding of common sense explanations.

It is for this reason that we have underlined conceptual issues in the first part of the book. Jaspars, Hewstone and Fincham discuss three basic issues in the first chapter, by considering the nature of common sense notions of causality, the social nature of attributions and the problem of the relationship between attributions and behaviour. The chapter also serves as an introduction to the book by providing a frame of reference in which most of the other contributions fit. Some of the conceptual problems discussed in the first chapter are dealt with at greater length in other chapters of the first part of the book. Shultz and Schleifer discuss the vicissitudes and complexities of various forms of attribution and present a 'pre-supposition' model indicating how attributions of cause and responsibility and, in turn, sanctions are related. Ajzen and Fishbein consider the importance of cognitive heuristics such as relevance and availability for the attribution process, thereby echoing the point made by Jaspars, Hewstone and Fincham, that we do not know nearly enough about the cognitive (encoding) processes involved in making causal attributions. Eiser also relates attribution processes to other aspects of social cognition, arguing that processes of social cognition and perception are primarily concerned with categorisation and perception and only secondarily with causal explanations. It seems to us that Eiser's point is well-taken and is especially important for the relationship of attributions to behaviour and for studying functional aspects of causal attributions, problems which are addressed in the last part of the first chapter and which occupy a great deal of our research effort at present.

The remaining parts of the book deal with three broad categories of determinants of attribution processes. Their importance has been recognised in the literature and is stressed in the first chapter. We have attempted to bring together some of the relevant literature and we have presented some of the research conducted at Oxford. Fincham presents a comprehensive review of developmental work in attribution and a review of his own studies on age differences in the attribution of causality and responsibility, Lalljee, Watson and White show how different types of events elicit different types of explanations (causal and non-causal) in children, and Elfriede Löchel presents evidence for sex differences in attribution at the very young age of four years.

The third section of the book starts with a chapter by Deschamps, who was one of the first to call attention to the social and especially the intergroup aspects of attribution theory, a theme which has been developed since by Hewstone. In the present volume, however, Hewstone has only focused on the role of language, as one of the social aspects of attribution which deserves attention. The work of Sally Lloyd-Bostock has already been mentioned; it illustrates a particular social dimension of attribution processes by relating research in social psychology to legal literature on jurisprudence.

In the final part of the book the implications of the person-situation debate, which has dominated personality research for the last 20 years, are taken up by Monson and Furnham, Jaspars and Fincham, It seemed odd to us at the time that two research traditions, attribution theory and the interactionist approach to the study of individual differences, which seemed to be concerned with very similar problems and which arrived at different conclusions were never directly related to each other. These last two chapters form an attempt to make such a comparison possible.

After all of this work was done we were of course curious to see whether the contributions presented in this volume would indeed offer some new perspectives in attribution research. Harold Kelley has graciously consented to write an epilogue to the present volume. It has become an epilogue in the true sense of the word, because it is not so much a direct commentary upon the contents of the book, as a further development of a latent theme which is present in several of the chapters: the importance of causal structures for understanding attribution processes.

In editing this book we owe a great deal to many people. Intellectually, we owe perhaps most to Heider's pioneering work on common sense psychology and Kelley's attributional elaboration of Heider's naive analysis of action. Heider also represents for us the combination of European and American traditions in the study of social behaviour, in a manner which we believe to be the most fruitful in contemporary social psychology. We also owe a great deal to the Department of Experimental Psychology at the University of Oxford and especially to all the members of the social psychology group who have shown a lively and critical interest in our work on common sense. If anyone should be mentioned specifically it has to be Michael Argyle who, through his own energetic and cheerful approach, has provided us with a stimulating work environment. Finally we wish to express our appreciation for the secretarial help received from the Department, in particular from Valerie Wills, and our gratitude to Henri Tajfel whose untimely death has deprived contemporary social psychology of one of its greatest contributors.

*January, 1983*                                        JOS JASPARS
                                                       FRANK D. FINCHAM
                                                       MILES HEWSTONE

# Contents

# Part I

# Theoretical and Conceptual Issues

# 1

# Attribution Theory and Research: The State of the Art

## Jos Jaspars, Miles Hewstone and Frank D. Fincham

## Introduction

Attribution theory has come to dominate research in social psychology. Since the earliest theoretical writings of Heider (1944, 1958a), Kelley (1967) and Jones (Jones and Davis, 1965) an enormous number of studies has been devoted to 'causal explanations given for events by ordinary people' (Kelley and Michela, 1980, p. 460). There is no need to review this prolific research activity during the past ten years, because this has been done quite recently in various publications (Fincham and Jaspars, 1980; Harvey, Ickes and Kidd, 1976, 1978; Kelley and Michela, 1980). However, a critical appraisal of some of the central theoretical notions and the available empirical evidence seems useful in the light of recent criticisms of attribution research (Ajzen and Fishbein, 1975; Anderson, 1978; Brewer, 1977; Buss, 1978; Hamilton, 1978; Kruglanski, 1975). Some of these issues will be discussed in other chapters of this volume, together with the results of empirical research conducted by the contributors. We will therefore consider some general, but funda-mental, issues concerning attribution theory and refer to other chapters for a more detailed discussion of specific questions.

In the first part of this chapter we will discuss the nature of attributions and explanations in common sense. In the second part we will investi-gate some determinants of attributions and explanations, in particular the social dimension of explanations. In the last part we will devote some attention to the consequences of attributions; this will focus on important, but unanswered, questions such as the relation between attributions and behaviour, and the accuracy of attributions. Finally, the present chapter will discuss some of the most promising possibilities for the application of attribution theory.

3

## The nature of attributions and explanations in common sense

Explaining an event constitutes an answer to the question of *why* the event happened. One way of explaining an event is by stating what caused the event. If science is the 'institutionalized art of inquiry' (Nagel, 1961, p. vii), attribution theory, in the widest sense of the term, apparently deals with the non-institutionalised or common sense way of answering 'why' questions. There are, to be sure, considerable and obvious differences between scientific inquiry and common sense explanations, which have been spelled out by philosophers of science (see Nagel, 1961, Chapter 1). However, the similarities between the scientist and the layman are apparently sufficient for attribution researchers to believe that modern methods of scientific inquiry can be used as a model for understanding explanations in everyday life. The work of H. H. Kelley (1967), G. A. Kelly (1955) and Heider (1958a) is explicitly based on this model of man-the-scientist. Viewed from an historical perspective, this is a curious inversion, because contemporary scientific inquiry has only gradually emerged from common sense during the last twenty-five centuries. In the past, ever since Aristotle's posterior analytics, the principles of valid inference have often been confounded with the psychology of reasoning. It took until the second half of the 19th century before the two were clearly separated in the history of logic (Kneale and Kneale, 1962, p. 738).

The first question to ask then is whether methods or techniques of scientific analysis, which have only recently been developed as prescriptive methods of inference, are likely to be plausible descriptive models of common sense explanations. Perhaps students of attribution processes should have paid more attention to the fate of Bayes' theorem as a descriptive model of human decision making and information processing, before putting all their attributional eggs into one explanatory basket. As Slovic, Fischoff and Lichtenstein (1977) recently concluded, until 1970 people merely appeared to be poor Bayesians, but since then it has seemed more likely that they were not Bayesians at all.

In attribution research the problem may be even more complicated. Notwithstanding the claim that attribution theory is interested in causal explanations given for events by ordinary people, many attribution studies do not deal at all with explanations, let alone with causal inferences, in common sense. In research concerned with the attribution of responsibility (Fincham and Jaspars, 1980) one is not dealing with individual, cognitive inference processes aimed at the explanation of the effects of another person's behaviour, but with a social act on the part of the attributor who demands that actors answer for their acts or the outcomes of their acts (see also Lloyd-Bostock, chapter 10). This use of the term attribution makes at least as much sense as the meaning which is ordinarily given to the word in attribution research, i.e. to ascribe, impute or refer an event, as an effect to a cause, since the original meaning of the concept does not refer to a mental act, but to such external acts as assigning, giving or paying (Latin: *ad-tribuere*). Ascribing or assigning an effect to a cause appears to be a metaphorical use of the original expression which can be considered as *one* form of explanation.

This short etymological excursion also indicates that we should be careful not to consider predictions as forward causal inferences by attributing a cause to an effect (as has sometimes been suggested; Ajzen and Fishbein, 1975; Anderson, 1974).

Another problem which is raised by the causal interpretation of attribution is that we are sometimes considering *unknown* causes to which an effect is attributed; it is a moot question whether such attributions can be regarded as explanations. Hence, attributing responsibility for an outcome to a person's actions or attributing a person's behaviour to something in the person do not seem to deserve the same theoretical status in attribution theory.

The second point to be made is that even if the meaning of attribution is confined to the imputation of unknown causes, or the assignment of an effect to another known event which is perceived or interpreted as the cause, asking 'why' questions may lead to a variety of responses, all of which might be considered as genuine explanations without necessarily being causal attributions (Kruglanski, 1979; Lalljee, 1981). Several authors have recently argued that explanations might differ in ways similar to scientific explanations, emphasising especially the distinction between causes and reasons (Buss, 1978, 1979; Harvey and Tucker, 1979; Kruglanski, 1979; Lalljee, 1981). Other distinctions could of course be made. Hart and Honoré (1959) distinguish between causes, reasons and opportunities, while other writers have seen behaviour as rule-governed (Argyle, Furnham and Graham, 1981; Harré, 1977), or to be explained genetically in Nagel's sense (Nagel, 1961). In short, philosophy of science suggests a variety of types of explanations most of which have so far not been considered seriously in attribution theory. Rather than attempt to develop here an exhaustive common sense philosophy of science or lay epistemology (Kruglanski, 1979) we want to stress the usefulness of the distinctions which have been made by legal philosophers like Hart and Honoré, because it has been argued that the notion of causation used in the law

is rooted in common sense. Hart and Honoré point out that philosophical notions of causation have always seemed irrelevant to the
lawyer and historian, because they are primarily concerned with causal
statements about particulars, whereas science and philosophy deal
with connections between types of events which can be formulated as
laws or generalisations. In the philosophical tradition of Hume and
Mill every singular statement is seen as an instance of one or more
general propositions asserting an invariable sequence. This implies
however that a major difficulty arises when generalisations are used to
identify the cause of a particular event on a particular occasion. How
does one distinguish between something which can be said to be the
cause and something which is only its occasion', 'a mere condition'
or 'part of the circumstances'? Normally one does not consider the
presence of oxygen as the cause of a fire, whereas the dropping of a
lighted cigarette would be considered as a cause in common sense
thinking.

Another major difficulty in applying the scientific notion of causality
to ordinary life is that there appear to be, both within the law and in
common sense, rational limits to the pursuit of causal connexions,
backwards and forwards in time (Hart and Honoré, 1959, p. 12). To
cite just one example: 'if a man has been shot it would usually be stupid
or inappropriate, though not false, to give as the cause of his death the
fact that his blood cells were deprived of oxygen, and equally
inappropriate to give the manufacturer's action in selling the gun to his
father from whom he had inherited it' (1959, p. 11). In summary, Hart
and Honoré argue that in common sense a cause is perceived as an
abnormal condition, a condition which makes the difference because it
is not present as part of the usual state or mode of operation of a thing,
but interferes with or intervenes in the normal course of events. A
voluntary human action intended to bring about what in fact happens,
and in the manner in which it happens, appears to be the prototype of
such an abnormal condition. It occupies a special place in causal
inquiries because it is seen as a primary or ultimate cause through
which we do not trace back the cause of a later event and to which we do
trace the cause though intermediate causes of different kinds. The
central notion of causality is however distinguished from cases where
one person causes another person to act by providing him or her with a
*reason* or *opportunity* for acting.

The first of the latter two cases is distinguished from a causal
relationship in the strict sense by the following features: (1) The second
person knows and understands the significance of what the first actor
has said and done, (2) The first actor's words and deeds are a part of the
second actor's reasons for acting, (3) The second actor forms the

intention to perform the action only after the first actor's intervention, and (4) Except in the case when the first actor has merely advised the second actor in question, he intends the second actor to do the act. Providing another person with an opportunity for acting is distinguished from causal relationships by the following two essential features according to Hart and Honoré: (1) Providing or failing to provide another with an opportunity to act must be a deviation from a standard practice or procedure, (2) The arguments on which statements of this kind rely are mainly hypothetical, showing what could have happened had the opportunity (not) been provided.

The distinctions made here are not incompatible with those made by attribution theorists in social psychology. The separation of voluntary human actions from other normal conditions is comparable to the distinction made between person and situation explanations in attribution theory. However, the addition of reasons and opportunities provided by other persons adds to situational explanations a new dimension, by differentiating the nature of environmental influences which can be personal or non-personal, where the latter can be separated into causal and non-causal influences. Moreover, it is also obvious that we can differentiate person explanations, since not all human actions will be perceived as voluntary; a distinction similar to the one suggested by Heider, between personal and impersonal causality, seems to be implied by Hart and Honoré.

COMMON SENSE NOTIONS OF CAUSALITY

The essence of this argument is that the common sense notion advanced by Hart and Honoré is different from the notion utilised in attribution theory. The crucial difference appears to be the productive, generative relationship between the antecedent condition and the subsequent effect, which is lacking in the notion of covariation. As originally conceived by J. S. Mill, and later used by Kelley (1967), covariation implies that a cause is 'that condition which is present when the effect is present and which is absent when the effect is absent' (Kelly and Michela, 1980, p. 462). The issue is important because it is not clear at the moment which of these notions of causality is entertained in common sense explanations. Kelley and Michela (1980) treat these notions on an equal footing by considering not only consistency, consensus and distinctiveness as antecedents of causal attributions, but also such factors as similarity, continuity in time and space, salience and primacy. Kelley and Michela argue that the link between information and causal attribution possibly involves a variety of psychological processes. At one extreme they see time-consuming processes of logical analysis such as covariation determining causal attribution; at the other extreme they consider processes of immediate perception which rely heavily on the earliest and most salient information. Quite recently, Kelley (1980a) has even put forward the general idea that children and adults may differ in this respect when making causal attributions.

The problem may however be more complicated than is suggested by Kelley and Michela. It may be that covariation information affects causal attribution only when certain other, more basic, conditions are met. Considering, for example, the conditions discovered by Michotte (1963) for the perception of causality – permanence of cause and effect and kinematic integration (together called ampliation by Michotte) – one wonders to what extent covariation information can override the effect of these conditions when they are not met. Thus, if the precise kinematic integration in Michotte's experiments is not achieved, because temporal and spatial contiguity is 'wrong', would repetition of the sequential motions of two 'objects' lead to a causal attribution to the first moving object: if almost any second object would move subsequently; the same second object would move all the time; but only when the same first object was present? This seems unlikely since Michotte has already shown that variations other than the crucial ones do not seem to affect perceivers' impressions very much. One could of course argue that we should not look for covariation of structural characteristics of the two objects in Michotte's experiment, but for covariation of the movements of the objects. But even if covariation is interpreted in this way it seems unlikely that repetition of the sequential events is going to affect the impression of causal relationship.

It is quite possible, though, that the conditions found by Michotte are only relevant when one is concerned with the more immediate perception of causality and not when time-consuming reasoning processes are involved. In order to test this hypothesis one could extend the notion of kinematic integration to social stimuli and contrast covariation information with it. Although this has not been done to the authors' knowledge, the idea is not inconceivable. Michotte's concept of causality is in fact a dynamic Gestalt principle. One social interpretation of this principle would be that an effect should be commensurate with its cause. Similarity of cause and effect, which has been mentioned as an information processing rule for attributing causes, could be considered as a special case of social ampliation and some results have been reported which confirm its importance (McCauley and Jacques, 1979; Shultz and Ravinsky, 1977). It should be noted that the importance of similarity between cause and effect was pointed out a long time ago by Duncker, Fauconnet, Huang and Heider (see Heider, 1944). According to Heider, the attribution of a change to an origin is a special case of cognitive or perceptual unit formation. Actor and act, act and outcome are integrated as cause and effect units on the basis of the same Gestalt factors which lead to figural unit formation in perception.

We propose that such factors may have played an implicit role in most covariation studies, in the sense that behaviour which is described in vignettes is always commensurate with the stimulus that gives rise to it. If one were to violate this principle it is unlikely that an observer would make attributions based on covariation. Perhaps such a Gestalt factor can be seen as a basic causal schema, affecting the impact of observed covariation in the same way as prior beliefs and expectations based on real world knowledge. In motion perception the perceptual system is adapted to what is ecologically given and mechanically possible. When new information is in conflict with what is possible or what ordinarily happens, as in Michotte's negative and paradoxical cases, the impression of causality does not arise.

Thus far we have argued that not all attributions can be considered as common sense explanations. In fact, it would make sense to regard attributions first of all as social acts, which imply an explanation and are entailed by it, but to acknowledge that such an explanation is not necessarily a casual inference. Other types of explanations for behaviour or outcomes of behaviour do occur in science and in common sense and should be part of a general theory of explanations. These two points are taken up in several chapters of this book (Shultz and Schleifer, chapter 2; Lalljee, Watson and White, chapter 6; Lloyd-Bostock, chapter 10) and will not be discussed further at this stage.

It has already been noted that, even when we restrict attribution theory to the making of causal inferences in common sense, different notions of causality may be involved. According to Kelley's ANOVA model, a cause is 'a condition which is present when the effect is present and absent when the effect is absent' (Kelley, 1967, p. 154). The second common sense notion of causality, discussed above, is the one given by Hart and Honoré, who regard a cause as a metaphorical human voluntary action which produces or brings about a change in the environment, or to put it differently, an abnormal condition which makes the difference. Both notions of common sense causality have their parallels in philosophy where, as Shultz has recently argued, they contribute the major division between the regularity and the generative theory of causality. Shultz has also conducted a number of interesting studies in which he has constrasted these two conceptions of causality in children and has shown that physical causation is primarily interpreted in terms of the concept of generative transmission. In addition to these two major positions, we have distinguished the Gestalt view of phenomenal causality as developed by Michotte and Heider. According to this perspective, a cause is a preceding event which forms a (dynamic) Gestalt with the effect.

Although this chapter is restricted to a critical examination of the covariation notion of causal attribution, since it is this concept of common sense causality which has played a dominant role in the attribution research so far, it should be clear by now that other notions of common sense causality and explanations in everyday life also merit attention in the future.

## THE INCOMPLETE DESIGN OF ATTRIBUTION STUDIES

In most attribution studies, aimed at testing Kelley's ANOVA model, subjects are presented with a short description of some response by another person and a few statements representing a combination of consensus, consistency and distinctiveness information regarding that response (e.g. McArthur, 1972). The additional information is, however, incomplete in most experiments if one regards Kelley's original 'cube' as the design which underlies the subject's implicit ANOVA. Normally, the subject is told only how the actor has behaved in the past with respect to the same entity, how others react to the same entity in the present and how the actor reacts to other similar entities. In terms of the ANOVA cube this means that the subject is only given one row, one column and one 'beam' of the total cube. If we were to take seriously the suggestion that subjects actually carry out an intuitive analysis of variance in order to make a causal attribution, this limited amount of information would surely cause serious problems. It represents an incomplete, fractional replication design in which the independent variables are not orthogonal. Even an explicit analysis of variance with the aid of a computer programme would not be easy and, in general, even impossible when the information is coded in the way suggested below.

A particular vignette or set of information might be represented as illustrated in Table I. If the information is coded in this way an analysis of variance would indeed be impossible because one cannot obtain the inverse of the matrix of the independent variables and their interactions. Of course, no one ever believed that subjects would actually calculate sums of squares or anything like that in

TABLE I   Suggested attributional coding of vignettes

---

1. John (P) laughs (B, C) at the comedian (S)
2. Almost everyone (P̄) who hears the comedian (S) laughs (B, C) at him
3. John (P) does not laugh (B̄, C) at almost any other comedian (S̄)
4. In the past (C̄) John (P) has almost always laughed (B) at the same comedian (S)
   Thus a formal representation of this vignette becomes:
1. (S, P, C) (B)
2. (S, P̄, C) (B)
3. (S̄, P, C) (B̄)
4. (S, P, C̄) (B)
Where  P, P̄ Indicates the presence or absence of the actor: John
       S, S̄ Indicates the presence or absence of the stimulus: The comedian
       C, C Indicates whether the behaviour occurs in the present (C) or
       in the past (C̄)
       B, B Whether the behaviour occurs (B) or does not occur (B̄) in the particular
       line of the vignette

---

order to make causal attributions on the basis of information of this kind, but that still leaves us with the problem that we do not have a precise model of the causal inference process which characterises the subject in an attribution experiment of this kind.

One possibility for a more precise model is a fairly literal interpretation of the notion of causality suggested by Kelley as the basis for the attribution process. This proposes that the subject, after having coded the information in the way suggested above, processes the information by considering for each of the conditions (person, entity, circumstance) whether it is present when the effect (behaviour) is present and absent when the effect is absent in the vignettes. In this way the subject might determine which condition is necessary and sufficient for the behaviour to occur in the story. Table II presents the eight possible combinations of information for vignettes like McArthur has used and the inferences which can be drawn according to the logical model suggested above.

As can be seen in Table II each of the informational configurations shows a one-to-one correspondence with eight possible attributions if we take into account all possible interactions of person, stimulus and circumstances and allow for a no response category. Although this model appears true to the original idea of Kelley's attribution theory, it is surprising that the theory has never been formalised or tested in this particular way. In fact, most studies have tested for main effects of consistency, consensus and distinctiveness, although it is very clear from Kelley's writings (Kelley, 1967, 1973) that the theory does not

TABLE II   Formalisation of McArthur's vignettes and predictions according to the logical model of causal attributions

| Vignettes | | Information combinations | | | | | | | |
|---|---|---|---|---|---|---|---|---|---|
| | | Cs D̄Cy | Cs D Cy | C̄s D̄ Cy | Cs D̄ C̄y | C̄s D Cy | Cs D C̄y | C̄s D̄C̄y | C̄s D C̄y |
| | s p c | B | B | B | B | B | B | B | B |
| | s p c̄ | B | B | B | B̄ | B | B̄ | B̄ | B̄ |
| | s p̄ c | B | B | B̄ | B | B̄ | B | B̄ | B̄ |
| | s̄ p c | B | B̄ | B | B | B̄ | B̄ | B | B̄ |
| Conditions | s | Su | [Su N] | | | N | N | | N |
| for | p | Su | | [Su N] | | N | | N | N |
| occurrence | c | Su | | | [Su N] | | N | N | N |
| of | sp | Su | Su | Su | | [Su N] | | | N |
| behaviour | sc | Su | Su | | Su | | [Su N] | | N |
| in | pc | Su | | Su | Su | | | [Su N] | N |
| vignette | spc | Su | Su | Su | Su | Su | Su | Su | [Su N] |
| Logical attribution | | ø | s | p | c | sp | sc | pc | spc |
| Kelley's prediction | | ps | s | p | psc | psc | sc | pc | c |

Where: Cs, consensus; D, distinctiveness; Cy, consistency; s, stimulus; p, person; c, circumstances; Su, sufficient condition; N, necessary condition; ø, no prediction possible. Bars (e.g. s̄, p̄, c̄) indicate the absence of a factor.

A causal inference can be made in each case by establishing whether a particular factor (s, p, c, sp, etc.) is a necessary and a sufficient condition for the occurrence of the behaviour in the vignette. If the behaviour occurs when a particular factor is present, the factor is a sufficient condition. If the behaviour does not occur when the factor is absent, the factor is coded as a necessary condition. If the behaviour occurs if and only if the factor is present the factor is both a necessary and sufficient condition for the behaviour to occur and hence a causal attribution is made to that factor. These conditions are indicated in brackets in the second part of the table.

predict any main effects of the three informational variables, but only effects of particular combinations of consistency, consensus and distinctiveness. The formal model of the theory presented in Table II reaffirms this emphasis, while other researchers have rarely made configurational predictions. To the extent that such predictions are made, they do not appear to accord with the predictions which we have derived from the original formulation of Kelley's statement about causality. In the study by Orvis, Cunningham and Kelley (1975) it is suggested that the information patterns for stimulus, person and circumstances attribution have a prototypical quality and that the subject, in making attributions, is influenced by the expectations expressed in these standard patterns. The predictions which follow from this model have been included in Table II; in four cases they are different from the predictions which follow from our own logical model.

Although the two models predict attributions to the main independent factors of person, stimulus and circumstances and to combinations of these factors, many attribution studies have not allowed for interactional explanations, or at least they have not given such explanations an equal chance as compared with main effect explanations. In McArthur's study, for example, the four interactive response alternatives are combined in one answer which asks for an attribution to some combination of the first three response alternatives. A proper test of Kelley's original idea should have allowed for all possible explanations, including the alternative of no explanation for the high consensus, high consistency and low distinctiveness condition. This information condition is in fact a very important one, because it is logically impossible to make a valid inductive inference when the event occurs universally within the domain of the information presented.

Because subjects are not allowed to refrain from making a causal attribution we cannot be sure that their responses to the universal information condition are a refutation of an inductive logic model. However, if subjects were to refuse to give an explanation in this condition, in a properly designed experiment, one would have to conclude that a strict application of an inference model could not explain all the responses. One possibility is, of course, that subjects may not code the information in the manner suggested. It may be that the missing information is completed on the basis of prior knowledge of the real world, thus rendering an attribution possible. The other possibility is that people do not make inductive inferences at all but operate in a deductive fashion as hypothesis testers (see Lalljee, 1981). This would seem to be a particularly interesting possibility in the case of the high consensus, high consistency and low distinctiveness condition, because such an event would require a universal law in order to explain that it occurs for everyone, all the time and under all circumstances. If all apples fall from all the trees, under all circumstances, no matter what the initial stimulus is, one has to move out of the world of empirical observations and into the realm of the imagination to find an explanation. It is highly unlikely that subjects in attribution experiments would, as a matter of course, have the imagination to derive their hypotheses from such general laws; after all, it took quite a while before someone discovered why apples always fall downwards! Nonetheless, it has been shown that subjects explain some general events as 'typical of our times' or our 'Western culture'. King (B. Jaspars, J. Jaspars, King, Pendleton and Rowe, 1981) has, for example, collected information on patients' explanations of their own illnesses and discovered that one dominant explanation for such general diseases as heart conditions and high blood pressure is typically of this kind.

Although it is impossible to test the suggested inductive logic model precisely, when the response format used is not compatible with the predictions which follow from the theory, one can nevertheless investigate the correspondence between published data and the predictions, in those cases where the model can be tested. Table III reproduces the results obtained by McArthur, as reconstructed from the figures published in her 1972 paper and her thesis.

TABLE III   Causal attributions for eight information combinations. (Data from McArthur, 1972)

| Causal locus | Information combinations | | | | | | | |
|---|---|---|---|---|---|---|---|---|
| | $C_s \bar{D} C_y$ | $C_s D C_y$ | $\bar{C}_s \bar{D} C_y$ | $C_s \bar{D} \bar{C}_y$ | $\bar{C}_s D C_y$ | $C_s D \bar{C}_y$ | $\bar{C}_s \bar{D} \bar{C}_y$ | $\bar{C}_s D \bar{C}_y$ |
| Stimulus | 1 | [62] | 1 | 7 | 18 | 11 | 1 | 4 |
| Person | 46 | 11 | [82] | 17 | 27 | 9 | 33 | 4 |
| Circumstance | 4 | 4 | 0 | [33] | 4 | 43 | 24 | 73 |
| Person × Circumstance | 36 | 18 | 9 | 6 | [36] | 4 | 2 | 0 |
| Rest | 13 | 5 | 8 | 37 | 15 | [33] | [40] | [19] |

Brackets indicate the predicted causal locus. McArthur did not publish separate results for interactive causal loci except for person × stimulus interactions. Cell values are estimated percentages.

As can be seen in Table III, there is *prima facie* good evidence for an inductive logic model of the attributions made in her experiment. The cell values in each column are always high where the model predicts the attributions, except for the columns where p × s × c explanations are predicted (see Table III). The latter result may be another artifact induced by the response language used (see Hewstone, chapter 9). An expression like 'the particular circumstances' might refer to either the situation at the moment (apart from the stimulus) or to the combination of person, situation and stimulus. A replication of the McArthur experiment, in which all response alternatives were given explicitly, found a much less pronounced effect of this kind; the p × s × c attributions were highest in the last column (Hilton, Jaspars, Lalljee, Lamb and Smith, 1981). In another experiment, in which the subjects were only asked to say 'why' a certain event had happened, the effect was even weaker (Hilton *et al.*, 1981). It should also be noted that, apart from the circumstance explanations, the logical model fits the data better than the model suggested by Orvis *et al.* (1975). This conclusion is confirmed in a number of other experiments (Hewstone, 1981; Hilton *et al.*, 1981).

The results obtained by McArthur clearly indicate interactional effects of consistency, consensus and distinctiveness for each of the attributions made, as is suggested by the theory. It is therefore curious to find that McArthur reports only main effects of these information variables in the summary table of her study (McArthur, 1972, p. 182), although in the text she discusses interactions which somewhat qualify these effects. If our interpretation of Kelley's attribution model is correct, there should not have been any main effects, because the model predicts, for all attributions, an effect which results from particular combinations of consistency, consensus and distinctiveness. Nevertheless, a large number of studies have been devoted to the study of consistency, consensus and distinctiveness as important informational variables in their own right and, adding empirical insult to theoretical injury, have reported a good many positive findings (Kelley and Michela, 1980). Such findings must mean that either the original model is not correct or that the use of analysis of variance in analysing the results of such studies is not appropriate. The latter explanation appears to be more likely, although it is ironic, to say the least, that those who propose a particular statistical technique as a model for common sense causal attributions do not seem to understand the technique itself. The crucial issue is that interaction terms in the standard analysis of variance are defined in a way that is not compatible with the notion of interaction implied by the theory. This can easily be seen when one obtains the sources of variation in a factorial experiment by using techniques of polynomial regression. The independent variables are then defined by contrasting the two levels of each variable as $+1$ and $-1$, interaction terms being defined as the product terms of the main variables. The implication of this procedure is that traditional ANOVA assumes the combined effect of two or more variables at the same level to be the same. In an attributional study this would mean, for example, that one expects the effect of the presence of consistency *and* consensus to be the same as the combined effect of inconsistency and lack of consensus. But this is clearly not what the theory predicts. The theory states that particular patterns of inform-

ation produce specific effects and hence it would be more appropriate
to define the interaction terms in advance, in accordance with the
theoretical notions. Pursuing this path, the interaction terms become
correlated with the main effect variables and with each other, but it is
still possible to analyse the results by linear regression methods. Such
an analysis has been conducted in a replication study of McArthur
(Hilton *et al.*, 1981). It shows that most of the variance is indeed taken
up by interaction effects, as the theory predicts.

PERSONAL AND SITUATIONAL CAUSALITY

Considering again the matrix presented in Table I, one might wonder
whether subjects always use the notion of causality suggested by Kelley
in its complete form. It is not impossible that subjects might give more
weight to the presence of a condition than to the absence of a condition,
or *vice versa*, for making particular attributions. The deviations from the
predicted results in McArthur's experiment (i.e. the off-diagonal
values) are highly suggestive in this respect. Re-classifying the results
of McArthur in terms of necessary and sufficient conditions, as is done
in Table IV, one can see immediately that the results for person,
stimulus and circumstance attributions show marked differences.

TABLE IV   Causal attributions to stimulus, person and circumstances in terms of
necessary and/or sufficient conditions. (Data from McArthur, 1972)

|  | Stimulus | | | Person | | | Circumstances | |
|---|---|---|---|---|---|---|---|---|
|  | N | N̄ |  | N | N̄ |  | N | N̄ |
| S | 62 | 1 | S | 82 | 46 | S | 33 | 4 |
| S̄ | 11 | 3 | S̄ | 21 | 12 | S̄ | 47 | 3 |

N, N̄ summarises those conditions where a factor was necessary or not necessary
S, S̄ summarises those conditions where a factor was sufficient or not sufficient
Cell values are means of estimated percentages

The results for stimulus or entity attribution conform to the notion
of a cause as a necessary and sufficient condition, since the attribution
to the stimulus is made mainly if the behaviour occurs when the
stimulus is present *and* does not occur when the stimulus is not present.
In the case of person attribution, the sufficiency condition becomes
much more important, whereas in the case of the circumstance
attribution necessary conditions appear to have more effect. This finding that a personal cause is seen more as a sufficient condition,

whereas situational causes are conceived primarily as necessary conditions, has very important consequences. One implication of this result is that neglect of consensus information should occur more strongly when making person attributions as compared with circumstance attributions. The results of McArthur's study in fact show this and it is an effect which has now been even more strongly confirmed by several other studies, analysed in the way suggested above (Hewstone, 1981). Another implication is that discounting (Kelley, 1973) should be asymmetrical in nature. When a subject is given information about the person and his behaviour, he or she should have less interest in situational information whereas the reverse should not be the case. This is in effect exactly what Fincham (1980) was able to show for adult subjects, especially when the described behaviour had severe outcomes.

It is not immediately evident why there should be a shift in the notion of causality when attributions are made to people or situations. One possible explanation could be that it would not make any difference, for all practical purposes in everyday life, whether the necessary condition is taken into account in person attributions, or the sufficiency condition in situational attributions. To understand, predict and control another person's behaviour in particular circumstances it might be relatively unimportant to know that other people also show the behaviour, or that the situation also leads to other behaviour. Whatever the case may be, it seems that attribution research might benefit from a content-specific notion of causality. When an event or behaviour is attributed to the person, attribution processes might be concerned only with the person as a sufficient condition for the event to occur. When behaviour is attributable to the circumstances, necessary conditions are more important and when the behaviour is seen as caused by a stimulus both conditions appear to be relevant. The findings reported above suggest that such variations in the subjective conception of causality do not introduce notions which are radically different from those suggested by Kelley, but simplifications which are perhaps adapted to the need for explanations in everyday life.

INDUCTIVE LOGIC OR PROBABILISTIC INFERENCES?

This analysis of attribution processes has so far assumed that subjects code the information presented to them in vignettes in a dichotomous fashion, allowing for a logical analysis. The information itself, however, suggests a probabilistic formulation. Expressions like 'almost everyone' 'almost any other' and 'almost always' suggest high probabilities of occurrence, just as the opposite formulations indicate low probabilities. Do people notice such gradations and are they used to make causal inferences? One could test this hypothesis by replacing the formulations of necessary and sufficient conditions with statements about the conditional probability of behaviour, given the person, the stimulus and the circumstances. With verbal information of the kind used in vignettes, no exact estimation of these probabilities is possible. But one could easily design an experiment in which the information was presented in a more precise, quantitative way. However, even in the case of vignettes, it is possible to distinguish five levels of conditional probabilities. These could be based on a simple count of the number of times the behaviour is mentioned in conjunction with any of the conditions (person, stimulus, circumstances), provided that the subjects code the information in the way suggested. The frequency with which the subjects make attributions to the person, the stimulus and so on can then be taken as the conditional probability of a 'cause', given the behaviour. The results of our replication study of McArthur's experiment, which will be published more fully elsewhere, have been re-analysed along these lines and are presented in Fig. 1.

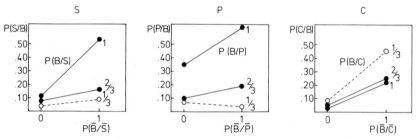

Fig. 1   Conditional probability analysis of causal attributions to stimulus, person, and circumstances. (Data from Hilton et al., 1981)
P(S/B), P(P/B), P(C/B) = Conditional probability of the cause (P,S,C) given the behaviour
P(B/S), P(B/P), P(B/C) = Conditional probability of the behaviour given the cause (P,S,C) = sufficient cause
P(B̄/S̄), P(B̄/P̄), P(B̄/C̄) = Conditional probability of absence of behaviour given absence of cause (P,S,C) = necessary cause

It can be seen in Fig. 1 that the subject hardly make a distinction between the different degrees of conditional probabilities. Attribution to the stimulus occurs only to a significant degree if the behaviour always occurs when the stimulus is present and not when the stimulus is absent. Attribution to the person occurs under similar conditions, but also to some extent when only the sufficiency condition is met. Attribution to the circumstances appears to be only affected by the necessary condition, as gradations of sufficiency do not make a significant difference.

    These results seem to suggest that subjects do not make use of probabilistic information in making causal inferences. But even if they did, it would be hard to explain the results obtained on the basis of a probabilistic model. The model which comes to mind immediately is, of course, Bayes' theorem, which has been suggested by Ajzen and Fishbein as a model for causal attributions (Ajzen and Fishbein, 1975; see Ajzen and Fishbein, chapter 3). There is almost no point in applying the Bayesian model to vignette studies of the McArthur type, because it is immediately evident that subjects do not use the probability of the occurrence of a condition, given the behaviour. If they did, they would have to, for example, make frequent attributions to P, S, and C in the high consistency, high consensus and low distinctiveness condition, which they very clearly do not do. This is not to say the Bayes' theorem might not be used by subjects when information is presented to them in quantitative form, but it does not seem likely that they do so in processing verbal information as presented in vignettes.

This problem leads on to a different question, dealt with only in a limited way in most attribution studies despite its importance for the external and internal validity obtained in most studies. Although the original formulation of Kelley's ANOVA model of attribution processes always refers to the observation of covariation of conditions and effects, most studies have not presented subjects with actual events which can be seen to covary with certain conditions. Instead subjects have merely been informed about covariation in terms of consistency, consensus and distinctiveness. This stage of affairs poses two quite significant questions. One should first ask whether subjects are in fact able to extract consensus, consistency and distinctiveness information from observed covariation and secondly one might ask whether this is the only information they obtain when observing the occurrence of natural events. The fact that people can apparently make use of Kelley's informational categories does not necessarily mean that they make use of these categories spontaneously. It would seem quite relevant therefore to conduct studies in which people are actually able to make such observations and to allow them to express their explanations in a free response format.

OBSERVING COVARIATION AND THE NATURAL CATEGORISATION OF CAUSES

In a recent study (B. Jaspars *et al.*, 1981) parents with children in secondary education were given class lists, report cards and A-level results of a complete sixth form for pupils who had failed their A-level examination in one particular subject. The information presented was varied systematically according to consistency, consensus and distinctiveness. An example of one set of information presented to the parents is given in Fig. 2 in the form of the ANOVA cube; the parents actually received the information in the natural format of class lists, report cards and examination results which happen to correspond with three faces of the cube.

ENTITY ATTRIBUTION

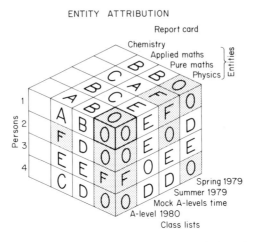

Fig. 2   Example of attributional information presented to Ss in A-level failure study. (Data from B. Jaspars *et al.*, 1981)

Parents were given ample time to inspect the information and then asked why they thought a particular pupil had failed an A-level in a particular subject. In a preliminary analysis the free responses of the parents were content-analysed using Kelley's attribution scheme (Bell, Contarello, Daniel, Debuschere, Jaspars, Jonas, Lorenzi and Velthuijsen, 1981). Coders appeared able to cast the parents' responses in terms of either Kelley's informational category patterns (i.e. consistency, consensus and distinctiveness) or in terms of attributional categories of person, subject, circumstances or combinations thereof. The parents did not, of course, give their answers in terms of the theoretical concepts. They would make observations such as, 'he has done badly in the past', 'he has been doing well in his other subjects', 'they seem to be a bad lot' or even 'it looks like the favourite horse stumbling over the last fence'. Such observations can easily be classified in terms of the informational categories of Kelley's theory, but that does not mean that one can also reconstruct the original response from the attributional categorisation. The most obvious example is the case of inconsistency. Parents often noticed a trend in the data, observing that a pupil was improving over time or doing less well than before. Such observations had to be classified as inconsistent (in the sense of irregular behaviour), but it seems fairly obvious that these different developments over time will not lead to the same attributions. A downward trend would probably lead to a person explanation, whereas an irregular trend might suggest a situational attribution.

Similar problems arise with the coding of explanations in the attributional categories implied by the ANOVA model. For example, subjects gave a large number of interactional explanations in terms of 'something having to do with the person' and 'something having to do with the subject'; but in one case this could mean lack of interest in the subject, and in another a personality clash between teacher and pupil. Although such attributions are formally similar they may lead to totally different behaviour on the part of an involved observer, such as a parent. In the first case the pupil might be advised to take another subject, in the second it would seem reasonable to change teachers or schools.

Another natural category of responses which could not be satis-factorily classified in the ANOVA system was formed by responses where the subject indicated a relation between person, situation and/or circumstances. A typical example would be one in which a lack of knowledge on the part of the pupil was blamed on poor preparation by the school for the examination. One could code such answers in terms of the direct cause of the failure, which is the lack of knowledge of the pupil, but it seems reasonable again to assume that the primary cause (i.e. the lack of preparation by the school) is more important as a determinant of the pupil's behaviour. As Kelley has pointed out before (Kelley, 1973), person and situation may not be independent of each other, an eventuality which creates serious problems for simple causal attribution as suggested by the ANOVA model. In such cases it would seem necessary to introduce causal networks for the explanation of common sense attributions (see Fincham and Jaspars, 1980 and Kelley's Epilogue, this volume).

The correspondence between what one might call a system of natural causal categories in the sense of Rosch (Mervis and Rosch, 1981) and the ANOVA categorisation thus appears to be a fairly complex, though not unsolvable, problem. To some extent the problem is reflected in attribution theory itself by the different categorisations used by Kelley and Weiner. Weiner's (e.g. 1974, 1979) categories seem to come closer to the natural categories used by our subjects and hence the corres-pondence between his categories and those suggested by Kelley is also somewhat unclear. Various attempts to relate the two systems have been made in the literature, by directly relating Kelley's dimensions of consistency, consensus and distinctiveness to Weiner's dimensions of stability, locus, and control. Any such direct correspondence appears unlikely, because Kelley's dimensions describe the information used for making attributions, whereas Weiner's classification refers to the causes themselves. It would thus make more sense to relate both systems at the level of causal attributions.

The one study known to the authors that allows for such a comparison is that of Frieze and Weiner (1971), in which information presented to the subjects was varied according to consistency, consensus and distinctiveness, but the attributions were made to ability, task, luck and effort. Inspection of the results obtained by Frieze and Weiner suggests that a person attribution in terms of Kelley's model is equivalent to an ability attribution in terms of Weiner's model, since such an attribution is predominantly given where one expects a P attribution in Kelley's terms, according to the results of other experiments like McArthur's. Task difficulty obviously corresponds with a stimulus attribution pattern and luck with a circumstance attribution. Effort is more interesting, because it tends to correspond with a P × S attribution in Kelley's terms. These relationships seem to confirm the suggestion made above that certain states in the person are directly related to the situation. This implies that classifying effort as a person factor is somewhat misleading, because it is, in effect, only a partial cause which is normally combined with a characteristic of the stimulus. At least, subjects do not seem to offer effort as a general explanation of behaviour, but normally in combination with a specific task.

The suggestion that natural categories of explanation can, in part, be translated in terms of an abstract ANOVA set of categories also indicates a way to combine the effect of prior expectations with the influence of new information presented to the perceiver. As Kelley has already suggested, the observation of only one instance of a person's behaviour may be sufficient for observers to make an attribution if they have recourse to a causal scheme (Kelley 1972a, b, 1973). A systematic way of investigating such expectations and suppositions would be to study the informational classification of behaviours in terms of consensus, consistency and distinctiveness, so that these *a priori* classifications could be taken into account when new information varying along the same dimensions is presented. There is already good evidence that suppositions about success and failure, and expectations about actors and behaviour in situations, affect attributions. Extrapolating from these studies to a more systematic approach would seem only a small, but important step. Thus Hewstone (1981) has studied the effect of implicit consensus in the form of attributions made for stereotypical and counter-stereotypical behaviour of boys and girls. When consensus information which confirmed or disconfirmed the stereotype was explicitly mentioned, the implicit consensus was ignored by public schoolboy subjects; they seemed to interpret the task as an exercise in logic based on covariation of cause and effect. However, when no explicit consensus information was given, subjects seemed to make use of the implicit consensus in the predicted way, although the results were not clear cut.

One final comment should perhaps be made about the relationship between abstract causal categorisation and the natural categories which people seem to use. In quite a few instances in our experiments (e.g. in the experiment reported by Löchel, chapter 7, this volume), subjects relate person and stimulus in their explanation, for example, by saying that a task is *too* difficult for a person or for themselves. Such a comparative reply seems to make good sense and is implied in Heider's concept of 'can' (Heider, 1958a). It suggests that subjects may in fact build up a cognitive representation of stimulus and persons by a subjective scaling process. A response like the one given above can be read off immediately from such a joint scale of persons and stimuli. When asked to locate a cause in either the person, the task or the circumstances a subject might simply report the relative position of the particular element on the scale. This may seem a complicated process, but it only implies that the subject builds up a rough picture of how many elements are dominated by the element in question on the scale. Such a scaling model of causal attribution does, in fact, predict the responses obtained in McArthur's experiment fairly well, but so far we have not been able to design an experiment which distinguishes between a natural logic and a subjective scaling model of causal attributions. Free responses given by subjects suggest, however, that a subjective scaling process should be considered as a serious competitor with the natural logic model outlined above.

CONCLUSIONS

This section has dealt with some of what we see as the major issues concerning the nature of attributions and explanations in common sense. We have emphasised the point, made recently by quite a few other attribution researchers, that explanations in common sense do not always take the form of causal attributions, but we have added that explanations in every day life are often an inherent part of such social acts as responsibility attribution and moral evaluation. In addition we have pointed out that, even if explanations are restricted to the making of causal attributions, the notion of causality may not be the one suggested by attribution theorists. The law and studies of event perception suggest different notions of causality which have so far received hardly any attention in attribution theory. Results of some replication studies of traditional attribution experiments suggest moreover that people do not always use the empiricist notion of causality in the same way. Personal causality appears to be conceived more as a sufficient condition, whereas situational causality tends to be seen as a necessary condition.

Considering the process aspects of causal attributions in common sense, we have argued that a strict interpretation of the so-called ANOVA model does not seem to be a likely model for the description of attribution processes. A more simple 'natural inductive logic' model, based on the empiricist notion of causality, appears to describe the results of attribution experiments fairly well if one takes into account that such a model is sensitive to the personal or situational nature of the cause. We suspect that such shifts in the notions of causality have until now gone undetected, because the analyses employed in attribution studies have been incompatible with the predictions following the ANOVA model.

Doubt has also been expressed concerning whether people do use the informational and causal categories suggested by various attribution theories. It does seem possible to relate the theoretical categories to natural categories, but it appears that certain distinctions are made by people which require a further differentiation of the theoretical taxonomies. Of special interest is the fact that subjects relate personal and situational causes in the form of a limited causal network, which may have important consequences for the relation of attributions to behaviour. The interdependence of causes suggests moreover an alternative model for describing attribution processes. Finally, we have pointed out that suppositions, expectations and real world knowledge could be incorporated within attribution studies in a more systematic fashion by analysing the implicit attributional categorisation of observed behaviours.

## Determinants of causal attributions in common sense

The first section of this chapter discussed the nature and process of causal attributions in common sense. To some extent this also involved a discussion of the determinants of attribution processes, since the effects of formal characteristics of information were considered. However, we have not paid any attention to the major external determinants of causal attributions. To what extent does causal attribution depend on the nature of the attributor, the nature of the person or persons whose behaviour is to be explained and the nature of the behaviour itself? It is to these problems that we now briefly turn, paving the way for more thorough discussions by various contributors to this volume.

ATTRIBUTOR, ACTOR AND BEHAVIOUR

There are obviously many personal characteristics which could be related to the making of causal attributions; one such characteristic that is currently receiving attention is that of *developmental* differences. However, major reviews of developmental research have appeared only recently (Sedlak and Kurtz, 1981; Fincham, chapter 5). The studies by Löchel and Lalljee *et al.* (see chapters 6 and 7) reflect the increasing interest in developmental aspects of attribution theory and there is no point in covering the same ground again in this chapter. Differences in *personality*, as the other major source of attributor influence on attribution processes, are introduced in the last part of this book (see chapters 11 and 12) and will, for the same reason, not be taken up here. It seems that the area of inter-individual and intra-individual differences in attribution processes is still a wide-open field of research which we have barely begun to investigate.

The same is probably true of the impact of the nature of *the actor* whose behaviour is to be explained. So far most research has concentrated on actor–observer differences, but it is obvious that many more relevant distinctions could be made. Sex differences are one clear example which has already received some attention (Kelley and Michela, 1980), but an extrapolation of the actor–observer difference may be fruitful in various ways. Until now actor–observer differences have mainly been studied for cases in which there is no relation between the two, but research in defensive attribution (Fincham and Jaspars, 1980) suggests that social relations may be quite important in making causal attributions.

An interesting example of the extent to which actor–observer differences can be influenced by the relationship between actor and observer is found in an early study by Jaspars (1968) on parents' explanations for the success and failure of their children. According to the Jones and Nisbett (1972) hypothesis, one would expect that parents tend to attribute the success and failure of their children to stable personality dispositions. Research on the explanation of success and failure (see Kelley and Michela, 1980, p. 468) suggests, in addition, that this tendency should even be strengthened in the case of success. Although the study by Jaspars does not contain a comparison of the explanations by parents and children, it is interesting to note that parents show a tendency to attribute the success of their children to external factors (family, themselves) and the failure to non-stable (motivation) factors in the children.

An example of a more controlled study in which an attempt is made to study the impact of the position of the observer in relation to the actor is an experiment by de Ridder (1980) in which attributions of 'evil intent' by an aggressor, a victim and a neutral observer were compared. It was expected that the victim would be inclined to attribute the aggressive behaviour more to evil intentions of the aggressor than a neutral observer, but no significant difference was found. Presumably this result arises because the observer identified more with the victim, and focused attention more on the victim, than the perpetrator.

Before considering the wider implications of the suggestion that the relationship between actor and observer may have an important effect on causal attributions made by the observer, we should not forget that the nature of the behaviour that is to be explained may also affect attributional processes. The verb effects reported by McArthur (1972), some of the language effects discussed by Hewstone in this volume (chapter 9) and the different explanations offered for success and failure all testify to the influence of the nature of what is to be explained on the explanation itself. Perhaps all these differences can be explained by the configural information implied by the behaviour; but, as Lalljee et al. explain in this volume, the differences in explanation may be more fundamental than simply a shift in the locus of causality. The nature of the explanation itself appears to change sometimes. Lalljee finds an interesting difference between the explanations offered for emotions and actions; the former more often receive causal explanations and the latter receive more 'reason' explanations. It could be that a good deal of the recent criticisms which emphasise the distinction between cause and reason explanations is in fact confounded with the difference between action, or more general instrumental behaviour, and emotions or expressive behaviour. Spinoza was probably the first to notice that one could make a distinction between these two forms of behaviour, in a causal sense, by arguing that: 'We act when anything takes place, either within us or externally to us, whereof we are the adequate cause' whereas passions imply 'that something happens with us or follows from our nature externally, we being only the partial cause' (*Ethica*, part III).

Thus the problem raised by Lalljee (1981) and others, could in part reside in the fact that when, we ask a person to explain an emotion, we are presenting the prototype of an effect and a causal explanation follows naturally. However, when we ask for an explanation of an action, we present the subject with the prototype of a cause in common sense and the subject gives a teleological, finalistic or reason explanation by referring to the effect of the act.

All the factors mentioned above, the nature of the attributor, the characteristics of the person whose behaviour is to be explained, the nature of the relationship between actor and observer and the type of behaviour which is to be explained presume that we are only interested in attribution processes at the individual or inter-individual level. These approaches do not consider the attributor or actor as representatives of social categories or human groups (Tajfel, 1981). It seems worth investigating to what extent attribution processes which have been studied without taking the wider social context into account operate in the same way when social categorisation is allowed to play a role. The following section therefore considers some of the possible effects of 'socialising' attribution theory, while Deschamps (see chapter 8) considers other aspects more extensively.

## The social dimensions of causal attributions

In the previous section of this chapter it was pointed out that making causal inferences is often an inherent part of social activities such as attributing responsiblity and making moral evaluations. It was also acknowledged that attributions may be affected by the (social) context in which they are made, defining the context mainly in personal and interpersonal terms. However, taking a wider perspective it is easy to show that the study of common sense explanations can be made more social in quite a few other ways. Figure 3 illustrates the main distinctions we wish to make.

The first question to ask when concerned with common sense explanations is whether we are concerned with the explanation of behaviour or with the explanation of outcomes of behaviour (the explanation of non-human events, although interesting enough, is not considered here). In the latter case we may be concerned with such direct outcomes of behaviour as accidents or with the explanation of more remote consequences such as particular social

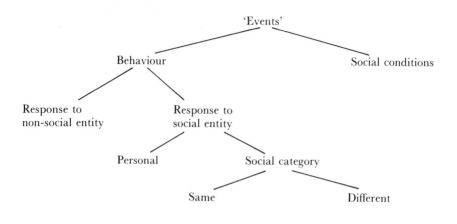

Resulting types of attribution

*Impersonal*          *Interpersonal*               *Intragroup*              *Intergroup*              *'Social'*

Fig. 3    Varieties of social explanada in causal attibutions

conditions like poverty, employment and criminality. The explanation of social conditions will not be elaborated here, but readers are referred to the publications by Furnham (1982), Hewstone (1981) and Hewstone and Jaspars (1982a). Focussing on the explanation of behaviour one can distinguish between behaviour which is a reaction to, or interaction with, the non-social environment and behaviour which is related to a social stimulus because it describes interaction with one or more other people. In this latter case the other persons may or may not be characterised in terms of social categories and, if they are, they may belong to the same social category as the actor or not. Taking all these distinctions into consideration we could speak about asocial or individual behaviour, interpersonal behaviour, intragroup and intergroup behaviour. Most experiments in attribution theory have been concerned with asocial and interpersonal behaviour and the interesting problem is therefore to see to what extent attribution processes operate in the same way when other people are categorised as own or other group members. In attribution studies such a social categorisation can play a role on at least two different levels. It can influence the characterisation of the stimulus person, whose behaviour is to be explained, or the description of the people about whom one receives consensus information. In addition the observer may or may not belong to the social category of the actor or the 'victim'.

These potential influences concern the generalisation across stimuli and other actors of the behaviour to be explained (by specifying the nature of consensus and distinctiveness). In many studies this has been done implicitly, by not specifying the consensus information (almost *everyone* else) and by indicating that behaviour generalises only across specific stimuli (e.g. other *comedians*). If we assume that generalisation depends to some extent upon the perceived similarity between elements, it is perhaps not surprising that consistency has usually been found to have more effect on attributions than distinctiveness and consensus. In the first case it seems reasonable to assume that a person's reactions in the present and the past to the same stimulus show a greater similarity than the person's reactions in the present to different stimuli; in the second case, this similarity is greater than the reactions of different people to the same stimulus at the present time.

Whatever the case may be, one could systematically vary the degree of similarity between the actor, other people and the stimulus persons by specifying the social category to which they belong. Hewstone (1981) has done just that in a series of experiments. In a replication of McArthur's experiment he found that, when consensus was limited to others of the same social category as the actor, it had a much greater effect on attributions than has previously been found (see Hewstone and Jaspars, 1982b). While these studies have 'socialised' attri- butions by means of relatively small manipulations of the stimulus materials, a more radically social perspective has also been taken. Thus Hewstone and Jaspars (1982c) examined the role of social influence processes in the development of attributions, and extended the research to realistic intergroup phenomena.

Finally Hewstone, Jaspars and Lalljee (1982) investigated the explanation of academic success and failure of ingroup and outgroup members. They demonstrated that attributions were based on socially shared representations; were related to the sociostructural positions of the two groups; and were made in a way likely to create, maintain or enhance the positive social identity of the ingroup, rather than in accordance with abstract causal schemata. A more complete dis- cussion of all these aspects of social attribution is presented in Hewstone (1981).

The findings of these studies and a few other experiments on intergroup attributions have been elaborated theoretically in two other publications (Hewstone and Jaspars, 1982a; Jaspars and

Hewstone, 1982). These chapters attempted to draw together research on ethnic stereotypes, intergroup relations and attribution theory. Research on social contact and intergroup relations has led to many contradictory results (Amir, 1969), although some understanding of the effects of social contact on ethnic prejudice has been obtained by specifying the conditions under which contact leads to either positive or negative intergroup relations. However, these conditions have not been put into a systematic framework which might lead to a more satisfactory explanation of intergroup relations. We believe that attribution theory offers such a framework, which may render the contradictory results obtained in the past more intelligible. Attribution theory applied to intergroup relations, moreover, leads to new and interesting hypotheses about the effect of social contact between members belonging to different groups.

Our major theoretical addition to the contact literature was an attributional analysis of stereotypes or, in general, of evaluative judgements of in- and outgroup members. Such judgements were seen as the outcome of an attribution process and not simply as distorted perceptions. This view makes clear why such personal evaluations take place in the first place, because one can argue that behaviour, which would normally lead to situational attributions, can lead to person attributions because of the added covariation with the observable social categorisation. Such an effect will probably be strengthened when contact between members belonging to different social groups is highly selective.

It also follows from an attributional point of view that different attributions will be made for in- and outgroup members when exactly the same behaviour is explained by an ingroup and an outgroup member, as shown originally by Taylor and Jaggi (1974); but it is also evident that a simple actor–observer model of these differences is not tenable, especially when the status of such groups in society is different and the outcome of the behaviour varies (see Jaspars and Hewstone, 1982).

Interaction between members of different groups, even when limited to a single occasion, can also be related to attributions. In particular it appears reasonable to assume that causal schemata such as discounting may play an important role because they can enhance the observer's social identity along positively valued dimensions (cf. Tajfel and Turner, 1979).

Another interesting implication of an attributional analysis of stereotypes is that such an approach shows why reality and stereotypes become indistinguishable when only ingroup consensus exists. One of the reasons why it is so hard to influence ethnic stereotypes may be that they possess all the characteristics of a veridical representation of reality. It is for this reason that we have suggested that attempts to influence negative outgroup judgements might benefit from a decomposition of perceived or attributed differences between ingroup and outgroup members, along the lines suggested by Cronbach (1955) for interpersonal perception (see Jaspars and Hewstone, 1982).

In the case of stereotypes or social attributions we have formally the same information as in the case of interpersonal perception. Similarities of auto- and heterostereotypes and attributions can be interpreted as overall 'accuracy' measures, which can be decomposed into a number of specific accuracy indices. Such an analysis would give us more precise information about the nature of the differences which are crucial and/or most amenable to social influence attempts.

### Consequences, applications and the relationship between attributions and behaviour

In their review of the literature on the consequences of attributions, Kelley and Michela show,

that attributions affect our feelings about past events and our expectations about future ones, our attitudes toward other persons and our reactions to their behaviour and our conceptions of ourselves and our efforts to improve our fortunes. (Kelley and Michela, 1980, p. 489)

We agree with Kelley and Michela that theories about the links between attributions and consequent responses have not been very sophisticated in the past. We do not claim to have all the answers to this problem, which Kelley and Michela regard as theoretically important, but we would like to make some comments at the end of this chapter about the issues involved in the analysis of attributional processes.

In studies of the attribution of responsibility and moral evaluation Fincham and Jaspars (1980) and Shultz and Schleifer (chapter 2, this volume) have already presented a formal model which implies that, in common sense just as in the law, causal attributions entail responsibility and responsibility entails sanctions of a positive or negative kind, depending on the nature of the behaviour outcomes. This entailment or pre-supposition model holds good for a variety of conditions (self–other, commission–omission, positive v. negative acts etc.) in experimental studies, but it comes under serious attack when applied to such real-life problems as the explanation of accidents (see Lloyd-Bostock, chapter 10, this volume). Are explanations then really determinants of behaviour, as the entailment models suggest, or are they justifications or reconstructions after the fact, which are determined by the behaviour of the actor? That is a question which has not yet been resolved.

One way in which the problem can be approached is by considering attributional information from a different perspective than that of Kelley's ANOVA model. If we reconsider the information available to the observer in terms of consistency, consensus or distinctiveness, we could argue that these informational dimensions in fact represent various types of probabilities for the occurrence of the behaviour to be explained. Consensus information has long been equated with base rate probability (see, more recently, Nisbett and Ross, 1980), but this line of thought can also be extended to conceive distinctiveness and consistency in terms of various aspects of the probability of occurrence of the behaviour. In the restricted sense given to the three dimensions in most experimental studies, one can show that consensus (Cs) is, in fact, the conditional probability (p) of the behaviour (B), given the stimulus (S) and the circumstances (C); consistency (Cy) is the conditional probability of the behaviour given the person and the stimulus (S), and non-distinctiveness (D̄) is the probability of the behaviour given the person and the circumstances.

$$\text{Thus:} \quad \text{Cs} = p \, (\text{B/S and C})$$
$$\text{Cy} = p \, (\text{B/P and S})$$
$$\bar{\text{D}} = p \, (\text{B/P and C}).$$

It can also be shown that for this restricted interpretation of consensus, consistency and distinctiveness the overall probability of the behaviour given the three types of information is:

$$p \, (\text{B}) = p \, (\text{B/S and C}) \times p \, (\text{B/P and S}) \times p \, (\text{B/P and C}).$$

It is doubtful, of course, whether the experimental data one could obtain to test this model are precise enough to distinguish between this multiplicative model and a simple additive model. In any case the multiplicative nature of the model follows only from the restricted interpretation of consensus, consistency and distinctiveness. It would therefore be sensible to proceed on the assumption that the probability of a certain behaviour occurring is a simple linear function of consensus, consistency, and indistinctiveness. The more people show a particular behaviour, and the more frequently a particular person shows the behaviour, and the more often it occurs in a variety of circumstances, the more likely it is that the behaviour will occur.

This probabilistic formulation of attributional information suggests a possible link between attributions and behaviour, if we recall that behavioural decision models and attitude models also contain a probability or expectancy component. It is easiest to illustrate the potential importance of attributional information for a person's behaviour by considering a particular example. In various studies King (see B. Jaspars *et al.*, 1981) has investigated attributional aspects of people's health beliefs. According to the health belief model (Maiman and Becker, 1974) people's health behaviour depends, among other things, upon the perceived risk of being affected by a particular illness and the perceived severity of the illness. As such, the health belief model is just a specific case of a general expectancy-value or behavioural decision model. What attribution theory possibly adds to the health belief model is a specification of the perceived risk. Is it likely that the person will contract the illness because of his or her own medical history, or because it is a very common illness or because the illness is widespread and can be contracted under a large variety of circumstances? It could be that certain risk components are much more important for understanding people's health behaviour than other risk components; hence a better prediction of their behaviour would be

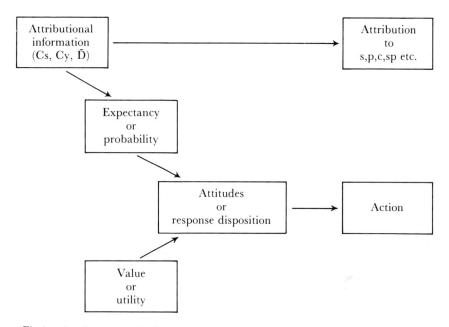

Fig 4.    Attribution, attitudes and action; a theoretical path diagram. The attitudes or response disposition can refer to the stimulus and/or the response as suggested by Fishbein

possible if such information were available. King (B. Jaspars *et al.*, 1981) has presented evidence from preventive health behaviour (attending screening for high blood pressure) which shows that attributional information can indeed improve the prediction of preventive behaviour over and above the predictions which can be derived from the health belief model.

If attributional information can be interpreted as specific probability information which, in combination with a value component, can form the heart of a behavioural decision model, it is also clear that attributions are not directly related to behaviour, because they are inferences made from the same information which is used to make decisions. The simplified diagram presented in Fig. 4 illustrates this point.

In order to see that attributions and behaviour are not directly related it is sufficient to realise that the same illness can have very different explanations (headache) but is often treated in the same way. For treatment or prevention it may not matter what the origin of the illness is, whereas explanations are at least in theory influenced by the specific pattern of consensus, consistency and distinctiveness.

It is quite possible that attributions might have a direct influence on behaviour, but the attribution-attitude-action (AAA) model has the advantage of being precise enough to be tested against such an alternative model by the methods of path analysis. Only one example of how attributions might be related to behaviour has been presented here. Other applications in clinical and educational psychology have also been attempted and are currently being extended (B. Jaspars *et al.*, 1981), but these will not be discussed here.

In general the attribution behaviour problem can be viewed as just one aspect of what one might call a *functional* analysis of attribution processes. As we have suggested at several places in the present chapter, causal attributions in everyday life are very often not just disinterested attempts to understand the behaviour of other people or the social world. In general they are explanations which are used for particular purposes: to predict, control, justify, communicate, express feelings or influence others. As such, attributions may be influenced by behaviour which is itself determined by other factors. However, this does not diminish the importance of an attributional analysis because one can now see how functional requirements may induce a particular representation of the attributional information, which by itself will also have an impact on a person's causal inferences. In this respect the problem of relating behaviour to attributions becomes formally the same as combining the influence of configurational information and observed covariation. This, according to Kelley (1973), is also one of the important areas of attributional theory which has as yet not been studied systematically.

## Conclusions

In this chapter we have considered some of the major issues in contemporary attribution theory and research. Quite a few of the recent reviews of the attribution literature have been rather critical of research on common sense explanations, pointing out that not all ordinary explanations take the form of causal inferences. Although we regard this form of criticism as partially valid, we do feel that there are more basic issues which have not yet been elaborated in attribution research.

We know a good deal about the informational determinants of causal inferences made by subjects in experimental situations, but it seems to us that we do not know nearly enough about the psychological and social *processes* involved in making such inferences in controlled experimental situations and in everyday life. Although an ANOVA model of causal attributions is able to predict inferences made by subjects in experiments with verbal vignette-type material, we do not know how such information is coded and how we proceed cognitively from this stage to making causal attributions. Unless we have a better understanding of this process it would seem premature to consider the much more complex problem of causal and non-causal reasoning in everyday life.

We have put forward a simple inductive logic model which is true to the original formulation of Kelley's attribution theory and we have shown that this model does predict, up to a point, inferences made by the subjects; but we have also shown that subjects may be using different notions of causality in dealing with personal and situational causes. We have also argued that the natural causal categories used by perceivers are not the same as those proposed by attribution theorists, although it does seem possible to relate the two category systems to each other. The advantage of working at two levels, with natural and theoretical attribution categories, is that such an approach allows us to bring together Kelley's configurational and covariational approaches in attribution theory. In addition, motivational and functional determinants can be combined with informational influences by considering the informational implications of the former.

Obviously we know far too little about other determinants of common sense explanations such as developmental and personality differences. No doubt a good many studies will be devoted to these problems, along the lines of some contributions to this book; but again it would seem that the social nature of attribution processes constitutes a more basic issue which has not been treated systematically in attribution studies. The heart of this problem is essentially the relationship between the attributor and the person whose behaviour is to be explained. As yet we cannot offer a coherent and comprehensive approach here: however, an integration of recent research on social categorisation and intergroup relations and attribution theory might be the most fruitful approach.

Finally we have offered a suggestion for studying the relationship between attributions and behaviour. This is one of the most important issues for a viable theory of causal attributions in common sense and as yet very little theoretical progress has been made here. Most predictions in the literature are based on plausible hunches without any attempt to make explicit the relations and processes involved. We have suggested an indirect relationship between attributions and actions by pointing out that an attributional classification of observed behaviour, as suggested by Kelley, has implications for the expectancy component of attitudes which are more directly related to behaviour in attitude and behaviour decision theories. Attribution theory makes an important contribution to such theories by specifying the nature of the expectancy component and in addition attribution theory can show how the concomitant explanations are related indirectly to the behaviour in a particular situation.

In short we have concentrated on three issues in this chapter: the nature of common sense causality, the social character of attribution processes and the relationship of attributions to behaviour. We have argued that these are some of the basic issues in attribution theory which so far have not been developed sufficiently and we have suggested various ways in which progress in studying these problems can be made.

# 2

# Towards a Refinement of Attribution Concepts

## Thomas R. Shultz and Michael Schleifer

### Introduction

This chapter deals with the issue of what gets attributed in psychological attribution. Does it matter for attribution theory whether one is attributing, for example, effects to causes or responsibility to persons? Will the underlying principles and processes remain the same across various attributional contents? Our claim is that widespread neglect of this issue in attribution research has created considerable theoretical confusion and has probably led to inconsistent findings as well. In particular, attributions of causation and responsibility and the assignment of punishment have often been carelessly combined in both theoretical analyses and empirical research. In an effort to disentangle some of these obscurities and deal with the effects of attributional content on attributional processes, we examine conceptual discussions in philosophy of science, law, and ethics. This literature is used to formulate and refine distinctions between central attribution concepts and to identify both relations among the concepts and variables likely to govern their application. The resulting psychological model of attribution contents and processes is evaluated in the light of new research which serves to modify the model and point the way towards future investigation.

### Attribution contents and processes: The classical theories

J. H. Harvey, Ickes and Kidd (1978a) point out that the classical theories of attribution focus principally on delineating the underlying processes by which attributions are derived. The goal was apparently to construct a broad and deep theoretical base that could account for any and all attributional conclusions which human observers might reach regardless of the content of the attributions. Such an approach has undeniable advantages including those of explanatory power and parsimony. Most of the modern attributional research (as highlighted, for example, in J. H. Harvey *et al.*, 1976, 1978a) has tacitly accepted these early theoretical assumptions and has sought to apply them to various problem domains in social psychology. The range of such applications has been truly extraordinary and includes topics as diverse as stuttering (Storms and McCaul, 1976), marital discord (J. H. Harvey, Wells and Alvarez, 1978b), learned helplessness (Dweck and Goetz, 1978), and moral behaviour (Dienstbier, 1978). The considerable success and consequent rapid growth of attributional approaches to social problems may have inadvertently contributed to the neglect of more fundamental theoretical concerns.

Although the content of attribution has not figured prominently in theorising about attributional processes, a sense of the variety of such contents can be obtained from a brief look at the classical theories. Heider (1958a) is widely acknowledged as the founder of modern attribution theory. He outlined, among other things, the processes involved in attributing *responsibility* to persons. 'Personal responsibility . . . varies with the relative contribution of environmental factors to the action outcome; in general, the more they are felt to influence the action, the less the person is held responsible' (p. 113). Heider proceeded to elaborate this conception in terms of a scale of five successive levels of responsibility (see chapters 1 and 5). For present purposes, one interesting feature of Heider's model is his tendency to slip back and forth between the attributional contents of *responsibility* and *causation*. In common parlance, one may attribute responsibility to persons, and events to their causes which in some sense may be persons. Heider defined his second level of responsibility in terms of *impersonal causation*: '. . . anything that is caused by $p$ is ascribed to him' (p. 113). And he defined his fourth level of responsibility in terms of *personal causation*, by which he seems to mean doing something with intent: '. . . only what $p$ intended is perceived as having its souce in him' (p. 113). Interestingly, none of Heider's other three levels of responsibility explicitly contained the notion of causation. They referred instead to issues of mere association or belonging (level 1), foresight of the consequences of action (level 3), and external provocation (level 5). Thus, although Heider was focusing on the attribution of responsibility to persons, he rather casually introduced the notion of attributing events to causes. In doing so, he made no systematic attempt to analyse possible differences between the two sorts of attribution. As Fishbein and Ajzen (1973) have rightly concluded, 'One immediate implication of Heider's analysis is that general measures of responsibility will tend to be ambiguous' (p. 150). The numerous investigators who have followed up Heider's insights into attribution of responsibility (e.g. M. H. Shaw and Reitan, 1969; M. E. Shaw and Sulzer, 1964) have likewise failed to distinguish clearly between the concepts of causation and responsibility. More recently, however, those 'Heiderians' who have included separate scales for the two concepts have in fact found that they yield somewhat different results (Fincham and Jaspars, 1979; Harris, 1977; see chapter 5 and below).

Historically, the second major influence on the emergence of modern attribution theory is generally acknowledged to be a paper by Jones and Davis (1965) on the attribution of *intentions* and *dispositions*. Following Heider (1958a) Jones and Davis reasoned that human actions are often explained by the attribution of stable, relatively invariant dispositions to the actor. They argued that the attribution of intention to the actor was a precondition for a dispositional attribution, and proceeded to formulate sets of principles for these two attributional steps. In this sense, the Jones and Davis model can be said to represent one of the few attempts to deal explicitly with the use of different rules for making different kinds of attributions. In their theory, the *knowledge* and *ability* of the actor were held to determine the attribution of intention. And given that intentionality had thus been established, the attribution of disposition was said to be governed by the principle of *correspondent inference*. As in Heider (1958a), correspondence between action and disposition was seen to decline insofar as the action was constrained by the setting in which it occurred. The greater the degree of correspondence, the stronger the dispositional attribution was supposed to be (see chapter 5, this volume). Presumably, the Jones and Davis model was meant to deal with notions of causal connections. Dispositions may cause intentions which, in turn, may cause actions.[1] Their model is also presumably relevant to the attribution of responsibility for action and outcome to the extent that intention of the actor may be considered as crucial to that issue (Bentham, 1789/1948). However, it is noteworthy that the concepts of causation and responsibility are not explicitly distinguished and discussed by Jones and Davis.

Perhaps the quintessentially process-oriented attribution theory has been that proposed by Kelley (1967, 1973). Kelley dealt explicitly with the problem of attributing events (usually behaviours) to their causes and delineated a highly abstract model of the processes by which such attributions are made. The model encompasses both covariation principles such as consensus, distinctiveness, and consistency, as well as configuration principles such as discounting, augmentation, and compensation (see chapters 1 and 5). The discounting principle, for example, specifies that a behavioural effect will more likely be attributed to an internal, personal cause to the extent that external environmental causes are not operative. These principles have been used to account for a vast array of diverse *causal* phenomena but without at all being applied to the actor's responsibility for action and outcome.

Thus, the three classical attribution theories (Heider, Jones and Davis, Kelley) have specified underlying processes for a variety of attributional contents but have invariably ignored or obscured distinctions between causation and responsibility. It is obvious that many sorts of things get attributed in psychological attributions, but the possibility that different types of attribution (specifically, causation and responsibility) depend on different principles has not been systematically addressed.

The apparently pervasive tendency to view the two concepts in an undifferentiated way perhaps stems from Aristotle's influential analysis of the assignment of responsibility for a tragedy at sea *Nicomachean Ethics*, Book 3). The Greek term which he used there (*aetia*) referred to both causation and responsibility. Such conceptual overlap was probably justifiable for a time in which animistic explanations were accepted as easily for the falling of a rock as for the consequences of human action. In our own age, it is less appropriate to confuse causation and responsibility because of the consensus that causation can assume a purely mechanistic or scientific role, quite apart from the intervention of some animate being (e.g. Harré and Madden, 1975).

## Conceptual obscurities in the contemporary literature

To a very large extent, the conceptual obscurities prevalent in ancient philosophy and in the initial contributions to attribution theory have been preserved in the contemporary literature. This appears to be true even in recent papers offering a variety of novel theoretical perspectives on attribution. For example, Brewer (1977) proposed an interesting re-interpretation of the phenomenon of *defensive* attribution in information processing terms. She predicted that responsibility would vary as a function of the difference between the perceived contingent probability of an outcome, given an action, and the non-contingent prior probability of that outcome. Although her model appeared to be largely successful in providing an alternative account of much of that literature, the concepts of causation and responsibility were not distinguished: '. . . the model proposed here equates responsibility judgements with assignment of *cause*' (Brewer, 1977, p. 63). Similarly, in an attempt to provide an attributional analysis of moral judgements, Ross and DiTecco (1975) sought to emphasise that both concepts are influenced by the same set of factors. They argued that moral standards (involving *oughts*) are subject to consistency and consensus information just as causal attributions are. This may indeed be the case, but it leaves unresolved the nature of the differences between causal and moral judgements.

The concept of responsibility has been confused not only with that of causation but also with the assignment of punishment for harm-doing. Hamilton (1978), for example, in offering an interesting account of the importance of social role requirements in attribution (see chapters 1 and 10), maintained that, '. . . responsibility refers to a decision about *liability for sanctions*' (p. 316). However, he clouds the distinction between responsibility and causation by asserting that, '. . . the key issue in causality is intent, what the actor meant to do' (p. 316). As will be seen below, there is considerable justification for regarding information on intent or volition to be crucial, not for judging causation, but rather for establishing responsibility, when defined independently of causation.

Occasionally, punishment judgements are taken as a summary assessment of an entire range of attributional concepts. For example, a recent experiment by Darley, Klosson and Zanna (1978) assessed the effects of a variety of mitigating circumstances on the punishment judgements of children and adults. Although their work shares with ours a recognition of the heuristic value of legal philosophy for the psychological study of attributions, their restriction of dependent measures to the assignment of punishment obscures a variety of important legal and moral distinctions. As will be seen below, there is good reason to believe that different mitigating circumstances operate primarily on particular attribution decisions. Effects on punishment judgements may well be indirect and hence mask a more subtle and more precise set of processes. We must agree with Fishbein and Ajzen (1973) when they conclude that, 'Much of the research in this area has been based less on systematic theoretical analyses of the attribution process than on intuitive hypotheses and speculation. It is perhaps for this reason that studies on attribution of responsibility have yielded contradictory and inconsistent conclusions' (p. 148). Further, it is our belief that a systematic, conceptual refinement of central attribution concepts such as causation, responsibility, and punishment will contribute to the removal of many of the current confusions.

Attempts to provide such conceptual refinement within the psychological literature have been rare and not notably successful. In his recent book on psychological attribution, Shaver (1975) recognised that causation and responsibility did not seem to be identical and hence undertook a conceptual separation of the two notions. However, his conclusion was not especially enlightening in terms of understanding the nature of their differences and possible inter-relations: '. . . (responsibility) can at times be equivalent to causality, at times more than causality, and at times less than causality' (Shaver, 1975, p. 111). Similarly, Pepitone (1975), in an analysis of the psychological basis for the legal system, recognised the distinction between judgements of causation and responsibility in certain well known legal cases but did not provide or refer to more systematic conceptual analyses of their differences.

## Some empirical signposts

It is interesting to note that a number of empirical investigations have included separate scales for attribution concepts and have often found that the scales yielded somewhat different results. Typically, no systematic theoretical rationale has been provided for either the inclusion of the separate scales or the divergence of the data. Several such investigations contained assessment of both causation and responsibility. For example Kelman and Lawrence (1972), in a national survey in the USA on the Vietnam war crimes trial of Lt. Calley, found that a number of respondents felt that Calley was morally and legally innocent even though his actions were seen to cause many deaths. Schroeder and Linder (1976) had subjects read a report of an industrial accident which varied in severity of consequence, number of previous accidents, and the extent of the actor's knowledge of the previous accidents. It was reported that ratings of responsibility, but not causation, were influenced by a number of interactive effects. In a study by Harris (1977), subjects from six years of age to adulthood watched videotaped scenes of a woman breaking a chair. Each of the scenes represented one of Heider's (1958a) five levels of responsibility, and the subject was requested in each case to attribute causation and *naughtiness* to the chair breaker. The interactive effects of age and level of responsibility were reported to be somewhat different for the two different measures. M. D. Harvey and Rule (1978) asked subjects to read an aggression story and an accident story and then factor analysed the ratings of act and action on a number of separate scales. The factor analysis yielded a *moral* factor loading on ratings of proper/ improper, right/wrong, controlled/uncontrolled, strong/weak, good/ bad, justified/unjustified, and praised/blamed, as well as a *causal* factor loading on ratings of intended/not intended, responsible/not responsible, and person/situation cause.

Several other investigations have included separate assessments of responsibility and recommended consequences (usually punishment, as the act typically had harmful consequences). For example, M. E. Shaw and Reitan (1969) requested subjects from several different occupational groups to make such judgements for actors in stories representing Heider's five levels. In their stories, the outcome varied in both positivity and intensity. For all occupational groups, it was found that recommended consequences (punishment or reward) were relatively more influenced by intensity of outcome than were responsibility ratings. (See the discussion of punishment, below for a more complete treatment of this and similar findings.) In a study by Phares and Wilson (1972), subjects rated the responsibility and three different scales of punishment for individuals involved in car accidents that varied in severity of outcome and the degree of ambiguity inherent in the accident descriptions. There was a significant main effect for scale of measurement indicating that the responsibility scale yielded different results from the three punishment scales. Subjects in an experiment by J. I. Shaw and McMartin (1975) also read about a car accident. In this case, the driver and/or the bystanders either suffered or did not suffer injury. The subjects rated the driver's responsiblity for the accident and sentenced him to a particular jail term. Different results were obtained for responsibility and punishment judgements in a curious interaction with gender of subject. Males punished less when the driver himself suffered and judged the driver to be more responsible overall than did females. Females punished the driver more when bystanders were harmed than when they were not harmed, but did not hold him more responsible. And finally, DeJong, Morris and Hastorf (1976) reported a study in which subjects read descriptions of fictitious criminal cases and then assigned punishment to the defendant. Eight different cases were used in a $2 \times 2 \times 2$ design which varied the severity of the crime, the degree of the responsibility of the defendant, and the fate of the defendant's accomplice (escaped or captured). Ratings of responsibility were included only as a check on the manipulation of responsibility. The findings indicated that, whereas punishment was affected by all three independent variables, responsibility ratings were affected only by the responsibility manipulation. Thus, there is considerable evidence in the attribution literature to support the assertion that judgements of causation, responsibility, and punishment are not really identical. The question still remains whether any theoretical sense can be made of such distinctions. The psychological literature, reviewed thus far, indicates that current and classical attribution theories have not yet generated such an analysis.


## Excursions into philosophy

It is our view that a great deal can be gained from examining the conceptual treatments of these notions provided by philosophers of science, mind, ethics, and law. As the above citation of Aristotle reveals, the concepts of causation, responsibility, and punishment have been a focus of study in philosophy for many more years than psychology has itself been separated from philosophy. Our reference to *classical* psychological theories of attribution in the 1950s, 1960s and 1970s further underscores the point that psychologists are just beginners in this enterprise. This was partly but very clearly recognised by Darley *et al.* (1978) in the introduction to their paper on mitigating circumstances:

There is a field of human activity that has been assigning judgments of innocence, guilt, liability, responsibility, and punishment to harm-doers for hundreds of years. This is the . . . legal system. It is our suggestion that psychologists consider drawing upon the moral judgmental principles embodied in the law as the basis for a model of the ordinary person's principles of moral judgment. (Darley *et al.*, 1978, p. 66)

(See also chapter 10; Fincham and Jaspars, 1980 and Leahy, 1979b.) Law is not the only source of possible conceptual inspiration for attribution problems, however. Ideas about causation, for example, are treated extensively within philosophy of science (e.g. Bunge, 1959; Harré and Madden, 1975; Mackie, 1974; Wallace, 1974). In addition the role of concepts such as *cause* and *reason* in the explanation of human behaviour has been thoroughly examined within the philosophy of mind, a fact noted and exploited in a recent conceptual critique of attribution theory by Buss (1978). Buss began his critique with a quotation that seems particularly apt for the present argument: 'The confusion and barrenness of psychology is not to be explained by calling it a "young science"; . . . (it) is not comparable with . . . physics, for instance, in its beginnings. . . . For in psychology there are experimental methods and *conceptual confusion*' (Wittgenstein, 1953, p. 232).

Unfortunately, the problem is that the attribution researcher seeking conceptual clarification within these areas of philosophy will find no quick and easy solutions. Indeed, part of the reason that concepts of causation, responsibility, and punishment have occupied the attention of philosophers for so long is that the proper analysis of these concepts has remained controversial. On many crucial issues there are still substantial disagreements and more than enough qualifications and exceptions to frustrate even the most diligent theory builder. Consequently, one is forced to pick and chose among a vast array of conflicting contributions; *caveat emptor* clearly applies to such an endeavour if it applies anywhere. One way to overcome the difficulties in interdisciplinary dialogues is to concentrate upon areas of consensus. This has been our own approach (Shultz, Schleifer and Altman, 1981; Shultz and Schleifer, 1982) as we have attempted to abstract a preliminary model of causal, moral, and punishment judgements from examining some of the leading works in these areas of philosophy and then to subject this model to empirical test. Our strategy was to focus on conceptual distinctions and conclusions that had obvious psychological relevance and on which there was at least some degree of agreement among contemporary writers. We tended to ignore many of the inevitable qualifications when these became too cumbersome to deal with in preliminary experiments. The remainder of the chapter reviews the theory and evidence resulting from this approach. We discuss below the derivation and testing of a model for judging causation, responsibility, and punishment in cases of harm-doing. The law and much of ethics have naturally focused on harm-doing as this has always been a critical matter of social concern. Finally, possible applicability of this model for making similar judgements of benefit-doing is discussed.

## Attribution processes in harm-doing

Treatment of harm-doing within Anglo-American law involves three principal decisions regarding: (*a*) establishing the cause of the harm, (*b*) determining who was responsible for it, and (*c*) assigning punishment or restitution (Harper and James, 1956; Hart and Honoré, 1959). Thus, our model focuses on the three variables of causation, responsibility, and punishment. It specifies the rules or principles by which each of these decisions is made, the informational content to which such rules apply, and the inter-relations among these decisions. In short, the model attempts to provide an information processing account of how judgements of harm-doing are made. Each of the three principal concepts in the model is discussed in turn.

CAUSATION

The conceptual analysis of causation has a long and interesting history in various sub-fields of philosophy including especially philosophy of science, but also philosophy of social science, philosophy of mind and action, and philosophy of law. Much of the discussion has focused on the nature of causation and on how and to what extent causation can be known. Views range from the sceptical Humean position (Hume, 1739/1960) that causation is an illusory construction of the human mind based primarily on the observed regularity of succession of two events to the *realist* position that causation does exist and can be known (Bunge, 1959; Harré and Madden, 1975; Mackie, 1974; Wallace, 1974; von Wright, 1971, 1974). Current consensus clearly favours the realist position on causation even among those whose approach may be termed neo-Humean (e.g. Mackie, 1974; von Wright, 1971, 1974). For many causal realists, the concept is best rendered in terms of a generative or productive relationship between either events (Bunge, 1959) or objects (Harré and Madden, 1975). By this is meant that the cause actually brings about the effect.

Recent research on the child's developing knowledge of physical (i.e. non-behavioural) causation has indicated that the generative view is fundamental to causal understanding from at least three years of age (Shultz, 1982). Whether the generative notion of causation can successfully account for human action and its consequences is somewhat more controversial. However, there is almost certainly no difficulty in conceptualising the connection between action and consequence in generative terms. Human actions do occasionally intervene in, and thus alter, the otherwise naturally unfolding course of events (von Wright, 1971) and it is clear that children do come to achieve accurate knowledge about such causal sequences (Piaget, 1977, 1978). It is rather the notion of the productive causation of human action that has invited controversy. A number of 18th century philosophers (e.g. Bentham, 1789/1948) maintained that human actions are caused by certain of the actor's mental states, variously described in terms of intentions, wishes, or volitions. This view was countered by several contemporary philosophers (Anscombe, 1957; Meldon, 1961; von Wright, 1971), but it still has a considerable degree of support (Davidson, 1963; Harré and Madden, 1975; Mackie 1974, 1977). Psychological evidence has suggested that young children consider intentional states to be causally related to the ensuing actions (Shultz, 1980; Shultz, Wells and Sarda, 1980).

In cases of harm-doing legal theorists have accorded the concept of causation a primary place. Essentially, the cause of the harm must be determined as a prerequisite to any consideration of legal liability or punishment (Harper and James, 1956; Hart and Honoré, 1959). For example, in their treatment of the law of torts, Harper and James (1956) maintained that:

The establishment of the requisite causal connection is . . . an element of a plaintiff's . . . action . . . to be pleaded and proven by him. And . . . the question of causal connection will determine the scope of liability – the extent of the injury or damage for which the defendant will have to pay. . . . Obviously the legal test includes a requirement that the wrongful conduct must be a *cause in fact* of the harm. (Harper and James, p. 1108)

If such a causal connection cannot be established, then questions of legal liability and punishment or restitution do not legitimately arise.

But how can such issues of causation of harm be determined? By what rules or principles is causation established? In general, legal theorists have advanced two somewhat different proposals, both of which derive from so-called *conditional* analyses of causation. Conditional analyses have, in general, attempted to account for causal connections in terms of the occurrence of one event being either a necessary or a sufficient condition or both for the occurrence of another event (Mackie, 1974; Nagel, 1961; von Wright, 1971, 1974). Necessary conditions are rendered in conditional logic as *q only if p*; sufficient conditions as *if p then q*. (In this notation, $p$ refers to the causal event, and $q$ refers to the effect event.) In legal theory, the analysis of necessary conditions involves the *but for* or *sine qua non* rule. Briefly, this rule specifies that a defendant's behaviour is a cause of some harm if and only if that harm would not have occurred except for the defendant's behaviour (Harper and James, 1956). Consider, for example, a boat captain who does not install life-saving floats on his boat and a passenger who falls overboard and drowns. Did the captain's behavioural omission in some sense cause the passenger's drowning? According to the *but for* rule, it depends on whether the drowning would have occurred even if the captain had installed the floats. If the passenger fell overboard and slipped under the water without anyone seeing him, then the captain's behaviour would not be considered a necessary condition for the drowning. On the other hand, if a crew member saw the passenger fall overboard and then searched in vain for a life float, then the captain's behaviour would be considered a necessary condition for the drowning. Our own research has found very

strong support for the use of the necessity principle in attributing
causation for harm in such cases (Shultz et al., 1981).

The legal analysis of sufficient conditions involves the so-called
*differentiating factor analysis* (Gorovitz, 1965), which is itself a conceptual
refinement of Hart and Honoré's (1959) distinction between normal
and abnormal occurrences. In brief, this rule specifies that the
defendant's behaviour is a cause of some harm if and only if that
behaviour differentiates the actual situation from some appropriate
standard. If the defendant's behaviour can be singled out as the one
relevant difference between the current, harmful situation and past,
harmless situations, then that behaviour can be regarded as a sufficient
condition for the harm. For example, in determining whether the
captain's behaviour was a cause of the passenger's drowning, this rule
would focus on a comparison of the present case against some normal
standard such as the past accident-free operation of the boat. If it were
typical not to install life-saving floats, then the captain's omission this
time does not differentiate the present case from the standard and,
hence, does not qualify as a sufficient condition for the drowning.
However, if it were typical for floats to be installed, then the captain's
behaviour does differentiate the present case from the standard and,
hence, does constitute a sufficient condition for the harm. Somewhat
surprisingly our research has indicated that subjects do not use the
sufficiency principle in assessing causation for harm in cases like this
(Shultz et al., 1981). Similarly, it was reported in a study of 'defensive'
attribution by Schroeder and Linder (1976) that differentiating factor
information had no effect on judgements of causation.[2]

The fact that subjects use the necessity but not the sufficiency rule in
reasoning about causation is rather curious since in the philosophy and
practice of science, both sufficient and necessary conditions are
typically regarded as critical for establishing causal connections
(Nagel, 1961). It is also the case that recent psychological research has
found that ordinary causal attributions are affected by sufficient, as
well as necessary, conditions even in young children (Bindra, Clarke
and Shultz, 1980; Shultz and Butkowsky, 1977; Siegler, 1976).
Consequently, we undertook further research in an effort to determine
why information on sufficient conditions was not readily used to make
judgements about causation. Our first step was to see if subjects could
use this information to judge whether the protagonist's behaviour
constituted a sufficient condition for the harm (Shultz et al., 1981).
This sort of decision would presumably be one step removed from
judging causation *per se*. If information concerning the extent to which
the protagonist's behaviour constituted a differentiating factor was not

viewed as relevant to a decision about sufficient conditions for harm, then this could by itself account for the fact that such information does not influence causal judgements. The results indicated that subjects did not use sufficiency information to judge sufficient conditions. The essence of sufficiency information is, of course, that the protagonist's behaviour either does or does not differentiate the current, harmful situation from other, normal situations in which no harm has occurred. An experiment was therefore conducted to determine if subjects could use sufficiency information to judge whether the protagonist's behaviour differentiated between the current, harmful situation and the normal standard (Shultz *et al.*, 1981). The rationale was that, if they could not even identify the behaviour as a differentiating factor, then the foregoing negative results for the sufficiency rule would be accounted for. The data indicated that subjects did view the behaviour as a differentiating factor in the *sufficient* condition but not in the *not sufficient* condition. The results from these experiments thus help to specify the difficulty that subjects have in using the sufficiency principle. It is clear that subjects do accurately identify whether or not the protagonist's behaviour is a differentiating factor, but they do not use that conclusion to determine whether the behaviour constitutes either a sufficient condition of or a cause of the harm. A deeper explanation of this will require further research, but a number of hypotheses seem reasonable at this point. Three of them are theoretical in nature, and two reflect primarily methodological considerations.

One methodological consideration (suggested by Jos Jaspars) is that the sufficiency rule might be used if the relevant judgements were made in a series of graded steps. For example, subjects could be asked first whether the behaviour constitutes a differentiating factor, second, whether it is a sufficient condition for the harm, and third, whether it is a cause of the harm. Such a graded procedure might serve to reduce the conceptual complexity of the decision process and thereby enhance subjects' use of the sufficiency rule. A second methodological consideration (suggested by Peter White) is that sufficiency information might be constructed somewhat differently. For example, the circumstances of the present drowning might be compared with other boats and captains currently operating rather than with the past operation of the boat and captain in question. These two alternatives are analogous to Kelley's (1967, 1973) consensus and consistency comparisons, respectively. Perhaps consensus information would have a greater impact on causal judgements in these cases than would consistency information; but, if so, this would conflict with other findings indicating that consistency information accounts for more variance in causal attributions than does consensus information (McArthur, 1972; see also Ruble and Feldman, 1976; Kassin, 1979).

Among the more theoretical explanations of the non-utility of the sufficiency principle is Mackie's (1974) argument that necessity implicates the notion of the *counterfactual conditional* whereas sufficiency does not. For Mackie (1974) a causal connection (say, between events $A$ and $X$) is most appropriately defined in terms of the counterfactual conditional: $A$ occurred, and $X$ occurred, and $X$ would not have occurred if $A$ had not. Mackie points out that such counterfactual assertions will hold if $A$ is necessary for $X$ but not if $A$ is only sufficient for $X$. Where $A$ is necessary for $X$, $X$ would not have occurred if $A$ had not occurred. But where $A$ is only sufficient for $X$, it is possible that $X$ would occur even if $A$ had not occurred; $X$ could occur, for example, as a consequence of causes other than $A$, since $A$ is not a necessary condition of $X$. Consequently, necessary conditions may be regarded as more essential to causal attribution than are sufficient conditions, at least under this particular interpretation of causation. It is not yet clear whether ordinary observers would view causation in this way, but such a possibility is at least consistent with our present results.

A second theoretical possibility (suggested independently by Frank Fincham) is that information on sufficient conditions may be taken into account in judging physical causation but not in judging psychological causation. The difference may be based on a reluctance to consider other, possibly past events when evaluating the causation of harm in social, moral, and legal contexts. Such relatively remote events are, as noted above, required to establish sufficiency but not to establish necessity. But why take remote events into account only in physical and not in psychological contexts? Perhaps the perceptual salience of the current harm captures the attentional capacity of the observer, leading her/him to ignore other, more remote pieces of information. Or perhaps the moral and legal aspects inherent in the evaluation of personal harm serve to enhance the psychological importance of the causal inquiry, suggesting to the observer that it may not be 'fair' to take remote events into account. The observer may feel no such compunction against considering remote information in a dispassionate analysis of purely physical causation. A third theoretical account of the non-use of sufficiency in causal analysis hinges on possible asymmetries in judging harm and benefit. In brief, it may be that an analysis of necessary conditions is critical for judging harm and that an analysis of sufficient conditions is critical for judging benefit. This argument is discussed more fully in the following section. These hypothesised explanations for the failure fully to utilise sufficiency information are currently being investigated in our laboratory.

Before leaving the topic of causation, it may be of interest to consider the possibility that principles for determining causal connections, such as necessity and sufficiency, may be reducible to probability calculus. Such reductionist arguments have in fact been made at both the conceptual (Suppes, 1970) and psychological (Ajzen and Fishbein, 1975; Brewer, 1977) levels. For example, as noted above, Brewer's (1977) model specified that attribution of responsibility (considered to be equivalent to that of causation) is a positive function of the difference between the contingent probability of the effect, given the protagonist's behaviour, and its base, non-contingent probability. It seems quite possible that probability values could be assigned to information categories reflecting variations in necessity and sufficiency in a way that would conform to either theoretical predictions or even data outcomes.

Whether the abovementioned assignments would carry any theoretical import is very problematic. First of all, there is no guarantee, and no current evidence, that subjects actually calculate these probabilities when reasoning about causal connections. It is, indeed, more reasonable to imagine that establishing such connections is essentially a dichotomous matter: event $A$ either caused event $X$ or it did not. Probabilities may be applied to the certainty or proof of causal connections without being inherently applicable to the connections themselves or to observers' understanding of those connections. The fact that causal judgements may be assessed on a continuous scale (probabilistic or not) in no way refutes this argument. Subjects may be quite flexible in providing researchers with all sorts of data that may bear little relation to how they actually deal with the phenomenon. Secondly, probabilistic conversions, even if successful, provide at best a relatively superficial account of attribution processes. This is because they leave untouched the various content variables which presumably determine the probability calculations. It would be important, for example, to know whether the relevant probabilities were determined by necessary v. sufficient conditions, physical v. psychological causation, or harmful v. beneficial outcomes. Satisfaction with probability estimates would hardly lead to consideration of deeper levels of explanation. In this sense, probability calculations may be regarded as a possible intermediate step between determining variables and causal conclusions. This conceptualisation, however, raises a third problem, namely whether such an intermediate step is psychologically redundant. If it contributes nothing to theoretical understanding, considerations of parsimony would argue for its elimination. Fourth, on a more conceptual level, it may be noted that convincing arguments have been raised against the possibility of probabilistic accounts of causation. In particular, Bunge (1973) stressed that probabilistic theories fail to deal with the essential issue of event generation. It is thus questionable whether there is any justification for analysing causal ideas in terms of probabilities.

RESPONSIBILITY

It has been noted above that the determination of causal connections can be a purely epistemic analysis, quite analogous to that which occurs in science. In contrast, responsibility is most often conceptualised in terms of a moral evaluation of a human action (Feinberg, 1968). Where the action results in harm, this evaluation is commonly construed in terms of the blameworthiness of the actor (Bentham, 1789/1948; Hart and Honoré, 1959). As will be seen below, where the action results in benefit, the issue becomes one of praiseworthiness rather than blame (e.g. D'Arcy, 1963). The possibility that concepts of responsibility and blame/credit are psychologically identical has received some empirical support in two recent studies. Lowe and Medway (1976) asked subjects to read a story about a person who produced personal outcomes varying in extremity and positivity. It was found that a measure of blame/credit correlated highly with one of responsibility and that both measures were influenced in similar fashion by differences in extremity of outcome. Similarly, Whitehead and Smith (1976) presented subjects with a story about an individual who bought a home expecting that an earthquake had varying chances of occurring. The story went on to state that the earthquake did occur and its effects were described in varying degrees of severity. Results indicated that measures of responsibility and blame correlated highly and were a positive, linear function of the expectancy of the earthquake.

It has been argued that many legal concepts are rooted in common sense moral reasoning and, in particular, that the notion of legal culpability is essentially equivalent to that of moral responsibility (Hart and Honoré, 1959; Mackie, 1977). Defendants are not, in theory, held legally responsible for harm unless they are also considered morally responsible for it. Contrary to the Aristotelian view sketched out above, contemporary legal theorists have maintained that legal/moral responsibility is conceptually distinct from issues of causation (Harper and James, 1956; Hart and Honoré, 1959). They have argued, for example, that a person could be judged not legally/ morally responsible for harm which s/he had in fact caused. That contemporary ordinary observers also hold this view is suggested by the results of the survey on the Calley case reviewed above (Kelman and Lawrence, 1972). Notwithstanding the conceptual distinctions between causation and responsibility, legal theorists have also stressed the nature of the relationship between the two concepts. This relationship can perhaps be expressed most efficiently in terms of the notion of *pre-supposition*; a judgement of moral responsibility presupposes one of causation. In other words, unless it can be established that the defendants actually cause the harm in question, there is no basis for even raising the issue of their moral/legal responsibility for it.

The one notable exception to this relationship within the law concerns the notion of *vicarious responsibility* (Hart and Honoré, 1959). For example, a father is sometimes held responsible for damages caused by his child, or management held responsible for harm caused to one worker by another. The argument here is that since people can be held responsible for harm which they themselves did not cause, then a judgement of responsibility does not invariably presuppose one of causation. However, it seems to us that such cases of responsibility without causation are quite rare and that the basis for their justification remains obscure. It may be, for instance, that the father or management is held responsible merely as a matter of policy based on their relative ability to provide financial compensation for the harm. Alternatively, perhaps a notion of implicit causation underlies attribution of vicarious responsibility. It may be believed, for example, that the father could have acted to prevent his son from causing harm or that management could have set up working conditions in such a way as to prevent one worker from injuring another. The notion of failure to prevent is undoubtedly a causal idea, and so perhaps vicarious responsibility does not actually represent 'responsibility without causation'. Finally, it is quite likely that responsibility is vicariously extended only with considerable misgiving, as if there were something inherently incorrect and unjust about it. At this point, very little is known about the psychological validity of vicarious responsibility.[3]

Returning to the less controversial and more common case where the harm is known to be caused by the person whose responsibility is being evaluated, how is this evaluation carried out? According to a variety of legal and moral theorists, judgement of responsibility in such cases is largely a matter of discounting various mitigating factors. Among the most commonly suggested mitigating factors are *voluntariness*, *foresight*, and *intervening causation*. The principle of *voluntariness* states that an actor is responsible only if the action that caused the harm was undertaken voluntarily (Feinberg, 1968; Fitzgerald, 1961; Harper and James, 1956; Hart and Honoré, 1959). By this is meant that the action was freely chosen without external coercion or pressure. Consider, for example, a construction foreman who omits to notify the electric company to shut off the power lines near his construction site. One of his workers, a crane operator, is electrocuted when the crane accidentally comes into contact with the live overhead wires. By the *but for* test, the foreman's omissive action can be said to have caused the operator's death. But if it was known that the construction company discouraged their foremen from waiting for power lines to be shut off, in order to avoid costly delays, then the foreman's responsibility for the death might be mitigated. Our own findings indicated that manipulation of voluntariness information strongly influences judgements of moral responsibility in this way (Shultz *et al.*, 1981). It has been well known in the psychological literature that an actor's 'responsibility' for the consequences of his/her actions is diminished by the presence of external coercion or force. This 'discounting' effect has indeed figured prominently in each of the three classical theories of attribution (Heider, 1958a; Jones and Davis, 1965; Kelley, 1973) as discussed above.

The principle of foresight specifies that an actor is responsible for the harm that s/he has caused only if the harm was a reasonably foreseeable consequence of the action (Harper and James, 1956; Hart and Honoré, 1959). For example, if the previously referred to construction foreman had been aware that most of the crane's work would be well away from the overhead wires, then perhaps his responsibility would again be mitigated. Our evidence indicated support for the mitigating effects of foresight information, but the magnitude of these effects was considerably less than for information on voluntariness (Shultz *et al.*, 1981). Foresight had been considered by Heider (1958a) to increase 'responsibility' over simple causality and was identified by Shaver (1975) as a 'dimension of causality'. Information on foresight was also included in an empirical investigation by Schroeder and Linder (1976) and was found to affect responsibility judgements as predicted.

The principle of intervening causation holds that an actor is responsible only if some independent cause of the harm has not intervened between the action and the resulting harm (Harper and James, 1956; Hart and Honoré, 1959; Prosser, 1971). In the above example, if it were known that the unusually soft ground collapsed under the weight of the crane, making the crane tilt and thus come into contact with the live overhead wires, this might also serve to mitigate the responsibility of the foreman. However, our preliminary experiments yielded no support whatsoever for the use of intervening causation in the mitigation of responsibility for harm (Shultz et al., 1981). Within the legal literature as well intervening causation has proved to be a rather controversial matter with respect to both the conditions under which it should be used and the precise locus of its effects. Prosser (1971) proposed that an intervening cause will be seen as a mitigating condition only insofar as its occurrence is not foreseeable in the circumstance. In contrast, Hart and Honoré (1959) argued that intervening causation affects judgements only when it comprises a voluntary human action. Subsequent research supports both of these propositions. The presence of an intervening cause was found to be more mitigating when the intervention was voluntary, as opposed to impersonal, and when it was unforeseeable, as contrasted with foreseeable (Fincham and Shultz, 1981). At first glance it may seem that mitigation via intervening causation could be conceptualised in terms of the familiar discounting effect referred to above (Heider, 1958a; Jones and Davis, 1965; Kelley, 1973). An intervening cause is, after all, another cause and knowledge of its operation might well lead subjects to discount the effectiveness of the initial action. However, this would be too simplified a view in that it would again neglect the influence of attributional contents on attribution processes. As noted above, an intervening cause is not merely another cause but is rather an event which intervenes in a causal chain already set into motion by some initial action. Current evidence shows that its presence does not invariably lead to discounting. This depends at least on its foreseeability and on the extent to which it comprises a voluntary human action (Fincham and Shultz, 1981).

PUNISHMENT

Issues of punishment and restitution concern the various consequences which may accrue to an actor for harm which s/he has caused and is responsible for. Such a conception seems fairly straightforward, and hence it might be imagined that punishment would not pose the same degree of conceptual difficulty that causation and responsibility do. And yet, as noted above in reviewing the literature, the concept of punishment has frequently been confused with that of responsibility and sometimes even with that of causation. Moreover, the principles governing its determination and the nature of its relation to those other two concepts must still be specified. For the latter issue, the notion of presupposition is once again useful. It is commonly held in jurisprudence that a consideration of punishment presupposes a judgement of moral/legal responsibility (Harper and James, 1956; Hart and Honoré, 1959). Unless a defendant has been found morally and legally responsible (i.e. guilty under the law) for harm that s/he has caused, the question of punishment does not legitimately arise.

Given that responsibility has been established, how is punishment actually to be determined? It is quite likely that the principles of punishment will vary with the particular goal or justification that is seen to underlie punishment. For example, people who believed that the primary purpose of punishment is to deter further crime would probably assign punishment on the basis of both the likelihood and the seriousness of future offences. Those motivated by retribution would probably use a simple seriousness rule so that the worse the harm, the greater the punishment. Considerable evidence for the prevalence of a retribution-based rule is already available in the psychological literature. Two experiments reviewed above (De Jong *et al.*, 1976; M. E. Shaw and Reitan, 1969) found that degree of punishment increased with severity of the harm. Vidmar (1977) reported similar results and, moreover, found a stronger effect for persons independently classified as high in retributive motivation than for those classified as low. A corollary of the retribution idea is that, insofar as an offender has himself suffered as a result of the offence, further punishment may be reduced. Some evidence for such mitigating effects has been reported by Leahy (1979b), Servedio (in Brewer, 1977), and J. I. Shaw and McMartin (1975).

Quite apart from such theory-based principles, it seems that punishment is sometimes based on the current demeanour of the offender, and her/his past record and general character. In a study of police discretion in the handling of juvenile offenders in a Canadian community, Doob (1979) found that the absence of previous offences and a 'correct and contrite' manner greatly lessened the likelihood of a court appearance. In our own research, unanticipated use of sufficiency information in the assignment of punishment was found to be mediated by assessments of the actor's character (Shultz *et al.*, 1981). In several experiments, we had noticed that actors were punished somewhat more if their behaviour was presented as not being sufficient for harm than if it was sufficient. Subsequent research showed that this 'reversal' of the sufficiency principle resulted from subjects viewing the actor as a relatively uncaring individual in the *not sufficient* stories. Information on the absence of sufficient conditions was conveyed in these items by specifying that the actor chronically behaved in this manner.

RELATIONS AMONG CAUSATION, RESPONSIBILITY, AND PUNISHMENT

In addition to identifying principles which determine each of the three types of judgements, the foregoing model has stressed their inter-relations. Explicitly stated, the assignment of punishment is claimed to presuppose a judgement of moral responsibility which, in turn, presupposes an attribution of causation. Within this model, it is to be expected that variables which affect a judgement would also influence those which it presupposes. For example, a principle which determines judgements of causation, such as necessity, should also have some effect on judgements of responsibility and punishment. Such carry-over effects have indeed been documented (Shultz, et al., 1981). Evidence has also indicated that principles affect their target judge-ments without also affecting presupposed judgements. For example, information on foresight influenced responsibility, but not causation judgements (Shultz et al., 1981); and severity of harm affected punishment judgements without also influencing responsibility judgements (DeJong et al., 1976).[4] It is possible to obtain an even clearer assessment of these presupposition relations by focusing on the differential degrees of remoteness among the three central concepts. In a psychological sense, judgements of causation and punishment should be more remote than judgements of either causation and responsibility or responsibility and punishment. Causal and punishment judgements are effectively two steps apart, whereas judgements in the latter two pairs are only one step apart. These remoteness predictions have received consistent empirical support from path analyses of the relations among the three types of judgement (Fincham and Shultz, 1981; Shultz et al., 1981). Invariably, the path coefficients between causation and responsibility and between responsibility and punish-ment have been found to be substantial. In contrast, path coefficients between judgements of causation and punishment were found to be negligible.

## The judgement of benefit

The variables of the foregoing model were found to account for a good deal of the variance in subjects' judgements of harmful outcomes. In a sense, this is not too surprising since the model was heavily influenced by conceptual analyses within the philosophy of law; and the law, of course, has always been primarily concerned with preventing or redressing harm. Thus the question arises as to whether this model would also account for variation in the judgement of beneficial outcomes. The distinction between harm and benefit is one on which the classical attribution theories (Heider, 1958a; Jones and Davis,

1965; Kelley, 1967, 1973) have been on the whole silent. Their tacit assumption has been that content-free attribution processes could explain reasoning about harmful or beneficial outcomes quite indifferently. Although some attribution studies (J. I. Shaw and Skolnick, 1971; M. E. Shaw and Sulzer, 1964; Sloan, 1977) have in fact reported differences between harm and benefit, these differences have not as yet attracted any theoretical concern. In moral philosophy, however, there have been a number of conceptual arguments for certain asymmetries in judging harm and benefit. The fact that each of our harm experiments (Shultz *et al.*, 1981) now has a mirror-image experiment with a beneficial outcome (Shultz and Schleifer, 1982) enables a systematic assessment of at least some of these conceptual asymmetries. Items for these benefit experiments were adapted from those of the harm experiments simply by portraying an action (e.g. installing life-saving floats, or having power lines shut off) as a possible contributor to the saving of an endangered person's life.

D'Arcy (1963) maintained that the criteria for judging benefit are in a sense stricter than those for judging harm. Contrary to a number of classical positions (e.g. Bentham, 1789/1948), he argued that establishing the actor's intention to produce harm is not critical to evaluating responsibility for harm. Rather, he claimed, it is sufficient in cases of harm to establish the less stringent criterion of negligence, defined as a lack of due care in thought or in action. As an illustration, consider the case of a person who drives his car at a dangerously high speed along a crowded street. Even if the driver possesses the best of intentions (e.g. to arrive somewhere on time, not to injure anyone, etc.), he is quite likely to be held morally and legally responsible, on the grounds of negligence, for any damage that he causes. In contrast, D'Arcy (1963) argued that it is intention, rather than 'negligence', which is crucial to the evaluation of responsibility for beneficial outcomes. People are unlikely, he wrote, to credit an actor for benefit which s/he brings about inadvertently or carelessly. Interestingly, there appears to be no English language term for an unintentional bringing about of benefit. Empirical support for this interesting asymmetry between harm and benefit in the judgements of ordinary observers has been found by Shultz and Wright (1982).

Schleifer (1966, 1973) raised the possibility that the relation between responsibility and causation is more remote in the case of benefit than in the case of harm. This could stem from a tendency to focus more on the actor in beneficial outcomes and more on the (harmful) outcome itself in cases of harm. Focus on the consequence, of course, would naturally lead to a consideration of the cause of the harmful outcome.

Empirical support for this differential remoteness was evident in a comparison of the path coefficients between causation and responsibility judgements across our harm (Shultz *et al.*, 1981) and benefit (Shultz and Schleifer, 1982) experiments. The relation between judgements of causation and responsibility was significantly stronger for harmful than for beneficial outcomes. At least this was true of those experiments where only causal variables (i.e. necessary and sufficient conditions) were manipulated. Furthermore, judgements of the protagonist's character were more strongly correlated with recommended reward than with recommended punishment.

Feinberg (1968) has emphasised the differential functions of judging harm and benefit. The primary function of judging harm is to prevent it, he claimed, and this can most efficiently be done by removing or preventing one of the necessary conditions for the harm. If a truly necessary condition is absent, the harm will no longer occur. In contrast, the function of judging benefit is to discover ways of producing or continuing it. Efficient production of an event is accomplished by ensuring the operation of one of its sufficient conditions. If a truly sufficient condition is present, the benefit will occur. Thus, insofar as observers are attuned to these differential functions, they should focus more on necessary conditions in the case of harm and more on sufficient conditions in the case of benefit. Our data, in fact, offer some support for this prediction. Regression models based on necessity accounted for considerably more variance in causal and moral judgements of harm than in causal and moral judgements of benefit (Shultz and Schleifer, 1982). It was also true that regression models based on sufficiency accounted for considerably more variance in judgements of benefit than in judgements of harm. However, it must be remembered that these effects of sufficiency information were actually the reverse of what would be expected by the sufficiency principle and more in accord with an evaluation of the actor's character (cf. Attribution processes in harm-doing). In this sense, the differential impact of necessity and sufficiency information on harm v. benefit is more consistent with Schleifer's (1966, 1973) view that the focus of attention is on the cause and consequence for harm and on the actor for benefit.

Thus, there appear to be a number of differences between harm and benefit in the way that causal and moral principles are applied. These differences document yet another instance in which an orientation to attribution processes must be tempered by a consideration of the conceptual content of the attribution. Except for the particular differences just cited, though, the results for benefit (Shultz and

Schleifer, 1982) corresponded quite closely to those obtained for harm
(Shultz *et al.*, 1981). Information on the voluntariness of the beneficial
action, for example, exerted powerful effects on judgements of causation, responsibility, and recommended consequences (reward) just as
it had for harmful actions. Compared with voluntariness, the variables
of foresight and intervening cause had much less impact on these
judgements in cases of benefit just as they did in cases of harm. Finally,
the pattern of the remoteness relations among the three types of
judgements was similar in both cases. In both realms, relations
between causation and responsibility and between responsibility and
recommended consequences were strong, whereas relations between
causation and punishment/reward were weak.


## Summary and conclusions

In this chapter we have argued for a conceptual refinement of some key
attribution concepts, namely causation, moral responsibility, and
punishment/reward. Some theoretical and empirical confusions were
identified in the attribution literature with respect to these concepts
and some degree of conceptual precision was attained by drawing on
analyses of these ideas in the philosophies of science, mind, law, and
ethics. It was argued that causation refers essentially to event
generation, responsibility to moral evaluation of an actor, and
punishment/reward to the recommended consequences for the actor.

   In addition, we established the influence of certain principles of
inference and their corresponding informational categories on these
causal, moral, and consequence judgements. The principle of necessary conditions (for the outcome) was found to exert a powerful
influence on judgements of causation and on the resulting judgements
of responsibility and punishment/reward. Use of the principle of
sufficient conditions (for the outcome) was found to be more problem-
atical. Subjects correctly identified the actor's behaviour as a
differentiating factor but failed to see the relevance of that information
to issues of sufficient conditions or causation. Various theoretical and
methodological interpretations of this problem with the sufficiency
principle are still under investigation. The principles of voluntariness
and intervening causation were also found substantially to mitigate
responsibility for an outcome even when the action in question was
portrayed as a necessary condition for the outcome. The mitigating
effects of intervening causation depended heavily on whether the
intervening cause represented a voluntary human action and was not

forseeable in the circumstance. The principle of foresight (of the resulting harm) was found to mitigate moral responsibility even when the harm was seen to be caused by the actor.

Relations among causal, moral, and consequence judgements were specified in terms of the notion of presupposition. A punishment/reward judgement was said to presuppose a judgement of moral responsibility which, in turn, presupposes a causal judgement. Path analyses of correlations among the three types of judgement were consistent with this view. Results on beneficial outcomes generally paralleled those on harm except that: (a) the necessity principle exerted greater influence in cases of harm than in cases of benefit, (b) there was more focus on the character of the actor in cases of benefit than in cases of harm, and (c) relations between causal and moral judgements were more remote for benefit than for harm. All of the foregoing results were anticipated to some extent by conceptual analyses derived from the philosophical literature. It was argued that process-oriented attribution theories should begin to take explicit account of these content variables. Findings reviewed here make it apparent that the application of processing principles depends on the particular kinds of attributional judgements being made. This, of course, greatly decreases the likelihood of a successful content-free theory of attribution.

The heuristic value of various branches of philosophy for the psychology of attribution has been emphasised throughout this chapter. What has not yet been stressed are the potential contributions of conceptually appropriate psychological research on attribution processes to the solution of certain philosophical issues. There are many instances in the philosophical literature where explicitly psychological assertions or assumptions are made, commonly without the aid of empirical data. A single and very broad example is Hart and Honoré's (1959) contention that the principles of jurisprudence are based firmly in common sense causal and moral reasoning. This point was stressed in opposition to the 'legal modernists' (cf. Morris, 1961) for whom purely pragmatic considerations predominate over causal and moral issues. Hart and Honoré may indeed be correct, but the absence of a conceptually sophisticated theory of ordinary causal and moral reasoning has made their proposition very difficult to assess. As psychologists gear their research to the important conceptual issues and distinctions raised by philosophers, this research will undoubtedly become more relevant to deciding among competing conceptual claims. Research reviewed here suggests that subjects untutored in moral, legal, and scientific issues do indeed exhibit a certain consensus on moral and causal ideas. More specifically, research has supported the use of several major principles and has identified psychological difficulties with others (e.g. the differentiating factor analysis of Gorovitz, 1965, and Hart and Honoré, 1959). Philosophers may eventually find it useful to incorporate such psychological data into their conceptual arguments, thus ensuring a more lively exchange of ideas between the disciplines.

## Acknowledgement

The preparation of this chapter was facilitated by a grant from the Department of Education of the Province of Quebec.

## Notes

1. We are aware of course that this claim is philosophically controversial, in that some would not accept that intentions can function as causes. For more on this, see Davidson (1963) and Shultz (1980).
2. The principles of necessity and sufficiency bear some relation to Kelley's (1973) schemata for multiple necessary and multiple sufficient causes, respectively. More specifically, it would seem that the use of one of Kelley's schemata would presuppose that the multiple causes have already been characterised as *necessary* or as *sufficient* for the effect. For example, on the assumption that each of two causes is sufficient to produce an effect, the operation of one of them may be discounted if it is known that the other is operative. The necessity and sufficiency principles, as considered here, may be said to generate the conclusions about the necessary and sufficient relations that are required by Kelley's schemata.
3. The notion of vicarious responsibility should not be confused with the related principle of *respondeat superior* in which a superior is held responsible for the acts of a subordinate who, in following orders, instructions, or policy causes some harm. Our data indicate that the underling is excused in such cases from a causal judgement, presumably because the superior is perceived as the primary cause of the harm (Shultz *et al.*, 1981). Thus, the argument that responsibility is entirely independent of causation gets no help here.
4. It has also been found that some variables, such as voluntariness and intervening causation, affect the presupposed judgement of causation nearly as much as they affect their expected target of responsibility (Fincham and Shultz, 1981; Shultz and Wright, 1982). At present, it is not clear whether this represents a carry-over effect (from responsibility to causation) or whether these variables are directly influencing causal judgements.

# 3

# Relevance and Availability in the Attribution Process

## Icek Ajzen and Martin Fishbein

## Introduction

A substantial proportion of basic research in contemporary social psychology deals with the processes that characterise naive interpretations of human behavior. Beginning with Heider's (1944) interest in causal attribution of a behavior or event, this field of inquiry has expanded to the point where it incorporates virtually any human judgement made within a social context. It is possible to classify these judgements into three broad categories. One type of judgement involves the *prediction* of future events. For example, a respondent may be asked to judge the likelihood of his own or another person's success on a given task or the likelihood that an act will result in a certain outcome. A second type of judgement involves, in its broadest sense, the task of *categorisation*. Sometimes individuals are asked to estimate the probability that a person is a member of an occupational, religious, political, or other group (e.g. a lawyer, an engineer, a Catholic, or a Republican). On other occasions, the categorisation involves judgements concerning the attitudes, personality characteristics, or other dispositions of a stimulus person. Such judgements may be considered a subset of categorisation since they can be interpreted as assigning the stimulus person to the class of people who possess the disposition in question. The third type of judgement, *explanation* is closely linked to Heider's original concern with the question of causal attribution. Here, the individual attempts to identify causes or reasons for the occurrence of a given action or event. Frequent concerns are explanations for success or failure on a task and for choice among alternatives. The judgement typically involves an estimate that a given factor, or class of factors, led to the observed event.

Although some investigators (e.g. Ross, 1977) regard all of these judgements as falling within the domain of attribution theory, we would argue that many social judgements are of only tangential relevance to this domain. Historically, attribution theory dealt with an individual's attempt to give meaning and coherence to the behavior of another person in terms of relatively stable dispositions of the person or the environment. According to Heider (1958a), 'dispositional properties are the invariances that make possible a more or less stable, predictable, and controllable world' (p. 80). Viewed in this light, it becomes clear that attributional judgements have as their starting point a behavior or a behavioral episode. The central issue addressed by attribution theory has to do with dispositional properties that allow the observer to give coherence and organisation to the actor's behavior. In attribution research, respondents have been asked to make two kinds of judgements that reflect this concern. Confronted with information about an actor's behavior (and often also about the circumstances under which it was performed and the effects it produced), an observer may be asked to specify the causes of the behavior or to draw inferences from it. In the first case, dispositional properties are used to explain the behavior (*causal attribution*), while in the second case the behavior is used to infer dispositional properties of the actor or the environment (*dispositional attribution*).

It can be seen that attributions are a special case of social judgements. Dispositional attributions are a subset of the class of judgements that involve categorisations whereas causal attributions are a subset of the class of judgements that involve explanations. However, both types of attribution are based on assumptions concerning the causal effects of dispositions on behavior. In causal attribution, these assumptions are used to explain the behavior whereas in dispositional attribution they are used to infer the dispositions. We believe that the term attribution should be used only with reference to these two types of judgement and our discussion in this chapter will be limited to this definition of dispositional processes. Although the basic principles underlying attributions may be equally applicable to other types of social judgements, we will make no attempt to review the literature in such areas as impression formation or predictions and other judgements under uncertainty. Only when it has direct bearing on the attribution process will this literature be considered.

## Fundamental components of attribution

The process whereby people arrive at causal or dispositional attributions is comprised of several separable components.[1] When people attempt to find explanations for an observed behavior or to draw inferences from it, they may be viewed as searching for hypotheses that could provide answers to these questions. One important issue that confronts attribution theory concerns the factors that influence the selection of these hypotheses. Clearly, people cannot formulate hypotheses about causal or dispositional properties that are not part of their cognitive repertoires. But even dispositions that are within a person's repertoire may not be available (Tversky and Kahneman, 1973), salient (Taylor and Fiske, 1975), vivid (Nisbett and Ross, 1980), or accessible (Bruner, 1957a; Higgins, Rholes and Jones, 1977) at the time of hypothesis generation.

The availability of dispositions sets only broad limits on the kinds of hypotheses that may be considered. Within the available set, dispositions are likely to be considered only if they are potentially capable of providing an answer to the attributional question (see Ajzen and Fishbein, 1978). For example, an observer attempting to explain why a woman had an abortion would not consider hypotheses that involve such dispositional properties as the color of her hair, her attitude toward snakes, or the location of the nearest shopping center. A complete analysis of the attribution process, therefore, must address not only the factors that influence the availability of dispositional hypotheses but also their perceived relevance.

After formulating one or more hypotheses, the observer will usually look for additional information or evidence to evaluate the validity of the hypotheses under consideration. Here, too, questions of the availability of evidence and its relevance to the hypothesis being tested are of major importance. Only evidence that is available and considered to be relevant is likely to be taken into account. The observer arrives at an attributional judgement by evaluating the extent to which the relevant evidence is consistent or inconsistent with the hypothesis under consideration. Consistent evidence is likely to increase the observer's confidence in the validity of the hypothesis whereas inconsistent evidence is likely to reduce his confidence.

In sum, the attribution process involves generation and validation of hypotheses concerning human behavior. Both the hypotheses generated and the evidence used to validate them are closely linked to questions of availability and relevance. Most theories of attribution have focused on the problem of relevance (or consistency and inconsistency) and have tended to ignore the question of availability. In fact, research designed to test these theories has usually examined attributional judgements in situations where both hypotheses and evidence were supplied by the investigator. In studies of dispositional attribution, the question of interest concerns the factors that influence reliance on the actor's behavior to infer a disposition, that is, the extent to which the behavior is perceived to be relevant for the disposition in question. For example, respondents may be told that a student advocated a certain position on an issue under conditions of high or low freedom of choice and are then asked to infer the student's true position on the issue. The investigator provides the dispositional hypotheses (that the actor favors or opposes a certain position) as well as the relevant evidence (the actor's behavior and presence or absence of situational constraints). In studies of causal attribution, the hypotheses provided by the investigator often involve a distinction between internal and external causes of behavior. The question here concerns the extent to which various kinds of evidence are used to infer an internal or external cause. For example, a respondent may be asked whether a student's success on an exam was due to ability (internal attribution) or ease of the exam (external attribution). In addition to these causal hypotheses, the respondent may be given evidence indicating that most or few of the other students in the class also passed the exam. The perceived relevance of this evidence is indicated by the extent to which it influences internal or external attributions.

In recent years, investigators have increasingly turned their attention to the role of availability in the attribution process. Initially, this research attempted to demonstrate that dispositional or causal attributions are influenced by the availability of hypotheses and evidence. For example, it has often been assumed that actors and observers make different attributions because different kinds of information are salient or available to them. Stimulated in a large part by Tversky and Kahneman's (1973, 1974; Kahneman and Tversky, 1973) work on cognitive heuristics, research in the attribution area has started to explore the factors that influence availability of hypotheses and evidence. It is argued that the intuitive strategies of information-processing identified by Tversky and Kahneman bias the use of information and hence produce systematic errors in attributional judgements. Since these biases are assumed to be related to the salience of information, to its storage in memory, and to its later recall, interest has shifted to the role of attention and memory in the attribution process. Although this research represents a new direction in the area of attribution, psychologists have of course long been interested in questions of attention and in processes that underlie organisation, storage, and retrieval of information. The challenge to investigators in the attribution area is not to demonstrate that earlier findings concerning attention and memory can be replicated with social stimuli, but rather to draw upon these findings in order to generate hypotheses about factors that may influence causal and dispositional attributions.

In this chapter, we will first discuss theories and research related to the question of relevance in the attribution process and then turn to some of the more recent developments concerning availability of hypotheses and evidence.

## Relevance of behavior and other evidence

Based on Heider's (1944, 1958a) work, a number of investigators have proposed theoretical accounts of attribution processes. As noted earlier, these theories address primarily the issue of relevance in attributional judgements. While they exhibit certain common features, they differ in terms of their major focus of interest and do not provide an integrated picture of attribution processes. In an earlier paper (Ajzen and Fishbein, 1975) we showed that Bayes' theorem could serve as a heuristic model to help interpret and integrate the diverse ideas and research findings concerning dispositional and causal attributions. The following discussion provides a brief summary of this approach and shows how a Bayesian analysis helps identify the relevance of behavior and other evidence for any given attributional judgement.

BAYES' THEOREM

Like attribution theory, Bayes' theorem is concerned with the formation or revision of beliefs in the light of new information. It is a normative model in that it describes optimal revisions in probabilities; that is, it describes how probabilities should change if the available information were properly utilised.[2] Thus, the theorem deals with revision in beliefs or hypotheses $(H)$ on the basis of new information or data $(D)$. In its simplest form, Bayes' theorem is expressed in eqn (1):

$$p(H|D) = \frac{p(D|H)p(H)}{p(D)} \tag{1}$$

where $p(H|D)$ is the posterior probability of the hypothesis given the datum; $p(D|H)$ is the probability of the datum given the hypothesis; and $p(H)$ and $p(D)$ are, respectively, the prior probabilities of the hypothesis and the datum.

If we let $\bar{H}$ stand for the complement of $H$ (i.e. $p(\bar{H}) = 1 - p(H)$), then by definition $p(D) = p(D|H)p(H) + p(D|\bar{H})p(\bar{H})$. Bayes' theorem can thus also be written as follows:

$$p(H|D) = \frac{p(D|H)p(H)}{p(D|H)p(H) + p(D|\bar{H})p(\bar{H})} \tag{2}$$

One interesting implication of Bayes' theorem as presented in eqn (2) is that no revision in belief should occur when $p(D|H) = p(D|\bar{H})$. That is, when the datum is equally likely whether or not the hypothesis is true, it should have no effect on the hypothesis. In fact, when $p(D|H) = p(D|\bar{H})$, these terms drop out of eqn (2), which then becomes

$$p(H|D) = \frac{p(H)}{p(H) + p(\bar{H})}$$

However, $p(H) + p(\bar{H}) = 1$, so that $p(H|D) = p(H)$; hypothesis and datum are thus by definition independent, and the latter should have no effect on the former when $p(D|H) = p(D|\bar{H})$.

When the difference between these two conditional probabilities is positive (i.e. when $p(D|H) - p(D|\bar{H}) > 0$), an upward revision in probability is expected. Conversely, when $p(D|H) - p(D|\bar{H}) < 0$, a downward revision should result. The greater the difference between $p(D|H)$ and $p(D|\bar{H})$, the more impact the datum in question should have on the posterior probability.

In many situations it is useful to consider two alternative hypotheses, $p(H)$ and $p(\bar{H})$, and Bayes' theorem can be stated with respect to each as follows:

$$p(H|D) = \frac{p(D|H)p(H)}{p(D)}$$

$$p(\bar{H}|D) = \frac{p(D|\bar{H})p(\bar{H})}{p(D)}$$

A computationally convenient form of Bayes' theorem in the case of two hypotheses is provided when the first of these equations is divided by the second:

$$\frac{p(H|D)}{p(\bar{H}|D)} = \frac{p(D|H)}{p(D|\bar{H})} \times \frac{p(H)}{p(\bar{H})}. \tag{3}$$

In eqn (3), $p(H|D)/p(\bar{H}|D)$ is the posterior odds with respect to Hypothesis $H$; that is, the extent to which Hypothesis $H$ is more or less likely than Hypothesis $\bar{H}$. Similarly, $p(H)/p(\bar{H})$ is the prior odds with respect to Hypothesis $H$.[3] Finally, $p(D|H)/p(D|\bar{H})$ is known as the *likelihood ratio*. This ratio is an index of the relevance or diagnostic value of the datum in question and indicates the degree to which the datum favors one hypothesis over the other.

Equation (3) is often written more simply as
$$\Omega_1 = LR\Omega_0, \tag{4}$$
where $\Omega_1$ is the posterior odds, $\Omega_0$ is the prior odds, and LR is the likelihood ratio. It can be seen in eqn (3) that the likelihood ratio is comprised of the two conditional probabilities considered earlier with respect to eqn (2), that is, $p(D|H)$ and $p(D|\bar{H})$. Again, when these two terms are equal, $LR = 1$, and no revision in probability takes place ($\Omega_1 = \Omega_0$). When $p(D|H)$ exceeds $p(D|\bar{H})$, the likelihood ratio becomes greater than 1 and, according to the theorem, the odds are revised in favor of Hypothesis $H$. Conversely, when $p(D|H)<p(D|\bar{H})$, $LR<1$, and the odds are revised in favor of Hypothesis $\bar{H}$.

A large number of studies have shown that beliefs tend to be internally consistent and that people revise their beliefs in an orderly fashion as a result of new information (Peterson and Beach, 1967; Slovic and Lichtenstein, 1971). The extent to which people can be described as Bayesian information processors, however, has been challenged in recent years (Fischhoff and Lichtenstein, 1978; Kahneman and Tverksy, 1972; Slovic, Fischhoff and Lichtenstein, 1977). Most of the criticism is concerned not with the internal logic of Bayes' theorem but with people's ability to make appropriate use of information to arrive at 'objectively accurate' prior odds and likelihood ratios. People's subjective probabilities may not correspond to objective probabilities based on the calculus of statistics for a variety of reasons some of which are considered below. From our point of view, the calculus of statistics that permits computation of objective prior odds and likelihood ratios is extra-Bayesian and people's inability to use it has little bearing on the descriptive accuracy of Bayes' theorem as such. In fact, there seems to be little evidence to suggest that the theorem fails to make accurate predictions when the respondents' *subjective* estimates of prior odds and likelihood ratios are used to predict their final judgements (see Ajzen and Fishbein, 1978).

In conclusion, Bayes' theorem specifies optimal revision of beliefs in light of new information. According to the model, the amount of change in a given belief or hypothesis is a function of the diagnostic value or relevance of the new item of information. The likelihood ratio thus identifies the extent to which a behavior and other items of evidence are relevant for a given causal or dipositional attribution. The theorem itself, however, has little to say about the factors that influence the degree to which some new item of information has diagnostic value for a given inference. This value has to be determined on the basis of other considerations. The different theories of attribution can be viewed as attempts to specify some of the factors that influence relevance or diagnosticity of information concerning a person's behavior or the context in which the behavior is performed. Below, we briefly consider theory and research concerning causal and dispositional attribution. For a more detailed discussion, see Ajzen and Fishbein (1975).

CAUSAL ATTRIBUTION

An actor's behavior can usually be attributed to a large number of causal factors. If the only information available to the observer is the fact that the actor has performed the behavior in question, causal attribution may prove quite difficult. Frequently, however, the observer will have some additional information about the actor, the behavior, and the conditions under which the behavior was performed. We now examine the effects of such additional information on the perceived likelihood of alternative causal explanations.

Following Heider's (1958a) distinction between personal and impersonal causation, theory and research on causal attribution has focused on explanation of an actor's behavior in terms of factors residing in the actor (internal attribution) as opposed to factors residing in the environment (external attribution). Theories of attribution attempt to identify factors that influence attribution of behavior to internal or external causes. Most work in this area is guided by Kelley's (1973) *covariation principle* which states: 'An effect is attributed to the one of its possible causes with which, over time, it covaries' (p. 108). The covariation principle is closely tied to the notion of consistency. Kelley's analysis deals with the degree to which the behavior in question is displayed consistently on different occasions ('consistency'), toward different objects ('distinctiveness'), and by different actors ('consensus').

In a typical study, respondents are given information about an actor's behavior, as well as additional evidence concerning its consistency, distinctiveness, or consensus. They are then asked to explain the behavior in terms of a set of alternative causal hypotheses provided by the experimenter. These hypotheses attribute the behavior to internal or external causes and occasionally also to a combination of internal and external causes. For example, respondents may be told that 'Ralph trips over Joan's feet while dancing', and that 'almost everyone (hardly anyone) else who dances with Joan trips over her feet'. To assess the effects of this consensus manipulation, they may then be asked to indicate which of the following four alternatives had caused the actor's behavior: (*a*) something about the actor, (*b*) something about the object, (*c*) something about the particular circumstances, or (*d*) some combination of the first three alternatives (McArthur, 1972). Similarly, in studies concerning explanation of success and failure, respondents may be told that a student passed an exam and that he or she had frequently (or rarely) succeeded on tests of this type in the past (consistency information). Here the respondents' task typically is to indicate the extent to which the student's success on the exam was caused by ability, effort, an easy test, or luck. The first two alternatives represent internal causes while the last two represent external causes (Frieze and Weiner, 1971; Weiner, Frieze, Kukla, Reed, Rest and Rosenbaum, 1971; Weiner and Kukla, 1970).

To apply Bayes' theorem to judgements of this kind, let $B$ stand for the behavior, $c$ for any of the possible causes specified by the experimenter, and $H_c$ for the hypothesis that $c$ caused $B$. The relevance or diagnosticity of evidence ($E$) concerning consistency, distinctiveness, or consensus is given by the likelihood ratio, $p(E|H_c)/p(E|\bar{H}_c)$.

As an illustration, consider the effect of consistency on attribution of success to an internal cause such as ability. Clearly, consistent success on a series of tests ($E_h$) is more likely under the hypothesis that the student's success was caused by his ability ($H_a$) than under the hypothesis that ability did not cause the success, i.e. $p(E_h/H_a) > p(E_h/\bar{H}_a)$. Conversely, lack of success on previous occasions ($E_l$) is more likely under the hypothesis that success on the exam in question was *not* due to ability than under the complementary hypothesis, i.e. $p(E_l|H_a) < p(E_l|\bar{H}_a)$. Given these differences between conditional probabilities, it follows that the likelihood ratio under high consistency is greater than the likelihood ratio under low consistency:

$$\frac{p(E_h|H_a)}{p(E_h|\bar{H}_a)} > \frac{p(E_l|H_a)}{p(E_l|\bar{H}_a)}$$

These considerations imply that consistency information is relevant for attribution of success to ability and that such attributions are more likely to occur when there is evidence for high (rather than low) consistency.

A Bayesian analysis can similarly be applied to the effects of distinctiveness or consensus information on causal attribution of a behavior to any given internal or external factor. In a previous paper (Ajzen and Fishbein, 1975) we showed that variations in consistency across occasions, objects and actors should influence the likelihood ratio in a manner compatible with Kelley's theorising. In the case of internal causal attribution, the likelihood ratio is expected to increase with evidence for high consistency, low distinctiveness, and low consensus. In the case of attribution to an external cause, the likelihood ratio should increase with the reverse pattern of evidence.

We also showed that it is possible to extend this analysis to evidence concerning consistency along other dimensions. Of particular importance is consistency among different behaviors performed by the actor. Campbell (1963) has argued that a person's attitude (and other dispositions) is evidenced by consistency in his responses toward the attitude object. In a similar manner it can be proposed that an observer attributes an actor's behavior to a given causal factor to the extent that other behaviors performed by the same actor are consistent with the proposed explanation.

Consider, for example, the hypothesis that Jim slipped and fell because he is clumsy. The perceived likelihood of this explanation should increase if Jim were also observed to spill his coffee, to drop his books, to burn his fingers while lighting a cigarette, and so on. In terms of the likelihood ratio, the subjective probability of the totality of this behavioral evidence will be higher under the hypothesis that Jim slipped because he is clumsy than under the hypothesis that his slipping was not caused by clumsiness. The total set of behaviors, including the slipping and falling, is therefore likely to be attributed to Jim's clumsiness.

A Bayesian analysis is also compatible with Kelley's (1973) *discounting principle* which deals with the effects of multiple plausible hypotheses on the likelihood that a given causal factor will be invoked to explain the actor's behavior. Consistent with the discounting principle, a Bayesian analysis suggests that alternative plausible hypotheses will tend to reduce the perceived validity of any given explanation. For example, success is less likely to be attributed to ability when there is evidence that most other people also succeeded, that is, when ease of task can serve as a plausible alternative hypothesis. Under the hypothesis that ability caused success, it is more likely that relatively few people succeeded than that most people succeeded. The likelihood ratio for the hypothesis that ability caused success is thus greater when ease of task cannot provide an alternative explanation.

To summarise our discussion thus far, we have tried to show that a Bayesian analysis of causal attribution can explain the effects of different kinds of evidence by considering its impact on the likelihood ratio. Such an analysis provides insight into the attribution process since it helps us gain information about the extent to which various types of evidence are consistent or inconsistent with a given causal hypothesis.

DISPOSITIONAL ATTRIBUTION

At the most fundamental level, attribution theory addresses the question of how people identify the causes of human behavior. In our preceding discussion we saw that these causes often refer to dispositions of the actor. Thus, a person's success on an exam may be attributed to ability and spilling coffee to nervousness. Because causal explanation often results in attribution of dispositions to another person, attribution theory has attracted the attention of investigators interested in person perception.

Inspired by Steiner's writings on decision freedom (Steiner, 1970, 1980; Steiner and Field, 1960) and Jones and Davis's (1965) work on attribution processes in person perception, research has dealt with the conditions under which a behavior will be attributed to a disposition of the actor. Three major variables have been investigated: the actor's perceived freedom of decision, the perceived desirability of his behavior, and the extent to which the behavior results in unique or uncommon effects. In the following discussion we briefly describe the application of Bayes' theorem to research that examines the effects of these three types of evidence on dispositional attributions.

*Perceived decision freedom.* Although it is possible to distinguish between different kinds of perceived decision freedom and to identify a variety of factors that may influence perception of freedom (see Steiner, 1980), there is general agreement that dispositional attribution will increase to the extent that the actor is perceived to have behaved under high freedom of choice. To investigate the effects of perceived decision freedom, Steiner and Field (1960) led respondents to believe that a confederate took a prosegregation stand in a group discusssion either because he was assigned to that role by the experimenter (low decision freedom) or of his own free choice (high decision freedom). Consistent with expectations, respondents were more confident in attributing a prosegregation stand to the confederate under high, than under low, freedom of choice.

The stronger attribution predicted under high decision freedom also follows from a Bayesian analysis. To demonstrate this, let $B$ stand for the confederate's behavior and $D$ for a disposition. Even before observing the confederate expressing a prosegregation position, the participants will have had some probability that the confederate was in favor of segregation. A dispositional attribution occurs when this belief is changed as a result of observing the behavior. In Bayes' theorem this implies a revision from prior odds, $p(D)/p(\bar{D})$, to posterior odds, $p(D|B)/p(\bar{D}|B)$. The behavior's relevance or diagnosticity for attributing the dispostion is given by the likelihood ratio, $p(B|D)/p(B|\bar{D})$.

It stands to reason that a behavior performed under low freedom of choice has little diagnostic value and is as likely to be performed with or without the disposition in question. Under high freedom of choice, however, the behavior is more likely to be performed when the actor has the appropriate disposition than when s/he does not. To put this more formally the likelihood ratio $p(B|D)/p(B|\bar{D})$ should be close to unity in the case of low decision freedom, while it should exceed unity under high freedom of choice. Consequently, expressing a prosegregation stand is of greater relevance to (i.e. more consistent with) the attribution of a corresponding attitude under high, than under low, decision freedom.

*Perceived desirability of behavior.* According to Jones and Davis (1965), when one assumes that the actor intended to produce the observed behavior, the lower its apparent attractiveness or desirability, the more likely it is that a dispositional attribution will be made. From a Bayesian point of view, a desirable behavior is likely to be performed whether or not the actor has the disposition in question, i.e. $p(B|D)\simeq p(B|\bar{D})$. In contrast, an unattractive behavior is more likely to be performed by a person having the appropriate disposition than by a person who does not (i.e. $p(B|D)>p(B|\bar{D})$). It follows that an undesirable behavior will tend to be more diagnostic than a desirable behavior.

In an experimental test of the desirability hypothesis, Jones, Davis and Gergen (1961) had subjects listen to a tape recording of a role-playing situation in which an actor was applying either to become an astronaut or a submariner. The instructions given to the actor (which were also recorded on the tape) made it clear that in the forthcoming job interview it would be desirable for the actor to respond in an inner-directed fashion (in the astronaut condition) or in an other-directed fashion (in the submariner condition). In the interview, the actor was heard to respond either in an inner- or other-directed fashion. After listening to the interview, subjects were asked to rate the actor's 'true' other- or inner-directedness.

It was found that undesirable behaviors (i.e. behaviors inappropriate for the job sought) had greater impact on dispositional attributions than desirable behaviors. The actor who behaved in an other-directed manner was more likely to be viewed as truly other-directed when he applied to become an astronaut (for which his behavior was inappropriate) than when he applied to become a submariner. Similarly, for the actor who behaved in an inner-directed fashion, attributions of inner-directedness were more likely in the submariner than in the astronaut condition. Direct support for a Bayesian interpretation of these results has been provided by Trope and Burnstein (1975). In a similar manipulation of behavioral desirability within a job interview situation, these investigators replicated the Jones *et al.* (1961) findings. They further showed that, as expected, the subjective likelihood ratios were higher for undesirable than for desirable behaviors.

*Uniqueness of behavior effects.* The analysis presented by Jones and Davis (1965) assumes that any outcome or effect produced by the behavior can provide the basis for a dispositional attribution. One important factor is the extent to which the action leads to *unique* outcomes, that is, to outcomes that would not be produced by alternative behaviors. The more uniquely that a given effect is associated with the actor's chosen alternative, the more likely it is that a dispositional attribution will be made on the basis of that effect.

Suppose that a person is planning a trip to Europe and that there are four package tours available within an acceptable price range. Each tour visits four European cities. Assume that the actor is observed to select Tour A, which among other cities includes Oslo. According to the uniqueness principle, if Oslo is a unique outcome of Tour A, an observer would be more likely to infer that the actor wants to visit Oslo than if all four tours visited Oslo.

In terms of a Bayesian analysis, uniqueness of outcomes should affect the diagnostic value of the behavior. Let $D$ stand for the actor's disposition (e.g. his desire to visit Oslo) and $B$ for his behavior (e.g. his choice of Tour A). Now consider the case in which Oslo is uniquely associated with Tour A. If the actor desires to visit Oslo, the probability that he will choose Tour A (i.e. $p(B|D)$ ) should be relatively high. Conversely, if he does not desire to visit Oslo, the probability of his choosing Tour A (i.e. $p(B|\bar{D})$ should be relatively low. The likelihood ratio $p(B|D)/p(B|\bar{D})$ would in this case be greatly above unity. In contrast, when Oslo is a common outcome of all the tours, the probability that the actor will select Tour A should be the same whether he desires to visit Oslo or not. In this case, the likelihood ratio will be close to unity. It follows that a behavior with a unique outcome is more diagnostic than one with an outcome common to other behavioral alternatives, and Bayes' theorem would predict stronger dispositional attribution in the former case.

To test this hypothesis, Ajzen and Holmes (1977) constructed four hypothetical situations similar to the touring example discussed above. For each situation, respondents were asked to estimate $p(D|B)$, the probability that the actor had the particular disposition (e.g. that he wanted to visit Oslo) given that he had chosen a certain alternative. In addition, measures were obtained of $p(D)$, $p(B|D)$, and $p(B|\bar{D})$. The results provided support both for the uniqueness hypothesis and for a Bayesian interpretation of the attribution process. Consistent with expectations, both the likelihood ratio $p(B|D)/p(B|\bar{D})$ and dispositional attribution increased significantly with the degree of uniqueness.

In conclusion, our discussion of dispositional attribution again illustrates the utility of a Bayesian analysis. By using Bayes' theorem it was possible to provide a common framework for examining the effects of diverse factors on the perceived relevance of behavior for a given dispositional attribution.

## MOTIVATIONAL BIAS IN ATTRIBUTION

The application of Bayes' theorem to attribution implies an observer who processes information about an actor's behavior in a systematic and reasonable manner. By way of contrast, attribution theorists have sometimes postulated certain more irrational tendencies on the part of the observer. The general idea is that people's attributions are biased by their needs, values, and desires. A great deal of research has been conducted to demonstrate the operation of such biasing factors as ego enhancement and defense (Johnson, Feigenbaum and Weiby, 1964; Miller, 1976), hedonic relevance (Jones and DeCharms, 1957; Jones and Davis, 1965), belief in a just world (Lerner, 1970; Lerner, Miller and Holmes, 1976), and defensiveness (Shaver, 1970; Walster, 1966). A complete review of this literature is beyond the scope of the present chapter; and it suffices to note that, by and large, there is little evidence that motivational factors of this kind exert pervasive biasing effects on attributional judgements. Many investigators have reached the conclusion that data in apparent support of motivational biases can best be interpreted as reflecting reasonable judgements in light of the available information (Ajzen and Fishbein, 1975; Miller and Ross, 1975; Nisbett and Ross, 1980).

This point can be illustrated by examining some of the research on the assumed biasing effects of ego enhancement and defense. In a study by Johnson et al. (1974) research participants served as arithmetic teachers on two consecutive trials. The simulated student did poorly on the first trial. Following the second teacher-student interaction, the student continued to perform poorly for some teachers and he improved for others. Teachers tended to attribute continued failure to the student, whereas they attributed improved performance to themselves. Similar results were reported by Beckman (1970), and Wortman, Costanzo and Witt (1973). Although these findings are consistent with a tendency toward ego-defensive attribution, alternative interpretations are available. For example, Kelley (1967) suggested that insofar as the teachers in the Johnson *et al.* (1964) study made a special effort on the second trial, the covariation of effort and success in the improvement condition would favor internal attribution, and the lack of such covariation in the continued failure condition would favor external attribution. As discussed above, this explanation is consistent with a Bayesian analysis, and it suggests a rational rather than defensive attribution process.

A related finding reported by Streufert and Streufert (1969) is that subjects tend to attribute their own success on a task to internal factors and failure to external factors. At first glance this finding also appears to indicate a defensive inference process in that subjects seem reluctant to accept blame for failure, while accepting praise for success. It should be clear, however, that the hypothesis of ego-defensive attribution is acceptable only to the extent that subjects make inferences on the basis of their *own* performance. The finding that the same difference in causal attribution obtains when subjects are asked to account for the performance of a hypothetical person (Frieze and Weiner, 1971) must therefore be interpreted as inconsistent with the notion of ego-defensive attribution.

If an ego-defensive bias appears untenable, Bayes' theorem suggests two alternative explanations of the obtained results. The first assumes that respondents perceive the experimental task as relatively difficult, with the effect that success has greater diagnostic value for the actor's ability than failure has for his lack of ability. As a result, success would be attributed to ability more than failure to lack of ability.[4]

The second explanation would hold if subjects expected to succeed on the task. Feather (1969; Feather and Simon, 1971b) either measured or manipulated a participant's prior expectations that he would succeed or fail on an anagrams task. Actual performance consistent with expectations was attributed to stable internal factors (skill and ability), while performance inconsistent with expectations was attributed to unstable external factors (luck). Thus, when subjects expected success they displayed the tendency found by Streufert and Struefert (1969) to attribute actual success to their own ability more than actual failure to their lack of ability. However, contrary to an ego-defensive bias, but consistent with a Bayesian analysis, when subjects expected to fail, they attributed actual failure to their own lack of ability more than they attributed actual success to their ability. Bayes' theorem thus accounts for the observed difference between inferences based on success and failure in terms of information processing without reference to irrationality or defensiveness.

COGNITIVE HEURISTICS

The conception that human judgement is based on reasonable use of available information has been challenged in an influential series of papers by Tversky and Kahneman (1971, 1973, 1974, 1980) and Kahneman and Tversky (1972, 1973). According to these theorists, people do not process information in a systematic manner but rather use simple strategies or heuristics as rules of thumb to arrive at their inferences. Tversky and Kahneman identified three major heuristics: representativeness, availability, and adjustment. Although these investigators were interested primarily in the psychology of prediction, it is also possible to apply their heuristics to attributional judgements.

In the context of attribution, the three heuristics can be described as follows. According to the *representativeness* heuristic, a behavior is likely to be attributed to a disposition to the extent that, in its essential characteristics, the behavior is similar to (or representative of) the disposition in question. Thus, hitting another person is more representative of aggression than is gossiping about that person. It follows that aggressiveness is more likely to be inferred in the former than in the latter case. The *availability* heuristic has two implications for the attribution process. First, when asked to draw inferences from a behavior (or to explain a behavior), dispositions that come most readily to mind are likely to be invoked. Second, and perhaps more in keeping with Tversky and Kahneman's description of the heuristic, the likelihood that a given disposition can be inferred from a behavior (or be used to explain it) is a function of the ease with which other evidence in support of the inference can be brought to mind. Finally, the *adjustment* heuristic suggests that in making an attributional judgement, observers start out with an initial hypothesis and revise it in light of new information.

It can be seen that the three heuristics identified by Tversky and Kahneman describe reasonable judgemental strategies that are quite compatible with the approach to attribution outlined earlier in this chapter. That is, representativeness corresponds to the concept of relevance or diagnosticity. A behavior that is representative of a disposition is consistent with it and thus has diagnostic value for the attribution. Both interpretations of the availability heuristic are compatible with our argument that hypotheses and evidence will be considered to the extent that they are salient, accessible, or available to the individual. Finally, the notion of adjustment is analgous to the Bayesian view that prior probabilities are revised in light of new information.

Clearly, then, it is quite reasonable for individuals to use these strategies or heuristics to arrive at their attributions. However, while recognising that such strategies can result in reasonable judgements, Tversky and Kahneman have proposed that their use will often lead to systematic biases and errors. In a recent paper, Tversky and Kahneman (1980) have turned their attention to causal schemas in human judgement and they have argued that people's reliance on their intuitive understanding of causal relationships biases their judgements and also leads to systematic errors. According to these theorists, people's reliance on a given heuristic or causal schema predisposes them to consider certain types of evidence and to disregard other information. Errors may result if the evidence considered is inappropriate or if the neglected information is relevant for the judgement in question. The problem, however, is not so much that errors may occur but that, according to Tversky and Kahneman, these errors are the result of *systematic bias* in the use of information. In the following discussion of this and related issues, we argue that although people may indeed fail to use all information available to them, there is little evidence for systematic bias and error in attributional judgements.

## Availability of hypotheses and evidence

In the introduction to this chapter we suggested that attributions are likely to be affected by the kinds of hypotheses and evidence available to the individual. There is general agreement that salience or vividness of information promotes recognition and recall (Bower, 1972; Wallace, 1965) and that information is likely to be encoded into readily accessible categories (Bruner, 1957a; Cantor and Mischel, 1977; Reed, 1972). In the attribution area, however, investigators have only recently turned their attention to these issues. A few studies have examined the effects of *perceptual availability* (salience, vividness) on attributional judgements (e.g. Arkin and Duval, 1975; Duval and Wicklund, 1972; McArthur and Post, 1977; McArthur and Solomon, 1978; Storms, 1973; Taylor and Fiske, 1975, 1978). These studies provide limited evidence that drawing attention to an actor increases attribution of behavior to that actor (Taylor and Fiske, 1975) and that making the environment more salient or vivid increases attribution of behavior to that environment (Arkin and Duval, 1975). It must be noted, however, that these effects have not always been obtained, that they are often quite weak, and that they do not generalise across all attributions (McArthur and Post, 1977; McArthur and Solomon, 1978).

Even fewer studies have investigated the effects of *cognitive availability* or accessibility on attributional judgements (Higgins, Rholes and Jones, 1977; Srull and Wyer, 1979; Wyer and Carlston, 1979). These studies have shown that behaviors are likely to be attributed to dispositions that were made salient or accessible by means of 'cognitive priming'. For example, in one of their experiments, Srull and Wyer increased the availability of 'hostility' as a dispositional category by inducing respondents to consider sentences that implied hostility. On a later unrelated task, respondents were found to attribute an ambiguous description of behavior to this disposition, so that the greater the amount of prior cognitive priming, the more the behavior was attributed to hostility.

There is also some evidence to suggest that once a category or hypothesis has been primed, it tends to continue to exert influence on attributions even if the evidence that initially produced the heightened availability of the hypothesis is subsequently discredited (Ross, 1977; Ross, Lepper and Hubbard, 1975; Ross, Lepper, Strack and Steinmetz, 1977b). For example, Ross, Lepper and Hubbard showed that false feedback concerning respondents' abilities to distinguish between authentic and fictitious suicide notes continued to influence the respondents' judgements of their own abilities after the feedback had been discredited in a debriefing session. This 'perseverance' of initial hypotheses is similar to the 'anchoring' effect of initial judgements in Tversky and Kahneman's (1974) adjustment heuristic. Heightened cognitive availability of a given dispositional or causal hypothesis is thus likely to guide attributions although, as Srull and Wyer (1979) have shown, cognitive availability tends to fade quite rapidly over time.

COGNITIVE BIASES: 'THE FUNDAMENTAL ATTRIBUTION ERROR'

Clearly, then, perceptual and cognitive availability determine at least in part the kinds of attribution that can be made. Some investigators, however, have gone beyond this conclusion to suggest that hypotheses and evidence available to an individual are systematically biased. The most important of these proposed biases can be traced to Heider's (1958a, p. 54) assertion that 'behavior . . . has such salient properties it tends to engulf the total field'. This argument implies that when observers attempt to explain an actor's behavior, they will tend to overestimate the importance of personal or dispositional factors and to underestimate the influence of environmental factors (Jones, 1979; Jones and Harris, 1967; Miller, 1976; Snyder and Frankel, 1976). In fact, this bias is assumed to be so pervasive that it has been called the 'fundamental attribution error' (Nisbett and Ross, 1980; Ross, 1977).

*Situational constraints.* The first experiment related to this issue was conducted by Jones and Harris (1967). In our earlier discussion we saw that decision freedom and desirability are found to influence dispositional attributions. Jones and Harris examined the simultaneous effects of those two factors. Subjects read a short essay on Castro's Cuba, which was either pro-Castro (with assumed low desirability) or anti-Castro (high desirability), and it was alleged to have been written either under conditions of free choice (high decision freedom) or by assignment of a course instructor (low decision freedom). On the basis of this essay, subjects were asked to infer the actor's attitude toward Castro's Cuba. Consistent with previous findings, the actor's essay was attributed to his attitude more under high than under low decision freedom and the undesirable (pro-Castro) essay had a stronger effect on perceived attitude than the desirable (anti-Castro) essay. In addition, the interaction between perceived decision freedom and behavioral desirability was significant. The effect of desirability was greater under high than under low decision freedom and the effect of decision freedom was greater for the undesirable than for the desirable behavior. Interestingly, even when the actor was described as having had no freedom of choice, subjects tended to attribute his behavior to his attitude, although to a lesser degree. This last finding was interpreted as evidence for 'behavior engulfing the field' and has been replicated across several different issues and choice contexts (Jones, Worchel, Goethals and Grummet, 1971; Miller, 1974, 1976; Snyder and Jones, 1974). According to the authors, the situational constraints under low decision freedom are sufficient to account for the actors' behavior and no dispositional attribution or 'correspondent inference' should be made.

This interpretation, however, has not gone unchallenged and it has been proposed that the findings may be due to artifacts inherent in the experimental situation. Perhaps most interesting is Kelley's (1972a) suggestion that there may have been a fair amount of perceived choice even in the presence of situational constraints. In a review of the relevant literature, Jones (1979) conceded that on the basis of available manipulation checks, this possibility could not be ruled out. In fact,

Ajzen, Dalto and Blyth (1979) have shown that dispositional attributions under no-choice conditions are eliminated when the possibility of artifact is minimised. Participants in one part of this study were simply told that a student wrote a pro- or anti-abortion essay either by assignment of the course instructor or by free choice. In contrast to previous experiments, neither the student's essay nor any other information about the student was made available. Statistically significant dispositional attributions in line with essay direction were made only under free choice conditions.

It may be argued that the findings of previous studies do not reflect a 'fundamental attribution error' but the effects of cognitive availability. We saw previously that ambiguous information is likely to be assigned to dispositional categories that have been made salient. Providing information that the actor wrote a pro (or con) essay may make the corresponding disposition salient (see also Cantor and Mischel, 1977). In previous investigations, participants were given various kinds of additional information about the actor and the essay which, although largely ambiguous, may have been used to infer the salient disposition. In support of this argument, Ajzen et al. (1979) showed in a second part of their study that dispositional attribution under no-choice conditions reappeared when irrelevant information about the actor was provided in the form of an ambiguous personality description.

The same explanation can also account for apparently conflicting findings reported by Snyder and Jones (1974) and Miller (1976). Using the standard paradigm in which observers read an actor's essay, Snyder and Jones showed that dispositional attributions were reduced to non-significance when the observer was aware that the essay contained arguments provided by the experimenter and were completely eliminated when observers were told that the actor merely copied in his own handwriting an essay written by someone else. In contrast, Miller (1976) reported that even when it was made explicit that the essay had been written by someone else, dispositional attributions were made to an actor who delivered the essay either on video- or audiotape. Our analysis suggests that the opportunity to watch or listen to the actor's speech provided information that may have been used to infer the attitudinal disposition salient in the situation.

Clearly, then, there is little evidence for a systematic bias on the part of observers to attribute an actor's behavior to dispositional rather than situational factors. In fact, Quattrone (described in Jones, 1979) showed that within the same attribution of attitude paradigm, it is possible to obtain external attributions even though internal factors should be sufficient to account for the stand taken in the essay. In this study, participants were told that the essay was perfectly consistent with the actor's attitude, but they nevertheless believed that subtle cues from the experimenter or the experimenter's attitude influenced the position expressed. That observers can and do often attribute an actor's behavior to external rather than internal factors has also been found in research dealing with differences in the attributions made by actors and observers.

*Actor–observer differences.* So far we have not made a distinction between attributions to another person as opposed to self-attributions. Since an actor may serve as an observer of his/her own behavior, an attributional analysis appears appropriate in both instances. However, disagreement exists as to the extent to which processes of self-attribution resemble those of attribution to another person.

The primary controversy concerns the amount and kind of information available to actor v. observer and the importance given to different items of information. Bem (1965, 1967) argued that the behavior in context and its effects constitute, in most cases, the major cues for making an attribution to the actor. Since these cues are available to both the observer and the actor, the two should make the same attributions. In contrast, others (Jones and Nisbett, 1972; Jones, Linder, Kiesler, Zanna and Brehm, 1968) have proposed that different information is available to actor and observer, and even when they have the same information, they tend to focus on different aspects of the behavioral situation. Specifically, Jones and Nisbett (1972) argued for a unidirectional difference such that 'there is a pervasive tendency for actors to attribute their actions to situational requirements, whereas observers tend to attribute the same actions to stable personal dispositions' (p. 2). According to Jones and Nisbett, this difference will obtain not only because of the actor's more detailed knowledge of the circumstances but also because different aspects of the available information are salient for actor and observer. Specifically, the actor's behavior is assumed to be most salient for an observer while situational factors take on greater salience for the actor. The fundamental attribution error is thus considered to be limited to the attributions of an observer whereas an actor's self-attributions are assumed to exhibit a systematic bias in the opposite direction.

Some of the early research on this issue dealt with actor–observer differences in the attribution of success and failure. Several investigations found significant differences between judgements of one's own versus another's ability following success or failure on a task (Feather and Simon, 1971a; Jones, Rock, Shaver, Goethals and Ward, 1968). Indeed, as empirical support for their hypothesis, Jones and Nisbett (1971) discussed the experiment by E. E. Jones *et al.* (1968) as well as three additional studies. Frieze and Weiner (1971), however, reported no significant differences between actor and observer in terms of causal attributions for successful or unsuccessful task performance. More importantly, Feather and Simon (1971a) showed that differences between actor and observer depend on the circumstances. Consistent with the Jones and Nisbett hypothesis, subjects were found to attribute another person's success to ability more than their own success. However, contrary to that hypothesis, another person's failure was judged to be due to external factors (such as bad luck) more so than was own failure.

The absence of systematic biases in the attributions made by actors and observers is documented in Monson and Snyder's (1977) review of the literature. After considering studies that appear to support the pattern of attributions postulated by Jones and Nisbett (e.g. Storms, 1973; West, Gunn and Chernicky, 1975), studies that show the opposite pattern of attributions (e.g. Miller and Norman, 1975), and studies that report both attributional patterns (e.g. Snyder, Stephan and Rosenfeld, 1976), Monson and Snyder (1977) concluded: 'We do not agree that there exists a pervasive tendency for actors to attribute their actions to situational influences and for observers to attribute the identical actions to dispositions of the actor' (pp. 106–107).

In sum, our review thus far has revealed no convincing evidence for systematic biases of a cognitive nature. To be sure, observers do under certain conditions attribute an actor's behavior to internal factors and seemingly neglect situational constraints. Under other conditions, however, observers not only take due account of situational constraints but may, in fact, disregard apparently relevant internal causes. It is thus just as reasonable to conclude that 'the situation engulfs the field' as it is to claim that 'behavior engulfs the field'. By the same token, actors and observers often make different attributions, but it is just as easy to find tendencies to make internal (rather than external) attributions among actors as it is to find them among observers.

COGNITIVE BIASES: USE OF HEURISTICS

The presumed cognitive biases discussed up to this point can be traced to Heider's suggestion that behavior engulfs the field. The growing interest in attributional biases has led investigators to postulate a variety of other tendencies systematically to misinterpret human behavior. The rationale for the proposed biases is not always readily apparent. For example, Ross (1977; Ross, Greene and House, 1977a) suggested that people tend to labor under the misconception that their own behaviors, judgements, and feelings are commonly shared while alternative reactions are relatively unique. As a result of this 'false consensus', observers are assumed to judge another's behavior (to the extent that it differs from their own) as deviant and therefore as revealing of the actor's stable dispositions. The likelihood of obtaining consistent support for this proposition must *a priori* be regarded as quite low when it is recalled that other social psychologists have in the past postulated a tendency toward 'pluralistic ignorance'. According to this hypothesis, people often consider their own thoughts and actions to be *different* from those of most others, and because they are reluctant to reveal this assumed deviance they fail to discover the existing consensus (Schanck, 1932). Pluralistic ignorance has, among other things, been invoked to account for the failure of bystanders to intervene in an emergency (Latané and Darley, 1968) and for the illusion of unanimity in 'groupthink' (Janis, 1972). It thus appears again likely that for every study showing a 'false consensus' effect we will also be able to find evidence demonstrating the opposite 'pluralistic ignorance' phenomenon.[5]

Perhaps of greater interest are some of the assumed cognitive biases that have their origin in Tversky and Kahneman's work on the use of heuristics in human judgement. Although these theorists concerned themselves largely with judgements of categorisation and prediction, their work has had a marked impact on research in the attribution area.

*Neglect of consensus information.* Most interest has probably been generated by the biases and errors that are assumed to accompany use of the representativeness heuristic (Kahneman and Tversky, 1973). Reliance on this heuristic to make probability judgements is said to result in serious errors 'because similarity or representativeness is not influenced by several factors that should affect judgements of probability' (Tversky and Kahneman, 1974, p. 1124).

One such factor is the prior probability or *base rate* of the judged event. To illustrate, consider one of the studies reported by Kahneman and Tversky (1973). In this study respondents were informed that a panel of psychologists had administered personality tests to 30 engineers and 70 lawyers or, depending on experimental condition, 70 engineers and 30 lawyers. They were also told that based on the interview and test data, the psychologists had prepared a brief personality description of every person tested. Respondents were shown five of these sketches, ostensibly selected at random, and were asked to judge in each case the likelihood that the person described was an engineer (or a lawyer). In actuality, the five personality sketches had been constructed such that they resembled, to varying degrees, the stereotype of an engineer or a lawyer. The results showed that the individuating information contained in the personality descriptions strongly affected probability estimates, whereas the population base rate was found to have little effect on these judgements. These findings were taken as evidence that in arriving at their estimates, respondents rely on the representativeness heuristic. Base-rate information, even though important by the normative principles of statistical prediction, is neglected since base rates do not constitute a representative feature of the engineer or lawyer stereotype.

Inspired by this work, Nisbett and Borgida (1975) suggested that judgements of causal attribution evidence a similar neglect of base-rate information. In the context of attributional judgements, base rates are usually provided in the form of *consensus* information, that is, information concerning the relative frequency of the actor's behavior. According to Kelley's (1967) analysis of the attribution process, when most people react to an entity in the same way as the actor (high consensus), the actor's behavior is attributed to external rather than internal factors. Internal attributions, on the other hand, follow from low consensus, that is, when few others behave like the actor.

Contrary to these expectations, several studies reported either no effect of consensus information on causal and dispositional attributions (Cooper, Jones and Tuller, 1972; Nisbett and Borgida, 1975; Nisbett, Borgida, Crandall and Reed, 1976) or underutilisation of consensus information in comparison to consistency and distinctiveness information (McArthur, 1972, 1976). However, other investigations have shown that even minor variations in the presentation of consensus information or in the assessment of its effects on causal attribution can greatly increase the utilisation of consensus information (Hansen and Donoghue, 1977; Ruble and Feldman, 1976; Wells and Harvey, 1977).

Perhaps of greater importance is the one line of research which has demonstrated consistently strong effects of consensus information. We saw earlier that like consistency and distinctiveness, consensus information greatly influences attribution of success and failure to ability, effort, task difficulty, and luck (see Weiner, *et al.*, 1971, for a review). When most people's performance is similar to that of the actor (high consensus), success or failure is attributed to external factors (task difficulty and luck), but under low consensus it is attributed to internal factors (ability and effort).

These findings make it clear that there is no pervasive tendency for people to neglect consensus information when arriving at attributional judgements. In fact, there is evidence to suggest that people can use not only consensus information but other types of base rate information as well (see Borgida and Brekke, 1980; Kassin, 1979 for reviews of relevant research). For example, Fischhoff, Slovic and Lichtenstein (1979) and Ginosar and Trope (1980) have recently shown that respondents take base rates into account when estimating probabilities in situations similar to those used by Kahneman and Tversky (1973). Our reading of the literature indicates that utilisation of base rate or consensus information depends on the information's perceptual salience and cognitive availability. As Nisbett and Ross (1980) have pointed out, relative to individuating information, base rates are rather pallid and abstract. It is, however, possible to increase the availability of such information by simply presenting it just prior to the judgement (Ruble and Feldman, 1976) or by varying it in a within-subjects rather than a between-subjects design (Fischhoff et al., 1979).

The importance of cognitive availability for the utilisation of base rate information has been demonstrated in a number of studies on the role of causal thinking in human judgement (Ajzen, 1977; Bar-Hillel, 1980; Tversky and Kahneman, 1980). The perception of causal relationships is basic to explanations of past behavior as well as predictions of future events. In the studies cited, respondents were found to use base rates appropriately when the base rates could be interpreted as having a causal effect on the predicted event. This finding can help explain the strong effect of consensus information on attributions following success or failure on a task. Information that most (or few) others also succeeded or failed provides evidence concerning the difficulty level of the task, and task difficulty of course influences task performance. This evidence can then be used directly to attribute success to an easy task and failure to a difficult task under high consensus, and more indirectly to infer high ability (or effort) from success on a difficult task and lower ability (or effort) from success on an easy task.

The main point to be made is that people can use base rate or consensus information just as they can use any other kind of information. Although it is true that base rates may sometimes have relatively low perceptual salience or cognitive availability, and may thus be underutilised, the same is likely to hold for other items of information. Thus, it should not be impossible to find situations in which consistency or distinctiveness information lack salience or availability and in which people rely primarily on consensus information. Research of this kind can provide evidence for the importance of perceptual and cognitive availability but it is unlikely to reveal, across a variety of situations, strong and systematic biases to disregard one type of information in preference for another.


## Conclusions

Attribution theory deals with the ways in which a person arrives at an explanation of observed or reported behavior. Closely tied to this process are inferences about dispositional properties of the actor and the environment that can be derived from the behavior. Obviously, people do not take into account all information of potential relevance to the causal or dispositional attribution they are asked to make. Selectivity in attention, perception, and memory all influence the hypotheses and evidence available to the individual at any given moment and hence the particular attribution he or she will make. We have repeatedly tried to show, however, that there are no *systematic* biases, either of a motivational or a cognitive nature even though people's judgements may deviate from normative expectations. Observers have been said to underestimate the effect of situational constraints on an actor's behavior and to overestimate the impact of personal dispositions, but the argument for a 'fundamental attribution error' of this kind is discredited by studies showing that observers can give full credit to the influence of situational constraints. Similarly, although actors and observers often differ in their attributions, the direction of these differences varies across situations, and no systematic biases can be discerned. In fact, it appears that both actors and observers will make use of any information they deem relevant, be it information concerning situational constraints or behavioral con-sensus, so long as the information in question is perceptually salient or cognitively available.

It was shown that an individual's attributions follow reasonably and systematically from the information that is *subjectively* available, and that these inferences can be described by a model such as Bayes' theorem. Using Bayes' theorem it was possible to provide a unifying framework for attribution theory and research by showing that available information is utilised and influences attributions to the extent that it is diagnostic of, or relevant to, the hypothesis in question. The diagnostic value of a given item of information can be gauged by considering its impact on the likelihood ratio in Bayes' theorem.

We would like to make it clear, however, that we use Bayes' theorem as a heuristic device, not as a description of the attribution process that is accurate in every minor detail. We would agree that people are 'not Bayesian' in the sense that they do not take into account all *objectively* available and demonstrably relevant information. Their subjective prior probabilities and likelihood ratios may well differ from objectively computed values. However, it is our contention that people may be viewed as Bayesian in the sense that, in arriving at their attributions, they make reasonable and systematic use of the information available to them.

## Acknowledgement

We would like to thank Amos Tversky for his comments on an earlier draft of this chapter.

## Notes

1. Similar ideas have been presented by Kruglanski (1980) in a more general analysis of knowledge acquisition.
2. A discussion of Bayes' theorem and its implications can be found in Edwards, Lindman and Savage (1963).
3. Odds are interpreted as in betting situations. Assuming that $\bar{H} = 1 - H$, prior and posterior probabilities can be directly transformed into odds, and *vice versa*. We shall frequently use the terms *odds* and *probabilities* interchangeably.
4. Let $S$ stand for success, $F$ for failure, and $A$ for ability. Given a difficult task, this argument assumes the following relation between the likelihood ratios: $p(S|A)/p(S|\bar{A}) > p(F|\bar{A})/p(F|A)$.
5. As support for the 'false consensus' hypothesis, Ross (1977) cited evidence of covariation between behavioral choice and estimated popularity of the chosen alternative. Rather than demonstrating false consensus, however, this covariation more likely reflects the influence of an intervening variable, namely, attitude toward the behavior in question. Individuals who believe that one alternative is more desirable than another may reasonably assume that others will choose this alternative as well as decide to perform it themselves.

# 4

# Attribution Theory and Social Cognition

## J. Richard Eiser

### Introduction

A quarter of a century ago, Floyd H. Allport started his book on *Theories of Perception and the Concept of Structure* by inviting the reader to imagine the reactions of a visitor from Mars on a guided tour round the busy and flourishing psychology laboratories of the time:

Impressed by all this experimental fervour he concludes that some great synthesis or awakening in psychological understanding must have taken place on earth, like the formulation of the cell theory in biology or the electro-magnetic field theory in physics. Turning at length to his guides he exclaims: 'I think I have seen enough of your laboratories. What you have shown me seems first-rate. Now, if you don't mind, I would like you to take me to the places where your systematic psychology is being developed. I want to see what your *theory* looks like'. At this the guides appear a little hesitant . . . (Allport, 1955, pp. 1–2)

If Allport's Martian were to make a return visit he would certainly notice a number of changes. Not the least of these would be the tremendous growth of activity in experimental social psychology from the status of a fringe area to a dominant specialty. 'This really is something new' he might say, 'I'd like to ask some of these social psychologists about their research, and the problems they are study-ing.' So he would start interviewing, keeping a count of the different topics within this specialty. But, knowing about his predilections from his previous visit, we could predict that he would soon break off from his survey in a state of high excitement. 'I knew this visit would be worthwhile' he might say, 'I've talked to sixty-four people this week who've said they're working on something called "attribution theory". Please, you must tell me what this "attribution theory" is.'

His guides at this point would shuffle uneasily, and after an exchange of pleadingly inquiring glances, one of these would diffidently start explaining 'Well you see, "attribution theory" isn't actually a *theory* in the strict sense of the word – it's more of a general perspective, or set of loosely related ideas. . .'

Attribution theory, as we have come to know it, is in great danger of overselling itself, and may indeed have already done so. In spite of all the vigorous experimentation, and the plethora of more or less replicable 'effects', the promising approach of some ten to fifteen years ago that had already (so the story went) disposed of the Goliath of dissonance theory with a casual flick of the wrist, has undergone comparatively little conceptual development. It has *not* matured into the coherent and unifying theory, of the kind that many of our colleagues and students (let alone any Martian visitor!) might have felt entitled to expect. Rather, it seems to have become more and more divided into specific sub-areas concerned with the testing of more and more limited-range hypotheses.

What then is likely to happen to attribution research over the *next* ten to fifteen years? A possible outcome is that it will collapse under its own weight, and the idea that there is any unifying set of principles called 'attribution theory' will be abandoned as an idle pretence. The work will go on, but researchers will be less and less concerned to call themselves attribution theorists. Indeed, this seems to be the trend of developments over the last decade, and there is little sign of it being halted or reversed.

There are many who would argue that the continuation of this trend is not only probable, but desirable – that the proper business of a scientific social psychology is not the formulation of integrative theoretical frameworks, but is indeed the testing of specific limited predictions in specific limited circumstances.

But there are dangers in this trend. If attribution theory, as *theory*, becomes stagnant, it will not simply be by-passed, it will be taken as symptomatic of much that is 'bad' about social psychology. There will be a backlash, and the backlash will carry away not only some of the more dispensable curios among attribution theorists' conceptual baggage, but also many of the more general advances of cognitive social psychology (see Eiser, 1980). There will be a rejection of a 'model of man' which is seen as too cool, cerebral and 'rational'; and an openness or vulnerability (depending on one's viewpoint) to approaches, however suspect, that erect a false dualism between cognitive processes on the one hand and emotional and motivational processes on the other, and treat the latter, which are assumed to be 'irrational', as dominant over the former. Human social behaviour, we will be told again, is essentially unreasoned, and the study of human social reasoning is a trivial irrelevance.

I cannot believe that such a scenario would represent anything but a most disastrously reactionary development for social psychology. It would be based on a false stereotype of the basic assumptions of attribution theory and cognitive social psychology in general. 'Attributional man' would be an ideal 'straw man', and would be afforded the same summary treatment as 'consistency man' or 'conformity man' or any similar pieces of our evolutionary history. This would not be a victory for empiricism, since such a treatment would take only selective evidence from the research actually accomplished within the attribution theory framework. Rather, it would be a victory for an even vaguer metatheoretical stance than that attributed to attribution theory.

But all this is premised on an 'if' – *if* attribution theory becomes stagnant. It is not stagnant yet, but something must be done, and soon, to prevent it from becoming so. I shall argue that the time has come to put some of the basic notions of attribution theory under critical scrutiny. Foremost among these are the concepts of phenomenal causality and naive psychology. It is typically taken for granted by attribution theorists that intuitive causal explanations are vital to our perception of our social world. I shall examine this assumption from the perspective of other research in cognitive social psychology concerned with processes of categorisation and prediction, and from a consideration of the logic of interpersonal descriptions. I shall argue that such ordinary language descriptions do not necessarily function as causal explanations, and that the causal attribution process is typically reserved for situations and events which appear otherwise unpredictable or difficult to categorise. The intended synthesis, therefore, is a broader social cognitive theory which relates attributions to other social cognitive processes and delineates the kinds of situations to which attribution theory will be most relevant (see also Langer, 1978; chapter 10 of this book).

## Phenomenal causality

To understand the present condition of attribution theory one has to go back to its roots, since some of the crucial turning points were reached before experimental research in the area even got off the ground. The tremendous debt which social psychology owes to Fritz Heider scarcely needs any further acknowledgement. However, the principle of *nil nisi bonum* can be a stultifying one for any science, and it is a poor mark of respect for a theoretical innovator to avoid re-examination of his basic ideas, particularly if not all his ideas have been equally well remembered.

Attribution theory, as we know it today, is still very much structured around the basic themes of Heider's early writings. These themes revolve around the notions of phenomenal causality and naive psychology.

Phenomenal causality refers to the individual's subjective impression of a causal connection between two or more objects or events. Heider and Simmel (1944) found that subjects would explain the movement of abstract geometrical figures in terms of apparent causal properties of the stimuli (e.g. object $A$ might be seen to push object $B$). In the same way, Heider (1944) argues, individuals will look for 'causal units' within social relationships. Persons can be seen as causal origins of changes, and from here springs the fundamental distinction between personal and impersonal causality. Persons are seen as capable of *spontaneous* action, that is, of setting things in motion without being pushed themselves. The notion of causal unit formation leads easily into Heider's balance theory of attitudes and cognitive organisation:

Attitudes towards persons and causal unit formations influence each other. An attitude towards an event can alter the attitude towards the person who caused the event, and, if the attitudes towards a person and an event are similar, the event is easily ascribed to the person.   (Heider, 1946, p. 107)

It is no mere coincidence that Heider treats this question of attribution of causality in essentially perceptual terms. As he has recently remarked, 'Attribution, of course, is just a close relative of perception' (Harvey, Ickes and Kidd, 1976, p. 12). In stressing the continuity between physical and social perceptual processes, his work is an important part of a more general tradition from the early 1950s onwards represented by people like Bruner, Helson, Hovland, Sherif, Stevens and Tajfel (cf. Eiser and Stroebe, 1972). What is special about Heider's approach is that the kind of perceptual theory he attempts to apply to interpersonal relations is one explicitly derived from Gestalt psychology. Notions of organisation, structure and Prägnanz seem more basic to Heider's way of thinking than notions of categorisation, attention, and stimulus detection. It would be unfairly polemical to suggest that Heider had no regard for these latter concepts, but they do not appear to contribute as strong a flavour to his approach.

An implication of this is that the close unity between physical and social perception in which Heider believed is *not* immediately apparent from a comparison of present-day research on attribution and on processes of perception. One important feature of this Gestalt heritage is the comparative neglect by most attribution theorists until very recently of the *probabilistic* nature of perceptual information and perceptual decisions. From this point of view one might argue that it is not that attribution theory is too cognitive, but that it is not cognitive enough. I shall return to this issue later.

## Naive psychology

Closely related to the notion of phenomenal causality is that of naive psychology. Perhaps Heider's single most important argument is that ordinary people's 'common sense' explanations and interpretations of their social world are a proper, and indeed essential, topic for study by social psychologists. There is no real dispute that individuals shape their behaviour as a function of their interpretation of events. As the wealth of empirical research on attribution processes has shown, moreover, such interpretations will vary predictably as a function of various personal and situational factors. Heider's concept of 'naive psychology', however, implies more than this. At its most basic level, it is assumed that such interpretations rest on perceptions of personal or impersonal *causality*. The distinction between personal and impersonal causality is explained by Heider in the following terms:

Of great importance for our picture of the social environment is the attribution of events to causal sources. It makes a real difference, for example, whether a person discovers that the stick that struck him fell from a rotting tree or was hurled by an enemy. Attribution in terms of impersonal and personal causes, and with the latter, in terms of intent, are everyday occurences that determine much of our understanding of and reaction to our surroundings. (Heider, 1958b, p. 16)

Heider's distinction between personal and impersonal causality is developed in the models proposed by Jones and Davis (1965) and Kelley (1967, 1972b). Both of these will be familiar enough to readers of this volume, but it may be useful to highlight a few of their basic assumptions.

Jones and Davis (1965, p. 222) assume that:

the perceiver typically starts with the overt action of another; this is the grist for his cognitive mill. He then makes certain decisions concerning ability and knowledge which will let him cope with the problem of attributing particular intentions to the actor. The attribution of intentions, in turn, is a necessary step in the assignment of more stable characteristics to the actor.

If a perceiver attributes behaviour to stable characteristics of the actor (e.g. if a generous act is attributed to the generous disposition of the actor), he is said to have made a 'correspondent inference'. A troublesome aspect of this approach is the idea that nothing can be said about an actor's dispositions unless the effects of his behaviour can be seen as intended. This is patently false. To say that somebody intended to act carelessly, spontaneously, stupidly, or forgetfully, is a strange use of language. Furthermore, there is an important logical distinction between describing an act as intentional, and describing the effects of that act as intended (Anscombe, 1963). These issues underly some of the conceptual difficulties which pervade the experimental literature on attributions of responsibility (Fishbein and Ajzen, 1973).

Within the Jones and Davis model, then, the notion of personal causality is treated in such a way that, paradoxically, persons *as persons* cease to be considered as causal origins. This comes about because it is assumed that, in the eyes of the perceiver, intentions are the outcome of specific personality traits or dispositions of the actor. In short, the view of common sense interpersonal descriptions proposed is that intentions are seen as causing behaviour, and traits are seen as causing intentions.

This elevation of traits, rather than persons, to the status of causal origins has caused no end of problems. This aspect of the Jones and Davis model does not seem to be a derivation from Heider, so much as from the 'impression formation' tradition which treated the question of person perception essentially in terms of how people perceive personality traits and how verbal 'trait descriptions' are processed. It also appears to be coloured by a trait-theoretical view of personality which many would now regard as outmoded.

One specific problem is over the distinction between reasons and causes. Looking for causal origins of intentions might seem to downgrade a person's intentions as reasons for action in their own right, and instead resurrect a more deterministic, non-volitional type of explanation. A recent exchange of views (Buss, 1978, 1979; Harvey and Tucker, 1979; Kruglanski, 1979) highlights the ambiguities in current formulations of attribution theory. Buss argues that 'Causes and reasons are logically distinct categories for explaining different aspects of behaviour' and that 'Attribution theorists have tended to project an exclusively causal framework onto the lay explanation of all behaviour and all explainers and are thus confused and confusing regarding causes and reasons'. (1978, p. 1311.) Harvey and Tucker argue that cause and reason explanations are not necessarily distinguishable in practice, and that Buss gives no operational criteria for distinguishing them empirically. Kruglanski's position is that reasons are distinct from causes only to the extent that causes can be defined either narrowly to exclude teleological (reason) explanations or more broadly to include both teleological and non-teleological explanations. Attribution theory, according to Kruglanski, adopts the broader definition of cause, and so *does* deal with reason explanations, though without giving them any unique significance.

This relates to a general difficulty with many psychological models of deciding at what point one is talking about actual behaviour or cognitive processes and at what point one is talking about what ideally ought to be happening. We are constantly reassured by attribution theorists that the rules of 'psychologic' are not necessarily the rules of logic. The argument can reasonably be made that ordinary people may be unaware of many of the distinctions recognised by philosophers. Yet 'philosophical' distinctions are not simply picked from thin air, but typically relate to distinctions (seen by philosophers) in the meaning, *that is in the use*, of concepts in ordinary language. The fact that ordinary people may not be able to verbalise such distinctions in the abstract does not mean that they cannot or do not make them. Naive behavioural explanations do not entail the naivety of behaviour.

Similarly, 'lay conceptions of personality' are distinguished from personality theory as studied by psychologists. It is quite consistent for instance to argue that ordinary people operate as naive trait theorists, but that trait theory is an incomplete view of personality, when viewed from the standpoint of psychological research. But then where is the evidence that ordinary people think in trait-theoretical terms? It comes primarily from the abundant use, in ordinary language, of adjectives applicable to persons, and the large number of experiments that have used such adjectives as stimuli, or as the basis for ratings and other dependent measures. But then, again, how is one to say that these adjectives are used as *trait* adjectives, in the sense in which personality theorists have used the term 'trait'? The answer, I fear, is that personality theorists have *assumed* that such adjectives (or a significant proportion of them) function as trait descriptions, and many attribution and impression formation researchers have interpreted their subjects' behaviour through the inherited perspective of this assumption.

There is a real difficulty in the context of attributions of personal characteristics in drawing a distinction between a normative model of how attributions *ought* to be made and a descriptive model of how in fact they are. This does not apply for instance, in the field of statistical or logical reasoning, where the correct solution to a problem can be defined *a priori*, and where descriptive models of reasoning processes can be compared directly with normative models. The difficulty I find with the Jones and Davis formulation is that it is very unclear where the hypothesised processes are assumed to represent a departure from some ideal, and where they are not. If their model represents only 'naive' processes of explanation, what would less naive processes look like? If, for instance, a given perceiver fails to take account of an actor's knowledge and ability, is this an imperfection of the model, or an imperfection of the perceiver's 'rational' attributional performance? If the latter, what normative criteria of 'rationality' are at work? To attempt to criticise the Jones and Davis model from a philosophical stance is like trying to hit a moving target: if one points out that the model makes curious conceptual assumptions, it can always be countered that it is only intended as a model of naive reasoning, and naive reasoning can make curious assumptions. But it is dangerous to use a presumed departure from rationality (on the part of ordinary people) as a defence in this way if one cannot state what *would* count as a rational process.

A far clearer picture of what might count as a 'rational' attribution process comes from Kelley's (1967, 1972b) version of the theory. Kelley does not say that people *ought* to make attributions in accordance with his model (any more than he would say that people *ought* to act in accordance with the 'rationality' embodied in the Thibaut and Kelley, 1959, version of exchange theory). Nonetheless, his model comes near to being a normative model in that regular departures from it can often be appropriately described as attributional 'biases'. Kelley presents it, however, not as an ideal, but as a 'naive version' of J. S. Mill's method of difference: the effect is attributed to that condition which is present when the effect is present and absent when the effect is absent. In place of the rather muddled philosophy of mind which Jones and Davis propose as the basis of naive psychology, therefore, Kelley proposes an orthodox, workaday scientific method which is so close to what most psychologists use themselves that they might well feel worried about calling it 'naive'.

But do our perceptions of one another, particularly as reflected in ordinary language descriptions, necessarily embody inferences of a cause-effect nature? Apart from recognising that we tend to talk about reasons and purposes in a rather different way from more 'exogenous' causes (Kruglanski, 1979), attribution researchers seem to take this assumption for granted. This assumption has been the central thesis of attribution theory ever since Heider's early concern with the notion of causal unit formation. It both defines and restricts attribution theory as we know it.

## Beyond causality

What then could be the antithesis of this assumption? Let me state it simply as a dogmatic assertion, and then examine the evidence for it:

*Processes of social cognition and perception are concerned primarily with categorisation and prediction and only secondarily with causal explanation.*

Let us go back to basics. Why do people make attributions? It is assumed that people seek to interpret and understand the behaviour of others, but to say this is just to restate the question in a new form: why do people seek interpretation and understanding? Heider's own answer was that attributions serve to simplify the individual's perceptual world, which otherwise would be impossibly complex.

Attribution serves the attainment of a stable and consistent environment, gives a parsimonious and at the same time often adequate description of what happens, and determines what we expect will occur and what we should do about it. (Heider, 1958b, p. 25).

Balance tendencies can be considered in essentially the same terms:

We also want to attain stable and orderly evaluations; we want to find the good and the bad distributed in a simple and consistent fashion. The codification in terms of positive and negative value is simpler when the positive features are grouped in one unit and the negative ones in another unit. (Heider, 1958b, p. 25)

A particularly useful way of considering balance as a form of cognitive simplification has been suggested by Jaspars (1965), based on an adaptation of Coombs's (1964) theory of preferential choice. According to Coombs, preferences can be interpreted in terms of the proximity of items of judgement to an ideal point in an underlying preference space, which could be unidimensional or multidimensional. If we consider a $p$–$o$–$x$ triad in terms of Coombs's model, then a positive self-evaluation places $p$ at or near the ideal point, and positive $po$ and $px$ relations can be represented as small distances between p and o, and between p and x respectively. If we further assume that a small $ox$ distance represents a positive $ox$ relation, and a large $ox$ distance a negative $ox$ relation, then Fig. 1 shows triads that can be represented in terms of a unidimensional preference space.

What is important about these triads is that four of them are balanced according to Heider's definition. The triad containing three negative relations, which Heider originally regarded as 'ambiguous', can be represented in terms of a unidimensional preference space, but only in the special instance where $p$ is at the midpoint of the underlying continuum (e.g. if $p$ is a political moderate who dislikes extremists of

Sign of each relation                J-scale

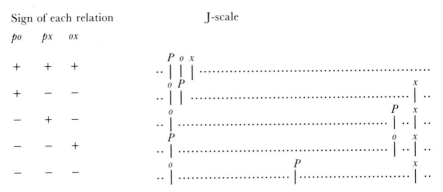

Fig. 1   Representation of triads in a unidimensional preference space. (From Eiser and Stroebe, 1972, p. 183)

both the left and right). With this exception, imbalanced triads cannot be represented in terms of a unidimensional preference space. Imbalance therefore implies greater cognitive complexity. Indeed, studies of individual differences in cognitive complexity have indicated that more cognitively complex individuals are more tolerant of cognitive imbalance (Streufert and Streufert, 1978).

Balance theory, then, can be presented in terms which emphasise simplificatory processes without insisting that such processes involve *causal* inferences or the formation of *causal* units. This is not to say that explanatory statements may not often exhibit balance properties. If we overhear a remark like 'I'm sure she only got promotion because her boss fancied her', we could say that some sort of causal inference is being made. The boss in question is seen as exhibiting the 'balance' tendency to assume that 'good' traits in a person (good looks, good work performance) go together. In that it exhibits this tendency, the behaviour of the boss is seen as predictable (no doubt too predictable!), and in some way explicable.

The *kind* of explanation that is involved here, however, is problematic and, indeed, much more may be involved than simple explanation. The degree of assumed intentionality is left unstated in this remark. Did the woman in question deliberately flaunt her attractiveness to gain promotion? Was the boss simply over-impressionable, or was he showing deliberate favouritism in the hope of some *quid pro quo*? We'd have to eavesdrop for a little longer for an answer, and perhaps we wouldn't hear one, but what we could say immediately was that the speaker (*a*) did not think too highly of the promoted woman; (*b*) did not think too highly of the boss for promoting her; and (*c*) was quite probably put out by the thought of how she herself compared or had been compared with the promoted woman. Thus, with the speaker attempting to maintain self-esteem, observing a positive relationship between the boss and the other woman, and disapproving both of the other woman and of the boss, we have all the elements of a classic balanced triad, with $p$ (the speaker) having a positive (if temporarily bruised) self-concept, a perception of a positive relation between $o$ (the boss) and $x$ (the other woman) and negative evaluations of $o$ and $x$ by $p$. This state of balance could be variously reinforced by the speaker's friend saying 'yes, you've been with the firm a lot longer than she has', or 'yes, I saw him really drooling over her in the coffee bar last week', or 'I think he's the worst of the lot – I'd hate to work for him' or 'I can't think what men see in her, to be honest'.

Looked at from the standpoint of attribution theory, one could say that this was an instance of a perceiver inferring causes from events. However, the attributional analysis has still a fair way to go. It is unclear how responsibility was assumed to be partialled out, whether calculated intentions or involuntary mental causes were involved, whether financial gain was a more or less important factor than the satisfaction of libidinous desires, and so on. But whilst the attributional analysis has hardly started, the restoration of balance, that is, of a simple evaluative structure, is essentially complete.

In all fields of psychology one can find evidence of how individuals cope with a complex stimulus environment through various processes of simplification. In a few instances it is plausible to think of such processes in causal attribution terms, but in very many it is not. This does not merely reflect the balance between social and non-social psychology – it applies to research in social psychology itself.

The idea that individuals exploit redundancy in stimulus information is fundamental to the principle of categorisation as applied to judgements of socially valued or neutral physical stimuli (Tajfel, 1959; Tajfel and Wilkes, 1963), of attitude statements (Eiser, 1971; Eiser and Stroebe, 1972) and of social groups (Tajfel, 1969, 1978). The basic effect is shown when subjects use information concerning the category-membership or position of stimuli in terms of one attribute or dimension (e.g. ethnic group membership) to discriminate between the stimuli in terms of another dimension (e.g. occupational status) believed by the subjects to be correlated with the first.

For instance, suppose someone said of a West Indian he'd just met at work 'I nearly fell through the floor when he said he was the new Area Manager – I thought he'd come about the vacancy in the packing office'. This person would be describing an event which violated his expectations – expectations based on an actual or imagined association between ethnic origin and occupational status in our society. Stereotypes may be thought of as accentuation of actual associations of this kind, or as fabrications of fictitious associations along similar lines. But do such stereotypes – or even more experientially based expectations – involve causal attributions? They can, but they needn't, and possibly more often than not, don't.

If we asked our speaker to say why he was surprised he *might* answer that he considered that prevailing social conditions made it very much more difficult for blacks than whites to obtain well-paid employment (an environmental attribution), or that he thought that blacks were all stupid or in other ways unsuitable for employment as managers (a personal attribution in terms of assumed group characteristics). In other words, we might get an answer which looked like an attempt at giving a causal explanation of the assumed relationship between ethnic origin and occupational status. However, it is just as conceivable that our question 'Why?' would be interpreted as a query about *whether* there was a basis for prediction (and hence surprise) rather than a request for *explanation* of the regularity. The kind of answer we might be given, then, could be a statement of the assumed basis for prediction – a 'justification' for the prediction itself rather than a causal explanation of the predictability.

If we confine ourselves to the question of how individuals make predictions, as opposed to attempting causal explanations, we again find strong evidence of simplificatory processes at work. One of the major influences in this area has been the research of Tversky and Kahneman (1974) on cognitive 'heuristics' (see also chapter 3). For Tversky and Kahneman, a heuristic is a simplificatory cognitive strategy employed by individuals when faced by uncertain information. The judgements which individuals make under such conditions frequently show systematic departures from normative statistical principles.

One such important bias is the neglect (except under certain conditions to be discussed below) of information concerning base rate probabilities of a particular event occurring by chance, or of a particular object or person belonging to a particular category. This kind of abstract information – equivalent to 'consensus' information in Kelley's model, tends to be disregarded in comparison with statistically less informative case descriptions of single concrete instances (Nisbett, Borgida, Crandall and Reed, 1976). People can also be shown to draw conclusions with excessive confidence on the basis of uncertain data and small samples, but to resist revising such conclusions in the light of contradictory evidence.

In such results, therefore, there is a bias in selection of information, and in the processing of such information to enhance apparent predictability. Such biases, by definition, leave open the probability of error, but it is a moot point whether they generally interfere with individual behaviour. We tend in our culture to talk of 'decisiveness' as a positive characteristic, and offer proverbs such as 'if you don't believe in yourself, nobody else will' or 'Don't change horses in mid-stream'. It could be argued that, in many real-life contexts, decisions have to be made in the absence of any adequate basis for prediction (Bonoma, 1977). It is also by no means an inconsequential coincidence that, by showing this kind of decision-making bias, individuals render their own behaviour more predictable to others, as well as to themselves. Conservatism in decision-making can thus enhance the consistency of the decision-makers' own behaviour, and lead to a recognisable behaviour as well as cognitive style – in short, to a personality.

It is interesting that science fiction writers who attempt to give particular computers, robots, automata, etc., individual 'personalities' tend to do so by emphasising some bias, blind spot, malfunction or 'human-like' deviation from mere exegesis of hard logic, which amounts, in terms of Kelley's model, to information of a kind of consistency and (by inducing contrast with 'normal' computers) lack of consensus.

## Beyond naive psychology

The above remarks imply the relevance of attributional concepts to perceptions of personality in a way that is similar to but still importantly different from the orthodox attribution theory view. The orthodox view states that, if such criteria as high consistency and low distinctiveness are satisfied, the observer *infers* a characteristic or personality trait in the actor from observation of the behaviour. I am saying instead that the appearance of high consistency and low distinctiveness means that the actor's personality appears recognisable, that is, the actor's behaviour appears to fit into recognisable categories.

This is the most fundamental aspect of ordinary language 'personality' descriptions – they are ways of categorising *behaviour* and their reference is actual or imagined behaviour by the actor, not some kind of insubstantial entity in the actor's consciousness or unconsciousness which cannot be directly observed. These descriptions are special kinds

of descriptions in that they assume and predict high consistency and
low distinctiveness – but not in that they refer to a logically separable,
unobservable, but still causally efficacious 'ghost in the machine'
(Ryle, 1949).

The starting point for a study of naive psychology or 'lay concepts of
personality' is such ordinary language descriptions of behaviour of
assumed consistency and distinctiveness. What can we say of such
descriptions as a general class? Do they entail a trait-theoretical view of
personality and a trait-determined view of behaviour? Allport and
Odbert (1936) found some 18 000 trait names in a standard English
dictionary. Of these 4504 seemed to describe 'consistent and stable
modes of an individual's adjustment to his environment' (Allport,
1937, p. 306). In making this selection, Gordon Allport was trying to
exclude adjectives referring to mere temporary states (e.g. *gibbering*,
*frantic*), metaphorical descriptions (e.g. *amorphous*, *prolific*) the predominantly evaluative descriptions, although he acknowledges that
this is a hard distinction to draw (e.g. *adorable*, *trying*). Those that are
left are assumed to be a relevant basis for the development of a
trait-theoretical view of personality.

A more mundane view is that this immense vocabulary has nothing
particularly to do with traits in the technical personality theory sense,
but is a device of labelling and commenting on recognisable features of
a person's appearance and observed behaviour and underlining this
recognisability. One can attempt to look for overall structural features
in any such vocabulary, and this is what Osgood, Suci and
Tannenbaum (1957) did in pioneering the use of the semantic
differential. Later generations of psycholinguistics might regard the
title of their book, *The Measurement of Meaning*, as imperialistic in the
sense that 'meaning' depends not only on the place of individual words
and concepts in a semantic space, but on the syntagmatic relationships
between words within (say) a sentence. However, it is significant, and
to their credit, that they did not call their investigation, as others might
have done, '*The Measurement of Personality*.' (After all, clinical case data
are reported.)

From this point of view, this vocabulary allows us to categorise and
simplify our perceptions of ourselves and others in ways which serve
(what I am arguing is) the more fundamental function of prediction.
Furthermore, as Osgood *et al.* show, our descriptive vocabulary
is very largely evaluative. As I have argued above, evaluative interpersonal descriptions are a way of rendering interpersonal relationships apparently more predictable and simple, through principles
of cognitive balance.

In all of this, is it necessary to assume that observers are looking for *causes* of the actor's behaviour within the actor's personality? This is far too narrow a view of the bases of predictability that can be implicit in such interpersonal descriptions. An alternative approach is to assume that we look for *themes* in the behaviour of different individuals in different situations.

Harré and Secord (1972) have argued for a 'dramaturgical' approach to the explanation of social behaviour, but they are not alone in recognising the fact that social behaviour is 'situated', that it unfolds in time, that it is shaped by social rules and conventions, and that we have different expectations concerning the roles of different participants. It is interesting that many of our technical terms have a strong echo of the stage – e.g. character, persona, role, actor, attitude (a posture struck by an actor). The idea that trying to explain someone's behaviour is like trying to understand the plot in a play has a very plausible appeal.

If this kind of approach is going to provide a new direction and vitality to attribution theory, however, it needs to be more than merely taxonomic. Aristotle introduced the idea of different kinds of causes, and attribution theorists are still arguing about it. Perhaps we might get on a bit more quickly if we took a different route. There is obviously a need for documentation and analysis of the roles and rules involved in specific social contexts, but it is not the sole, nor even arguably the special, responsibility of social psychology to carry this out. Where there is a special need for psychological inquiry is in discovering how 'world knowledge' – knowledge of the roles and rules involved in any social context – affects cognitive, perceptual and behavioural processes.

An example of how the dramaturgical metaphor can be applied in such a way as to generate hypotheses about cognitive processes, is the theory of cognitive scripts (Schank and Abelson, 1977). This has been taken up by researchers in such fields as artificial intelligence and psycholinguistics as a way of conceptualising how predictions, based on world knowlege, influence cognitive processes, such as those involved in understanding the meaning of a passage of narrative prose.

This approach is fundamentally different from the view that trait-descriptions point to the causes of observed behaviour. Instead, it is argued that the understanding of sentences and longer passages relies upon implicit schemata that are often not made at all explicit in the text itself. For example, the sentence 'I like apples' is clearly taken to mean 'I like to eat apples' even though eating is not mentioned. Interpersonal descriptions may contribute to our understanding of events in many ways other than saying that a particular behaviour was *caused* by a particular characteristic of the actor.

The difference between the script theory and attribution theory approaches can be partly seen by considering the following example:

(1) 'John was always the last person to leave the office. He was a very ambitious man.'

In terms of attribution theory, we have evidence for consistency ('always') and lack of consensus ('the last person'), and this invites us to look for a specific cause for John's behaviour, which we find in his personal trait of ambitiousness. We therefore make an internal attribution as distinct from an external attribution to role requirements as in:

(2) 'John was always the last person to leave the office. It was his job to lock up.'

If we went through the well-worn procedure of asking subjects to rate how much John's behaviour was due to his 'personality' or the 'situation', we would certainly obtain differences between (1) and (2). But here some interesting points arise. For a start, (1) and (2) are quite compatible with each other. Furthermore, it is a *special* kind of personality attribution that is involved in (1) and a *special* kind of situational attribution that is involved in (2). To understand *how* (1) and (2) are easily understood, we need to know what implicit information is conveyed by each. If all that were involved was a choice between an internal and external attribution, it would be difficult to see why (1) and (2) are more easily understood than:

(3) 'John was always the last person to leave the office. He was a former alcoholic.'

or

(4) 'John was always the last person to leave the office. The dentist's surgery was open till 6.30 p.m.'

Again, (3) and (4) could be compatible with each other, and (3) invites a rating of greater 'personal' causality than (4), but a great deal more cognitive work needs to be done in each before they are readily interpretable.

One way of looking at this is in terms of the 'scripts' implicitly involved. The script of 'working at the office' makes it easy to relate 'being last to leave' to either 'being ambitious', or 'having to lock up'. In each case, though, a wealth of 'world knowledge' is brought into play, and, as a result, information can be got across very concisely.

In (1) we readily imagine John as someone who wishes to impress his superiors and gain promotion and, with this goal in mind, voluntarily works harder than his colleagues. In (2), we take it for granted that the person who locks up has to be the last to leave, as otherwise people would be locked in for the night. All this is simple and obvious enough, but unless these assumptions are made, the connections are totally mysterious.

What is mysterious about (3) and (4) is that the second sentence of each passage seems to have nothing to do with the script 'working at the office' which is set off by the first sentence. To make sense of (3), we have to add something like 'He wanted to avoid being asked by his colleagues to go for a drink after work'. This shifts the focus of the passage to a script about 'how to stay off drink'. To make sense of (4), we need to add something like: 'He used to wait for Jenny to get off work and walk home with her'. We can now guess that Jenny worked at the dentist's surgery (though in what capacity is still unspecified), and we can infer some kind of bond between John and Jenny which, depending on how it is specified, can set off a 'courtship' script, a 'working couple' script, a 'father and grown up daughter' script, or whatever.

Whereas attribution theory asks how people *explain* their experience, the main question asked by script theory is:

How do people organize all the knowledge they must have in order to understand? How do people know what behaviour is appropriate for a particular situation? To put it more concretely, how do you know that, in a restaurant, the waitress will get you the food you ask for whereas if you ask her for a pair of shoes, or you ask her for food on a bus she will react as if you had done something odd?   (Schank and Abelson, 1977, p. 36)

Understanding comes from predictability, and predictability from world knowledge. Attribution theory seems to have little to say about how such world knowledge is acquired or organised.

### Towards a possible synthesis

CAUSAL SCHEMATA AND PREDICTION

Although I have argued that the search for predictability may be more 'basic' than the search for explanation, it is clear that being able to explain events usually renders them more predictable. The question then arises: when someone is faced with a mass of information, what information will s/he select in order to feel able to make a prediction?

Ajzen (1977) and Tversky and Kahneman (1979) have suggested that information which is causally relevant, i.e. fits into a causal schema, has more influence on prediction than equally informative data which does not seem to be causally relevant. Ajzen refers to this as the 'causality heuristic' (see also chapter 3).

Tversky and Kahneman (1980) give a number of examples of where what they call 'causal inferences' take precedence over 'diagnostic inferences'. One problem which subjects were asked was as follows:

'Which of the following events is more probable?

(a) That a girl has blue eyes if her mother has blue eyes

(b) That the mother has blue eyes, if her daughter has blue eyes

(c) The two events are equally probable.'

Although the correct answer is (c) of 175 subjects 106 said (a), 34 said (b), and 35 said (c). The argument is that subjects think of the daughter's eye colour being causally dependent on that of the mother, but not *vice versa*.

Another example is where subjects have to say which of the following probabilities is higher:

$P(R/H)$ – The probability of home fuel rationing in the US during the 1990s, assuming a marked increase in the use of solar energy for home heating during the 1980s.

$P(R/\bar{H})$ – The probability of home fuel rationing in the US during the 1990s, assuming *no* marked increase in the use of solar energy for home heating during the 1980s.

The possible causal relation between $R$ (rationing) and $H$ (solar heating) is that H should have, if anything, a negative effect on the need for $R$. However, Tversky and Kahneman argue, it seems unreasonable to suppose that the amount of energy saved by solar heating would be enough by itself to stave off an impending crisis.

The diagnostic implications of $H$ on $R$, however, are positive. That is, an increase in $H$ can plausibly be seen as a sign of an underlying shortage of energy from other sources, and such a shortage would make $R$ *more* likely.

Thus subjects who looked for a causal effect of $H$ on $R$ should say that $P(R/\bar{H}) > P(R/H)$, whereas those that looked for the diagnostic implications of $H$ for $R$ should say that $P(R/H) > (R/\bar{H})$. In fact, 68 of 83 subjects chose the first response.

This has important implications for the perceived relationships between personal characteristics, actions, and the consequences of actions, with which, of course, attribution theory is centrally concerned. Essentially, it suggests that people should have no great difficulty in constructing causal or explanatory schemata around these relations, *provided the inferences required of them are in a particular direction*, namely, from personal characteristics to actions, and from actions to consequences. This direction of inference is precisely opposite to that implied by the Jones and Davis (1965) model. Thus, people should find it easier to answer questions of the form 'How would someone like this behave?' or 'What would be the likely effect of this kind of behaviour?' than questions such as 'What kind of person would exhibit this behaviour?' or 'What kind of behaviour would produce these consequences?'. It is questions of the latter kind, however, which are typically asked of subjects in attribution experiments. In other words, although attribution theory continually talks about causality, in fact, when it comes to making personal attributions, subjects are required to reason diagnostically.

CAUSAL SCHEMATA V. CAUSAL UNITS

In view of all this, what definition of cause is defensible in attribution research, and how useful is the cause–reason distinction? We can discard for all but the most extravagant cases a crude deterministic view according to which people are impelled by traits or autonomous drives to act in particular ways. Once this is done, my own view is that the usefulness of further conceptual distinctions is something to be demonstrated rather than assumed. What Tversky and Kahneman (1980) refer to as causal inference is simply inference from one event to another assumed to occur as a consequence of the first. Causal schemata, in other words, typically unfold in time. In the same way, Schank and Abelson (1977) talk of causal chains to refer to sequences of linked events within a script, without dwelling on the kind of cause involved.

From the point of view of script theory, moreover, the 'basic' distinction between personal and impersonal causality is by no means crucial, or always easy to apply. Consider the Schank and Abelson restaurant script – the customer asks the waitress for some food and the waitress brings it to him. The question of how far the behaviour of the two 'players' is 'determined' by personal or impersonal causes is not a particularly helpful one. The point about the 'causal' schema involved in this script is that it involves behaviour in a predictable and familiar cultural setting. The 'players' are performing recognisable roles. Yet it is nonsense (except possibly in terms of an extremely deterministic conditioning theory) to say that the fact that the customer was sitting at the table *caused* him to order a given dish, or that the words he spoke to the waitress *caused* her to go and get it for him.

Behaviour which is highly predictable from knowledge of roles and social conventions may still be (typically) purposeful and voluntary. The customer could choose not to order, or to order something different, and the waitress could choose to ignore his order, or bring him something different. We can also assume that the customer has chosen to be a customer and the waitress to be a waitress (although, of course, they cannot choose to switch roles in mid-scene). Yet although we are dealing with purposeful choice, an orthodox attributional analysis would have to emphasise the 'causal' influence of the 'impersonal' situational factors. This is because causal *units* (in Heider's theory) are concerned with instrumental relationships – what makes something happen. Causal *schemata*, on the other hand (in script theory and the work of Tversky and Kahneman) are representations of what follows predictably from what. A doctor might prescribe a pill to a patient and the patient may happily take it, both 'knowing' that the symptoms will be relieved, without either necessarily having any real idea of how the pill can make this happen.

Regarding the cause–reason distinction, the argument that inter-personal attributions are frequently teleological – i.e. phrased in terms of reasons and purposes – might, paradoxically, be taken as evidence for the priority of what Tversky and Kahneman (1979) call *causal* inference over diagnostic inference. Faced with the task of constructing an explanatory scheme around a given piece of behaviour, it could be that individuals find it easier to look forward to what might be the consequences of that behaviour (and hence, by implication, the goal which the actor was seeking to achieve), than to look backwards to what possible personal or impersonal antecedents might have led to the behaviour occurring. (This is yet another argument against having intentions placed in between dispositions and acts as they are in the Jones and Davis model.)

Having raised the question earlier in this chapter as to whether the judgemental processes involved in attributions are in fact causal, let me now suggest an answer, that individuals can frequently reason in terms of causal schemata, but that they tend to do so by attempting to predict *what follows from* perceived factors or events. Thus, they may predict behaviour from knowledge of persons, or goals, and consequences from behaviour. Unless specifically asked to do so, they are less likely to infer antecedents. Such a bias is arguably behaviourally adaptive, in that it gears up the perceiver to anticipate future states of affairs. However, the formation of causal *units* in Heider's sense is concerned with more than anticipation and prediction. It is concerned with instrumentality and the balance of dynamic relations in the context of a total structure.

SCRIPTS AS CAUSAL SCHEMATA

The main emphasis of script theory is on the preconditions for understanding, rather than for causal explanation. Although Schank and Abelson talk of 'causal chains', nothing more contentious is implied than knowledge of one event leading on to another. Nonetheless, if someone can explain the relationship between a sequence of events, this is as good as saying that s/he understands what is going on and so can predict what will happen.

Making attributions and inferences then, according to this view, is to fill in the missing or unstated parts of a script. The ability to fill in a script is the ability to make predictions and to use causal schemata derived from world knowledge. The question of how world knowledge, as opposed to experimental instructions and hypothetical data, influence predictions and attributions, is one to which attribution research has given insufficient regard. The imaginary examples I used earlier in this chapter – the promoted secretary and the West Indian area manager – rely, for the point I was trying to make with them, on culturally specific world knowledge. If such world knowledge were inaccessible, any intelligibility in my argument would be quite beyond redemption. A more concrete instance of the attributional relevance of world knowledge is provided by evidence of how assumed social group characteristics and the context of intergroup relations influence attributions (see Hewstone and Jaspars, 1980a and chapter 9).

To some extent, I feel that the Gestalt heritage of attribution theory is responsible for its preponderant concern with abstract formal relations at the expense of content. Script theory is in many ways an attempt to reintroduce content into another area hitherto rather restricted by a reliance on abstract formal models of syntactic and semantic structures. Social psychology has much to learn from this experience. If we are interested in real social behaviour and in how real social events are interpreted, let us adopt methodologies consistent with this aim. Then, perhaps, we might have theories which are both general and applicable.

## Ambiguity and the engagement of the attribution process

We thus have arrived at a view of social cognition according to which individuals can think in terms of causal relationships and construct causal schemata out of their perceptual input. Such schemata, however, have content and are articulated within specific social contexts, rather than being pure formal logical structures or Gestalten. Moreover, it appears that such schemata are used predominantly for prediction rather than explanation, for inferring effects from causes rather than *vice versa*. Attribution theory, however, is concerned with how people infer causes from effects, so does this mean that it is much ado about nothing – a grand theory about a phenomenon not found except under artificial laboratory conditions?

The answer I would give is an emphatic 'no', but neither would I support the imperialistic claims of attribution theory, as hitherto developed, to a position of undisputed hegemony within the study of social cognition. My answer of 'no' is based on the simple facts that individuals can make attributions of causality and responsibility if called upon to do so in particular situations, and that many individuals spend a large part of their working lives attempting to answer questions of 'why?' including the whys of human behaviour.

But the point is that these are *special* types of activity, which stand out from a general background of prediction and predictability. In many situations, discerning a person's intentions is nothing very mysterious or problematic. Anscombe (1963, p. 8) makes this point: 'If you want to say at least some true things about a man's intentions, you will have a strong chance of success if you mention what he actually did or was doing'.

But what happens when events do not fit into a readily available schema, or when different schemata or scripts compete for plausibility? When this occurs individuals have to consider information diagnostically. Suppose a warehouse on a busy road is destroyed by a fire. Someone not too immediately concerned might be content to think only of what might *follow on* from the fire – whether there would be traffic hold-ups and s/he should take a different route to work, whether some goods would be in short supply in local shops, and so on. On the other hand, the police and inspectors of the insurance company would be very concerned with detecting signs that the fire could have been started deliberately. Suppose also that there were signs of arson, and it turned out that the night watchman had left a back window unlocked – was this unintentional, or was he in league with the arsonist? This would be the kind of attributional question required of a jury. The accuracy of any particular script or schema here has consequences. The acceptance of a particular script is an event in itself, from which particular effects will follow.

One thing that is special about the activities of jurors, scientists and diagnosticians generally, is that they stand outside the temporal context of the events they are attempting to explain. Actors, on the other hand, move forward in time with the events they are predicting. The focus of attribution theory has been on cognitive processes of the 'stop and think' variety.

What, then, is it that primarily makes people 'stop and think'? I suggest that it is the experience of uncertainty over what to do next and what is likely to happen. If we can find the correct explanation for a person's behaviour, we can decide how to react towards him or her, and predict how s/he is likely to behave in the future. Attribution theory presents this business of finding explanations as essentially problematic – and so it is, in the abstract. In just the same way, understanding language is problematic, in the abstract. But, just as from the perspective of a literate native speaker, understanding actual spoken or written language is something which seems to require almost no thought at all, so, from the perspective of a participant in culturally familiar settings, it is usually quite obvious why people are doing what they are doing.

In many concrete situations, familiar and appropriate scripts are readily accessible and can be used to provide concise and coherent descriptions of what is going on. In an important minority of cases, however, actors can seem to forget their lines, or to be playing parts from different plays; or observers can feel like viewers who cannot work out what programme they are watching. It is under these circumstances that the attribution process is engaged. It is with reference to these circumstances that the experimental literature on attribution processes has to be evaluated. But it is also the special nature of these circumstances which must be recognised if the attributional approach is to provide a more general theory of social cognition.

# Part II

# Developmental Aspects of Attribution Theory

# 5

# Developmental Dimensions of Attribution Theory

Frank D. Fincham

## Introduction

Attribution theory is most commonly associated with social psychology. It not only dominates the research reported in social psychology journals (Pleban and Richardson, 1979), but has also replaced cognitive dissonance theory as the major conceptual framework in this area. There are indications, however, that attribution theory is also beginning to influence areas of psychology which have not traditionally been associated with this approach. One such field is developmental psychology. The present chapter traces the increasing impact of attribution theory in this area and critically assesses both its current and potential contribution to developmental research. In addition an attempt is made to indicate further points of contact between the two areas.

The first developmental research conducted within the framework of attribution theory appears to be Shaw and Sulzer's (1964) widely cited study on responsibility which, perhaps not surprisingly, appeared in a social rather than developmental psychology journal. Although the above association is almost as old as attribution theory itself, it should not therefore be construed that attribution research has a long history in developmental psychology. Despite a few notable exceptions (e.g. Baldwin and Baldwin, 1970), the attribution approach only began to emerge in developmental literature towards the mid-seventies. This development was closely related to changes in developmental psychology. The most important of these was the emergence of social cognition as a legitimate and important field of study. Traditionally, social development had been investigated almost exclusively within the framework of psychoanalytic and social learning theories (Shantz, 1975), neither of which showed a strong cognitive orientation. It was only under Piaget's influence that the study of cognitive development captured the imagination of researchers interested in children. During the 1960s this was largely limited to logical problem solving, although the extension of this work to social perception was readily apparent early in the next decade. It heralded the beginning of a boom in developmental research on social cognition.

In the first major review of this new research area Shantz (1975) noted that 'research and theories of adults' interpersonal understanding have had very little impact on developmental research' (p. 259). However, Flavell (1971, p. 272) had earlier pointed out that our understanding of development is necessarily influenced by our conception of the mature organism, the adult. In a later publication he specified more precisely the value for developmental psychologists (Flavell, 1974) of adult studies on interpersonal inferences. Shantz (1975) similarly points to the value of such social psychological investigations but it is clear from her research review that little use had been made of the attribution framework.

Research was quick to fill this gap. It became increasingly apparent that social cognitive development did not display the relative unity that appeared to characterise thinking about the physical world. Not surprisingly, more research outside of Piaget's cognitive developmental framework began to emerge and a spate of attribution oriented studies followed. As in social psychology, attribution theory was not seen as a 'theory' pertaining to a particular content area *per se*, but rather as a research approach or framework. Consequently, its influence is apparent in several very diverse areas of child development research. A brief overview of these is given before each is considered in more detail.

In its broadest conception attribution theory has been characterised as an examination of how people arrive at answers to the question 'why?' (Kelley, 1972a). Considered in these very general terms it is not surprising to find that attribution theory has even been quoted with respect to person perception studies regarding children's descriptions of persons and explanations of events. For example, Leahy (1976) suggests that the increasing qualification of trait descriptions provided by older adolescents may reflect an increasing use of Kelley's (1967) attribution criteria and hence awareness of behavioural variability. Similarly Guttentag and Longfellow (1977) include content analytic studies of children's descriptions (e.g. Livesey and Bromley, 1973; Secord and Peevers, 1974) in their review of social attributions. (The relationship of attribution theory to children's explanations and descriptions is dealt with in chapter 6.)

Attribution theory is, however, more correctly identified as the study of perceived causality. Consequently, one area in which one might have expected it to have an impact is in the study of children's notions regarding causality. Although this has indeed been the case it must be pointed out that developmental research on causality has traditionally been limited to physical causality. The contribution of attribution theory to this field of investigation is, however, relatively small when compared with the study of situations where a person acts in relation to some object (human causality) or other person (interpersonal causality). With regard to the latter, most recent research has centred on the use of causal schemes and the related principles of discounting and augmentation (Kelly, 1972b). As attribution theorists do not distinguish sharply between cause and responsibility the earlier mentioned work on responsibility attribution can also be seen as falling into this category. The present chapter focuses on the contribution of attribution theory to these areas of developmental research. However, the perception of causality (physical, human and interpersonal) is clearly distinguished from responsibility attribution.

The above topics do not exhaust the areas in which attribution theory has begun to affect developmental studies, nor do they comprise the only major influences. Equally important is the role of attribution theory in the achievement motivation literature (cf. Weiner, 1974; Weiner, Frieze, Kukla, Reed, Rest and Rosenbaum, 1972). Developmental dimensions of this work are reviewed elsewhere in this volume (chapter 7), but it is worth noting that the attribution analysis developed in the achievement domain has been applied to moral judgements (Weiner and Peter, 1973; Weiner, Kun and Benesh-Weiner, 1978), social motivation (Weiner and Kun, 1980), mastery and emotions (Weiner et al., 1978) with some success. Where appropriate, reference will be made to such research.

It is also apparent that attribution theory can be studied in relation to characteristics of both the perceiver and perceived which may show age-related differences (e.g. sex, race, personality etc.). Investigations in these areas often tend to derive from other conceptual frameworks and to use the attribution approach merely as a methodological tool. While not wishing to deny the importance of such work the present chapter is limited to research which explores the developmental nature of fundamental attribution principles. Lest any confusion arise in relation to such principles it remains finally to delimit what the term 'attribution theory' precisely designates. Attribution theory is probably best identified with the work of Jones and Davis (1965), Kelley (1967, 1972a, b, 1973) and especially Heider (1944, 1958a) as conceptual advances over and above these earlier and by now classic statements have been limited (Jones, 1978, Jones and McGillis, 1976; Kelley and Michela, 1980). Consequently, it is in relation to these core 'theories' that developmental research will be examined.

## The perception of causality

PHYSICAL CAUSALITY

In order to appreciate fully the contribution of attribution theory to the areas under review it is necessary to summarise briefly what is known about each. Because of the dominant role of cognitive-developmental theory in the child development literature, this inevitably leads one to the work of Piaget. In the study of physical causality it is again Piaget's (1927/1969) writings which initiated and stimulated much of the research. It should be emphasised that, as the present chapter primarily concerns attribution theory, only rather brief and summary statements of Piaget's views can be given. Appropriate reference is made to the original literature for the reader interested in pursuing Piagetian ideas.

*Piaget on causality*

*The Child's Conception of Physical Causality* (English translation, 1927) is often seen as Piaget's contribution to knowledge in this field (e.g. Weiner and Kun, 1980). In this work Piaget used an observational and largely verbal approach. For instance, he examined the kind of 'why' questions young children asked and speculated on the developmental history of the underlying notions of causality they express. More direct investigations were made by interviewing children of different ages and asking them questions about a number of physical phenomena (e.g. why the wind blows, why the boat floats, etc.). Piaget identified seventeen different types of causal explanations and three major processes in the child's development. At first, the child extends the properties of the self to the universe, but during the course of time begins to distinguish between motivation and physical causality (Piaget's 'subjectification of causality'). Early on, therefore, the child confuses psychological relations with physical ones (the notion of precausality). Secondly, the child's early causal explanations imply an immediate and almost extra-temporal relation between cause and effect. Simple juxtaposition is sufficient to establish a causal connection for there is no interest in how the cause brings about the effect. With time the child begins to pay attention to intermediary events and temporal factors (what Piaget calls the 'formation of series in time'). The third development is the establishment of a reversible series (in Piaget's terms 'the progressive reversibility of cause and effect').

It is this last process which hints at what Piaget (1974) considers 'the main question raised by causal explanations' (p. xi), namely, the relationship between logical operations, which are purely formal, and understanding causality, which is an ontological acquisition. Indeed, he even sees causality in terms similar to those used in his theory of intelligence. A causal explanation shows 'through what transformations' an effect is produced and how it relates 'to certain transmissions from the initial stages'. Both 'production' and 'conservation' (*ibid.*, p. 1.) are involved. It is this question regarding the primacy of operations versus causality which provides a tie between his early book and *Understanding Causality* (1974). The overtly 'experimental' approach adopted in this later work is clearly motivated by this question and according to Piaget provides a clear answer to it.

Piaget's position is perhaps best illustrated by outlining one of his studies as it gives some indication of the nature of this later work. In an experiment on mediated causal transmission (experiment R2, Piaget, 1974, p. 12) a child observes a moving marble strike the first in a row of marbles. The last marble in the row rolls away from the rest which do not move at all. Children explaining this phenomenon understand that causal transmission is purely internal and mediated by the row of stationary marbles only at 7 or 8 years of age, before which time Piaget had long ago concluded 'no genuinely physical explanation could be given of natural phenomena' (1927/1969, p. 267). More important, however, it also coincided with the age at which children acquired that ability to make transitive inferences. Piaget then goes on to argue that such inferences are necessary for solving the causal problem. In essence, this later work tries to show that any causal explanation is essentially an attribution of operations to the world of objects and therefore reflects the cognitive development of the subject.

Both of Piaget's works can be criticised for the heavy demands made on the child's comprehension and verbal ability. Neither examines the child's responses in terms of discrete behaviours or judgements. The question of judgements v. explanations as developmental criteria has recently given rise to some considerable debate (cf. Brainerd, 1978, 1979; Jamison and Dansky, 1979) as it generally has not been recognised that the latter lag considerably behind the former. It is therefore not clear whether Piaget's work deals with the causal reasoning or, rather, with linguistic development regarding this concept. Its utility with regard to the latter is also open to question. For

example, Hood and Bloom's (1979) recent analysis of causal expressions in young children's discourse shows that 2–3-year-olds have some
understanding of causal relations. Moreover, they found that children
first made causal statements which later led parents to ask causal
questions. Only after they had learnt to answer these inquiries did
children themselves ask 'why?' questions (approximately 30 months).
Equally important in the present context is that no evidence was found
for causal relations based merely on juxtaposition. Such findings
question the very infrastructure on which Piaget bases his claims.

   Despite the above criticisms, it is Piaget's early, largely verbal, work
which dominates research on causality.[1] However, nearly all subsequent studies have investigated childhood animism (Brainerd, 1978,
p. 119). Readers interested in this work are referred to Looft and Bartz
(1979) and especially Laurendeau and Pinard (1962) who have
summarised much of the early work and conducted several replication
studies. Apart from a conceptual (Shultz, 1980) and empirical
(Bindra, Clarke and Shultz, 1980) attempt to challenge the primacy of
operations there has been virtually no attempt to evaluate Piaget's later
work. Lately, however, it has been noted that Piagetian research deals
almost exclusively with the content of causal explanations and says
very little about their form or structure (e.g. Shultz and Ravinsky,
1976; Weiner and Kun, 1976). Like Kun (1977), the present author
considers this awareness to have emerged because of the impact of
attribution theory. Whatever its source there is little doubt that
recognition of the distinction stimulated research on physical causality.
Moreover, researchers turned largely to attribution theory for causal
principles which might be used to investigate development.

*Attribution research*

It is worth noting that not all the studies quoted in this section make
explicit reference to attribution theory. Some investigators (e.g.
Siegler, 1976) tackle issues raised by other researchers (Shultz,
Butkowsky, Pearce and Shanfield, 1975) who have drawn directly from
attribution writings. In some studies the link with attribution theory is
even less direct. It is quite likely that such studies reflect the Zeitgeist
created by the impact of attribution theory in this area and are
therefore included where appropriate. The present section also contains research which may include the judgement of human actions, as
it is not always possible to determine whether all the stimuli used in a
particular experiment are limited to examples of physical causation.
First the child's use of covariation and contiguity as causal principles is
examined. The question of temporal order in cause–effect relationships

is then addressed before finally considering the distinction between facilitative and inhibitory causes in children's causal reasoning.

*Covariation.* The covariation principle is fundamental to Kelley's (1967) attribution model. According to this Humean notion people attribute an effect to one of the possible causes with which, over time, it covaries. Many of Kelley's (1972b) observations derive their validity from this principle and its importance would be further strengthened by showing that covariation is a 'primitive' test used even in young children's causal judgements.

Siegler and Liebert (1974) tested 5–6- and 8–9-year-olds' knowledge of covariation (referred to by the authors as 'regularity') by having them indicate which of two possible machines (A or B) resulted in the onset of a light (X). For different groups X occurred either 100% or 50% of the time following the insertion of a card into A ('the card programmer'). The relationship between B (a 'computer' with flashing lights and clicking sounds) and X was random. It was found that by the sixth trial, older children on the 100% machine A schedule were more likely to perceive A and not B as the cause of X than those on the 50% machine A schedule. No such difference was found for the younger children, even at the end of the 12 trial experiment. Similar age differences were found for an 'overall' judgement and hence Siegler and Liebert (1974) concluded that covariation only emerges as a determinant of causal judgements in late childhood. As no predictions had been made (owing to the absence of previous research) the authors were only able to offer several possible *post hoc* explanations for this result. However, Siegler (1975) replicated this result and showed that it was not due to artifacts such as memory difficulties, response set or the brevity of the exposure period. The crucial variable seemed to be the young child's perceptual distractibility which prevented her/him from searching for and finding the temporally invariant relationships implied by the covariation principle.

Consequently, Shultz and Mendelson's (1975) demonstration that even children of 3–4 years old use the covariation principle does not seem to conflict with Siegler and Liebert's (1974) initial findings. Children of 3–4, 6–7, and 9–11 years observed six events in which effect X varied consistently with cause A, and inconsistently with cause B (the child was presented with the series AX, B, AX, *AB*X, B, *AB*X where italics indicate the simultaneous occurrence of causes A and B). Thus, for instance, a bell would ring whenever a marble was dropped into a box from the left hand side, but not when it was dropped into the box from the right hand side. In all age groups causality was more frequently attributed to the consistent covariate, an effect which was slightly stronger in the two older age groups.

Whether covariation information is fundamental to young children's causal judgements is, however, not established by the above finding. For instance, Siegler (1976) in another 'computer simulation' study provides data which suggest otherwise. Although motivated by research on causal schemes (see p. 130) Siegler's manipulation of sufficient and necessary causes (see chapter 1 for research on adults use of sufficiency and necessity information) involves a partial replication of his first study (Siegler and Liebert, 1974). His 'necessity and sufficiency' and 'necessity only' conditions are identical to the 100% and 50% schedules described above. In the case of 'sufficiency only' information, the effect occurred not only each time the cause was present, but also on other occasions. Finally, when the cause was neither necessary nor sufficient for the effect to occur (control condition) random pairing was used. Both 5-year-old and 8-year-old subjects were influenced by the necessity and sufficiency information, although in slightly different ways (a check on the perceived cause and effect relationship was included this time). When both conditions were present (100% schedule) all subjects correctly chose the covarying cause while their absence (control condition) led to random responding in both groups. However, 5- year-olds also identified as the cause an event which was only a necessary or only a sufficient condition for the effect. In contrast older children did not use this information in any systematic way. The younger group therefore did not base their judgements on covariation alone, but rather seemed to operate on the basis of contiguity. It is this principle which Siegler uses to explain the younger children's judgements. Evidence regarding the child's use of contiguity in causal judgements is now examined.

*Contiguity.* Often covarying events are temporally contiguous. While Kelley (1971) recognises that the covariation principle assumes a temporal relation between cause and event, neither he nor his followers has investigated its precise nature. Thus, Michotte's (1963) early work still remains the most important in this field. It will be recalled that temporal and/or spatial contiguity (juxtaposition) between events of whatever kind is a feature of young children's causal explanations. Hence even where covariation is used it is possible that subjects are responding in terms of this principle.

Siegler and Liebert (1974) also varied the temporal relationship between cause A and effect X in their experiment. Hence X occurred either immediately after A or five seconds later (the temporal relationship between cause B and X was random). The results showed that regardless of age effect X was more likely to be attributed to A when there was no delay. This seems to suggest that contiguity is a more fundamental concept than covariation. A similar test between the two principles was made in an experiment by Mendelson and Shultz (1976). They noted that when allowed to choose between a temporally contiguous cause which varied inconsistently with the effect and a covarying but non-contiguous cause, children invariable chose the former. However, they went on to argue that when given some rationale for the delay children would use covariation information. The 'rationale' comprised rubber tubing connecting the box into which a marble is dropped (cause), and the box in which a bell rings (effect). In the complementary condition the bell rang in the same box into which the marble was dropped. In each case a 5 second delay did or did not occur. The results confirmed their hypothesis and showed that neither principle was fundamental for the children ($M$ age = 5–10) tested, as each might be used depending on the conditions. The crucial question thus becomes: when is each principle applied? This issue has yet to be investigated.

Tests of the covariation principle often present stimuli which are also spatially contiguous. The principle of spatial contiguity might similarly influence causal judgements even though it is not specifically considered in Kelley's analysis. Piaget's (1927/1969, 1974) work suggests that this would be especially true of young children. An attempt to replicate Michotte's 'launching effect' without having the two objects actually touch (Lesser, 1977) provides some evidence on the child's use of spatial contiguity in causal judgements. Even after training in cause-at-distance (via the use of magnets) 6-year-olds and to a lesser extent 9-year-olds confused cause and effect. It thus seems that while children are highly dependent on spatial contiguity as a causal cue they are not as reliant on temporal contiguity. However, the correct use of temporal cues presupposes that the child has some notion that causal relationships are temporally ordered.

*Temporal order.* The assumption that causes precede or co-occur with effects is taken for granted by adults, but the belief may not be shared by children. Understandably, this issue has not been considered by attribution researchers who have worked exclusively with adult subjects, and can only be traced to attribution theory to the extent that it can be seen as a special case of temporal contiguity.

According to Piaget (1927/1969) young children do not understand causal order and will readily endorse sentences such as 'the man fell off the bike because he broke his arm'. Corrigan (1975) empirically verified that only 31% of children considered such sentences 'wrong' which seems to support Piaget's conclusion. However, 89% thought the correct causal sentence was 'right'. Such ambiguity also characterises Kuhn and Phelps' (1976) demonstration that 5-year-olds did not choose the correct causal sentence to describe a pictured series of events. For instance, the sentence 'the water spills because the chair gets wet' was chosen as often as the correct alternative 'the chair gets wet because the water spills'. As the authors themselves point out, this may reflect a syntactic problem rather than one of causal under-standing. The same cannot be said of Shultz and Mendelson's (1975) experiment which produced similar results. Subjects observed two instances of an event sequence AXB (e.g. marble in one side of box, bell rings, marble in other side) and had to choose as the cause of X either A or B. The youngest group ($M$ age = 3–7) tended to choose the event which followed X as the cause, whereas older children correctly chose the preceding event. While Shultz and Mendelson (1975) acknowledge that this may reflect a conceptual reversal of the causal sequence in young children they prefer to explain their results as a recency phenomenon.

Two recent studies suggest that the above findings may indeed reflect deficiencies in linguistic and memory skills. Kun (1978) showed subjects pictorial sequences of the form 'A caused B caused C' and asked for the cause of B. Even 4-year-olds answered correctly and chose A more often than C. It should be noted, however, that this task is structurally different from that of Shultz and Mendelson (1975) insofar as event C is a consquence of B rather than some random event which might have been a potential cause. The change makes a subtle difference, for if children do emphasise production or generation in causation (Piaget, 1927/1969) the second task is much easier. Although Kun (1978) does not address this problem she carefully eliminates other possibilities such as response bias and order of events which might explain her different results. In a final study even 3-year-olds were found to answer 'why?' questions with antecedent events. Finally, it should be noted that, unlike the previous studies. Kun uses human actors in some of the causal sequences. In this respect her results are supported by A. Brown and French (1976) who found that preschool children are capable of correctly reconstructing or completing a causal sequence of events involving a young girl.

Bullock and Gelman (1979) used a simple mechanical apparatus in which a marble inserted in the side of a box released a 'jack in the box' to show that 3–5-year-olds do indeed pick a prior event as a cause. They argue that Shultz and Mendelson's (1975) task may have involved too limited a set of demonstrations on the basis that their own subjects rendered more confident judgements in a later phase of the study. The argument is not convincing as their subjects, unlike those in the earlier study, used temporal cues after only two trials. They go on to claim that when pitted against spatial contiguity, temporal order was still used. Unfortunately, simply moving the part of the box where the marble is inserted from the central 'jack in the box' hole was not an adequate manipulation of spatial contiguity given their apparatus. As the authors themselves say, they studied causal judgements on the basis 'of inferences drawn from what must have occurred after the ball disappeared rather than on events directly sensed' (Bullock and Gelman, 1979, p. 91). It is quite possible that their subjects would, like Lesser's (1977), have denied causality had they been shown that the marble remained in the disconnected section of the box.

*Facilitatory and inhibitory causes*. Up to this point reference has been made to cause only as an undifferentiated concept. However, as Kelley (1972b) correctly points out, causes may be of different kinds. Some may assist or facilitate the effect, whereas others may preclude or inhibit it. Shultz and Mendelson (1975) studied such causes by including an additional one (e.g. a blue car on top of the box – C) as well as the normal causes (e.g. marble in either side of the box – A, B) for effect X. Hence sequences such as $ACX$, A, B, $BCX$, $BCX$, A, B, $ACX$ (where italics denote the simultaneous occurrence of two causes) were presented in the case of facilitatory causes. Each time C was present the effect X occurred. In the inhibitory cause condition X accompanied both A and B *except* when C was present. Three-year-olds correctly distinguished the causal status of C in these two conditions, but gave more correct responses in the facilitatory case. This is perhaps not surprising as closer examination shows that the facilitation problem used is simply one of covariation which subjects had readily coped with in an earlier phase of the experiment. The application of the covariation principle in the inhibitory condition is not as straight-forward as it involves a negative relation which is generally learnt more slowly even by adults (Slovic, 1974).

Any doubt regarding the young child's ability to understand the nature of inhibitory and facilitatory causes is dispelled by two brilliantly conceived perceptual analogue studies. Kassin and Lowe (1979) had subjects view two triangles simultaneously approach and enter a house. One, however had encountered an obstacle. Ninety-three percent of kindergarden children chose this latter triangle as the one which wanted to get in the house more. In contrast, only 40% were able to explain their response. In similar vein Kassin, Lowe and Gibbons (1980) contrasted a triangle which was pushed by another object with one which moved spontaneously. As younger subjects tended to view the 'push' as an aversive stimulus rather than a facilitatory cause, a further experiment was conducted in which one of the triangles was carried towards the house. In this latter condition all subjects chose the spontaneously moving triangle. Again age differences emerged only in the subjects' ability to explain their response.

*Comments*

It is the dependent variable, verbal explanation v. discrete judgement, which in fact characterises the difference between Piagetian and attribution oriented research in this field. The use of discrete judgements in attribution studies manifests an attempt to tap competence rather than performance variables. As such it reflects the current re-examination of Piagetian work, which is so prevalent in many areas of developmental research (cf. Brainerd, 1978, 1979; G. Brown and Desforges, 1977; Fincham, 1982a; Siegel and Brainerd, 1978). However, it goes beyond a mere reaction to Piaget and represents a new focus on the principles which children might use. Those examined are old philosophical principles which have been introduced to contemporary psychologists largely through attribution theory. Clearly this work is only beginning, and at present has been limited to examining Kelley's writing.

Although correspondent inference theory (Jones and Davis, 1965; Jones and McGillis, 1976) offers little in this domain as it deals primarily with intentional events, there is much of value in Heider's (1944, 1958a) original work which has not been considered. In fact, the very notion of unit formation via causal integration which gave rise to attribution theory implies a dynamic interaction between parts within the unit. Do, as Heider asked, effects influence origins (causes) and *vice versa*? Can they be assimilated or contrasted? Awareness of the fact that attribution theory arose largely from Heider's attempt to apply Gestalt principles to social perception takes one further back to the original work on perception (e.g. Koffka, 1935; Kohler, 1929). Are there other principles in this work which have not been applied to social perception but which may be useful in studying children's conceptions of physical causality (e.g. closure, Prägnanz)? One study which does indeed go back to Gestalt literature demonstrates children's use of similarity in causal judgements (Shultz and Ravinsky, 1976). As well as moving backward there is much also to be gained from moving forward in the attribution literature. For example, salience has emerged as a factor in making attributions (cf. Taylor and Fiske, 1978) and may be especially important to young attributors with limited cognitive abilities.

It would be sad if this exploration merely comprised the testing of such principles with children of different ages. Thus far there has been little attempt to integrate this new work with what is known about cognitive development. We need to know why some principles might be used in favour of others. Each needs to be 'unpacked' in terms of the cognitive demands it makes and its basic components studied. In this respect pitting one principle against another may yield much valuable information and become less of an arbitrary 'hit or miss' procedure. Moreover, attention should be given to whether children's use of various principles is qualitatively distinct. For instance, if young children are prepared to consider a post-effect covariate as a cause, their use of the covariation principle means something different from that of adults. Is covariation implicated in precausal thinking so that the child mentions the most obvious covariate (e.g. a stone's colour) for an effect (e.g. its sinking in water)? The child's readiness to make causal connections coupled with his/her use of the various principles reviewed above suggests that an important task is to determine how content comes to affect causal judgements with increasing age. In short, a theory relating to the child's acquisiton and use of causal principles is required. In seeking such a theory Paiget's valuable insights should not be ignored despite the deficences apparent in his work.

On a methodological level there is one issue which requires mentioning. Most of the research cited tries to avoid testing factual knowledge or learned responses by using materials which are novel and unfamiliar to the child. However, in doing so several dangers arise. First, there is the possibility that the task becomes so bewildering that it inhibits the young child from attending to the relevant stimuli. Siegler's (1975) 'computer' is, according to his own findings, a case in point. Secondly, one wonders just what the responses to some of these strange tasks mean. Consider the situation where a marble dropped into the side of a box leads to a bell ringing inside the box only when a blue car is present. Or where a piece of metal picks up a thumbtack only when a dark blue pipe cleaner is coiled around it (Shultz and Mendelson, 1975). Perhaps children's 'correct' responses say more about their readiness to entertain magical causal explanations than anything else for one wonders just how adults would respond to such tasks. The most worrying feature of these materials is that they may yield a false picture of the child's capabilities. Children tested 'out of context' appear to behave differently from those seen 'in context'. How else does one explain the very different results obtained by Bullock and Gelman (1979) and Shultz and Mendelson (1975) with regard to temporal ordering? Both experiments use structurally identical tasks and even the apparatus is similar, except in one major respect. Instead of being exposed to an association between the experimenter's action and a ringing bell Bullock and Gelman's (1979) subjects interacted with a puppet whose action triggered a 'jack in the box'. One need only recall that young children were able to conserve when interacting with a toy bear who 'accidentally' spills his drink (McGarrigle and Donaldson, 1974) but not when tested by an adult, to realise how important this change of context can be.

The above analysis creates a dilemma regarding methodology. On the one hand there is a need to avoid materials which merely reflect the child's exposure to adult causal explanations. On the other, there is evidence that some familiarity with the task yields more mature responses (Berzonsky, 1971). Even adults offer precausal explanations when questioned on events outside their sphere of competence (Ausbel and Schiff, 1954). Research tends to err in favour of the first consideration in its use of novel materials, and while it has been shown that children can use causal principles much earlier than one might have expected this could still be a conservative estimate. Attention needs to be paid to the presentation of such principles in a context more familiar to the child. It is only one step further to investigate children's use of causal concepts in naturalistic settings which may give an even more accurate picture of their ability. Consideration of Hood and Bloom's (1979) data shows that 3-year-olds' spontaneous causal expressions made no reference to physical causality. Although aware of physical causality they spoke of causality in terms of intentions and motives. Moreover, this was largely 'social' in that it referred to an intention to act or requested a listener to act. In fact, there is some evidence that 'mature' causal judgements appear much earlier for social situations than physical ones (Fein, 1973). It is to the child's understanding of causality with regard to human action that we now turn.

CAUSAL SCHEMES (HUMAN AND INTERPERSONAL CAUSALITY)

For some strange reason most investigations of social causality have examined causal schemes.[2] The notion of a causal scheme was introduced into attribution theory by Kelley (1972b) and denotes 'a conception of the manner in which two or more causal factors interact in relation to a particular kind of effect' (1972b, p. 152). When repeated observations are not possible and complete covariation data are missing, subjects can still make attributions by filling in missing cells of the matrix. Consequently a scheme is simply 'an assumed pattern of data in a complete analysis of variance framework' (1972b, p. 152). Understanding the covariation principle thus forms the basis for schematic thinking which derives from experience in observing cause–effect relationships. Indeed Kelley explicitly makes the link with development in characterising causal schemes as a subset of the cognitive schemes studied by Piaget. He even uses the term 'reversibility' in pointing out that the implicational relationships between the elements are bidirectional. Effects can be used to predict the presence/absence of various causes and *vice versa*. It is possibly because of this connection that research on causal schemes attempts to offer more overtly developmental explanations for its findings.

*Multiple necessary and multiple sufficient cause schemes*

The simplest causal configurations considered by Kelley (1972b, 1973), are those where the attributor distinguishes between the presence or absence of two causes and an effect. The presence of only one cause may be considered sufficient for the effect (sufficient cause scheme) or else both causes may be required (necessary cause scheme). Much of the pertinent developmental research has been initiated in part by work on intrinsic motivation (Deci, 1975; Lepper, Green and Nisbett, 1973) and therefore focuses on the former scheme.

In a classic demonstration Lepper *et al.* (1973) were able to undermine nursery schoolers' self-motivated desire to draw pictures by giving them extrinsic rewards for drawing. It is assumed that either intrinsic interest or reward alone is sufficient for engaging in such behaviours. Presumably, the child who draws without reward attributes her/his actions to an internal cause or interest and is intrinsically motivated. When an external reward is present s/he seemingly attributes the drawing to the external incentive and therefore discounts the intrinsic enjoyment of the task. Although this interpretation suggests that very young children operate according to the multiple sufficient cause scheme, research which directly investigates its use is somewhat more ambiguous.

Initial evidence cited with respect to schematic thinking also came from the moral judgement literature. Like the intrinsic motivation research this yielded only an indirect measure, as attributions had to be inferred from evaluative judgements. This work is considered in the next section on responsibility and hence only direct investigations of the scheme are presented here. As in moral judgement research both single story and story pair presentations have been used. A study by Shultz *et al.* (1975) is representative of the former tradition. They presented 5-year-olds, 9-year-olds, and 13-year-olds with a particular behavioural event (e.g. 'Johnny is afraid of the dog'). Subjects were also given information regarding the presence or absence of one cause (known cause) and had to infer the status (present or absent) of another. One cause was always internal to the person (e.g. 'Johnny is usually afraid of dogs') while the other was external (e.g. 'the dog is very large'). Among 5-year-olds inferences regarding the presence or absence of the second cause were unrelated to the presence or absence of the first, stated cause. In contrast the 9-year-olds and the 13-year-olds tended to infer the presence of the unknown cause when the known cause was absent, but not when it was present.

These results therefore stand in sharp contrast to those obtained by Lepper *et al.* (1973) on intrinsic motivation. Surprisingly, they also show that the nature of the known and inferred cause makes little difference. The nature of the given cause did, however, show some effect when a slight complication to the basic scheme for multiple sufficient causes was introduced. In a second phase of their experiment Shultz *et al.* (1975) used an inhibitory external cause. The behavioural effect (e.g. 'Johnny is afraid of the dog') was supposed to be suppressed by its presence (e.g. 'Johnny is with his father') but not its absence (e.g. 'Johnny is alone'). Except for this change the procedure used was identical to that outlined above. It was found that the mean proportion of times the inhibitory external cause was inferred to be present was 0.10, whereas the corresponding figure for the internal cause was 0.75. As this main effect was independent of the presence/absence variable and hence not relevant to schematic predictions,[3] Shultz *et al.* (1975) analysed inferences of internal and inhibitory external causes separately. Only 13-year-olds' responses differed in the schematically predicted manner. The inhibitory external cause was inferred to be present more often when the internal cause was present than when it was absent. Similarly, the internal cause was inferred present more frequently when the inhibitory external cause was present. However, these differences, while statistically reliable, may not be very significant. It should be remembered that the vast majority of subjects in this age group inferred the external cause to be absent (more than 90%) and the internal cause to be present (over 77%). Hence the differences found pertain only to small percentages of the responses. Given the example Shultz *et al.* (1975) quote, it is not clear whether their results reflect the rather late (and very slight) emergence of schematic reasoning in regard to inhibitory causes or rather the weakness of their stimulus materials. How plausible is the presence of the child's father as an inhibitory external cause which would suppress the child's fear? On the basis of this example alone one might well question whether adults' responses would conform to the pattern predicted.

Shultz *et al.*'s (1975) conclusions are indicative of the more overtly developmental interpretation given in this area. They argue that the youngest subjects' inability to use the scheme lies in their tendency to focus on only one aspect of the problem and not the various sources of information. It is the ability to consider two dimensions simultaneously which constitutes the essence of concrete operational thought and hence they argue that the use of the MSC scheme is related to the development of concrete operations. They go on to say that the use of inhibitory causes is logically more difficult than the simple MSC scheme and hence these are understood only in the period of formal operations. Finally, the familiar concept of *décalage* is used to explain the difference between these results and those on intrinsic motivation. Before presenting a later study of theirs which pursues this difference further, let us consider one which uses the method of story pair presentation.

Smith (1975) had subjects choose between two stimulus stories in which a child stood before two toys and chose to play with one of them. In one story the child was described as making the choice in the presence of an extrinsic facilitatory cause (a parent's command, reward or obligation). Kindergarten, second grade, fourth grade, and college students had to decide which child wanted to play with the toy and how much each wanted to do so. The results indicated that the youngest subjects responded randomly and chose each child with equal frequency. Scheme-consistent responses were apparent among the second grade children and increased until the fourth grade. No difference was found between the latter group and college subjects.

In considering these findings Smith (1975) shows some sensitivity to an important problem. It is commonly accepted that use of the MSC scheme implies the use of Kelley's (1972a) discounting principle whereby 'the role of a given cause in producing a given effect is discounted if other plausible causes are also present' (p. 8). But neither discounting nor the MSC scheme suggest that a second cause should be inferred as absent given the presence of the first. Rather, there should be uncertainty about its presence which presumably would lead to random responding. In questioning his subjects with regard to their choices Smith (1975) noted that they unequivocally attributed the choice behaviour to the extrinsic cause when it was present (kindergarten children excluded). He suggests two possible explanations.

First, the forced-choice question may have implied that only one story character was intrinsically motivated and that the other was not. Secondly, subjects may simply have been responding to the presence or absence of the extrinsic cause. When present, subjects might have immediately attributed the choice to it but when absent the choice would have been internally attributed. Attributions are most likely made with little uncertainty. This 'partial scheme' does not therefore require the simultaneous consideration of both causes and could conceivably be used by very young children.

Neither of the above possibilities is negated by Shultz et al.'s (1975) results as 13-year-olds tended also to infer the absence of the unknown cause when the known one was present. However, approximately half of the 9-year-olds inferred the presence of the unknown cause. The crucial question of interpretation arises. The problem is how to distinguish the proper use of the MSC scheme from the use of the 'partial scheme' except via the above argument regarding uncertainty. This leads one to the counter-intuitive conclusion that the 9-year-olds used a MSC scheme whereas 13-year-olds were only able to use a partial scheme. Smith (1975) even argues that the ability to consider multiple sufficient causes is a component of the capacity to use formal operational thought. Whatever the correct interpretation it seems that Shultz et al.'s (1975) conclusion that 9-year-olds and 13-year-olds use the MSC scheme may be incorrect. What may be just as important as the difference between inferred causes given the presence or absence of known causes, is the distribution of responses when the known cause is present. Despite the possible confounding of the partial and full scheme there has been no attempt to investigate this problem in subsequent research (but see Experiment 1). Consequently, when referring to the use of the MSC scheme with regard to this research it is obviously qualified by the constraints outlined above.

From these two initial studies there is clearly disagreement as to whether the MSC scheme is a concrete operational or formal operational acquisition. Both sets of findings, however, agree that in contrast to work on intrinsic motivation, young children cannot use this scheme. Subsequent research has taken two forms. On the one hand there is an attempt to show that young children can and do use the MSC scheme under certain conditions. On the other, it is argued that pre-operational subjects exhibit a qualitatively different form of reasoning and in fact use an additive rule, whereby the presence of an extrinsic cause increases the intrinsic liking for a chosen object.

There are two obvious differences between the research which might account for the differing results obtained. First, the child may be more advanced in understanding his/her own behaviour than the behaviour of others. Certainly the research on perspective taking (cf. Chandler, 1977; Shantz, 1975) supports this possibility. Alternatively, s/he may experience difficulty in making attributions about hypothetical as compared to real behaviour. Shultz and Butkowsky (1977) report unpublished research which assessed these possibilities. Some support was found to suggest that 5-year-olds used the MSC scheme only when judging another person's real behaviour. They attempted to provide more convincing evidence for this effect by having 5-year-olds infer the presence/absence of unknown causes for behaviours which were presented either verbally or by means of videotape. The procedure and materials were similar to those used in their earlier study (Shultz et al., 1975). The results are clear-cut. For roughly half of the responses the unknown cause was inferred to be present, except in one condition. When the known cause was absent the unknown cause was invariably (96%) inferred for the video-tape presentation.

If, as Shultz and Butkowsky (1977) maintain, this indicates that young children can use the MSC scheme, the earlier analyses which tie its use to operational thought are inappropriate. However, it seems quite likely that responding in terms of a scheme consistent pattern is possible without co-ordinating the two sources of causal information. For instance, a sequential processing strategy whereby the first plausible cause encountered is seen as sufficient for the effect and all others are ignored, is also consistent with the obtained results. No such alternative account is given. It is simply noted that performance variables (e.g. the ability to conceptualise hypothetical behaviour) might be responsible for the difference found. However, the real-hypothetical explanation also seems inadequate as Kun (1980) has recently shown that this age group not only infer with confidence the presence of a second cause from the absence of a first, but also are not confident about the presence of the second cause when the first is known to be present.

Both the above findings stand in sharp contrast to the second line of research which tends to focus on the discounting principle. Starting from the observation that Smith (1975) did not assess story recall, Karniol and Ross (1976) quite reasonably argue that young children's random responding might merely have reflected memory failure in the constraint or extrinsic factor present condition. Utilising a similar story choice technique they ensured accurate recall and employed parallel story sets within each type of constraint to determine whether subjects consistently used the discounting principle. In their experiment the constraint comprised either a maternal command or reward. As predicted the percentage of children who chose the unconstrained protagonist as the one who 'really wanted' to play with the chosen toy increased from kindergarten through grade one and two to college subjects. Of particular note, however, is the finding that the majority of the kindergarten and grade one children consistently chose the constrained story character and explained their choice by reference to the external constraint (i.e. the protagonist *wanted* to play with the toy because of the reward or command). They thus viewed the extrinsic cause as an added incentive for playing with the toy, an effect which was more pronounced in the reward condition.

One possible explanation for this finding is semantic, in that young children might interpret the question of 'want' as one which includes the protagonist's wanting the reward or wanting to please her/his mother. In a second experiment Karniol and Ross (1976) rule out this possibility by simply substituting 'like' for the word 'want' in their questions. The number of kindergarten and first grade children who consistently chose the constrained protagonist was reduced by approximately a half (68%–39% and 63%–26% respectively) whereas those consistently using the discounting principle more than doubled (9%–32% and 29%–62%, respectively). A sequence effect was also found which showed that the change was not merely due to the different wording. More specifically, discounting occurred more frequently in the command-followed-by-reward sequence than its inverse.

Despite the latter result Karniol and Ross (1976) note that over one third (39%) of the kindergarten children consistently made the wrong choice and suggest that young children use an additive, rather than discounting, principle. They go on to argue that this result may reflect a difference in the meaning ascribed to the extrinsic cause. 'Adders' might not see the constraint as an attempt to influence the protagonists' behaviour, but rather as defining its desirability. 'Discounters' on the other hand should be aware of manipulative intent. As commands offer more unambiguous evidence of manipulative intent the decreased incidence of adding in this condition supports their interpretation. Before evaluating it any further a few observations need to be made.

First, the 'additive rule' proposed by Karniol and Ross (1976) is very loosely applied. In order to test whether their results are evidence of adding, rather than multiplying or any other combinative rule where the response is a positive function of the variables investigated, the subjective values of the stimulus factors need to be systematically varied. Functional (Anderson, 1974) or conjoint (Tversky, 1967) measurement techniques are ideally suited to this purpose. Secondly, the extrinsic cause was repeated in each story to ensure recall, with the second repetition being prefaced by the cue word 'remember'. It has been suggested that the salience of this manipulation might have misled some children (especially those eager to please an adult inquirer) to believe that the desired response was the one which the experimenter so forcefully emphasised (Fincham, 1979). Thirdly, the fact that children can so readily discount when a condition such as sequence of presentation is varied suggests that the additive phenomenon may say more about the task characteristics than the child's capabilities. Given this apparent shift surely the most important question is not to ask whether children add or discount, but under what conditions they may engage in one or the other.

Karniol and Ross (1979) seem to mis-state the problem when they later set out to study the 'developmental shift' from the use of an additive to a discounting rule. However, their attempt to uncover the process underlying these different rules is fundamentally sound. Without emphasising the constraint they were able to replicate their previous finding and show an increasing use of the discounting principle from grades one through three. In this experiment the children were also asked why the constraint person had offered the reward to the protagonist. A significant, but low, correlation ($r = 0.39$) was found between awareness of manipulative intent and discounting. A second experiment investigated the possible direction of this influence by making the manipulative intention more salient to 'adders'. One group saw a model infer a manipulative intention when exposed to the experimental stories, whereas the other was exposed to a non-manipulative interpretation of the reward offer. While the former as a group used discounting more frequently following this experience, only one subject discounted consistently and six of the remaining eleven did not do so at all.

It seems that awareness of manipulative intent is at best only a partial explanation for young children's adding. Recent research, moreover, suggests that awareness *per se* may not be the crucial factor. Cohen, Gelfand, Hartmann, Partlow, Montermayor and Shigetomi (1979) found an age-related change from adding to discounting only when the reward offered was material and not social (praise). Significantly, even college subjects did not distinguish between a protagonist acting for no reward and one acting for a social reward. It could be argued from these findings that what is crucial is not the reason for which the reward is offered, but whether the reward is itself one which might indeed influence a person's behaviour. Results from a probe question support this interpretation as younger children were less likely to perceive the presence of the material reward as indicating that the child would not have helped otherwise. Even greater difficulty emerges when trying to reconcile Karniol and Ross' (1979) explanation with Kun's (1980) recent work. Kun (1980) found the adding-discounting 'age shift' for stories about play (drawing) but not non-play behaviours (eating, helping, sharing, fighting and stealing). She argues that the tenet 'good things go together' is appropriate in the context of play, but not elsewhere.

From the research to date the exact process(es) underlying the 'additive principle' remain unclear. Whether this indicates a difference in the young child's perception of stimuli, a limit on her/his cognitive ability to use the discounting principle or a lack of awareness as to when it should be used, is not known. The indications are that it is the latter and attention should therefore be turned to an analysis of the conditions where it is found. It also remains to determine whether the early use of what appears to be the MSC scheme is rather the result of a more elementary cognitive strategy.

The other major scheme discussed by Kelley (1972b) has not provoked much controversy. This is partly due to the fact that there has been very little research on children's understanding of multiple necessary causes (MNC). It will be recalled that Kelley (1972b) suggests this scheme is evoked to account for extreme effects or when both causes are weak. It is the former which has been used to investigate the scheme in developmental research. For instance, Shultz *et al.* (1975) had their subjects also judge extreme versions of the behavioural effects used to examine the MSC scheme. Only 13-year-olds' inferred the presence of the unknown cause more when the effect was extreme than when it was mild as predicted by this scheme. Not surprisingly, they conclude that the MNC scheme is part of the formal operation package. However, Kun (1977) reports that Shultz *et al.*'s (1975) manipulation of outcome intensity was inadequate as she found that children did not assess their extreme and mild behaviours differently. She presents evidence to show that even 5-year-olds believe that greater effects have greater causes (see following section).

Some evidence relating to the use of MNC schemes comes from a study by Erwin and Kuhn (1979) which investigates the child's understanding of whether two possible motives or external causes might conjointly underlie a single act. They found that the majority of kindergarten children denied that behaviour might be multiply determined and concluded that this awareness only develops in adolescence. While such research may help in understanding the development of the MNC scheme, this particular study is unfortu-nately equivocal. It is quite possible that by asking the children which cause was 'right', whether one was 'wrong' and 'how can they both be right?', they clearly implied that only one cause was permissible. Such demand characteristics are more likely to have influenced younger children. It thus appears that there is little evidence on the use of the MNC scheme. It is this observation which partly motivated the following experiment.

**Experiment 1.** Several 'loose ends' and interpretational problems have been outlined in reviewing the above research. First, work on moral judgement is still cited as evidence for the use of various schemes. It is implicitly assumed that moral judgements are mediated by causal inferences. Secondly, appropriate tests to examine the use of an MSC scheme have not been made. Typically, the extent to which a second cause is inferred when the first is known to be present is compared to the case where the first cause is known to be absent. It has been argued that the distribution of responses in each condition is more important. Third, whether the given, or known, cause is present/absent may be of some importance. It is probably easier for children to infer the presence of a second, unknown cause when the first is known to be absent than *vice versa*. Fourth, little attention has been paid to the possibility that inferring internal and external causes may reflect different processes. Finally, adequate investigation of the child's use of the MNC scheme remains to be conducted. The present study attempted to address these issues.

Before presenting the experiment it is worth noting the predictions that would be made on the basis of Kelley's schemes. According to the MSC scheme, a second cause should readily be inferred when the first cause is known to be absent, but should lead to uncertainty when it is known to be present. Whether internal or external, the nature of the two causes should make no difference. However, it is argued that because actor and act form such a strong perceptual unit so as to lead to 'overattribution to persons' (Jones, 1979), 'the fundamental attribution error' (Ross, 1977) or 'persons as the prototypes of origins' (Heider, 1944) one might expect the nature of the cause inferred (internal or external) to make some difference especially for young children. More specifically, there should be some tendency to infer the presence of an internal cause given an external one according to the above 'error'. For the very same reason the presence of an internal cause should lead attributors to infer the absence of an external one. Similarly, when an external cause is known to be absent, an internal one should be readily inferred. But when it is the internal cause which is known to be absent the external cause may not be as readily inferred. In short, there is reason to suspect an interaction between the presence/ absence of a known cause and the nature of an inferred cause. An increase in outcome intensity is likely to accentuate the above effects but should, according to the MNC scheme, only lead subjects to infer the presence of a second cause when the first is known to be present.

Negative outcome stories were administered to 5-year-olds, 9-year-olds and to adults. A possible internal or external cause for the action was known to be either present or absent. All subjects were asked whether the second cause was present and in addition rated the story protagonist on a pictorial blame scale. As predicted, interactions between the presence/ absence of the known cause, the nature of the inferred cause (internal v. external), and age emerged on both measures. In addition, second order interactions involving outcome intensity were also found in both cases. Consequently, the results for each condition were examined separately.

Judgements of blame were related to causal inferences in only one condition. When an external cause was given for a mild outcome, subjects tended to attribute greater blame when the internal cause was inferred to be present. Although no significant interaction with age was found, the size of the difference did increase with age. Significantly, it is this condition which characterises much of the relevant moral judgement research (e.g. Baldwin and Baldwin, 1970; Berndt, 1977; Darley, Klosson and Zanna, 1978). Results regarding the inference of the unknown cause are slightly more complex. Table I shows the conditions under which the unknown or second cause was inferred to be present (italicised) or absent using a simple binomial test. As predicted, the external cause was inferred to be absent when the internal cause was known to be present. In contrast, when the extrinsic cause was present there was uncertainty regarding the presence of the internal cause regardless of age.[4] However, with extreme outcomes adults did infer the internal cause to be present as use of the MNC scheme would predict. The first finding supports the earlier argument regarding overattribution to persons, but the latter is entirely consistent with Kelley's scheme analysis. It was also hypothesised that it would be easier to infer a second, unknown cause when the first was known to be absent. This prediction was supported as more adult-like responses were given when the known cause was absent, especially for extreme outcomes. Moreover, this effect was most marked when the external cause was absent and supports the idea that intentionality may not be inferred from positive information, but rather from the absence of situational explanations (Fincham and Jaspars, 1980).

TABLE I   Age groups where the unknown cause was inferred to be present (italicised) and absent

| Outcome | Known cause | | | |
| --- | --- | --- | --- | --- |
| | Present | | Absent | |
| | Internal | External | Internal | External |
| Mild | 2*, 3 | | *3* | *2, 3* |
| Severe | 2*, 3 | *3* | 2,* *3* | *1, 2, 3* |

* Marginally significant (p<0.10) whereas p<0.01 for all other entries.
1, 5-year-olds; 2, 9-year-olds; 3, adults.

The present study suggests that inferences concerning the presence of internal and external causes are not merely inverse images of the same process. Similarly, deciding on the presence or absence of a second cause when one is already present seems different to doing so when the first cause is absent. It could also be argued that internal causes have a status different from that of their external counterparts. For instance, it is possible that the former more readily explain the behavioural effect (especially for young children). It has been pointed out that person and act seem to form a very natural unit which might be the reason why younger subjects more readily infer the presence of an internal cause when an external one is absent than *vice versa*. This process might also explain why the MSC, rather than MNC scheme, was used for extreme outcomes when an internal cause was known to be present. In short, these results suggest that there may be several different processes at work and that children's ability to use MSC and MNC schemes may be related to these. Finally, it is worth noting that this study, like all the research cited thus far, does not actually test the discounting principle. Typically, subjects have to infer the presence of a second cause and are not given situations for which two causes are known to be present. The same can be said of the adult literature and Kelley's own examples.

*Compensatory causes and graded effects schemes*

More complicated schemes arise when degrees of cause and effect, rather than their mere presence or absence, are distinguished. In essence, such schemes represent generalisations of the MSC and MNC schemes and are considered under the titles 'compensatory causes' and 'graded effects' in Kelley's (1972b) work. In the first case causes are calibrated against each other, and act in a mutually compensatory manner. For example, if an effect remains invariant an increase in the strength of one cause will be accompanied by a decrease in the second. Graded effects, however, occur when variation in the strength of causes is associated with changes in the strength of effects.

The only developmental work on these schemes appears to have been done in the achievement motivation domain (Kun, 1977; Weiner and Kun, 1980). In an early study (Kun, Parsons and Ruble, 1974) children between 5 and 10 years of age predicted performance from ability and effort information. All saw performance as a monotonically increasing function of ability and effort. In later work Kun (1977) distinguishes between a 'magnitude-covariation schema' and a 'compensation-schema' which roughly correspond to Kelley's compensatory causes, and graded effects schemes. She found that both schemes were present in 5-year-olds, although the former continued to develop until 9 years of age. A further complication was introduced by distinguishing direct from inverse compensation. The former occurs when two opposing causes (e.g. effort, task difficulty) change in the same direction and hence require the same operation (e.g. adding) on both causes. In contrast the latter involves inverse operations as two like causes change in opposite directions.

Although Kun's (1977) results are quite complex, and cannot be presented in full, a few observations are apposite. First, Kun argues that the three schemes as mentioned (magnitude-covariation, direct compensation and inverse compensation) parallel the principles of extremity (use of MNC scheme for more severe outcomes), augmentation and discounting in attribution theory and claims that they emerge developmentally in that order. The first scheme is fully developed in the 5-year-old while the second, although present, continues to emerge until 9 years. The last scheme, however, was only used by 9-year-olds. While it is not possible to evaluate fully these results it should be noted that they are qualified by the fact that effort attributions were easier to make than ability attributions. Again, the actual causes inferred were of some importance. A final noteworthy finding was that prior to the emergence of the compensation scheme children perceive a positive relation between ability and effort when performance is held constant. Kun (1977) explains this as a halo effect and posits the existence of a 'halo scheme'!

The 'halo scheme' is directly analogous to the earlier mentioned additive principle and constitutes an alternative explanation for

Karniol and Ross' (1976, 1979) finding. In similar vein, the inverse-compensation scheme can be used to describe many of the findings which purport to demonstrate the use of the MSC scheme. However, making this link draws attention to the fact that it was still possible to use a sequential, rather than simultaneous, processing strategy to infer the absence of ability/effort in Kun's experiment. If, as she suggests, inverse compensation is a concrete operational acquisition, multiple rather than dichotomous levels of each cause are needed. The problem, therefore, remains as to why younger children did not use 'inverse compensation' in her study. Whatever its problems Kun's (1977) careful analysis of scheme usage represents an advance on much of the earlier mentioned work and places the MSC and MNC schemes in a more general framework.

*Patterns of causes*

A final variety of schemes Kelley (1972b) considers comprise the interplay between *sets* of causes. Although some fairly complex systems are considered, developmental research is limited to investigation of rather simple patterns. In fact most of this work is not seen in terms of schematic analysis, but seems instead to be a by-product of the attempt to investigate Kelley's (1967) earlier ANOVA model. Investigations of consistency, consensus and distinctiveness along the lines followed by McArthur (1972) are understandably not possible with children. Consequently, developmental studies typically present information about only one dimension from which an attribution is then made. In this way the effect of information pertaining to each dimension on person/entity attributions is determined.

Only one study to date has varied information along each of Kelley's dimensions. Di Vitto and McArthur (1978) correctly point out that covariation evidence along each dimension differs in the causal factor it identifies (distinctiveness = agent; consensus = entity; consistency = agent or entity). They go on to argue that the utilisation of such information to make causal inferences about the complementary causal factor (person or entity) requires in addition the application of the discounting principle. Hence, by simply asking for attributions about both agent and entity (or target of agent's action) the developmental path of these two principles can be investigated. Five to six, 8–9, 11–12 and 18–20-year-old subjects were presented story pairs depicting the same act, but differing in the level of consistency, consensus or distinctiveness information (high or low). As predicted, consensus and distinctiveness information were found to provide the least direct information about causes in the agent and target respectively. Moreover, college students in general made choices consistent with Kelley's model. No age differences emerged with regard to distinctiveness information and agent attributions, but this information was not used in the expected manner until adulthood. On the other hand an age difference emerged for consensus information even when making target attributions (correct use from 8–9 years on), an effect which was even more marked for agent attributions (from 11–12 years on). As in the adult literature (cf. Kassin, 1979) consensus was, however, found to have a relatively weak impact compared to distinctiveness information. Finally, all ages used consistency information to make agent attributions whereas only 8–9 and 11–12-year-olds did so in relation to targets.

These results seem to indicate several developmental trends in the use of consensus, consistency and distinctiveness information. They also suggest that all age groups were able to use the covariation principle, whereas discounting was developmentally emergent. Two further findings are worth noting. First, agent attributions were overall more frequent and much easier for children to make. Thus once again, the special role of persons as causal agents seems to emerge. Secondly, approximately one third of the youngest subjects tended to use information that the cause was present in the agent/target to infer that it was also present in the target and *vice versa*. This additive effect occurred in the absence of manipulative intentions and is perhaps best accounted for by the 'halo scheme'.

Despite these interesting and provocative results Di Vitto and McArthur's (1978) study contains two major flaws. They speak of causal attributions, but in fact asked subjects for moral evaluations ('niceness' and 'meanness'). While these two different kinds of judgements may be related (cf. p. 155) they are not necessarily identical. In addition the manipulation of consistency and distinctiveness also poses a problem when acts can be morally evaluated. For instance, subjects' judgements of 'John has never given Doug a cupcake' might reflect a concern with evaluating John's repeated lack of sharing rather than an attempt to locate the cause of the action. Similar points could be made about John's not giving cupcakes to anyone else (distinctiveness). These problems also arise in the interpretation of a study by Leahy (1979a) where children awarded money to prosocial story protagonists whose acts differed in distinctiveness and consistency. As in Di Vitto and McArthur's (1978) experiment all subjects used this information in the manner predicted by Kelley's model (only actor attributions were made).

Recent research by Ruble, Feldman, Higgins and Karlovac (1979) managed to circumvent the dependent measure problem by asking subjects whether an object was chosen because of something about the actor (person attribution) or something about the item (entity attribution). Their study was limited to investigating whether consensus information was used when no information was available about choice (target) items. Using a videotape presentation in which four adults were seen to disagree with the choice, even 4-year-olds and 5-year-olds were found to use consensus information appropriately making person attributions for low, and entity attributions for high, consensus. The authors account for their discrepant results in terms of the real–hypothetical distinction noted earlier (Shultz and Butkowsky, 1977). However, there are other important differences between the two experiments. Subjects in the earlier study (Di Vitto and McArthur, 1978) made a comparative choice between agents (and targets) acting under different consensus conditions whereas those in Ruble *et al.*'s (1979) study chose between the agent and the target. These are essentially different tasks. A second study where the subject her/himself chose the item was also conducted. Although a measure of other people's liking of the object was obtained it was not directly analysed in terms of person/entity attributions. In separate analyses it was simply noted that both entity attributions and the number of other people liking the object decreased with age.

Although intended as a generalisation of their first study this manipulation involves a conceptually different sort of consensus information. Kassin (1979) distinguishes the explicit consensus (Kelley type) used in the first study from normative expectancies (Jones and McGillis, 1976) which are tapped in the second. There is a great deal of evidence to suggest that these represent very distinct sorts of consensus and hence the abovementioned experiments provided an opportunity to test possible developmental differences in the use of these two types of consensus information. Ruble *et al.*'s (1979) self–other manipulation is also interesting in that their results contrast with the actor–observer or divergent perspectives hypothesis (e.g. Jones, 1976; Jones and Nisbett, 1972; Monson and Snyder, 1977, see also chapter 11). In both experiments adults made more attributions to the person whereas the reverse was true for young children. In addition there is the question of why adults chose person attributions in the first experiment where the manipulation of consensus suggests that they should have responded equally in terms of entity and person? Neither of these latter problems are recognised in the original study yet they provide interesting possibilities for future research.

The results discussed thus far conflict with a final study by Leahy

(1979b). Testing 13-year-olds and 18-year-olds he found that only the latter group were affected by the number of judges who shared an impression of a target person. It is not possible from his rather inadequately reported study to determine why this should be so. Furthermore, his attempts to manipulate consistency and distinctiveness are unclear. Indeed, one questions the utility of publishing such results when 'significant three and four way interactions are not reported' (Leahy, 1979b, p. 189). In the absence of further research the precise developmental status of consistency, consensus and distinctiveness information remains questionable. However, it does seem that even very young children do behave in accordance with Kelley's predictions when appropriately tested and when no other information is available.

*Comments*

It should be noted that the distinctions between studies reviewed in the above sections are sometimes rather blurred. For instance, in some of the MSC scheme studies, the stimulus item described uses consistency information (e.g. Shultz and Butkowsky, 1977). The majority of the items used, however, are typically not described in such studies and one is thus not able to examine features of the stimulus items which might be related to scheme usage. This may prove crucial, for if different developmental patterns do indeed exist with regard to consistency, consensus and distinctiveness this might account for some of the inconsistent results obtained to date. A rapprochement between the ANOVA model and scheme usage also has other advantages. For example, an awareness of the former shows that consistency information is not an appropriate means of manipulating the presence/absence of a cause in the agent (internal) or entity (external) as it yields information pertinent to both.

Perhaps the most fundamental omission in the literature is as obvious as it is simple. Kelley (1972b, p. 169) points out that a thorough knowledge of schematic functioning involves an understanding of the conditions which evoke different schemes. In a developmental context this assumes even greater importance. Recently, cognitive developmental researchers have moved forward to ask, not whether children can think logically, but under what conditions they do so (Bryant, 1977). Research on causal schemes might profitably follow this lead as it is clear that children do in some contexts use adult-like causal schemes, whereas in others they do not. One of the obvious differences between these is not only the medium of presentation (verbal or video), but also the content of stimulus items. Although no clear pattern is readily discernable some obvious distinctions can be made. Perhaps the most fundamental of these is between causal connections where the target/entity is either a physical object or a person. There seems to be a qualitative difference between choosing an object and acting in relation to another person which often involves awareness of psychological states, recursive thinking and so on.

The importance of content in schematic causal reasoning has recently been emphasised in adult research. Reeder and Brewer (1979) cogently argue that the particular dimension along which an attribution is made affects the inference process involved. Their analysis stems largely from Jones and Davis' (1965) model which seems to have been ignored in developmental research. However, it is noteworthy that much of the research contrasting free v. constrained choices is closer to the attitude attribution paradigm associated with correspondent inference theory (e.g. Jones and Harris, 1967) than to Kelley's work. Consider Thibaut and Riecken's (1955) and Jones, Davis and Gergen's (1961) well-known studies which Kelley (1972a) quotes in presenting the discounting principle. Protagonists in these experiments act either in accordance with, or against, situational demands. The comparison here is conceptually different and perhaps even easier than evaluating a constrained act versus one which is freely chosen and in which role demands are absent (the toy choice paradigm described earlier). Indeed, it is such a distinction which might also account for Kun's (1980) findings regarding play and non-play behaviours. Four of the six non-play behaviours are moral actions with implicit role demands and hence may involve 'easier' comparisons. The above argument also suggests that neutral and moral behaviours should not be considered as a whole (e.g. Di Vitto and McArthur, 1978), but separately.

Despite the implicit connection between correspondent inference theory and the abovementioned developmental research, no reference is made to Jones and Davis' (1965) work. The one exception is a study by Costanzo, Grumet and Brehm (1974). Because it is misquoted as showing that children are more likely to infer an intrinsic factor in the presence of an external constraint (e.g. Karniol and Ross, 1979), it is worth brief consideration. Costanzo et al. (1974) showed films in which a protagonist initially chose a toy to play with, but was either unable to reach it or was ordered not to do so and hence played with the alternative toy. In the complementary unconstrained condition the actor either merely played with the chosen toy or received adult approval while doing so. Subjects were then questioned about the actor's attitude to both toys. They found that the degree to which toy liking corresponded to adult sanction was inversely related to age. Although this held only for 'liking' and the 'unplayed with toy' much has been made of this result. What tends to be overlooked, however, is that all ages (5–6, 8–9 and 11–12 years) clearly saw free acts as more correspondent with the actor's attitude as predicted by correspondent inference theory. Moreover, no strong age difference emerged on a behavioural choice item (which toy would the actor take home?) as only 14 of the 60 subjects in the constraint condition mentioned the unchosen (adult specified) toy, a finding which was not strongly age-related. To the extent that adult sanctions made a difference then, this was only within the constraint condition and when compared with a physical-environmental obstacle.

The point of mentioning Costanzo et al.'s (1974) study is not solely to draw attention to its actual, rather than purported, findings. Rather it is reported to show in addition that developmental analogue studies can be derived from correspondent inference theory. While the issues investigated are in many ways similar to research emanating from Kelley's work there are important differences between the approaches (Jones and McGillis, 1976). The hope is that by expanding the initial framework within which research on causal schemes is performed a clearer developmental picture will emerge. In this respect Reeder and Brewer's (1979) analysis offers a clear lead for researchers interested in correspondent inference theory.


## Attribution of responsibility

The link between cognitive developmental and attribution theories is most explicit in work on developing conceptions of responsibility. For instance, both Heider and Piaget who respectively stimulated research in these two traditions freely quote from Fauconnet's classic work in expounding their own views. Yet there are important differences in the way that Piaget and Heider talk of responsibility. These become clear when considering each theory.

### PIAGET'S WORK

*The Moral Judgment of the Child* (English translation 1932) was written after Piaget's first book on causality and comprises the last of five volumes marking his early work in genetic epistemology. As Piaget (1973) points out 'I published them without taking sufficient pre-cautions concerning the presentation of any conclusions, thinking they would be little read and would serve me mainly as documentation for a later synthesis to be addressed to a wider audience' (pp. 122–123). This is readily apparent from reading the work and is reflected in many ways. For example, Piaget talks of stages, yet in a far less formally systematised manner than in later work. More importantly, however, the child in this work is more of a 'social' being than in any other of Piaget's writings. Indeed, it is the child's changing experience of the social environment that constitutes one of the major catalysts for changing moral judgements. What are these judgements?

From his investigation of nine dimensions of moral thinking Piaget distinguishes two broad stages, or more precisely, phases which he labels heteronomous and autonomous morality. The first reflects both the moral constraint of adults and childish egocentrism. It leads to *moral realism*, according to which the child regards duty 'as self-subsistent and independent of the mind, as imposing itself regardless of the circumstances in which the individual may find himself' and observes 'the letter rather than the spirit of the law' (Piaget, 1932, p. 106). Most importantly, however, 'moral realism induces an objective conception of responsibility' (*ibid.*) which Piaget uses as the criterion for its existence. Consequently, acts are not evaluated in accordance with motive or intention, but in terms of their objective consequences and their conformity with established rules. As the child enters the peer group and experiences relationships of mutual respect and equality, autonomous moral thinking emerges. Subjective responsibility, or judgements based on intentionality, begin to characterise the child's thought.

More detailed expositions of both Piaget's theory and the voluminous research literature it has spawned are readily available (e.g. Hoffman, 1970; Lickona, 1976; Tomlinson, 1980; Wright, 1971). It suffices in the present context to note that the distinction between subjective and objective *responsibility* constitutes the essence of Piaget's theory. Much of the subsequent Piagetian research has focused on this difference and replication studies (e.g. Boehm, 1962; Boehm and Nass, 1962; Johnson, 1962; MacRae, 1954) generally support Piaget's views. However, increasing awareness of the theory's limitations has led to considerable conceptual advances (Kohlberg, 1969, 1971, 1976) and a great deal of methodological refinement in testing the original theory (cf. Armsby, 1971; Berg-Cross, 1975; Gutkin, 1972; Hebble, 1971; Imamoglu, 1975). It is against this background and an emerging dissatisfaction with Piaget's theory in the seventies, that the attribution studies on responsibility should be seen.

ATTRIBUTION RESEARCH

Attribution oriented studies on changing conceptions of responsibility are largely an historical accident. They stem from the manner in which Heider (1958a) describes several criteria or levels (see Table II) according to which responsibility can be ascribed. He sees them as 'successive *stages* in which attribution to the person decreases and attribution to the environment increases' (Heider, 1958a p. 113, emphasis added). From his presentation it is not clear whether Heider intends his levels to represent developmental stages in the cognitive developmental sense or not. Nonetheless by pointing out the similarity between his criteria of causality and intentionality and Piaget's notion of objective and subjective responsibility, he implies that the levels are age-related.[5] Clearly, this was not his intention for he has recently written 'I did not want to imply that they followed each other in time . . . [but] thought of this only as a simple way of presenting . . .

TABLE II   Heider's levels of responsibility attribution

| Level | Definition |
|---|---|
| I   Association | According to the global concept manifest at this level, 'the person is held responsible for each effect that is in any way connected with him or that seems in any way to belong to him' (Heider, 1958a, p. 113). |
| II   Causality | Anything 'caused by (a person) $p$ is ascribed to him. Causation is understood in the sense that $p$ was a necessary condition for the happening, even though he could not have foreseen the outcome however cautiously he had proceeded . . . the person is judged not according to his intention, but according to the actual results of what he does . . . what Piaget (1932) refers to as 'objective responsibility' (*ibid.*). |
| III   Foreseeability | Here '. . . $p$ is considered responsible, directly or indirectly, for any after effect he may have foreseen even though it was not a part of his own goal and therefore still not a part of the framework of personal causality' (*ibid.*). |
| IV   Intention | At this level 'only what $p$ intended is perceived as having its source in him. This corresponds to what Piaget has called subjective responsibility' (*ibid.*). |
| V   Justification | Finally '. . . even the $p$'s own motives are not entirely ascribed to him but are seen as having their source in the environment . . . responsibility for the act is at least shared by the environment' (*ibid*, p. 114). |

different forms of mental structure with different cognitive "depth" '
(personal communication, 13 December, 1978). Notwithstanding his
disclaimer, it is these levels which gave rise to the first developmental
research in attribution theory.

Whatever it was intended to be, Heider's model offers several
refinements to Piaget's description of responsibility. First, global
association represents a level even more basic than objective responsibility. It expresses what Fauconnet considers to be a fundamental
element of responsibility, namely, its 'expanding and contagious
nature' (cited in Piaget, 1932, p. 343). Given a developmental interpretation it could be seen as an example of syncretistic thinking in
which no distinction is made between causes, effects and unrelated
phenomena (Piaget, 1926). In the remaining levels Heider clearly
separates accidental acts from intentional acts and within each
category makes distinctions overlooked by Piaget.

The first of these distinctions concerns the foreseeability of the effects
an actor accidentally produces. Unintended acts with foreseeable
outcomes are clearly distinguished from similar acts where the
outcome is not foreseeable. In addition to covarying motive and
outcome intensity some of Piaget's story pairs differ along this
dimension, further confounding the interpretation of his findings (e.g.
Piaget, 1932, p. 118). Heider also offers an elaboration with respect to
subjective or intention-based responsibility. The fourth level is described in terms of *intention* which is entirely internal to the actor whereas
the actor's *motives* are seen as partly external at his last level. Heider
apparently sees 'intention' and 'motive' as separate concepts where
Piaget, like many attribution theorists (e.g. Jones and Davis, 1965),
uses them interchangeably. Despite the possible advances it offers over
Piaget's two phase theory, most research on Heider's model has been
conducted by social rather than developmental psychologists. Moreover, in comparison to the cognitive developmental literature relatively
little work on responsibility has been done within an Heiderian
framework.

Tests of Heider's scheme tend not to use a strict stage interpretation
of the levels, but merely examine quantitative variations in response
patterns across age. Perhaps the most widely cited is that of Shaw and
Sulzer (1964) which is prototypic of research in this area, and hence
serves to illustrate some of the difficulties with these studies. Stories
concerning a boy named Perry were administered to two different age
groups (6-year-olds to 9-year-olds and college students) who rated his
responsibility for story outcomes which differed in both valence and
intensity. Each contained only the minimum information to be
classified at one of Heider's levels. Some support was found for

age-related changes regarding some of the levels (a levels × populations interaction) although the exact nature of these differences has to be inferred in the absence of explicit tests of the differences between age groups or between levels within each age group. More importantly, the results are open to alternative interpretations. For example, Harris (1977) shows how the use of only two groups differing so widely in age may have yielded results which merely reflect differential understanding of the task requirements. This possibility is not unrealistic in view of the large group testing procedure and the use of the rather complex term 'responsibility' in eliciting responses from young children.

Several crucial problems relating to the operationalisation of Heider's levels (cf. Fincham and Jaspars, 1979) create further interpretational difficulties and impose severe limitations on subsequent research by Shaw and his associates (e.g. Shaw and Schneider, 1969b; Shaw, Briscoe and Garcia-Esteve, 1968). This is implicitly recognised by these researchers who have tried to develop new stimuli. A more adequate set of Perry stories has been constructed, but has to date only been used in a cross-cultural study (Shaw and Iwawaki, 1972). As an alternative 'abstract structures' such as 'Steve caused something to happen that was a little bit bad. He intended to cause it. Is Steve responsible for the bad thing he caused?' have also been used. The abstract nature and linguistic complexity of such stories is obviously prejudicial to the young child's performance and is likely to inflate developmental differences. In any event these later studies primarily investigate the effects of cultural (Garcia-Esteve and Shaw, 1968; Shaw, 1967; Shaw et al., 1968; Shaw and Iwawaki, 1972; Shaw and Schneider, 1969a) and IQ (Shaw and Schneider, 1969b) differences on responsibility attribution. Where age differences are reported they take second place to the above variables.

The importance of operationalising Heider's criteria appropriately is illustrated in two recent developmental studies using subjects of similar age (6-year-olds, 8-year-olds, 10-year-olds, 12-year-olds, and college students). Harris (1977) responded to the earlier mentioned methodological criticisms by varying Heider's levels in the context of a single behavioural situation. Hence, his videotape recordings showed a young girl walking into a room and either accidentally damaging a chair by sitting on it (levels one to three), or intentionally kicking (breaking) it (levels four and five). Consistent with previous research results, an age × levels interaction was found for judgements of naughtiness. Closer examination, however, revealed that none of the five age groups tested distinguished between Heider's first three levels, despite a successful manipulation check of these criteria, while only older subjects differed in their responses to any adjacent level pair (e.g. levels one and two, two and three etc.).

In contrast, all age groups distinguished at least one adjacent level pair in a study by Fincham and Jaspars (1979) where several rather more natural and familiar behavioural contexts were presented. Moreover, each group distinguished between all the levels in the manner predicted by Heider, the age × levels interaction resulting from a relatively greater differentiation with increasing age. These findings cannot be purely fortuitous, as a similar use of Heider's criteria was again found when the study was partially replicated on an independent sample of six-year-olds (Fincham, 1981). Keasey (1977a) also cites unpublished data, which similarly suggest that there is little increase in the use of Heider's criteria in 6-year-olds, 8-year-olds and 10-year-olds, precisely because they are already used by the youngest age group.

Further corroborative evidence, but of a rather different sort, comes from an interesting study by Sedlak (1979). In a multidimensional scaling analysis she showed that 8-year-olds, 11-year-olds and adults utilise Heider's criteria in their cognitive representation of stimulus stories. However, the salience (relative weight) of this dimension in predicting moral judgements did increase with age. Although this result requires replication in view of the extremely small sample used, and the fact that the structure found depends heavily on the precise questions asked in presenting the stimuli, it also supports the view that age differences are merely quantitative.

The studies cited above are united by the fact that they all use Heider's levels to define variations in the stimuli presented. Thus the protagonist may be related to the outcome in various ways (e.g. mere association, intention, etc.). Considered in these terms the criteria can, by reversing intentionality (level four) and justification (level five), be used to construct vignettes where the action-outcome becomes increasingly attributable to internal (personal) factors with each level. Yet Heider sees his criteria as defining 'cognitive depth' or response levels. From this perspective attribution of responsibility should be cumulative in the sense that people responding in terms of a more differentiated criterion such as justification should not attribute responsibility when confronted with stimuli portraying more 'primitive' levels (e.g. association). Conversely, someone using the criterion of association is likely to assign responsibility to stimulus characters portrayed at all levels. It is therefore apparent that the above two dimensions in combination generate a classification scheme representing the pattern of a perfect Guttman scale (cf. Fishbein and Ajzen,

1973). Two questions result: do Heider's levels actually function in this cumulative manner and, if so, are those response patterns related to age?

Fincham and Jaspars (1979) tested both the scalability of Heider's levels and the allied question as to whether they represent developmental stages. Using a fairly stringent criterion (a single cut off point determined by the presence/absence of perceived cause/blame) a Guttman scale was found for blame judgements. Eighty-seven percent of the sample constituted pure scale types. Most respondents based their absolute ascription of blame on intentional (even where the act might be justified) and foreseeable actor-produced accidents. The criterion of justification (Heider's last level) did, however, serve to mitigate or reduce judgements of blame in comparison with a similar act committed without justification, even though it did not (except in 19 cases) constitute an excusing condition.

Turning to the related question of developmental stages, analysis of the age-by-scale-type distribution revealed no clear age-related pattern. However, a greater proportion of adults than of any other age group used the abovementioned criteria of foreseeability and justification while some younger children, unlike adults, made no distinctions between the levels. It thus appears that Heider's model does represent a single cumulative dimension at least with regard to perceived blame, although the use of this structure was not found to be clearly age-related.

Research to date therefore suggests that a developmental interpretation of Heider's model is not as appropriate as was initially thought. Developmental differences seem to arise, not so much because different age groups use different criteria, but because they use the criteria to differing degrees. However, this should be seen as a tentative rather than a final conclusion in view of the restricted lower age limit used thus far. No attempt has been made to investigate children younger than six years, possibly because of the severe methodological difficulties this would pose (cf. chapter 7). But, if the levels are indeed learned with age, an alternative may be to investigate their use in groups with limited or deprived learning experiences. One such study (Fincham, 1982b) showed that culturally deprived 6-year-olds and 8-year-olds only used the basic principles of association and causality (levels one and two) in assigning blame, suggesting that the levels may indeed be learned in the order implied by Heider. Such results emphasise the need for research with preschool subjects. In the absence of such investigations, the precise developmental status of Heider's model will remain unclear.

Whatever the precise developmental status of Heider's levels model its use in developmental studies has yielded results which stand in marked contrast to those found in traditional Piagetian studies. It seems that children are able to make fairly sophisticated judgements at an early age when appropriately tested. In addition the levels model seems to raise issues which are potentially of great interest to developmentalists. However, it is noteworthy that Heider's work in this area, like Piaget's, is only a very minor part of his more general analysis of 'naive' or common sense psychology. It is perhaps precisely because responsibility is not fundamental to their theories that neither writer gives a satisfactory account of the concept of responsibility. This is not the place to offer such an account, nor is it necessary to do so as a detailed analysis has recently been made by the present author (Fincham and Jaspars, 1980). Nonetheless, it seems reasonable to suggest that an adequate conception of responsibility is a necessary prerequisite for meaningful developmental research. Consequently, some issues raised by an attributional approach to responsibility attribution and which may be especially important in developmental research, are now considered. Lest it appear otherwise, it should be stated that the areas chosen are representative rather than exhaustive and reflect in part the author's research interests.

*Cause, responsibility, blame, sanctions: An entailment model*

In Piaget's (1932) writing responsibility seems to be equated with moral judgement for as he himself concludes 'the psychological data of child *morality* suggest to us an interpretation of *responsibility*' (p. 334, emphases added). The matter is not, however, so simple. The interpretation Piaget offers is between objective and subjective responsibility which, as pointed out earlier, are defining characteristics of heteronomous and autonomous morality. An integral part of autonomous moral thinking (and hence subjective responsibility) is the sense of justice which Piaget investigates mainly via children's conceptions of punishment. Indeed, Piaget even suggests that young children's evaluations often reflect material consequences because these consequences are related to severity of punishment. Consequently, it is not surprising that Piagetian researchers use a variety of dependent measures in assessing moral judgements. Similar confusion arises in attribution studies, but there is in addition a further problem. In his early work Heider (1944) frequently uses the word 'responsibility' in discussing phenomenal causality. Even though his levels model is presented in a chapter on naive (causal) analysis of action, Heider never directly defines responsibility or states the extent to which it is synonomous with or related to perceived causality. Not surprisingly, his criteria are sometimes seen as levels of 'causality' (e.g. Hamilton, 1978).

It could, however, be argued that because Heider's second level of responsibility reflects mere causality, at least in the sense that the person's act was a necessary condition for the outcome, judgements of responsibility do by and large entail judgements of causation (except for global association). Such a suggestion presupposes that people do in fact answer questions of cause and responsibility differently, which is an open empirical question. Two developmental studies address this issue. Although the word 'responsibility' has been utilised in research with children (e.g. Shaw and Sulzer, 1964) both understandably used simpler terms which even the youngest subjects were able to understand. Harris (1977) found differing response patterns for perceived naughtiness and causality while Fincham and Jaspars (1979) found similar results using the term 'blame'. In the latter study 81% of subjects had correctly attributed causality by level two. However, it was noted that none of the child groups showed the adult pattern for perceived causality as their responses tended to follow a similar pattern to those for blame. Closer inspection revealed that the majority of the subjects acted as predicted and ascribed greater causality than blame, a pattern which was marginally related to age (6 years = 72% of total responses, 8 years = 76%, 10 years = 80%, 12 years = 83%, and adults = 90%).

Once sensitised to the issue of how various judgements may be related one can similarly suggest that punishment judgements (or sanctions in general) entail those of cause and blame. Such an entailment model is also proposed by Shultz and Schleifer (chapter 2) and Fincham and Shultz (1981). A slightly more elaborate version which, in addition, distinguishes responsibility from blame, cause and punishment is discussed by Fincham and Jaspars (1980). There is emerging a great deal of evidence to show that adults do respond to these various concepts differently (cf. above references). In contrast there appears to be little evidence regarding children's response to them, nor when an entailment relationship begins to emerge. It may turn out that the interchangeable use of various dependent measures in research with young children is not important as they respond to them similarly. There is some evidence to suggest this is the case. Nonetheless, children obviously do not continue to respond in this way and it seems important to determine when a change in response pattern occurs if we are to correctly interpret previous research.

*Outcome valence*

The above suggestions presumably hold for both positive and negative outcome events, as neither Piaget nor Heider specify any differences between judgements of events varying in outcome valence. More accurately, both tend to focus exclusively on negative behaviours, a tradition which has been maintained in Kohlberg's more recent work (Eisenberg-Berg, 1979). It was an attribution oriented study which first questioned this practice. Baldwin and Baldwin (1970) while fully cognisant of Heider's levels model specifically propose and test a naive analysis of kindness. By doing so they implicitly question the symmetry of positive and negative evaluations. These authors showed that adults' implicit notions of kindness rest on the assumption that only (a) intentional acts and (b) behaviours which do not also reflect self interest, lack of choice, obedience or the fulfilment of social obligations are judged as kind. These concepts not only developed at different rates, but some young children also tended to respond in the opposite manner to adults. For example, kindergarten children consistently chose and justified compliance with an adult command to share as kinder than spontaneous sharing. It was such findings which were initially quoted as evidence of an additive principle.

In contrast, structurally identical stimuli portraying negative events have yielded very different findings. For example, Darley et al. (1978) found that the presence of legal defences which limit legal responsibility also mitigated ordinary moral judgements, regardless of age (6-year-olds, 9-year-olds and 24-year-olds). Where both positive and negative outcomes have occasionally been included in experiments results tend to be rather inconclusive as different story contexts and outcome intensities are used to portray positive and negative acts, thereby reducing their comparability (e.g. Imamoglu, 1975; Shaw and Sulzer, 1964; Weiner et al., 1978). Moreover, the two studies which specifically investigate outcome valence (Costanzo, Coie, Grumet and Farnill, 1973; Sedlak, Thompson and Sands, 1982) pose interpretational difficulties. By varying motive (good or bad) and outcome (positive or negative) orthogonally it is not clear whether it is the greater use of motive information for differently valenced outcomes or the lesser reliance on outcome for differing motives which is the criterion against which development should be measured.

**Experiment 2.** An experiment was therefore conducted in which the same story context was used to portray an actor who intentionally produces a positive result (e.g. help build another child's toy tower) or its inverse negative outcome (e.g. knock down another child's toy tower). The action was portrayed as obedience to an adult, as due to reciprocity or as spontaneous. It was argued that young children because of their hypothesised orientation towards punishment (Piaget, 1932) would respond differently to positive and negative acts. More specifically, the young child's respect for adult commands favours the discounting principle in negative evaluations (reduces blame) but works against it for positive outcomes (increases positive evaluations) produced under adult direction. Hence the relative difference between obedient and spontaneous acts should initially be much greater for judgements of naughtiness than kindness, but should disappear with age and the emergence of an autonomous morality. It was further hypothesised that because reciprocity norms mediate the development of this morality (Piaget, 1932) they are unlikely to affect young children's judgements regardless of outcome valence. However, to the extent that their concern with punishment leads them to learn that it can be avoided by justification, it might influence their judgements of negative acts.

A latin square design was used to administer stories to 24, 5-year-olds, 9-year-olds and adults. Each subject was asked to indicate how 'naughty' or 'kind' the protagonist was on a pictorial rating scale. In addition, they had to choose the 'naughtier/kinder' protagonist when obedient and reciprocal acts were compared with spontaneous ones. As both forms of measurement yielded similar results only those for comparative judgements are given. Table III shows the frequency with which the spontaneous actor was chosen. As predicted, negative acts were discriminated in an adult like manner before their positive counter-parts. Moreover, within each condition the concept of reciprocity was understood later than that of obedience.

TABLE III  Frequency of comparative responses which distinguish between the stories in the hypothesised direction

| Age | Outcome valence | | | |
| --- | --- | --- | --- | --- |
| | Negative | | Positive | |
| | Reciprocity | Obedience | Reciprocity | Obedience |
| | COMPARISON | | | |
| 5 years | 12 | 20 | 4 | 9 |
| 9 years | 22 | 21 | 11 | 20 |
| Adults | 22 | 24 | 23 | 24 |

As outcome valence did not effect adults' judgements, the differential development found does not seem to be accounted for by reference to adult functioning. However, such a conclusion may be misleading. First, the stimuli used in the study were extremely simple, and it is possible that with more subtle manipulations adults will be found to have more elaborate notions regarding blameworthy rather than praiseworthy behaviour. There is some evidence that judgements of praise are more closely tied to perceived causality than blame which has its own rules of assignment (cf. Fincham and Jaspars, 1983). Secondly, the rules which govern society tend to be far more explicit with regard to prohibited negative behaviour than prescribed positive alternatives. This is consistent with the fact that feedback for bad, but not good, actions is necessary (and is more likely given) for peaceful coexistence. There thus appear to be good *a priori* reasons for believing that adults may have systems differing in complexity for evaluating positive and negative acts which might be related to the above finding.

In the absence of evidence to support such claims the results are perhaps best explained in terms of Piaget's theory. A fundamental desire for the young child is to avoid parental punishment. Consequently s/he soon learns that parents do not punish children who can justify their harm-doing. Initially, children appeal to adult obedience, the concept with which they are most familiar. It is only later with the emergence of a morality based on co-operation that they turn to reciprocity. The question of justification does not arise in relation to positive outcome behaviour which might explain the later use of such principles in this context.

*Comments*

By placing the above study in a Piagetian framework it should be clear that Heider's model is not seen as a panacea for developmental research on responsibility attribution. While it might offer some clear advantages to Piaget's two stage model, this is not to suggest that Piaget's work should be neglected. On the contrary, there is still a great deal of value in Piaget's writings which might be used to refine attribution theory. A clear example of this is Piaget's (1932) work on collective or communicable responsibility (pp. 231–250). This is different from global association as it concerns an investigation of whether it is justifiable to punish the group to which an offender belongs. The importance of social categorisation in attribution research has only recently been noted (Hewstone and Jaspars, in press; Jaspars and Hewstone, 1982) and empirically evaluated (Fincham and Hewstone, 1982) but has not yet led to any developmental research.

Another distinction Piaget draws is between practical and theoretical moral reasoning and he devotes a great deal of energy to
discussing why children are able to make judgements on the plane of
action which they are unable to make on a hypothetical level. The
importance of such differences has not yet been noted in attribution
research. However, there is also a great deal of common ground
between Piaget's work and attribution theory with respect to a related
distinction. Piaget observed that younger children often made judgements about themselves in terms of intentions whereas the actions of
others were evaluated according to consequences. Only two Piagetian
studies have investigated this issue, but with conflicting results
(Keasey, 1977b; Nummendal and Bass, 1976). The divergent perspectives hypothesis (chapter 11; Jones and Nisbett, 1972; Jones, 1976;
Monson and Snyder, 1977) also predicts a difference between actor and
observer, but does not account for why this difference should disappear
with age. Contrary to both viewpoints stable self–other differences have
not emerged in research using Heider's levels (Fincham, 1981;
Fincham and Jaspars, 1979). These negative results may, however, be
accounted for by the fact that in both conditions hypothetical stories
were used. Under such conditions it is possible that because the actions
of the 'self' are described to the subject in the same manner as the
'other', they appear to be equally 'salient' and hence behaviour does
not 'engulf the field'. Whatever the mechanism underlying this result
there appears to be a great deal of scope for developmental research on
actor–observer differences especially in view of the research showing
age-related differences in perspective taking (cf. Chandler, 1977;
Flavell, 1974; Shantz, 1975).

Just as attribution research may broaden the base for investigating
self–other differences in development, it may also further the study of
intentions. Much of the developmental literature on the child's use of
intention cues in judgements of human behaviour comes from moral
judgement research (Karniol, 1978) but this provides only indirect
evidence of children's perceptions of intention. The reason why
research on intention has only recently become an independent field of
study may be due in part to the absence of a theoretical framework for
the judgement of intention. Yet attribution theory offers such a
framework. Although Kelley (1967, 1972a,b) does not treat personal
and impersonal causality separately, both Jones and Davis (1965)
and Heider (1958a) clearly specify criteria for inferring the presence
of intentions.

A final expansion suggested by the writings of attribution theorists pertains more narrowly to the investigation of moral evaluations. In a paper which has been virtually neglected in subsequent research Kelley (1971) proposed that the moral evaluation process is based on the processes of reality and achievement evaluation. More specifically, the moral nature of acts is, like Heider's (1958a) *oughts*, perceived as belonging to an objective reality and hence its evaluation is a matter of external attribution. Like reality, it is consensually validated. In contrast, the moral evaluation of persons involves judgements of personal causation. As in achievement settings the major criterion here is distinctiveness. Kelley goes on to derive three principles from this proposition which respectively stress the conflict of the reality and achievement systems, the possible emergence of different moralities (one system might be emphasised more than the other) and the contamination of moral judgements by achievement and reality evaluations. The last mentioned, where 'is' and 'ought' tend to be confused, characterises precisely the young child. It seems quite possible that the reality system is more basic than that of achievement, and it is the development of the latter which stimulates moral growth. Such developmental hypotheses remain pure speculation as the only research in this respect is limited to showing that intent replaced objective outcome as the main determinant of both achievement and moral judgements (Weiner and Peter, 1973). Although one might question whether moral evaluations can be described in terms of only these two systems[6] the value of such ideas for developmental research seems clear.

Kelley's (1971) distinction between the evaluation of acts and persons is also of some conceptual importance. In developmental research especially, these two different judgements have often been confused. They may only be synonymous when high correspondence is inferred, an inference which is likely to be age related. However, Fincham and Jaspars (1980) argue that this distinction is not the most important in talking of moral and responsibility judgements. Consideration of legal material shows that the primary question is whether the outcome can be said to be derived from the person's act. Only then does the question of responsibility arise. In law this involves accountability according to legal rules and may therefore pertain to an omission as well as an actual overt act. In most of the research on responsibility attribution such issues have not been recognised. This is rather surprising as both Heider and Piaget often refer to examples of crime etc. in quoting Fauconnet. It is in relation to questions such as duties, act-outcome relationship, etc. that the strongest developmental findings are likely to emerge. Recent research on adults (cf. chapter 2;

Fincham and Jaspars, 1980) and children (cf. Darley *et al*., 1978; Leahy, 1979a) which investigates the utility of legal notions for everyday thinking augurs well in this respect. Not only does it herald a greatly refined conception of responsibility but also the emergence of more adequate developmental research in this field.

## Retrospect and prospect

It is apparent that attribution theory has begun to have a major impact in developmental psychology. To some extent the nature of this influence reflects the state of attribution research in social psychology. In a recent review of the adult literature Kelley and Michela (1980) distinguish 'attribution theories' which study the antecedent-attribution link, from 'attributional theories' concerned with the attribution-consequences relationship. They note that while the majority of research investigates the former, it is the latter where important theoretical development is necessary. Similar observations and comments can clearly be made about attribution oriented developmental research. Perhaps more importantly, Kelley and Michela (1980) point out that while attribution theory deals with the causal distinctions made by ordinary people these have ironically been little investigated. This omission in developmental studies assumes even greater importance as it is possible that such distinctions change with age. Moreover, there is no recourse to our own intuitions as possible participants or subjects of our own study, as in adult research. In this respect work such as Löchel's (chapter 7) is of considerable importance. It is also necessary to determine the natural contexts within which such attributions occur, a need which again remains unfulfilled in both social and developmental research.

There are also important ways in which the child literature differs from its adult counterpart. Most obviously there are many aspects of attribution theory which have not been tested with subjects of different ages. Moreover, within the areas investigated certain questions appear to have become associated with particular contents. There is a need for cross fertilisation, which is slowly emerging. There is also a sense in which the developmental literature exceeds the bounds of adult research, the work on physical causality being a case in point. Such extensions seem inevitable as many of the assumptions normally taken for granted cannot be made when working with children. Indeed, the development of some of the work on causal schemes shows social psychologists' increasing awareness of this fact. In part, the attempt to eradicate tests of irrelevant performance variables in favour of measuring true competence also stems from the increasing interest shown by developmental psychologists in attribution theory. Following the observations of both Shantz (1975) and Flavell (1974) more research is beginning to appear in child development journals.

It might seem from the present chapter that research at the interface of developmental psychology and attribution theory is primarily in the interests of the former. The exchange appears to have been unidirectional as the developmental psychologists' interest in attribution has not been parallelled by a strong move towards developmental research in social psychology, nor perhaps should it be. Yet attribution theorists such as Heider and Kelley have implicitly recognised that the child is father to the man and have not ignored developmental findings. Heider (1944) begins his analysis of persons as the prototype of causal origins by arguing that the tendency to attribute change to persons is an early ontogenetic achievement which can even be seen as necessary for the development of causal thought. Both Piaget's concept of animism (the tendency to attribute life to inanimate objects) and Werner's idea of 'physiognomic perception' (a preference for interpretation in terms of dynamic rather than static properties) in children are discussed as possible bases for the phenomena. However, Heider also suggests that personification might be explained by the very simplicity of origin organisation, where various changes are attributed to a single source rather than several different ones.

In a more recent statement on attribution theory, Kelley (1973) takes up the question of simplicity in attribution. He quotes both Piaget's (1932) work on moral judgement and Baldwin and Baldwin's (1970) study of kindness to show the increasing complexity of attributions with age and goes on to argue that the preference for simple causal explanations persists into adulthood. Although no explicit connection is made between other problems considered and a developmental perspective it is not difficult to do so. For instance, in discussing the gap between his covariation and configuration models Kelley (1973) asks what he sees as a crucial question: 'How do a priori causal beliefs affect the intake and processing of further information bearing on the attribution problem?' (p. 119). One answer to such a question is clearly developmental and it could even be argued that a complete answer must inevitably include a developmental dimension. Such speculations are not entirely convincing, yet the point remains that major attribution theorists have had recourse to the developmental literature in attempting to solve problems in attribution theory.

Explicit recognition of the reciprocal relationship between attribution theory and developmental research may lead to an even more fruitful interchange than that outlined above. Whether this marriage occurs or not it seems that attribution research on children has fast become an established practice. Currently, it is still possible to conduct a fairly exhaustive review of such studies in a chapter such as the present one. However, there are indications that the major impact of attribution theory on developmental research is still to come. Rather than being a mere downward extension of attribution theory using non-adult subjects the hope is that a more truly developmental attribution theory will emerge. Only then will any marriage between developmental and social psychology begin to be mutually beneficial and only then will the newly emerging area of developmental social psychology come of age.[7]

## Notes

1. There are of course some notable exceptions such as Olum's (1956) investigation of the developmental dimensions of Michotte's experiments on the perception of causality.
2. The term 'scheme' is used in preference to 'schema' (Kelley, 1972b) to distinguish what is considered to be an operative (scheme) rather than figurative (schema) aspect of cognition (Piaget and Inhelder, 1969).
3. Shultz et al.'s (1975) reasoning is open to question as the ensuing analysis of the MSC scheme indicates (see especially Experiment 1).
4. This result poses an interpretational difficulty. It is quite possible that the young children's responses reflect random judgements whereas those of adults may indicate genuine uncertainty. The pattern of the youngest children's responses in the other conditions favours the above interpretation.
5. The causality–objective responsibility association can only be approximate. Objective responsibility refers to judgement in terms of outcome and conformity to rules and is not restricted to impersonal causality or unintentional acts.
6. Kelley himself suggests in a footnote that the system of reciprocity may also underlie moral judgements.
7. Since this chapter was written three complementary papers on children's attributions have appeared (Kassin, 1981; Ruble and Rholes, 1981; Sedlak and Kurtz, 1981). Together the four reviews published to date provide an exhaustive account of developmental attribution research.

# 6

# Some Aspects of the Explanations of Young Children

Mansur Lalljee, Margaret Watson and Peter White

## Introduction

In a previous publication, Lalljee (1981) has attempted to analyse the layman's explanations by distinguishing between processes at three levels: the intrapersonal level, which is concerned with what goes on inside people's minds; the interpersonal level, which is concerned with what develops between people; and the societal level, which is concerned with culturally shared beliefs, assumptions and expectations. Though all these levels are interrelated, attribution theory has been concerned essentially with the intrapersonal level of analysis. However, the intrapersonal processes involving how we arrive at an explanation for an event may be largely guided by societal beliefs about the event. Further explanations are provided to other people on particular occasions and so a number of features of the interpersonal context are important. Explanations also have to satisfy conditions of interpersonal and cultural appropriateness. Both the interpersonal dimension and the societal level of analysis are ignored by attribution theory, resulting in an impoverishment of the theory at the intrapersonal level as well. All three levels of analysis must be taken into account in any psychology of explanations.

This chapter falls into two main parts. In the first part, some of the general ideas mentioned above will be elaborated with reference to explanations by children. The first section examines the idea that different types of events are explained in systematically different ways and explores some of the implications for the study of the development of explanations in children. The second section stresses the importance of understanding the child's assumptions and hypotheses about what is going on; while the third section looks in further detail at some of the interpersonal processes involved. The second part of this chapter takes up the point that different events are explained in different ways and reports on two empirical investigations of children's explanations.

## Some general considerations with particular reference to explanations in children

EXPLANATIONS: CAUSAL AND NON-CAUSAL

The conception of explanation predominant in attribution theory is that of causal explanation. Attribution theorists have assumed that causal explanation is the paradigm case of explanations both in science and in everyday life. This assumption has been challenged in a paper by Buss (1978). Following the distinction suggested by Kruglanski (1975), between actions and occurrences, Buss argues that while causal explanations may be generally acceptable for occurrences, explanations of human actions (particularly of one's own actions) are more appropriately formulated in terms of reasons. As examples of actions, he includes behaviour such as 'responses on intelligence tests, the expression of attitudes and opinions, the translation of sentences and decision behaviour. It is clear', he continues, 'that these kinds of behaviour are intentional, conscious and willed *actions* rather than occurrences' (p. 1318). Occurrences are events which happen to people, rather than behaviour they perform. Into this category come displays of emotion and physiological states. In this section the applicability of causal explanations to different types of event will be discussed, followed by an exploration of some implications for the development of explanations.

Buss's arguments have recently been challenged by Kruglanski (1979) and by Harvey and Tucker (1979). Kruglanski takes issue with Buss on philosophical grounds claiming that reasons are in fact a special sort of cause and not a logically different type of explanation. Harvey and Tucker (1979) question the distinction between actions and occurrences, pointing out that there is no clear way of deciding what constitutes an action and what an occurrence. People do, after all, have some control over their emotional states and often have little control over their abilities which may be to some degree genetically determined. Further, they argue, to attempt to distinguish between these two classes of events in terms of the actor's intentions also does not work, since there are no adequate criteria for deciding whether or not something was intentional.

The distinctions between cause and reason and between actions and occurrences both raise important questions for the study of explanations. However, it is unnecessary for the psychologist interested in the layman's explanations to enter into the debate concerning the philosophical differences between reasons and causes. The empirical questions concern the different conditions under which explanations in terms of goals and explanations in terms of antecedent conditions are offered, and the differential consequences of offering one type of explanation rather than another. In order to investigate this question one does not have to decide whether or not reasons and causes are in some philosophical sense similar types of explanation. What one does have to do is to depart from the traditional practice in attribution studies of using as dependent variables ratings of attributions of causality to person and situational causes, and to allow people to provide explanations for events in their own words.

Similarly the differences between what Buss refers to as actions and what s/he calls occurrences may well be unclear. There may be no specific criteria for distinguishing those events which a person intends and over which he has control from a variety of other types of events. For the psychologist interested in explanations the question is not 'What is the "real" difference between actions and occurrences?' but 'How are different types of events explained?' It seems likely that what are conventionally regarded as actions are explained in terms of goals while other aspects of human behaviour, for instance emotions, may be explained more in terms of antecedent events. This question is investigated empirically in the second part of the chapter.

These issues raise interesting questions for the development of explanations in children. If different types of explanation are relevant for different sorts of events, how do children acquire this differentiation? In the West, the distinction between animate and inanimate is sharp and distinct, and causal explanations are generally regarded as appropriate for events in the physical world. Piaget (1929) suggested that the child's conception of the distinction between the animate and the inanimate and between the conscious and the unconscious is very different from that of the adult. Thus the young child ascribes consciousness to things that move such as clouds and the wind; at a later stage, consciousness is only attributed to those things that move of themselves, rather than being caused to move by some outside agency; and finally consciousness is restricted to the animal world.

More recently Brooks-Gunn and Lewis (1978) point out that the infant has to learn to distinguish between the social and the non-social. In one sense, this distinction comes early. They claim that by the age of two months, infants make different responses to the face than they make to other objects. However, differentiation between social and non-social objects will change as a function of growing social knowledge. A child may, for instance, classify dogs as human, because they are often treated in similar ways by some people, but with increasing social knowledge children learn to classify animals as non-human.

The distinction between the animate and the inanimate and between the human and the non-human is related to a different range of explanations that are offered for these different classes of object. According to Piaget's early work (Piaget, 1929) the young child seems to attribute goals to human and non-human and indeed to animate and inanimate alike. It is only gradually that the use of goal explanations is limited to exclude the inanimate. Along with the classification of animals as non-human must come the realisation that the range of explanations that is generally permissible to explain their behaviour is not identical with that for explaining human behaviour. For instance, we do not normally accord animals a moral sense or explain their behaviour in moral terms. Lest the distinctions that are made by Western society are seen as in some sense inevitable, it is worth pointing out that different cultures attribute greater continuity between classes of being and ascribe life and agency in ways that are very different from that of the West (Lévy-Bruhl, 1928). Thus investigating the culturally appropriate ways of explaining different sorts of events is an important part of a psychology of explanations, and the acquisition of such distinctions is a relevant problem for the understanding of the development of explanations in young children. This issue will be addressed in one of the studies to be reported in the second part of this chapter.

The early use of animistic explanations has frequently been explained in terms of the child's failure to grasp the notion of causality (Piaget, 1930). Such an explanation no longer appears to be tenable. Hood and Bloom (1979) present evidence to support the view that very young children do show understanding of causal relationships. They analysed the naturalistic conversations of children interacting in the home with an adult and found that children of about the age of two years already showed understanding of causal relationships. However, Hood and Bloom do not adequately distinguish between causal explanations and explanations in terms of goals. Clearer evidence for the young child's understanding of causality comes from recent experimental work, some of which has been provoked by attribution theory. Kun (1978) has shown that 3-year-old children can identify antecedent events as causes, and Shultz and Mendelson (1975) support the view that children of that age can use covariation information as a basis for making causal judgements (see chapter 5).

Thus it does not appear that the child's early animism can be explained in terms of a lack of understanding of causality. Piaget (1929) also suggests a range of other processes including the progressive differentiation of the self. An alternative explanation would be in terms of the explanations provided to the child. The child is not only the recipient of explanations but also seeks them out. Piaget (1926) reports that the first 'why?' questions of the child concern human action. If so, the child may generally be provided with goal explanations, which are then perhaps generalised to other events. Berzonsky (1971) has suggested that unfamiliar events invoke more magical and animistic explanations than do familiar ones, and Hood and Bloom also argue that the failure to appreciate the nature of the child's causal thinking may have been due to the use of problems and questions which are far removed from the interests of the child.

So far the discussion of the child's explanations has been in terms of causes and of reasons. It has been proposed that although the young child does have some understanding of both sorts of explanations, s/he may more frequently be offered goal explanations, and thus resort to them in cases of unfamiliarity. However, action takes place in a sequence of events. Sometimes events long preceding may be the cause of an event and events in the distant future may be the actor's goals. Hood and Bloom (1979) remark that the explanations presented by their subjects (aged 24–40 months) focused on events that were closely related in time to the event being explained. It is reasonable to suppose that the child gradually learns to make more distant connections with the development of memory and the growth of social knowledge.

While causes and reasons may be two important types of explanation, a variety of other types of explanation are also common in Western culture. Three sorts of explanation – explanations in terms of categorisation, rules and chance – deserve special mention in the present context, since hypotheses can be formulated concerning their development. Behaviour is frequently explained by referring the individual case to a class. For the child, two pervasive instances of this are age and sex. For instance, the aggressive behaviour of a particular child may be explained by saying 'He's a boy'. Behaviour is also frequently accounted for in terms of rules. Rules of the school and of the playground form an important part of the life of the school-age child. Finally, events are sometimes explained in terms of chance. All three types of explanation are related to a range of issues in cognitive development studied by Piaget and his associates (see Flavell, 1963). Thus categorisation involves some notion of class inclusion and explanations in terms of rules and in terms of luck would be expected to develop alongside the growing awareness of the rule concept and the growing understanding of the nature of chance in other spheres of the child's activities.

ATTRIBUTIONAL PRINCIPLES AND CHILDREN'S ASSUMPTIONS

One of the considerable strengths of attribution theory as developed by

Kelley is the enunciation of a range of general principles to characterise the processes involved in making causal attributions (Kelley, 1967, 1972a, 1973). Kelley distinguishes between cases where the attributor has information from multiple observations and cases where he or she only has information from a single observation. In the former case, Kelley suggests that people use covariation information with regard to the three dimensions of persons, entities and time (consensus, distinctiveness and consistency) in order to make causal attributions. In the latter case, the attributor takes the configuration of factors into account. Kelley maintains that where there are a variety of plausible causes for an effect, the role of any particular cause in producing that effect is discounted (the discounting principle). In this section, certain studies concerning the use of these attributional principles will be considered with a view to stressing the importance of understanding the assumptions and hypotheses that the child may have about an event.

The suggestion that consensus, consistency and distinctiveness information are influential in determining an adult's attributions of causality has received considerable support. Experimental formats which have presented subjects with information of this sort show that people do use such information when making causal attributions, though the importance of information concerning the behaviour of other people (consensus information) is not entirely clear (see Kelley and Michela, 1980). By varying the information presented to their subjects, Di Vitto and McArthur (1978) have shown that 5- to 6-year-old children do use consistency and distinctiveness information in the manner predicted by Kelley. The results for the use of consensus information are not clear-cut.

Kelley's model of man as an inductivist who appears to count instances of the behaviour of the individual over time and entities, and also instances of the behaviour of other people, has been criticised by Lalljee (1981). Although people may use consensus, consistency and distinctiveness information when this information is presented to them, it may not be the information they ordinarily use when making attributions (see chapter 10). Rather than engage in an inductive search, people may quite simply seek information that will test hypotheses they have about why an event occurred. This alternative approach would suggest that a person has a store of hypotheses as to why an event occurred. Rather than engaging in the sort of search implied by Kelley, the person may then seek specific information enabling her/him to corroborate certain hypotheses.

This alternative model could be tested by asking people to seek information before providing explanations and analysing the questions they ask. Such an approach would lead to a different range of developmental questions. What are the hypotheses that children have about different events? Where do they come from and how do they change? One may speculate that the young child derives hypotheses through familial sources as well as through more general cultural sources such as books and television. The changing social life of the child through interactions in schools and with other groups in society would be important sources for the formation of new hypotheses. Perhaps the more general information search implied by Kelley occurs at a later stage in development since each of Kelley's three dimensions involves integrating a considerable amount of information. Further, even a young child has access to information about how certain people in the environment, for instance members of the family, behave over time with reference to a number of entities. Thus one would expect consistency and distinctiveness information to be relevant earlier than consensus information, since the young child may only have limited access to information about how a variety of other people behave in a particular situation.

Research into attribution processes has generally ignored the fact that people have hypotheses about events, many of which may be derived from general cultural sources. Kelley does stress the importance of the person's previous beliefs and assumptions about what is going on in those cases where the individual does not have access to covariation information (see Kelley, 1973). His strictures here are particularly relevant to developmental studies where the young child may have assumptions about what is going on which are very different from those held by adults. However, his ideas here have largely been ignored. The power of the discounting principle has led to an emphasis on studies which seek to explore whether or not young children make use of this principle when making causal attributions. The evidence for this is equivocal, and it is worth considering the implications of this.

In order to operate in terms of a principle such as discounting, two factors are relevant: certain cognitive capacities and certain beliefs about the ways in which events are related. This can be clarified through an example that has been used by Smith (1975) and by Karniol and Ross (1976) in their work in this area. The experimental material consists of a pair of stories. In Story 1 the target child is faced with the choice of playing with either of two toys and plays with one of them. In a comparison story (Story 2), the target child is described as facing the same choice and the subject is then informed that the target child's mother offers him a reward for playing with one of them. The target child plays with the toy. The subjects are asked which of the two target children really wanted to play with the toy. Children operating in terms of a discounting principle should maintain that the former wanted to play with the toy, since in the latter case there are two plausible causes – internal factors such as the child's wants and external ones such as the offer of a reward. In the first study by Karniol and Ross (1976) only 9% of kindergarten and 33% of grade 2 children adopted a discounting model, as compared with 75% of college students. However, 68% of kindergarten and 50% of grade 2 children maintained that the child who was offered a reward would want to play with the toy *more* than the one who was not offered the reward – a result in the direction opposite to that predicted by the discounting principle.

There are a variety of plausible explanations for this result, some of which are discussed by Karniol and Ross. The fact that the children do respond differently to cases where the target is offered a reward shows that they take into account the fact that two causes are operating. This would render invalid explanations based on the notion that the child cannot take into account more than one cause. It could of course be that in some way the inferences required by the discounting principle are more complex than cases where the child attributes greater motivation to the child who was rewarded.

An alternative explanation may be sought in terms of the assumptions that the child makes about what is going on. The young child may be interpreting the question concerning the motives of the target children in the two stories in different ways. Thus the stories may be presented in a time sequence as follows:

Story 1: Want T1 → Play → Reward
Story 2: Want T1 → Offer of reward → Want T2 → Play → Reward

In Story 1, the question concerning the target child's motivation clearly refers to Want at Time 1 (Want T1). In Story 2, it is ambiguous. Thus the older child or adult may interpret the question concerning the child's motivation to play with the toy with reference to Want T1; whereas the younger child may interpret the question with reference to her/his motivational state after the offer of reward (i.e. Want T2). With this in mind it is easy to see that the young child may well perceive the reward as enhancing the motivation to play with the toy. Assuming that they started out with the same initial motivation, the child who gets the reward is likely to be more motivated to play with the toy.

Further, the intentions attributed by the child to the mother will also have an important bearing on the use of a discounting principle. In the adult world, it may be assumed that if $X$ tells $Y$ to do something, $X$ probably would not have told $Y$ unless he thought that $Y$ would not otherwise have done it. $Y$ may not have intended to perform the action for a number of reasons such as not knowing that it ought to be done, or not wanting to do it. The child may make different assumptions about the conditions of such instruction. The mother could be interpreting the child's wants, telling her/him to do what s/he wants to do, rather than instructing the child to do something s/he would rather not do. Indeed a subsequent paper by Karniol and Ross (1979) demonstrates the point that the intentions the subject attributes to the mother are crucial in the invoking of the discounting principle.

Finally, young children use the discounting principle more frequently when the external force is a command rather than a reward (Karniol and Ross, 1976). Though adults may see these two forces operating in similar ways, young children apparently do not. More specifically, they may believe that the mother is less likely to use a command to interpret the child's wants, less likely to use a command except in cases where the child does not want to do something, than she is to use a reward. Commands are not seen as increasing wants. This may of course be a perfectly accurate reflection of the mother's treatment of the young child. Whether or not it is, is a question amenable to empirical investigation.

This discussion of the study by Karniol and Ross has attempted to show the importance of understanding the young child's assumptions in investigations of cognitive principles. Baldwin and Baldwin (1970) have shown that young children have a different conception of kindness from older ones, and a recent paper by Sedlak (1979) argues that young children attribute intentionality in systematically different ways from older children. However, it is not just the intentions and plans that the child attributes to the other that are important, but the entire gamut of assumptions and expectations that need to be explored. The types of explanation that children provide for different types of events – which one would expect to be related to their hypotheses about why the event occurred – are explored in the studies reported in the second part of this chapter.

INTERPERSONAL PROCESSES

So far we have been primarily concerned with the intrapersonal processes to which attribution theory has been traditionally addressed. It has also been pointed out that explanations are acquired in interactions with other people and that the type of explanation appropriate for an event is socially defined. In the previous section we have stressed the importance of investigating the assumptions that a child brings to a situation and that these assumptions are often different from those of adults. In this section we will stress the importance of the interpersonal processes involved in the presentation of explanations.

The general model implicit in attribution theory is that on encountering an event, a person makes an attribution of causality to personal or situational factors. An alternative model would be that an individual has at her/his disposal a range of explanations each of which is partly true. The explanation that a person provides on any particular occasion may then depend upon a variety of factors which have been discussed by Lalljee (1981).

The nature of the relationship is one factor which may determine the appropriateness of an explanation. An important function of an explanation is to apportion blame and responsibility. However, the explanations that are considered acceptable or indeed relevant in one context and to one person may not be relevant in a different context and to another person (see chapter 10). The appropriate excuse for negative behaviour at school may be different from that at home; and the explanations one gives to one's peers for one's behaviour may be very different from the explanations one provides to adults. Besides the relationship between the interactors, interpersonal context may take a different form. Grice (1975) has argued that one of the over-riding principles of conversation is to be informative. Do not tell the other person what s/he already knows. This simple postulate implies that people should provide different explanations depending upon the assumptions they make concerning the knowledge of the person to whom the explanation is being presented.

The idea that people provide different explanations as a function of interpersonal context, can be related to the growing interest in the young child's communicative competence. Reviewing the literature in the area, Flavell (1977) points out that even 3-year-old children are sensitive to the needs of different listeners; and Shatz and Gelman (1973) have shown that 4-year-old children use linguistically less complex utterances when talking to 2-year-olds than they do when talking to peers or adults. It is now accepted that a person's behaviour varies as a function of the situation (Argyle, Furnham and Graham, 1981). However, little attention has been paid to the way in which the content of speech varies as a function of the situation, and even less to the way in which children adapt their explanations to suit the relationship. Providing appropriate explanations to relevant others is one aspect of social skills, and such questions can be profitably considered as an important part of the child's social development.

The social aspects of explanations are also frequently ignored in research on the development of moral judgement. There are of course a variety of ways of denying responsibility for an apparently untoward act. One of these involves denying that the act was intentional. When young children present such an excuse has not been investigated. It implies some recognition of the distinction between intentional consequences and the accidental consequences of an act, and also the knowledge that 'I didn't mean to' may constitute an adequate excuse for one's behaviour in a variety of situations. There has of course been considerable research into whether or not young children use information concerning the intentions of others in making judgements of praise or blame. Though early studies suggested that the moral judgement of the young child was primarily in terms of the consequences of an act, a recent review of the literature by Karniol (1978) argues that even young children do use intentionality as a criterion in making moral judgements (cf. Fincham and Jaspars, 1980).

However, there do seem to be certain conditions under which the young child makes judgements of blame in terms of intentions. That is the situation where the actor's intention is a positive one but the outcome is negative and severe. Thus for instance, a child who is helping to lay the table and accidentally drops a whole lot of dishes, is considered more blameworthy than the child who deliberately breaks only one item of crockery (Armsby, 1971). It has been suggested that this might quite simply be a reflection of the child's greater likelihood of encountering the parent's disapproval and anger in the former case than in the latter. Though such an argument may well provide part of the explanation, it is in danger of overlooking important processes that may be at work. It is well known that in legal contexts the foreseeability of an event and taking due care are relevant factors in decisions of culpability (Cross and Jones, 1964). There is clearly an analogy in everyday life. A frequent charge against someone who has accidentally done some damage is 'You should have taken more care'. The greater the importance of what is at stake (for instance carrying a lot of dishes), the greater the care that a person is expected to take. But the boundaries of the applicability of such an accusation may not be clear, and indeed fulfil important social purposes by being ambiguous. The younger child may be more uncertain about when such an accusation may be invoked and how to defend her/himself against such a charge. The rules governing the invocation of such excuses as 'I didn't mean to' and defences against accusations such as 'You didn't take enough care' become relevant questions for understanding the explanations a person provides of her/his own behaviour and that of others.

The notion that the child's social development involves the learning of socially appropriate forms of justification leads one to look at some of the work on 'moral' development in a different light. The research of Kohlberg and his colleagues (see Kohlberg, 1969) may be seen as presenting a list of socially appropriate justifications for behaviour. Are these justifications unique to *moral* behaviour? Without debating the definition of morality, one may reasonably argue that there are likely to be strong continuities between forms of justification for all sorts of events in everyday life. Explanations in terms of avoiding punishments or satisfying one's needs, in terms of the approval of others or respect for authority are surely explanations that people provide for many forms of their behaviour. Continuities between legal excuses and those regarded as acceptable in everyday life have been demonstrated. Thus Darley, Klosson and Zanna (1978) presented subjects with a range of negative behaviour which was described as having taken place in the context of conditions which a court of law would regard as mitigating circumstances. They found that even children in grade 1 used these situational constraints to mitigate punishment. Brown and Lalljee (1981) have found that the continuity between the excuses offered by the layman and those recognised in law also holds for the spontaneous excuses presented by adolescents for criminal acts. The relevance of legal concepts for understanding attributions of responsibility is discussed by Fincham and Jaspars (1980). More generally, Scott and Lyman (1968) have provided an analysis of excuses and justifications in everyday social life.

These forms of legitimation are likely to be considerably influenced by factors such as social class and culture. Reviewing studies of socialisation, Robinson (1972) reports that distinctions have frequently been drawn between various linguistic forms of control. Thus 'positional appeals' involve reference to general status categories such as age, sex and position within the family. 'Big boys don't behave like that' is an explanation provided to the child, and one which the child presumably takes over and incorporates into his or her own repertoire of acceptable explanations. Positional appeals seem to be used with equal frequency by middle-class and working-class mothers. Middle-class mothers however tend to use more 'personal appeals'. These are explanations in terms of the affective and behavioural consequences of an act. Thus one would expect middle-class children to explain and justify their own behaviour in terms of its consequences more frequently than working-class children would. Culture too will play a dominant role. Garbarino and Bronfenbrenner (1976) have convincingly argued that authority-oriented, peer-oriented and collective-oriented forms of moral justification are related to general societal processes. If we are to understand the explanations a person offers for her/his behaviour and for that of others, these societal factors must also be investigated.

## Two investigations into children's explanations

STUDY 1: THE EXPLANATIONS PROVIDED FOR ACTIONS AND EMOTIONS

One of the fundamental starting points of the studies to be described in this section is that different types of events are explained in systematically different ways and that one objective of a psychology of explanations is to investigate how different types of events are explained. It has already been pointed out that, in the West, a clear distinction is drawn between the animate and the inanimate and that different explanations are considered appropriate in each case. Physical events are appropriately explained in terms of efficient causes while human behaviour and biological processes may be explained in terms of goals. There may, however, be further sub-divisions which are less obvious.

The distinction between actions and occurrences discussed by Kruglanski (1975, 1979), Buss (1978, 1979) and Harvey and Tucker (1979) which was examined in the first section of this chapter is one possible candidate. Buss suggests that emotional states are occurrences and Averill (1974) has proposed that the conception of emotions as somehow more biological, reactive and less under the person's control, which in Western thought can be traced to Plato, is the result of myth and simplistic conceptualisation rather than fact. Indeed McArthur (1972) provides some evidence that actions are explained more in terms of the person than are emotions; and emotions are explained more in terms of the situation.

The difference between actions and emotions was one of the central distinctions considered in the first study to be described. Since the distinction must be acquired, it is plausible to argue that young children will not see the difference as distinctly as will older children. One of the points that has been consistently stressed in the first part of this chapter is that people generally have a whole range of background assumptions and expectations about events, and that those held by young children may be very different from those held by older children and adults. Understanding how the young child views different types of events is not just relevant to the study of attribution processes, but is itself a contribution to the social psychology of childhood.

Averill (1974) also argues that emotions function as socially acceptable ways of denying responsibility for one's actions and has produced some evidence in support of this view (Averill, De Witte and Zimmer, 1978). This would be particularly relevant for explaining negative outcomes in terms of negative emotions, since there is litle rationale for denying responsiblity for positive outcomes. Insofar as situational explanations are ways of denying responsibility, negative emotions should be seen as more under situational influence than positive emotions. In an attempt to distinguish between different actions, the moral quality of the act was taken into account as a further independent variable. It would be consistent with the argument just proposed concerning positive and negative emotions that one might in general explain negative actions in terms of situational factors and positive ones in terms of the person. Reviewing research on attributions for success and failure, Kelley and Michela (1980) point out that success is generally attributed to the person and failure to situational causes. Of more specific relevance is the evidence from studies by Taylor and Koivumaki (1976) who show that negative behaviour is explained in terms of the situation while positive behaviour is explained in terms of the person. Such an outcome would also be expected from the view that social encounters are generally organised in ways which are concerned with the preservation of face (Goffman, 1955). Goffman suggests that interactors are not simply concerned with their own self-image, but are generally concerned with enabling the other interactors too, to maintain a positive identity. Finally if the general model of action in this culture is in terms of goals (Buss, 1978), then neutral actions should most clearly be explained in terms of the actor's goals.

Besides the hypotheses that the distinctions between actions and emotions and positive and negative events are more clear-cut for older children than for younger ones, developmental differences can also be expected in the different types of explanations invoked. Considerable research has been provoked by the work of Jones and Nisbett (1972) and of Nisbett, Caputo, Legant and Maracek (1973) into differences in attributions between actors and observers (see Ross, 1977). One explanation of the observer's tendency to make attributions primarily in terms of the actor has been in terms of perceptual input (Storms, 1973). The behaviour of the actor is supposed to engulf the perceptual field of the observer, and hence the behaviour is explained in terms of the actor rather than in terms of situational factors. The development of these differences has not yet been explored. Young children are thought to be more influenced by perceptual input than older ones

(Flavell, 1977), and so would be expected to make more person attributions.

So far the guiding hypotheses for the study to be described have been discussed in terms of person and situation explanations. The distinction between attributions of causality to personal or situational factors is central to attribution theory. It has been argued (Lalljee, 1981) that by treating this distinction as crucial, the heterogeneity of explanations that fall within each of these categories has been ignored. Explanations in terms of a person's goals may be treated very differently in terms of prediction, control and responsibility than explanations in terms of personality traits. Further, Taylor and Koivumaki (1976; see also chapter 12) report low correlations between attributions to the person and attributions to the situation when rated on separate scales. Since the work to be described was aimed primarily at exploring the child's conception of different types of events, it was considered essential to present them with the opportunity to give explanations in their own words. The content analysis of such data would of course be guided by some of the main hypotheses investigated.

Thus two sets of hypotheses were tested. With reference to the difference between actions and emotions it was hypothesised: (1) actions will be explained more in terms of the person's goals or some characteristic of the person, while emotions will be explained more in terms of factors in the situation or past events through which the event described was inescapable; and (2) naughty actions and negative emotions will be explained more in terms of situational factors or past events, than will good actions and positive emotions. Developmental differences were also expected: (1) these distinctions will be more clear-cut for older than for younger children, and (2) younger children will offer more person explanations than older children.

*Method*

*The stimulus material.* The stimulus material for the study consisted of vignettes familiar in the study of attribution processes. Positive and negative emotions where chosen on the basis of the theoretical work of Tomkins (1962) and success in cross-cultural work (Ekman, Friesen and Ellsworth, 1972). Tomkins amongst others (e.g. Averill, 1974; Osgood, 1966) points out that there are fewer positive emotions than negative ones. Thus the emotions used in the study were: happy (positive), and angry, sad and afraid (all negative). To illustrate: 'Once there was a boy whose name was Jack. One day Jack was happy. Why do you think he was happy?' Six actions were described. The two conventionally good acts were instances of sharing and tidying; the morally neutral acts were drawing a picture and watching television; and the naughty acts were those of lying and stealing. To illustrate: 'Once there was a boy called Tom. One day Tom was naughty! He went into a shop and when nobody was looking, he stole some sweets. Why do you think he stole the sweets?' Two alternative forms of these stories were developed, one where the target person was a child of the same sex as the subject, and the other where the target was an adult (with some adjustment for the appropriateness of the event e.g. the adult stealing some coffee rather than some sweets). As a result of attempting to portray the events in a reasonably naturalistic way, the action stories were longer than the emotion stories.

*Subjects.* The subjects were 60 children (22 aged about 5 years, 20 about 7 years and 18 about 9 years) from two state schools in Buckinghamshire. Thirty-one were male and twenty-nine female, divided approximately equally over the three age groups. The schools served a fairly heterogeneous, though predominantly middle-class, area. Each child was tested by a female interviewer who read out each of the stories in a predetermined random order, and allowed the child to respond. One boy (aged 5) refused to respond to any of the items, and was therefore discarded, leaving an effective total of 59 subjects. The interviews were tape-recorded unobtrusively, the recordings transcribed and content analysis performed on the data.

*Content analysis.* The data from six pilot subjects were used to explore what content analysis would be most appropriate for the data, and to set up the category scheme that would be used in the analysis. A broad framework was elaborated, though the final analysis was performed on four main categories which accounted for 90% of the data. Part of the initial framework consisted in ordering explanations along a temporal dimension which overlaps with the cause–reason distinction. Explanations in terms of past events, explanations in terms of some current aspect of the situation and explanations in terms of future states were thus distinguished. Within the past and future categories a distinction was attempted in terms of those factors that were temporally close to and those that were temporally distant from the event described. However, explanations in terms of temporally distant events did not occur, and so the attempt to make such distinctions was abandoned. The temporal character of the scheme was maintained and explanations in terms of past events, present situation and future states were three of the four categories finally used.

Attempts were also made to distinguish between a variety of explanations in terms of the characteristics of the person. Distinctions were attempted between traits and states, but they proved impossible to code reliably. Explanations in terms of social categorisation were also sought, but these occurred rarely. So all three types of explanation were included in a 'person characteristic' category. Explanations in terms of regularity (e.g. He always does it) and chance (It was just luck) were also sought, but they did not occur in these data. Thus the four categories on which the analyses were performed were:

(1) *Explanations in terms of past events*
These refer to explanations in terms of events that preceded the event being explained. (None of these in fact referred to previous behaviour by the actor.) For instance: 'Because his Mummy didn't give him any sweets'.

(2) *Explanations in terms of the current situation*
These were explanations in terms of some process or event that is occurring while the event is taking place. For instance: 'Because the sweets were tempting'.

(3) *Explanations in terms of some characteristic of the person*
These explanations usually referred to some trait or temporary state of the person. They also included explanations where some aspect of the situation was mentioned but where the explanation seemed to be primarily in terms of the person. For instance: 'Because he was greedy' or 'Because she liked it'.

(4) *Explanations in terms of future states (goals)*
These were explanations in terms of some future state towards which the actor was aiming. They were identified as explanations that could readily be changed into the form 'in order to . . .'. For instance: 'For his friends'.

It should be pointed out that categories 1 and 2 can be seen as two different types of situational causality; category 3 is a person category of a potentially causal nature; while category 4 is closest to Heider's notion of personal causality (Heider, 1944; 1958a).

The extent of inter-rater agreement was established by two of the present authors (M.L. and M.W.) independently coding 25% of the data. Complete agreement about their classification was achieved for 91% of the explanations.

*Results and discussion*

*Actions and emotions.* The results of the types of explanations offered for actions and emotions including details for each event separately are presented in Table I. With regard to action–emotion differences, the results are clear-cut. Actions are explained primarily in terms of goals and in terms of the person characteristics, while emotions are explained in terms of the current situation or in terms of past events. In order to evaluate these differences statistically, the following analyses were performed. For each type of explanation, the relative frequency of its use by each subject in response to action stories and in response to emotion stories was established. These relative frequencies were then compared by performing sign tests for large samples (Siegel, 1956). For each of the four categories of explanation, the differences in the frequency of usage between actions and emotions were significant beyond the 1% level (two-tailed). (Only results that are significant at or beyond this level in these studies are discussed.)

| | No. | Past event | Current situation | Person characteristic | Goal | Uncodable | No response |
|---|---|---|---|---|---|---|---|
| | | | | *Actions* | | | |
| Stealing | 59 | 11.9 | 0 | 62.7 | 13.6 | 10.2 | 1.7 |
| Lying | 59 | 18.6 | 0 | 18.6 | 42.4 | 8.5 | 11.9 |
| *Naughty* | 118 | (15.3) | (0) | (40.7) | (28.0) | (9.4) | (7.1) |
| Tidying | 59 | 25.4 | 0 | 10.2 | 47.5 | 16.9 | 0 |
| Sharing | 59 | 5.1 | 3.4 | 57.6 | 18.6 | 10.1 | 5.1 |
| *Good* | 118 | (15.3) | (1.7) | (33.9) | (33.1) | (13.5) | (2.6) |
| Drawing | 59 | 3.4 | 22.0 | 28.3 | 37.3 | 5.1 | 3.4 |
| Watching TV | 59 | 0 | 1.7 | 39.0 | 55.9 | 1.7 | 1.7 |
| *Neutral* | 118 | (1.7) | (11.9) | (33.9) | (46.6) | (3.4) | (2.6) |
| *All actions* | | (10.8) | (4.5) | (36.2) | (35.9) | (8.8) | (4.1) |
| | | | | *Emotions* | | | |
| Happy | 59 | 37.3 | 25.4 | 22.0 | 0 | 8.5 | 6.8 |
| *Positive* | 59 | (37.3) | (25.4) | (22.0) | (0) | (8.5) | (6.8) |
| Sad | 59 | 52.5 | 11.9 | 23.7 | 1.7 | 1.7 | 8.5 |
| Cross | 59 | 78.0 | 3.4 | 8.5 | 0 | 0 | 10.2 |
| Afraid | 59 | 23.7 | 30.5 | 3.4 | 0 | 25.4 | 16.9 |
| *Negative* | 177 | (51.4) | (15.3) | (11.9) | (0.6) | (9.0) | (11.9) |
| *All emotions* | | (47.9) | (17.8) | (14.4) | (0.4) | (8.9) | (10.6) |

Category of explanation

The differences between positive and negative emotions were evaluated in a similar way. For each type of explanation, the relative frequency with which it was used by each subject in response to the positive emotion story and in response to the negative emotion stories was calculated. These relative frequencies were then compared by performing sign tests. The data are presented in Table I. There are no significant differences in the frequency of usage as a function of the quality of the emotion.

In order to evaluate the statistical significance of the differences in type of explanation as a function of the moral quality of the act, a Friedman's two-way analysis of variance by ranks (Siegel, 1956) was performed for each of the four categories of explanation. The data are presented in Table I. There are no significant differences as a function of moral quality for any of the four types of explanation.

Examination of the data presented in Table I suggests that while the moral quality of the action does not seem to be relevant to the type of explanation offered, there are marked differences as a function of the particular act. Thus stealing and sharing are both explained primarily in terms of some characteristic of the person, whereas lying and tidying are both explained primarily in terms of the person's goals. To evaluate these differences, sign tests were performed for both these explanation types (i.e. person characteristic and goal) on all possible comparisons over the four stories, stealing, lying, sharing and tidying. Similar patterns of results emerged for both the goal and the person characteristic categories. Stealing is significantly different from lying and tidying; and sharing too is significantly different from lying and tidying. However, stealing was not different from tidying. The significant differences are all at probability levels of 0.005 (two-tailed) and below.

These results suggest an alternative hypothesis to the one tested in the study. The moral quality of the act may be less important than the nature of the event itself. Both sharing and stealing can be seen as different aspects of the same theme – that of the give and take of property. If the nature of the event rather than its quality is the critical factor, one might also expect this to apply to emotions. Happy and sad are sometimes seen as opposites in a way in which happy and angry or happy and afraid are not. Following the general line of reasoning just developed, one would expect happy and sad events to be explained in similar ways. In fact, sign tests performed comparing the differences in each type of explanation as a function of the happy and sad stories showed no significant differences.

*Age differences.* Table II presents the explanations provided as a function of age. For each subject the frequency of use of each type of explanation was established and the extension of the median test (Siegel, 1956) was calculated across the three age groups. None of the differences is significant. Developmental differences in the presentation of different types of explanation for actions and emotions were also examined. For each type of explanation, the difference between the relative frequency of that explanation for actions and for emotions was calculated, and the extension of the median test was calculated across the three age groups. The results were not significant.

TABLE II    Study 1: Distribution in percentages of type of explanation as a function of age

| Age (yrs) | No. | Category of explanation | | | | | |
|---|---|---|---|---|---|---|---|
| | | Past event | Current situation | Person characteristic | Goal | Uncodable | No response |
| 5 | 210 | 25.2 | 9.5 | 30.0 | 19.0 | 6.2 | 10.0 |
| 7 | 200 | 24.0 | 11.0 | 29.5 | 19.0 | 10.0 | 6.5 |
| 9 | 180 | 28.3 | 8.9 | 22.8 | 27.2 | 10.0 | 2.8 |

Thus there were no main developmental differences. It seems that 5-year-old children explain the events portrayed in similar ways to the 9-year-olds. The difference between actions and emotions appears sufficiently central to the culture that 5-year-olds clearly recognise that different types of explanation are relevant for these different classes of behaviour. Though there was a tendency for explanations in terms of goals to increase with age and for explanations in terms of person characteristics to decrease, the differences were not significant. The method of presentation of the material could be a critical factor here. If younger children are more influenced by perceptual input then clearer developmental differences may be obtained if the stimulus material takes the form of visual material rather than the vignettes used in the present study.

*Sex and target.* Median tests were performed to investigate sex differences in the type of explanation provided. The differences were not significant. Whether the target described in the story was an adult or a child also had no significant effect on the type of explanation provided. These differences too were evaluated through sign tests.

STUDY 2: THE EFFECTS OF MORAL QUALITY, THEME AND FAMILIARITY

The first study provides support for the hypothesis that different types of events are explained in systematically different ways, and thus validates one of the starting assumptions of this work. Further, distinguishing person explanations into those that refer to the actor's goals and those that refer to some characteristic of the person is clearly relevant. It seems that stealing and sharing are explained primarily in terms of the actor's characteristics while other actions such as lying are explained primarily in terms of the actor's goals. This distinction would have been completely lost if the data had simply been classified into person and situation categories. The next study to be described sought to investigate systematically the differences in explanation offered as a function of theme, while also attempting to replicate the earlier negative results concerning moral quality.

The first study also provided another lead that was followed up. Most children seemed to explain the stealing item in very similar ways. These were invariably explanations such as 'He didn't have enough money' or 'Because she was poor'. It is likely that the children who served as subjects in this experiment were less familiar with stealing than with the other events presented in the study. Though the children have little first hand experience of stealing, they have some explanations for it that are common in the culture. For events with which they have more experience, they develop more differentiated and diverse explanations. Brown and Lalljee (1980) have shown that adolescents' explanations for crimes which they have heard of from the media (crimes such as murder and rape) are less varied than their explanations for offences such as shoplifting and taking and driving away for which the main source of information is the neighbourhood. This would lead to the prediction that subjects will provide a greater variety of explanations for those events with which they are familiar than for those with which they are unfamiliar. Thus the second study involved three independent variables: (1) Moral quality, (2) Theme, and (3) Familiarity.

*Method*

*Stimulus Material.* The stimulus material consisted of vignettes similar to the ones used in the earlier study. The stories embodied three themes, each with good and naughty versions. They were: truth/lie; give/take; help/hinder. Two instances of each of these six events were constructed. One instance referred to an act with which the subject would be reasonably familiar (e.g. knocking someone down) and another version to an act with which the subject would be unfamiliar (e.g. pushing someone off a boat). Familiarity with events was decided in consultation with teachers and others who were familiar with the sort of children from which the subjects were to be drawn. Two sets of 12 stories each were developed to avoid repetition of essentially the same story to different subjects. Each set was then arranged in two random orders.

*Subjects.* The subjects consisted of 44 children (22 male and 22 female), of about the age of 7. Nearly equal numbers of children came from each of two state schools in Oxford, one serving a working-class area, the other a middle-class area. The children were interviewed individually by one of two female interviewers in a quiet room in the school. The children were read each of the stories and asked why the event described had occurred. Which order of presentation each child received was randomly determined. The responses were tape-recorded unobtrusively, the recordings transcribed and content analysis performed. The recording from one boy turned out to be spoilt, leaving an effective number of 43 subjects.

*Content analysis.* The data from 12 pilot subjects were used to refine the category system. The four categories developed in the first study served as a basis for the analysis of the explanations. The person characteristic category was subdivided. In the initial study any explanation which seemed to be primarily in terms of the person was included in the person characteristic category. Here, however, an attempt was made to distinguish those explanations which were exclusively in terms of the person and those which made some mention of the situational factors as well. Thus, besides a person characteristic category, a person and situation category was created. This included such items as 'He liked it' and 'Because he was his friend', which on the earlier analysis would have been included in the person characteristic category. The earlier study had also provoked some explanations in terms of the moral quality of the act. Thus with reference to some good acts, the children replied that the target person did it because it was a good thing to do. Intrinsic justification was therefore included as a separate category in this analysis. These categories accounted for 90% of the data. The extent of inter-rater agreement was established by two of the present authors (M.L. and P.W.) independently coding 16% of these data. Complete agreement about their classification was achieved for 95% of the explanations. A Spearman's Product Moment correlation on the number of explanations in each category elicited by the two interviewers over all the data was 0.92.

*Results*

*Good v. naughty.* The results for the explanations provided for good and naughty actions are presented in Table III. For each type of explanation the frequency of its use by each subject in response to good and naughty stories was established, and sign tests were performed to evaluate the significance of the differences. The results are broadly similar to those obtained in Study 1. Only the intrinsic justification category shows a significant difference beyond the 1% level (two-tailed). The category is used significantly more frequently for good actions than for naughty actions – where, not surprisingly, it does not occur at all. The differences between the other categories are not significant.

*Theme.* The percentage of explanations in each category as a function of theme is presented in Table III. For each type of explanation, the results for each theme were compared with each of the others and the differences evaluated through sign tests. Differences beyond the 1% level (two-tailed) were found for three of the categories: goal, current situation and P + S. Goal explanations are offered significantly more frequently for the truth/lie theme than for the help/hinder theme. The difference between the help/hinder and give/take themes is not significant. The current situation and P + S categories are both offered significantly more frequently for the give/take and for the help/hinder themes than for the truth/lie theme; but the differences between the give/take and the help/hinder themes are not significant.

These results are similar to those of Study 1. The truth/lie theme is explained primarily in terms of the person's goals, whereas the give/take theme (and the help/hinder, which was not used in Study 1) is explained primarily in terms of the relationship of the person and the situation (a category which in the previous analysis would have been merged with the person characteristic category).

TABLE III Study 2: Distribution in percentages of type of explanation as a function of type of event

| Type of event | No. | Past event | Current situation | P+S | Person characteristic | Goal | Intrinsic justification | Uncodable* |
|---|---|---|---|---|---|---|---|---|
| Good | 258 | 2.4 | 6.6 | 24.0 | 12.4 | 37.6 | 8.1 | 8.9 |
| Naughty | 258 | 0.8 | 5.8 | 25.6 | 18.2 | 38.4 | 0 | 11.2 |
| Give/Take | 172 | 1.7 | 8.7 | 39.0 | 20.3 | 12.2 | 3.5 | 14.5 |
| Truth/Lie | 172 | 2.3 | 1.2 | 0 | 10.5 | 73.3 | 6.4 | 6.3 |
| Help/Hinder | 172 | 0.6 | 8.7 | 35.5 | 15.1 | 28.5 | 2.3 | 9.3 |
| Familiar | 258 | 1.9 | 7.0 | 17.4 | 19.8 | 39.5 | 5.0 | 9.3 |
| Unfamiliar | 258 | 1.2 | 5.4 | 32.2 | 10.9 | 36.4 | 3.1 | 10.9 |

The category of explanation header spans: Past event, Current situation, P+S, Person characteristic, Goal, Intrinsic justification, Uncodable*.

*These figures included 8 instances of no response.

*Familiarity.* The percentage of explanations in each category as a function of familiarity is shown in Table III. Sign tests were used to evaluate the differences in the frequency of each type of explanation as a function of the familiarity of the event described. The P + S category is used significantly more frequently for the unfamiliar events than for the familiar events ($p < 0.001$). None of the other differences is significant.

In order to test the hypothesis that the variety of explanations for familiar events is greater than for unfamiliar events, a different type of content analysis was developed. The explanations for each event were classified on the basis of similarity of meaning. Whereas the previous analysis would, for instance, have included all explanations in terms of person characteristic in the same category, this new analysis attempted to distinguish between different person characteristics. For instance, the explanations 'she was naughty' and 'he was excited' would on the earlier analysis both have been classified as instances of the person characteristic category. In the present analysis they were distinguished as meaning different things. Similarly, explanations of lying in terms of 'not to get into trouble' and 'to get the other boy in trouble' are both instances of goal explanations. However, they stress different things, and would for the present analysis be put into separate groups. Of course, except in cases where the explanations are identical, there is no entirely adequate way of deciding whether or not explanations are similar in meaning and any classification of this sort would have to be validated by ensuring that the same level of similarity has been used for different types of events.

Thus for each event, the explanations provided were divided into categories on the basis of their similarity of meaning by two of the present authors (M.L. and P.W.). These categories were ranked in order of the number of instances in each category (e.g. most frequently used category, second most frequently used category and so on), and the number of explanations in categories of each rank was summed for the familiar and unfamiliar events separately. The cumulative distributions for familiar and unfamiliar events are shown in Table IV. Differences in the cumulative distributions was evaluated with the Kolmogorov–Smirnov test (Siegel, 1956). The difference between them is significant at the 0.001 level (two-tailed). Examination of the data shows that the difference is accounted for by the number of explanations in the first ranked category. For unfamiliar events, 56.5% of the explanations were accounted for by the most frequent explanation offered for each event, for familiar events, the figure is 38.2%.

TABLE IV   Study 2: Cumulative frequency, in percentages, of explanations accounted for by categories of similar meaning

| Type of event | Categories rank-ordered in terms of frequency of use | | | | | | | | | | | |
| | 1 | 2 | 3 | 4 | 5 | 6 | 7 | 8 | 9 | 10 | 11 | 12–16 |
|---|---|---|---|---|---|---|---|---|---|---|---|---|
| Familiar | 38.2 | 54.7 | 66.1 | 72.4 | 77.1 | 81.0 | 84.5 | 87.3 | 89.7 | 91.7 | 93.7 | 100 |
| Unfamiliar | 56.6 | 72.7 | 80.3 | 85.1 | 89.5 | 92.7 | 95.1 | 97.1 | 98.7 | 99.7 | 100 | |

In order to ensure that different levels of similarity had not been used in categorising the explanations for familiar and unfamiliar events, similarity ratings were obtained from 20 volunteer adult subjects from the Subject Panel at the Department of Experimental Psychology of Oxford University. Members of the panel were paid for their participation. The analysis was intended to check the following: (1) That explanations placed in the same category were more similar than explanations drawn from different categories; and (2) that there was no significant difference in degree of similarity as a function of familiarity.

For each story, these subjects were presented with explanations drawn from the most frequently used category, the second most frequently used category and from the other categories. Similarity ratings were obtained (1) comparing explanations within the most frequently used category (comparison 1) (2) comparing explanations drawn from the second most frequently used category (comparison 2); and (3) comparing explanations drawn from the most frequently used category with those drawn from less used categories (comparison 3). Two analyses of variance were performed on these data. One involved comparison 1 and comparison 2; the other involved comparison 1 and comparison 3. The critical results for the present purposes show that explanations in the same category are seen as more similar than explanations drawn from different categories; and that the main effects for familiarity and the interaction of familiarity with comparison are not significant. Thus it seems that the cumulative distributions reported earlier are not simply an artefact of different degrees of similarity for familiar and unfamiliar events, and that there is indeed a tendency for the children in this study to use more varied explanations for events with which they are familiar than for events with which they are unfamiliar.

*School and sex.* Median tests were calculated to evaluate the differences in the three most frequently used categories (goal, personal characteristic and P + S) as a function of school and of sex, but none of the differences was significant.

## Discussion

The studies taken together provide confirmation for some of the starting assumptions of this research and raise a number of questions. Even 5-year-old children have clearly differentiated explanations for actions and emotions, and any developmental differences will have to be sought before this age. Actions are explained primarily in terms of a person's goals and personal characteristics; whereas only on one occasion was a goal explanation offered to explain emotions. Explanations in terms of personal characteristics are offered both for actions and for emotions, but significantly more frequently for actions. Emotions are generally explained in terms of past events or in terms of some current aspect of the situation, though these explanations were also used to explain actions.

One of the clearest and least expected results of these studies is the easily discernible effect of the nature of the event itself, the theme, as we have referred to it, of the event. Though these were clear, and replicable, their explanation is not obvious. In the introduction to this part of the chapter we suggested that actions would be seen as under the person's control and goal oriented, while emotions would be seen as reactive to the environment and less under one's control. The results provide confirmation of this view. However, the sharpness of the distinction has perhaps obscured the point that within each of these categories different types of event are also differentially located along a continuum of attributed control. Quite simply, some actions may be seen as more under the individual's control than others. The explanations for such events are primarily in terms of the actor's goals. The events that invoked most goal explanations concerned lying and truth telling. These are verbal acts. Verbal acts are seen as being more under the individual's control than, for instance, non-verbal behaviour (Argyle, 1975). Both the give/take theme and the help/hinder theme did not involve words. Similarly explanations for happy/sad emotions invoked more person explanations than did fear or anger. This might be because the latter are seen as less under the individual's control than the former. Thus, rather than the clear-cut distinction between actions and emotions postulated at the beginning of these studies, it would be more fruitful to consider the range of human behaviour as lying on a dimension of perceived control, with preferred forms of explanation related to them on that basis. It is important to stress that *perception* of control, rather than some notion of actual control, is considered the crucial factor.

It was suggested earlier that the difference between actions and occurrences should not be seen as absolute and that the psychologist interested in the layman's explanations should be concerned with finding out what explanations are generally offered for different types of events and the implications of these explanations. Thus by offering different kinds of explanation a person may attempt to enhance or reduce apparent control over an event. Though the notion of theme is no doubt in need of further theoretical analysis a general taxonomy of events in terms of the layman's perceptions of control would be a clear step forward from the present work. In order to develop such a taxonomy, the ideas developed by Schank and Abelson (1977) concerning primitive acts may be of assistance. Their primitive acts include ATRANS (which is concerned with the possession of something), MTRANS (which is concerned with the transfer of mental information), and PROPEL (which is concerned with the application of physical force to an object). Some of the others are INGEST (commonly concerned with the intake of food, liquid and gas) and MBUILD (involving the construction of new information from old information). It does seem that the give/take theme is an instance of ATRANS, the truth/lie theme an instance of MTRANS and the help/hinder theme an instance of PROPEL. A summary of Schank and Abelson's complex ideas concerning primitive acts is not attempted here, but rather we direct the interested reader to a possible theoretical framework for a taxonomy of actions which may be related to systematically different types of explanation.

Unlike the work of Taylor and Koivumaki (1976), there were no differences in the explanations for good and naughty acts. There could be a variety of explanations for this. The subjects in the Taylor and Koivumaki studies were adults whereas in the studies reported here they were children. An alternative possibility is in terms of culture, the Taylor and Koivumaki studies being carried out in the USA. Kelley (1972a) suggested that one function of making person attributions is to establish control over an event. Perhaps Americans are more generally willing to believe that positive outcomes are under the control of the individual than are the British. Further, the specific items that were used in the Taylor and Koivumaki studies were different from those used here. In view of the consistent and powerful effects of theme discussed earlier, it would be surprising if this had nothing to do with the difference in the results obtained.

The notion of familiarity was introduced to examine its relationship with the variety of explanations offered. The general model implicit in the investigation is that people have a general cultural conception concerning why an event occurred. With greater individual experience they acquire a range of different explanations. The fact that for an unfamiliar event there is a greater tendency to offer the same explanation and for a familiar event to provide a wider range of explanations supports this view. The only category of explanation that showed a difference as a function of familiarity was the P + S category. These explanations are offered more frequently for unfamiliar events than for familiar ones. Perhaps unfamiliar events need more explaining and more complex explanations, involving a number of factors, are offered. To study complexity the relevance of asking people to explain events in their own words is clear.

The studies reported in this paper are a contribution to understanding the nature of these explanations and how they are to be classified. It is primarily at a societal level of analysis that we see the present contribution. We would argue that they will form the backdrop for processes at other levels, which have been considered in the first part of this chapter, but have not been investigated empirically. For instance we would expect explanations of lying in terms of goals to be more generally acceptable than explanations for sharing in similar terms. The explanation for telling a particular lie will of course also depend upon other factors, such as who is receiving the explanation. We would also expect it to be relevant to the process of searching for an explanation. Thus the search for an explanation for lying would first be in terms of the goals of the actor and would show a very different pattern from the search for explanations for sharing. We have argued that the relationships between processes at the intrapersonal, the interpersonal and societal level are integral and that all three levels must be taken into account in a psychology of explanations. Demonstrating these connections empirically is a job for the future.

## Acknowledgements

The studies reported in this chapter were funded by a research grant from the Social Science Research Council to Mansur Lalljee. We wish to thank the schools involved who so generously gave their co-operation and assistance. We would also like to thank Mrs Greta Edwards who assisted in the conduct and analysis of the first study and Dr Kathy Sylva and Dr Jos Jaspars for their comments on earlier drafts of the chapter.

# 7

# Sex Differences in Achievement Motivation

Elfriede Löchel

## Introduction

In this chapter the attribution model of achievement motivation (Weiner 1972, 1977a; Heckhausen 1972, 1973, 1977, 1978) will be used to investigate sex differences in attitudes towards achievement behaviour. The purpose of the chapter is two-fold. First a review of literature on sex differences in achievement motivation and attribution, including adult and developmental studies, is given. In the second part, data from a study on 4-year-olds will be reported. The study also had a more general developmental objective, namely, to find out how early sex differences in self-attribution of success and failure emerge. The question of whether 4-year-olds do causally attribute their own achievements, and of which causal factors they use, is inseparable from investigating sex differences in attribution at such an age. In presenting the results general developmental considerations will therefore be discussed together with the findings on sex differences.

Previous research on adult subjects and children above the age of 10 years shows that the sex differences found in achievement motivation and attribution do not favour females. 'Self-derogatory' as opposed to 'self-enhancing' attribution patterns (Nicholls, 1975), 'learned helplessness' (Dweck and Repucci, 1973), and 'fear of success' (Horner, 1972) are the three main concepts used to describe females in discussions of achievement motivation, attribution and behaviour. In the present study predictions in terms of these concepts were made for causal attributions given by 4-year-olds after success and failure in masculine and feminine tasks. The aim of the study was to detect the beginnings of these disadvantageous sex differences.

In the present context the origins of sex differences in achievement behaviour are seen in sex role *socialisation*. The term socialisation stresses that there are demands and expectations made of the child by a given society and culture. Sex role demands are only one system of norms which guide the process of socialisation. The stereotypic ascription of mutually exclusive sets of qualities and activities to the sexes is not arbitrary, but is related to the actual division of labour between the sexes and the lower social status of females in society. Achievement is one of the main areas in which the sexes have traditionally been distinguished as work and achievement have for centuries been seen as part of the male role, whereas the activities ascribed to the female role were limited to the domestic sphere and were both economically and socially regarded as 'non-work' (Oakley, 1974). Only during this century has the polarisation with regard to vocational achievement been blurred by the (limited) opening up of the vocational area for women (Fransella and Frost, 1977). It is assumed that these dual role demands are peculiar to the socialisation of females with regard to achievement and that they might explain the relative disadvantages of females in the achievement domain when compared with males.

The process of sex role socialisation is, however, highly complex. There is general agreement that the acquisition of sex roles takes place through processes of social learning (reward and punishment, explicit instructions, modelling) as well as through the process of cognitive development (construction of gender identity) (Maccoby and Jacklin, 1974, pp. 275–348; Weinreich, in Chetwynd and Hartnett, 1978). This view can be applied to the specific behaviour under investigation here. At least two ways of learning sex-specific self-attributions regarding success and failure are possible. First, socialisation agents can explain to the child her/his performance on the basis of sex. Secondly, children can actively incorporate all information on sex differences from the outside world and can draw conclusions according to their self-categorisation as a 'girl' or a 'boy' from about 3 years on (Kohlberg, 1966). Both possibilities point to the importance of adults' attributions. Sex-specific, self- or other-attributions by socialisation agents, whether given explicitly or inferred by the child, are relevant for the development of gender-specific self-attributions. For these reasons research on adults is carefully considered in formulating the hypotheses of the present study.

More specifically, the structure of the present chapter is as follows: First, non-attributional research on sex differences in achievement motivation will be mentioned insofar as it relates to the development of hypotheses on attribution differences. Reasons why an attributional model of achievement motivation is more suitable for conceptualising sex differences will then be discussed. Thirdly, research on sex differences in attribution will be reviewed and the dimensions along which they might be expected are noted. For this purpose adult studies are given as much weight as developmental ones. Finally, this framework is used to introduce the author's own research.

## Sex differences in achievement motivation

Achievement motivation is a construct which was initially developed and tested on exclusively male samples (Atkinson, 1958; McClelland, Atkinson, Clark and Lowell 1953). Only when it became apparent that the construct was not valid for female subjects was this irregularity addressed[1] (see Veroff, McClelland and Ruhland, 1975) and females' lower and less intrinsic achievement motivation rejected (cf. Bierhoff-Alfermann, 1977, pp. 46–53; Maccoby and Jacklin, 1974, pp. 161f.). Sex differences in achievement motivation came to be conceived of not as quantitative, but in terms of the particular way in which females relate to achievement because of their dual social role. Horner (1972) conceptualises this specific female relation to achieving as a 'motive to avoid success', or 'fear of success' (as an addition to the two conflicting tendencies of 'hope for success' and 'fear of failure' in the classical approach to achievement motivation). Horner argues that female success, unlike that of males, will not have purely positive social consequences, because it is regarded as unfeminine (especially in traditionally masculine professions like medicine or science). With regard to socialisation this means that girls are brought up according to a double standard. They are encouraged to do well at school and to plan careers, but at the same time they are expected not to 'beat' men, and must be prepared to fulfil a domestic role towards them. This conflict may be described as 'wanting to succeed, but not too much' (Maccoby and Jacklin, 1974; p. 140).

## The attribution model of achievement motivation

The history of achievement motivation research reflects a general trend within psychology towards more cognitive approaches during the past 15 years. Work by Weiner (1972, 1977a), Meyer (1973), and Heckhausen (1972, 1973, 1977, 1978) is representative of the cognitive model of achievement motivation which is used in the present study. In this model causal attributions are seen as mediating cognitions between objective performance outcomes of an individual and her/his

subsequent achievement behaviour. They are assumed to be effective
prospectively in motivating an action and retrospectively in the process
of evaluation. Causal attributions of achievement outcomes are treated
as independent variables which have been shown to determine the
amount of measured achievement motivation, its direction (whether
fear of failure or hope for success) and actual achievement behaviour
(variables like choice of tasks, amount of effort, persistence). Investigating causal attributions, therefore, might provide an understanding
of sex differences in achievement motivation and behaviour which is
more specific and qualitative than the global approaches previously
utilised (e.g. Horner, 1972). The advantages of using an attributional
approach to sex differences in achievement motivation are readily
apparent.

(1) *As a cognitive model it takes account of the individual's active effort to make
sense of all the information that s/he receives about sex differences from the outside
world.*

The cognitive developmental approach (Kohlberg, 1966; Ullian,
1976) and personal construct theory (Fransella and Frost, 1977)
maintain that children do not passively react to stimuli, but actively
construct their own sex roles. Contradictory information, for example
the dual role expectations relating to women, is dealt with in cognitive
terms. Causal attributions could, for instance, be used as a conflict-
solving strategy which is what Feather and Simon (1973) indicate
actually happens. Subjects who had been classified as showing fear of
success (according to Horner's, 1972, projective method) attributed
their own success in an experimental task less to the external factors of
luck and task difficulty than did the subjects without fear of success.
There were no differences, however, in the use of the internal factors of
ability and effort. Thus fear of success, subjects, when accounting for
their success, seemed to minimise the importance of external (rather
than to highlight the importance of internal) factors. 'Wanting to
succeed, but not too much' appears to be paralleled by 'taking
responsibility for success, but not too much'.

(2) *The attribution model is useful for pointing out immediate practical
consequences of cognitions. It allows for a distinction between advantageous and
disadvantageous attributions in the context of sex differences.*

Following Heider (1958a), Weiner (1972) classified the four basic
causal factors of ability, effort, task difficulty, and luck according to the
dimensions of locus of control (internal–external) and stability
(stable–variable). He predicted, and confirmed in a series of studies

(Weiner, 1972), that the degree of internality of causal attributions determines the intensity of *affect* which is experienced after a performance, while the stability of a causal attribution determines future *expectations* and thereby instrumental achievement behaviour. In other words, more pride or shame will be experienced if the individual feels responsible for her/his success or failure. If an outcome is believed to have a stable cause it will be expected to occur again and if success is expected in the future, instrumental achievement behaviour is likely to be shown whereas if failure is expected the individual will not bother to try. Although other factors usually influence these basic relationships (cf. Heckhausen, 1978) much research has shown that they are essentially valid (e.g. Weiner, 1972, 1977a). These ideas are discussed in more detail below when presenting our own data.

(3) *The attribution model permits the different cognitions that individuals hold about themselves to be structured in terms of a 'self concept'. Consequently, sex differences may be dealt with as differences in self concepts.*

The notion of 'self concept' used comprises a theory held by individuals about themselves (Epstein, 1973). In the present context, the term is used to denote a specific sub-structure of self concepts, that is, the self concept of one's own ability. Meyer (1973), Heckhausen (1973), and Weiner (1977a) show that individuals classified according to the nature of their achievement motivation (either fear of failure or hope for success, measured by the conventional projective method, see McClelland *et al.*, 1953) could also be distinguished by their attribution patterns, which served to maintain a self concept of either low or high ability. Independent of actual ability or achievements, both groups are biased in explaining the causes of their performances. Persons with a self concept of high ability are characterised by the authors as attributing success to *internal* factors (ability or effort) and so are internally reinforced by feeling proud. Failure, in contrast, is attributed to *variable* factors, thus maintaining hope for success and the possibility of increasing effort. The shift from the dimension of locus of control to the dimension of stability is essential as it implies that this group of individuals may take responsibility for both success and failure. It is not the externalisation of failure they choose, but its changeability. Opposed to this strategy, individuals with a low self concept tend to attribute success to *external* factors (task difficulty or luck), which renders affective self-reinforcement impossible, and failure to *stable* causes, mainly lack of ability. These descriptions indicate how biased attribution patterns serve to maintain self concepts.

(4) *Sex differences in attribution patterns which serve to perpetuate different self concepts in both sexes can partly explain the maintenance of females' disadvantageous social status.*

If females are given lower social status and are believed to be less competent (see below), this should be reflected when self concepts of ability and causal attributions of performance are measured. Nicholls (1975) provides an example of this. American fourth graders worked on an angle-matching task, in which the pattern of success and failure was manipulated by the experimenter. Nicholls' purpose was to test predictions about attributions following a logical v. a biased strategy. He found significant sex × outcome interactions for the ability and luck factor. Girls showed a self-derogatory bias in their ability attributions in attributing failure much more to poor ability than success to high ability. On the luck factor, however, boys showed a significant self-defensive (or self-enhancing) bias as they attributed their failure more to bad luck than girls did.

Heckhausen (1973) points out that self concepts – even if they lack validity at the beginning – can operate like self-fulfilling prophecies. If girls are led to believe in their own inability, this will in the long term decrease their instrumental achievement activities and thus narrow down the possibilities of learning and acquiring skills.

(5) *The attribution of behaviour by relevant observers (socialisation agents) may be seen as one way of transmitting sex role stereotypes*

This point was alluded to in the introduction and will not be elaborated in this chapter. Some of the studies cited in the following section indicate, however, that there do exist similar biases in self- and other-attributions which can be linked to prevailing sex role stereotypes.

## Sex differences in achievement attributions

Previous research relevant to the present study can be classified by the two criteria of self v. other attribution and adult v. developmental studies. Studies on adults are included in this review for two reasons. First, the small number of developmental studies (see below) requires that one consider research on adults in determining the dimensions on which sex differences in attribution might occur. Secondly, it is in this research literature that a model has been proposed (Deaux, 1976) to explain the link between sex role stereotypes and attributions in terms of expectations. This model applies to self- and other-attributions, and will briefly be introduced here.

ADULT STUDIES

Whereas in the previous section causal attributions were considered as independent variables which determine cognitive, emotional, and instrumental behaviours, their use as dependent variables is now considered. Deaux (1976) argues that a person attributing causes to her/his own or someone else's behaviour uses two sources of information before arriving at the final attribution, namely, the actual behaviour itself in a given situation and the expectancies concerning this behaviour. Causal attributions are seen as a 'function of the match or mismatch between these two sets of information' (Deaux, 1976, p. 336). One important source of expectancies is categorical assumptions about social groups (see chapter 8) such as the stereotypes linked with the category of sex. Observers will have expectancies regarding the behaviour of individual males or females which are based on sex role stereotypes. Consequently they will causally attribute and judge the observed behaviour relative to these expectancies (Deaux, 1976, p. 336). According to existing sex role stereotypes (Broverman, I., Broverman, D., Clarksen, Rosenkrantz and Vogel, 1970; Rosenkrantz, Vogel, Bee, Broverman, I. and Broverman, D. 1968;) males are expected to be 'competent' (competent, independent, competitive, objective, logical, ambitious, self-confident), whereas females are expected to be 'expressive' (tactful, gentle, aware of feelings of others, able to express tender feelings). The expectancy-model assumes that expectancy-confirming performance (i.e. success in males, and failure in females) should result in attributions to stable causal factors whereas expectancy-disconfirming performances (female success and male failure) should be attributed to variable factors (Feather, 1969).

In presenting the evidence relating to this model studies on self- and other-attribution will be presented separately and in each case data on ability and effort/motivation attributions will be dealt with. On the grounds of the expectancy-model Deaux and Emswiller (1974) predicted that, given equally good performance on a masculine task, males' performance should be attributed more to skill (stable factor) and females' more to luck (variable factor). The reverse was predicted for feminine tasks. It was assumed that in sex-typed tasks expected competence was higher for same sex than for opposite sex performers. The results for both sexes revealed, however:

(1) A main effect of sex of stimulus person as males were rated more

skilful than females, independent of task.

(2) A sex of stimulus person by sex of task interaction. There were sharp differences in ratings between male and female stimulus persons on the masculine task. As expected, males' performance was attributed more to skill, females' more to luck. But there were no differences on the feminine task. Thus the prediction that males would be seen as less skilful on female tasks was not confirmed.

The fact that identical male and female performances are attributed to different causes could explain the frequently found differences in the evaluation of identical male and female performances (e.g. Goldberg, 1968; Friend, Kalin and Giles, 1979; McArthur, 1976; Ward, 1979). The study suffers, however, from methodological problems as it uses a unidimensional rating scale only and, in addition, it confounds the two dimensions of stability and locus of control. This is not true of the following studies.

Feldman-Summers and Kiesler (1974) measured the four causal factors separately and found a more complicated pattern of attributions, in addition to sex-of-subject differences. Subjects evaluating the performance of stimulus persons of both sexes in laboratory tasks attributed more *motivation* to female problem solvers, regardless of level of success. In a second study where subjects were given stories about successful doctors there was the same main effect of sex of stimulus person on the effort/motivation attribution. However, there were also significant interactions with sex of subjects. Males attributed the success of male as compared with female physicians more to ability. At the same time, male subjects attributed the success of female physicians more to motivation and task easiness. Female subjects, however, had a different pattern of attributions: they perceived the male physician as having an easier task and also attributed the success of a female doctor more to motivation.[2]

In addition to these two studies which provide attribution data for success situations only, Feather and Simon (1975), varied success and failure in stories about males and females in different occupational fields. They showed that not only was male success more often attributed to the stable factor of ability than was female success, but also that female failure was more often attributed to a stable lack of ability than was male failure. Moreover, while succeeding males were rated much more positively than failing males, females were more positively rated when they failed than when they succeeded.

Studies of this kind indicate that stereotypes of males competence and female incompetence actually influence attributions of performance by others, at least in experimental situations. Such attributions are likely to maintain exisiting stereotypes. Furthermore, if self-stereotyping parallels stereotyping by observers, detrimental effects on the achievement behaviour and self concept of females can be predicted.

One of the self-attribution studies confirming this hypothesis is that by Deaux and Farris (in Deaux, 1976). Subjects solved an anagram task where success and failure and sex-linkage of the task were manipulated. Of the four causal factors (luck, ability, effort, difficulty), *ability* yielded the main sex difference. Men used it more often to explain their success, whereas women used it more often to explain their failure. As in Deaux and Emswiller's (1974) study these differences were most clear-cut for masculine tasks.

For ability attributions the data seem to be clear and compatible with the explanatory scheme based on expectations, whereas the data on self-attributions of *effort* are more complicated. First, there are studies showing no sex differences in effort for self-attributions (Nicholls, 1975; Deaux and Farris, in Deaux, 1976). This could be explained by a ceiling effect assuming that all subjects expended maximal effort in the experiments (see Deaux, 1976, pp. 344f.). But from the expectancy-model it also follows that effort as a temporary causal factor should be used more often by males in the case of failure (and should therefore increase their persistence), and by females in the case of success. The role of effort is a very crucial one, as it is the only causal factor which can be changed by the subject intentionally taking into account her/his ability as well as environmental difficulties. Especially in the case of failure, only effort attributions can lead to task persistence. In this respect Bar-Tal and Frieze's findings (reported in Deaux, 1976) on sex differences are most interesting. Ability attributions of success differentiated high and low achievement-motivated males only. Females, even when they were high in achievement motivation, attributed their failure to lack of ability, whereas they attributed success to effort. This is a strategy which serves to maintain a low concept of personal ability. In the face of such vicious circles it seems pertinent to ask: how do such attributions develop and how could they be changed?

Two conclusions can be drawn from the evidence on adult sex differences. First, ability and effort attributions in conjunction with outcome condition (success or failure), distinguish between males' and females' differing expectancies concerning their own competence. In order to find out whether sex role stereotyping affects children it is necessary to look for sex differences in these causal factors or their developmental equivalents. Are success and failure attributed differently by boys and girls? Could the attributions used be indicative of different expectations of competence? Secondly, type of task (masculine or feminine) has to be taken in to account as it differentially determines the expectation of competence for both sexes.

## DEVELOPMENTAL STUDIES

Developmental research on causal attribution has not paid much attention to intergroup differences such as those relating to sex and there are very few studies on sex differences in achievement attribution which have been carried out with children. One of them is Nicholls' (1975) study, cited earlier. Dweck and her colleagues (Dweck, 1975; Dweck and Bush, 1976; Dweck, Davidson, Nelson and Enna, 1978; Dweck and Gilliard, 1975; Dweck and Repucci, 1973) have worked with a similar age group and attempted not only to determine what sex differences exist, but also to clarify their origins and to develop strategies for their modification.

Dweck interprets the specific sex differences she found in terms of the concept of 'learned helplessness'. This concept is defined by Seligman (1975) as the cognition of independence between one's own behaviour and its consequences and can be an experimentally created, situation-specific expectancy as well as a more generalised personality trait. The latter typifies depressive patients, of whom the number of women is twice that of men (Hoffmann, 1976). The notion can also be used to conceptualise some people's behaviour in achievement situations.

Dweck and Repucci (1973) showed that generalised learned helplessness in children (fifth graders) and the experimental condition of real helplessness (i.e. unavoidable failure) interacted. Subjects suffering from performance deterioration in the presence of an experimenter who had given failure feedback only, but not in the presence of a 'success experimenter', were classified as 'learned helplessness'. Their measures on the Intellectual Achievement Responsibility Questionnaire (Crandall, V. C., Katkovsky and Crandall, V. J., 1965) showed that these subjects, compared with persistent ones, took less responsibility for success and failure. Although there were no differences in ability attributions, persistent subjects made significantly more *effort* attributions than helpless subjects in the case of *success*. In the case of *failure* there were significant differences in effort attributions between the helpless and persistent groups, as well as between the male and female groups. This means that helpless subjects, as well as female subjects who had not been classified as helpless, did not attribute failure to motivational deficiencies, and were therefore unlikely to increase their effort. It thus appears that female as well as helpless subjects are more prone to deterioration of performance in the face of failure. As the performance deteriorations were specific to the experimenter who had provided failure feedback only, this hints at the role of social interaction in the development and change of expectations.

In another study, Dweck and Bush (1976) demonstrated the differential effect of peer v. adult failure feedback on boys and girls. Whereas failure feedback given by adult evaluators improved performance and persistence in boys and impaired performance in girls, the effects were reversed with peer evaluators. This is explained in terms of different interaction and feedback patterns for boys and girls with peers and adults, especially teachers. As teachers usually criticise boys more than girls, and more often because of lack of discipline or motivation than because of work-related matters, boys can sustain a self concept of high ability even in the face of negative feedback. They may attribute negative feedback externally (to the teacher) or internally, to unstable, non-intellectual aspects of their behaviour. Girls, in contrast, are rarely criticised by teachers, because they behave in a more disciplined way, and work more neatly and industriously than boys. Consequently, they are more likely to take failure feedback as a valid assessment of their intellectual abilities. The validity of this explanation was shown by Dweck, Davidson, Nelson and Enna (1978) who actually assessed these patterns of feedback in natural classroom situations and then produced the expected effects in the laboratory. Dweck and Bush's (1976) results again seem encouraging with regard to modifying attributions, because they do not conceptualise 'learned helplessness' in girls as a stable, general personality trait, but rather as a logical and agent-specific reaction to certain interaction patterns.

Dweck (1975) in fact shows how learned helplessness attitudes can be changed by means of reattribution training which aimed at teaching subjects to take responsibility for failure and ascribing it to lack of effort. Though this is further proof of the central role of effort attributions in the face of failure, the study does not provide any follow-up data and does not use measures different from the training methods. It therefore seems doubtful whether the effects were lasting.

No other developmental studies on sex differences in achievement attribution are known to the author. Moreover, there is a complete lack of research on children below school age. This may partly be explained by the time-consuming measurement techniques needed for research with non-reading children. Natural tasks and oral questioning methods (rather than questionnaires) have to be used while non-verbal stimuli and responses also need to be considered. Another problem for attribution research with pre-operational children is that interindividual differences cannot necessarily be regarded as stable. Nor can they be equated with comparable differences in adults. The confounding of sex differences and cognitive developmental differences, which creates an experimental as well as theoretical problem, will be considered in more detail in discussing the study reported below. Apart from methodological difficulties, attribution research on pre-school children might also have been neglected because achievement behaviour is often not practically relevant before school age. However, by the time children enter school advantageous or disadvantageous attribution patterns can already have been established (cf. Falbo, 1975).

## Experimental evidence regarding causal explanations in four-year-olds

PURPOSE AND HYPOTHESES OF THE PRESENT STUDY

The main purpose of this study was to investigate sex differences in the causal explanations of 4-year-olds. As argued in the introduction however, this goal cannot be reached directly. Sex differences at this age presuppose that 4-year-olds make consistent and meaningful causal attributions. Consequently, such differences cannot be specified precisely in advance, because they are most likely related to the causal explanations 4-year-olds use. As investigation of the nature of 4-year-olds' causal explanations regarding success and failure was seen as a necessary precondition for analysing sex differences, two sets of hypotheses were tested.

*Hypotheses*

*General developmental hypotheses*

(1) Four-year-olds will make causal attributions for their own successes and failures if asked to give reasons for their performances.

(2) They will use causal explanations which are different from the classical factors found in adult research (Heckhausen, 1978).

*Hypotheses on sex differences*

(3) There will be sex differences in the causal explanations 4-year-olds give for their own successes and failures in masculine and feminine tasks. Three general expectations were formulated with regard to the direction of the sex differences.

(4) A self derogatory bias will be manifest for girls, as opposed to a

self enhancing bias for boys (Nicholls, 1975). This prediction was derived from previous findings on adults and older children showing the influence of sex role stereotypes which ascribe higher competence to male persons.

(5) The direction of the sex difference will favour 'learned help-lessness' attitudes in girls, as found by Dweck (e.g. Dweck and Repucci, 1973). It could not be expected, however, that the same attribution pattern found in older children would occur, as the use of 'effort' as a causal factor is unlikely in this age group (Heckhausen, 1978; Nicholls, 1978).

(6) On the basis of females' 'fear of success' (Horner, 1972) and their dual role expectations, it was predicted that girls would choose attributions which were likely to diminish the ambivalence of success.

METHOD

*Subjects*

Fifty subjects participated in the study, 25 girls and 25 boys (age range 4–0 to 4–11). They were drawn from a variety of nursery schools and playgroups in and around Oxford, which differed in many respects (e.g. social backgrounds, amount and quality of playing and teaching materials, size of groups, structuring of activities etc.).

*Materials*

Previous research has shown that sex-linked tasks influence success and failure attributions, because they create different expectations in the two sexes. In this study 'masculinity' and 'femininity' of tasks was defined in two ways. The first concerned *performance* differences which have been found between the sexes. According to Maccoby and Jacklin's review (1974) the only clear-cut and consistent performance differences exist in *verbal* skills (superiority of girls) and *spatial* skills (superiority of boys), although these differences are not stable before early adolescence. Secondly, there are *preference* differences. Maccoby and Jacklin's review (1974) also shows definite sex differences in the preference of toys and activities from the age of three onwards. Some of the most frequently found examples are boys' preference for gross motor play, transportation toys, blocks and manipulating physical objects. Girls prefer fine motor play and 'artistic' activities. Therefore, *building and manipulating* and *fine motoric play* were chosen for the sex typing of tasks in terms of preference differences.

*Independent and dependent variables*

There were two independent variables, outcome (success or failure) and sex-linkage of the task which was defined in terms of either preference or performance. Fully crossing these variables led to eight experimental conditions (see Table I). The administration of the eight tasks was counterbalanced incompletely (Selg, 1971) to avoid order effects. The sequences chosen avoided the simple alternating of success and failure, and the occurrence of more than two successive failures or successes (this could be too frustrating in the case of failure and could determine expectancies too strongly under both outcome conditions). Thus each child was tested under all eight experimental conditions. Following each successful/unsuccessful performance the child was asked 'Why do you think you could (not) do that?'. An open-ended question was necessary to determine which causal factors were used by this age group.[3]

TABLE I   Design overview

| | Task | | | |
|---|---|---|---|---|
| | Masculine | | Feminine | |
| | *Preference* Building and manipulating | *Performance* Spatial skills | *Preference* Fine motor, artistic play | *Performance* Verbal skills |
| Success | 1 | 2 | 3 | 4 |
| Failure | 5 | 6 | 7 | 8 |

1, Building an aeroplane out of wooden parts and screws ('meccano'); 2, Block design WISC, simplest form; 3, Completing the drawing of a man; 4, Describing a picture; 5, Undo screws which are fixed too tightly; 6, Block design WISC, difficult form; 7, Maze tracing task for higher age level; 8, Vocabulary task for higher age level.

*Procedure*

The eight tasks were administered to subjects individually. The instructions were as follows: 'I have come to find out what children can do and why they think they can do it. I wonder if you can do the games I brought with me? The first one is . . . [e.g. building an aeroplane] . . .'. The child was shown the materials. 'Do you think you will be able to do that?' The instruction and the first question served to make the dimension of success and failure salient to the child, and to help her/him understand the following questions more readily. All answers were recorded on prepared sheets. If the child did not answer, the

TABLE II   Definitions and examples for the five main categories

| Category | Examples | Definition |
|---|---|---|
| (1) Can, know | –because I don't know how to play this sort of game<br>–I can't do it very well<br>–I know how to do it<br>–because I could<br>–I don't know what it means<br>–I can't do hard things | Explanations by specific knowledge or skills (opposed to explanations by general ability in trait terms)<br>All explanations using can/could and know/know how<br>Explanations using the word 'can' even if they contain task difficulty expressions |
| (2) Difficulty | –it's quite hard<br>–it's a bit difficult<br>–it wasn't easy<br>–because it's easy-peasy<br>–it's too stiff<br>–they are too tight<br>–it's too hard for me<br>–this is too difficult for a boy like me | Explanations by ease or difficulty of the task when used as such and not adverbially with a knowledge attribution (see above)<br>Explanations referring to tightness, toughness of the screw-task<br>Explanations which relate degree of difficulty to own person |
| (3) I don't know | | Only if appearing literally in this form, indicating that the subject does not know any reason or explanation for her/his performance<br>Not: 'I didn't know', 'I don't know how to do it' |
| (4) Learned | –I've been doing it at home<br>–My mum showed me how to do it<br>–I've seen them before<br>–because I learn how to read<br>–I've never done this before<br>–I haven't been doing it for a long time | Explanations referring to previous experience with the same material or activity, e.g. being taught, learning, seeing, practising, doing something before – or to learning activities in other areas |
| (5) Age | –because I'm four<br>–because I'm only four and nine months<br>–I'm not big enough to do it yet<br>–I'm too small to know<br>–because I'm old enough to do it<br>–because I'm a big girl<br>–because my hand is too small yet<br>–I am not very strong yet | Explanations by age or size<br>Explanations by size of parts of the body<br>Explanations in terms of physical strength |

experimenter repeated the question. Only if there were no answers on both questions was this coded as 'no answer'. Preceding and following the presentation of the experimental tasks an experience of success was provided with toys familiar to the subjects. This was designed to elicit co-operation from the subjects and to counteract any negative effects of failure on the children's emotions and subsequent expectations.

RESULTS AND DISCUSSION

*Causal explanations of four-year-old subjects*

*Results.* One of the two major aims of the study was to find out what kind of causal explanations, if any at all, were used by children aged four. Answers given in a pilot study were used to construct various response categories. In order to analyse the present data 17 categories were defined. A neutral observer who did not know the purpose of the experiment was trained in the application of the categories, and then classified the experimental data. Inter-rater agreement occurred on 84% of the 464 answers. In some cases the disagreements were resolved by referring to the definitions, in others by discussion.

In both the pilot and main study five categories (*can* (27%), *difficulty* (22%), '*I don't know*' (11%), *learned* (8%), *age* (6%) ) made up 74% of the answers (see Table II), while each of the other categories occurred in less than 5% of the cases.[4]

The data showed unambiguously that 4-year-olds do causally attribute their performances to a variety of factors. It is also clear that the causal explanations given do not fit the conventional locus of control/ stability scheme as applied to adult achievement attributions (Weiner, 1972). Thus both the developmental hypotheses of this study were confirmed.

*Discussion*

*Nature of the data.* Before discussing these results, some consideration ought to be given to the nature of the data. Because they are entirely verbal two inevitable problems result. First, 4-year-olds are still in the process of language acquisition and do not talk independently of a concrete context. Secondly, being necessarily based on verbal data attribution theory is very much a theory concerning the language of causal explanations (see chapter 9). Both problems are interlinked in the present data. In forming categories subjects' answers had to be taken literally. It is obvious that in a developmental study different cognitive concepts of '*difficulty*' or '*can*' might be involved when the subjects use the same linguistic expressions as an adult. Therefore a specific developmental interpretation will be attempted after considering the behavioural implications of these results.

*Behavioural implications.* The lack of explanations (*'I don't know'*) has not been found in any other study. However, the presence or absence of causal explanations of an individual's own performance is indicative of the relation individuals establish between their own person and achievements. It can be assumed that the more important an area of behaviour is for a person, the more complex cognitions s/he will have about it.

Causal explanations of achievements do not only serve to associate or dissociate an outcome from one's own person, but also by doing this in a particular way serve to maintain the nature (hope for success, fear of failure) of one's self concept. Dissociating oneself from one's performance could express an attitude of indifference towards achievement outcomes, or it could be a defensive strategy which avoids feedback about one's ability. Developmentally, both strategies would be disadvantageous, for the cognitive link between person and outcome is a necessary precondition for the acquisition of achievement motivation (Heckhausen, 1978). From the researcher's point of view, the lack of a causal attribution makes it impossible to predict systematic effects on expectations, emotions, and further achievement strivings. All that can be said is that the lack of explanations in the case of success will diminish the internal reinforcement value of success, and in the case of failure it will mean uncontrollability.

Explanations in terms of *age* have never been dealt with in attribution research. This is surprising insofar as a great deal of every individual's social experience is structured according to age (e.g. schooling) and age is used to build rank orders (e.g. salaries made dependent on age). Age is likely to be most salient in the extreme ranges of the age distribution (childhood and old age). From the child's point of view, it creates a rank order of strength, knowledge, status and power. Further, age attributions do not only imply social comparisons (with siblings, peers) which are often explicitly made by adults towards the child, but also comparisons with one's own previous performance. So in the case of success an age attribution ('because I'm big enough') may very well create satisfaction and pride in the child and takes the character of an internal cause which is based on an individual performance standard ('now I'm big enough'). In the case of failure, however, 'I'm not old enough' removes the responsibility from the child, and the same causal factor as before shifts to an external meaning. Nobody can be blamed for her/his age. At the same time, hope for success can be maintained, for although age cannot be changed intentionally it will certainly change.

To refer to *learning* as a possible causal explanation of success or failure seems a most obvious way of thinking. Like age, learning is a very salient factor in children's cognitions, and together with age is probably most visible during childhood. The practical consequences of making attributions in terms of learning can take two directions. As it is a variable and internal factor it is useful in the case of failure to maintain expectations of success and perseverance in the long term. If a person explains her/his failure as due to not yet having learned the necessary skills, s/he believes that it can be changed by learning as opposed to an ability attribution. As distinct from effort, however, learning cannot be controlled immediately, but only in the long term. Learning attributions in the case of success lay more stress on the process of acquiring knowledge, rather than the outcome which is emphasised more by 'can' or 'ability' attributions. It could therefore be hypothesised that persons who are less sure about their own ability and possession of knowledge would prefer attributions to learning in the case of success.

*Difficulty* is the only causal factor which may be subsumed under Weiner's scheme. However, as will be seen, difficulty attributions given by 4-year-old subjects cannot be equated with adult difficulty attributions because of the different levels of cognitive concepts involved. It may be maintained, however, that difficulty attributions are centred on the task more than on the individual and imply uncontrollability.

Although the main aspects of *can/know* attributions will be treated in the following section, a general, non-developmental characteristic needs to be mentioned, the distinction between attributions to (general) ability v. (specific) knowledge. In this study general ability was used as a causal explanation in only 4.1% of the cases compared with 26.7% for can/know attributions. This again points to the shortcomings of the conventional classification scheme which only refers to general ability. In the area of education the distinction becomes practically relevant for self- and other-attributions, as specific knowledge (as opposed to general ability) can be seen as changeable through internal and external factors. It can even be assumed that can/know attributions are more relevant to the self concept of individuals, because general ability, though internal, may be experienced as something given, but not intentional (Sohn, 1977; Weiner, 1977b). With reference to Weiner's classification scheme two factors did not emerge. The absence of luck attributions is not surprising, as the tasks were apparently ones of skill rather than luck. The lack of effort attributions, however, which have been relevant in attribution research on adult women, poses general developmental questions.

*Developmental interpretation.* The most difficult problem in studying sex differences in 4-year-olds is that there is no established body of knowledge on the general cognitive development of causal concepts for success and failure. Heckhausen (1978) concludes (after reviewing the developmental literature on achievement attribution in terms of a cognitive-developmental framework) that there must be a sequence of phases in the development of causal concepts in which *task difficulty* attributions precede *'global competence'* attributions, which will then be differentiated into *effort* and *ability* attributions (see Nicholls, 1978). The existence of a global concept of one's own competence can be seen in the present data. In their answers the 4-year-old subjects never used effort as a causal factor. The most frequently used categories were instead 'can/know' and 'task difficulty'. This is exactly what Krüger (1978, reported in Heckhausen, 1978) found for 3- and 4-year-olds when she asked them for the causes of performances like lifting objects or blowing pieces of cotton wool towards a goal.

Again, it must be pointed out that neither 'difficulty' nor 'can/ know' attributions can be equated with the same causal factors known from research on adults. A difficulty or ability/knowledge attribution made by an adult ideally results from a multidimensional processing of information which 4-year-olds are cognitively not yet capable of. Unless the three dimensions of consistency, distinctiveness, and consensus information (Kelley, 1967, 1973) can be integrated, no realistic estimate of one's own ability will be possible. Instead centering on one aspect or the other is likely to occur (for further discussion of this problem, see Heckhausen, 1978). Thus a pre-operational subject's preference for difficulty attributions, for instance, would not have to be stable but could be the consequence of cognitive uncertainty and arbitrary centering on one aspect. If this were true, the reliability of a sex difference in difficulty attributions would be diminished as long as it had not been shown that this centration was systematically related to sex.

*Conclusions for investigating sex differences.* The data suggest that the second major set of hypotheses relating to girls' self-derogation, learned helplessness, and diminution of ambivalence of success, can be tested. It must be remembered, however, that the assessment of sex differences at this age is likely to be confounded with cognitive development. Sex differences, found at this stage, do not necessarily have to be stable, but could simply reflect developmental differences. Nonetheless it can be argued, that if developmental differences are systematically linked to sex, this will not reduce the reliability of the sex differences found. Further, if the nature of the sex difference is similar to stable adult sex differences and can be linked to sex role stereotypes as a point of reference, the validity of the difference will be strengthened.

*Sex differences in relation to success and failure and type of task*

*Results.* The two ways of sex-typing tasks (by preference and performance differences) did not lead to systematic differences, and therefore were not distinguished in the 2 × 2 × 2 (sex × outcome × type of task) ANOVAs carried out for each causal explanation.

*Can.* It was found that boys give more *can* explanations for feminine (masculine = 29; feminine = 39), and girls more for masculine tasks (masculine = 33; feminine = 23). In other words, the direction of the sex difference is reversed for the two types of tasks. This interaction effect of sex × type of task is statistically significant ($F$ [1,48] = 8.70; p<0.01). It appears as if both sexes took more responsibility for sex-inappropriate tasks as opposed to sex-appropriate ones. Closer inspection of the data reveals that the influence of outcome condition has to be considered (sex × outcome × type of task interaction: $F$ [1,48] = 2.77; p<0.25). Whereas boys use more *can* explanations for feminine tasks under both success and failure conditions, for girls the masculine-failure condition is distinct from all others (see Table III). Girls tend to use *can* answers more if they fail in masculine tasks. On the other hand boys use *can* explanations under all conditions.

TABLE III    Frequency of responses in relation to outcome and type of task for girls and boys (in parentheses)

| Category | Task—Outcome | | | |
| | Success | | Failure | |
| | Masculine | Feminine | Masculine | Feminine |
|---|---|---|---|---|
| *Can* | 11 (14) | 12 (19) | 22 (15) | 11 (20) |
| *Difficulty* | 8 (12) | 6 ( 9) | 26 (25) | 5 (13) |
| *I don't know* | 10 ( 1) | 8 ( 2) | 9 ( 8) | 11 ( 4) |
| *Learned* | 8 ( 2) | 10 ( 4) | 5 ( 1) | 5 ( 2) |
| *Age* | 6 ( 5) | 2 ( 4) | 3 ( 3) | 3 ( 0) |

*Difficulty.* There are highly significant effects of outcome ($F$ [1,48] = 24.08; p<0.001), type of task ($F$ [1,48] = 72.2; p<0.001), and outcome × type of task interaction ($F$ [1,48] = 26.13; p<0.001). More *difficulty* attributions appear under failure as opposed to success, and following masculine as opposed to feminine tasks. Under failure in masculine tasks the frequency of *difficulty* answers is far higher than under the three other conditions. The sex × type of task interaction ($F$ [1,48] = 3.2; p<0.10) as well as the sex × outcome × type of task interaction ($F$ [1,48] = 3.3 p<0.10) are marginally significant. Boys under all conditions (except masculine-failure) give more *difficulty* answers than girls, especially after failure in feminine tasks. As can be seen in Table III, the masculine-failure condition minimises the sex difference, whereas feminine-failure emphasises it.

*I don't know.*   Although there is not a strong main effect of sex ($F$ [1,48] = 3.43; p<0.10) this is remarkable, as tests on the main effect of sex necessarily are less sensitive because sex is confounded with other differences between the groups (Winer, 1962, p. 299). Girls say '*I don't know*' far more often than boys (see Table III). This is true for all conditions except masculine-failure where the boys' use of 'I don't know' answers increases (see Table III, sex × outcome × type of task: $F$ [1,48] = 3.08; p<0.10).

*Learned.*   For this causal explanation a significant main effect of sex was found $F$ [1,48] = 4.89; p<0.05). Girls use it more often than boys, and this is true for all conditions. Moreover, the main effect of outcome approaches significance ($F$ [1,48] = 3.39; p<0.10). A success condition is more likely to evoke a causal explanation in terms of learning. In other words, the highest number of *learned* answers is given by girls under success conditions, whereas the lowest number of *learned* answers occurs for boys under failure. (This is summarised in Table III.)

*Age.*   A significant main effect of type of task ($F$ [1,48] = 4.57; p<0.05) shows that more *age* explanations are given following masculine tasks. Further, there is a marginally significant sex × outcome × type of task interaction ($F$ [1,48] = 3.60; p<0.10). Whereas for boys there is a difference between masculine and feminine tasks under the condition of failure (they give more *age* answers for failure in masculine tasks), girls differ between masculine and feminine tasks only under the condition of success (they give more *age* answers for success in masculine tasks).

*Summary.*   Table IV summarises the results in relation to the hypotheses regarding sex differences. The prediction that there would already be sex differences at the age of 4 was clearly confirmed.[5] As can be seen in Table IV the three hypotheses regarding sex differences were confirmed to different extents and on different causal factors. Girls' self-derogatory v. boys' self-enhancing attributions were found for all

TABLE IV  Summary of results, relating the findings within each causal factor to the hypotheses on the direction of sex differences

| | Can | | Difficulty | | I don't know | | Learned | | Age | |
|---|---|---|---|---|---|---|---|---|---|---|
| Sex of subjects | Girls | Boys | Girls | Boys | Girls | Boys | Girls | Boys | Girls | Boys |
| Frequency | 56 | 68 | 45 | 59 | 38 | 15 | 28 | 9 | 14 | 12 |
| ANOVA Main and interaction effects | Sex × type of task $p<0.01$ Sex × outcome × type of task $p<0.25$ | | Sex × type of task $p<0.10$ Sex × outcome × type of task $p<0.10$ | | Sex $p<0.10$ Sex × outcome × type of task, $p<0.10$ | | Sex $p<0.05$ | | Sex × outcome × type of task $p<0.10$ | |
| Girls' self-derogatory attributions | Girls use fewer *can* attributions than boys under all conditions except masculine-failure | | | | (a) Girls give more *I don't know* answers than boys, in general; they give no explanations for their successes | | Girls give more explanations in terms of *learned* than boys, especially under success | | Girls explain their unexpected success in sex-inappropriate tasks in terms of *age*, whereas | |
| versus Boys' self-enhancing attributions | Boys use *can* attributions more often than girls; they use *can* to explain their successes as well as failures | | Boys give more *difficulty* explanations than girls especially under feminine-failure conditions | | Boys lack explanations to the same extent as girls *only* under the masculine-failure condition | | | | | | Boys use *age* to defend their failures in masculine tasks |
| 'Learned helplessness' attributions in girls | Girls give more *can* attributions under masculine-failure than under other conditions | | | | Girls give more *I don't know* answers than boys, in general; they give no explanations for their failures | | Girls give *learned* explanations predominantly under success, not under failure | | | |
| Attributions to diminish ambivalence of success in girls | | | | | (b) Girls give more *I don't know* answers than boys, in general they give no explanations for their successes | | Girls give more explanations in terms of *learned* than boys, especially under success | | | |

causal factors. The hypothesis that attributions would favour attitudes of 'learned helplessness' in girls was confirmed in the case of *can, I don't know*, and *learned*. The prediction that girls would prefer attributions which can diminish the ambivalence of success was confirmed for *I don't know*, and *learned*.

*Discussion. Can.* The previous discussion of *can/know* as a causal factor showed that it serves to create links of responsibility between person and performance. In traditional terminology it is an internal causal factor, and therefore relevant for self-induced emotional rewards or punishments following achievements (Weiner, 1972). However, it is also a stable factor (acquired knowledge) in the case of success and a variable factor (potential enlargement of knowledge) in the case of failure.

It was found that boys make *can* attributions equally often under success and failure (33:35) thus using its dual character. Such a strategy is likely to provide confidence in one's performance. Girls use *can* less frequently than boys and do not make the same use of it as a strategy for self-enhancement. They use it more often under failure (33) than under success (23). Hence they will not obtain the positive internal reinforcement of success as often as boys. Linking failure rather than success to their own self concept will also lead to negative emotional consequences and expectancies of failure in the future. Boys increased their *can* attributions for sex-inappropriate tasks for both failure and success. Unlike girls they take responsibility for succeeding in sex-inappropriate tasks and do not avoid linking that with their self concept. Thus the present data confirm what has been found in various other studies. It is in line with boys' (men's) expectations to be able to do girl's (women's) tasks, but not the reverse (e.g. Deaux and Emswiller, 1974). In sum, the hypothesis of a self-enhancing attribution bias in boys and a self-derogatory one in girls was confirmed for the causal factor of *can*.

The only outcome condition in which girls do not give fewer *can* attributions than boys is masculine-failure and the difference here is very small (see Table III). As has been shown, *can* attributions in the case of failure could serve to maintain hope for success and to encourage effort, if lack of knowledge were seen as changeable. Since girls use *can* attributions mainly if they fail in sex-inappropriate tasks it is unlikely that they see lack of knowledge as changeable. It may be assumed that lack of knowledge in a sex-inappropriate task will not have detrimental effects on the self concept as long as this concurs with the gender role prescribed by society. It will, however, prevent the person in question from acquiring knowledge in that area. Thus girls' *can* attributions seem to favour 'learned helplessness' attitudes in sex-inappropriate tasks.

*Difficulty.*    Failure in masculine tasks evokes the highest number of *difficulty* attributions for both sexes, whereas failure in feminine tasks reveals a sex difference as boys more often than girls believe that the task is too difficult (Table III). The boys' estimate is realistic because sex-inappropriateness of a task is very likely to mean less experience and skill in it. It is interesting, however, that failure in a sex-appropriate task leads to *difficulty* attributions only if the task is masculine. If girls fail in a sex-appropriate task they do not excuse it by pointing to the difficulty of the task. There is an underlying assumption, shared by both sexes, that masculine tasks are more difficult than feminine ones. As Deaux's (1976) review indicates, masculine tasks and activities are usually believed to involve more skills because of the higher status they are given in society and because of the higher competence attributed to the male stereotype. This could explain why boys give *difficulty* explanations for failure in sex-appropriate tasks to a greater extent than girls do. Such attribution patterns, however, have a self-derogatory bias for girls and a self-enhancing bias for boys.

*I don't know.*    The lack of causal explanations for one's own performance and its predominance among girls deserves special attention. As causal explanations of one's own success and failure are an integral part of achievement motivation (following the theory of Weiner and Heckhausen), their absence might also indicate a lack of this motivation.

Girls, not knowing the reasons for their success, will be deprived of the positive internal reinforcement (feeling proud or satisfied) which is a function of self-attributions (Heckhausen, 1978). Further, their expectations of future success will not be affected in a very systematic way, if there is no attribution of success to stable or to variable factors. If the expectations are inconsistent, however, the instrumental achievement behaviour (e.g. approaching or avoiding achievement situations; effort expenditure) will be inconsistent, too. Thus, whereas *I don't know* answers are self-derogatory as such, they are particularly so insofar as they imply not taking responsibility for success.

Boys hardly use *I don't know* answers except in the masculine-failure condition. This pattern makes sense, for if we assume that boys' expectations of success must be highest for perceived masculine tasks, then their experimentally manipulated failure in these tasks must seem inexplicable to them. Thus *I don't know* answers in the case of boys could reflect a very specific and sensible reaction to the discrepancy between expectation and performance. As girls are usually found to have lower expectations (e.g. Crandall, 1969) even for sex-appropriate tasks, there is no comparable discrepancy which could plausibly explain their reactions.

Until now, *I don't know* answers have been interpreted as an actual lack of causal explanations. Alternatively, they could be seen merely as a linguistic response pattern. *I don't know* explanations are likely to have a different history of reinforcement in boys and girls. In a society where achievement pressures and expectancies of higher competence are directed towards the male sex, *I don't know* is not a very suitable answer for boys and is unlikely to be accepted by adults. Girls' *I don't know* answers, on the other hand are readily accepted and thus reinforced, since 'not knowing' conforms to the feminine sex role stereotype. Thus even if the sex difference in *I don't know* answers is seen in terms of a verbal response pattern rather than a true difference in causal attribution, it clearly has self-derogatory implications for girls.

Not knowing the reasons for their own achievement outcomes also implies that girls do not know how to control their failure. Failures (like successes) will be seen as arbitrary. According to the theory of learned helplessness (e.g. Dweck and Repucci, 1973; Seligman, 1975) the consequences of not feeling in control of one's failures will be feelings of hopelessness, a lack of persistence, and deterioration of performance in the case of failure feedback. If there is no effort to overcome failure, however, there will also be no chance of contradicting the 'learned helplessness' attitude through success.

If there are reasons to assume conflicting achievement demands towards girls (because of the conflicting demands of the social role of women), the refusal causally to explain one's own achievements could be one way of escaping this conflict by cognitively distancing oneself from one's own achievements.

*Learned.* In order to understand girls' preference for this kind of causal attribution, its nature and definition need to be borne in mind. An answer was classified under the category of *learned* if it referred to any previous experience or familiarity with the material or activity in question. Compared with the category of *can/know* (which is preferred by boys) *learned* refers to the process of acquiring knowledge rather than the result of such an acquisition.

The girls in this study seem not only to be more aware of the necessity of the process of learning, becoming familiar with things, but also explain their successes predominantly in these terms. An explanation of success in terms of 'having learned how to do it' or 'having seen this before' (as opposed to 'knowing how to do it') is likely to diminish the internal reinforcement value of success. *Learning* does not, like knowledge, refer to ability, but to the need for training in and familiarity with something. Thus the data again confirm the hypothesised self-denigrating, rather than self-enhancing, attributions of girls.

In the case of failure, *learning* attributions could have the useful function of defending the self concept, by maintaining hope for future success and encouraging effort. This possibility, however, is used less often by girls (see Table III). The low number of *learned* attributions under failure may reflect girls' perceived uncontrollability of failure.

As a *learning* attribution is likely to weaken the link between a successful performance and the person, it can also be seen as a suitable strategy for solving the typically female conflict between positive and negative connotations of success. This interpretation is strengthened by the fact that girls actually give *learned* attributions predominantly under success conditions.

*Age.*   Causal explanations in terms of *age* can have, as explained, the dual function of being self-enhancing in the case of success and not self-denigrating in the case of failure. For young children age is also an indicator of competence and status. The main effect of type of task, showing that more age attributions are given for masculine tasks, can therefore be explained by the higher status and higher competence which are stereotypically linked with the concept of masculinity.

## Summary and conclusions

The main finding of the present study is that there already exist sex differences in achievement attributions at the age of four years. The direction of the sex differences is the same as in adults and can be linked to the prevailing sex role stereotypes which ascribe higher competence to males than to females: (*i*) girls show a pattern of attributions which is clearly self-derogatory in its consequences; (*ii*) there are indications of an attitude of 'learned helplessness' in the use of three causal factors; (*iii*) with regard to two causal factors, girls seem to use attributions in such a way as to diminish (now or at some later stage of development) the ambivalence of success which is rooted in the incompatibility of the female stereotype with successful achievements.

The fact that sex differences found in adults are apparent at such an early age is relevant to both developmental and practical (educational) concerns. All the sex differences found in this study have been shown to be clearly disadvantageous for girls. The attributions given by girls prevent the development of achievement motivation and confidence in their own ability, and do not prepare them for coping effectively with failure. The study suggests that by the time children enter school these biased attribution patterns already exist. It can be expected that teachers will share the same sex role stereotypes as the primary socialisation agents. Thus the self-attribution patterns, apart from maintaining themselves, are likely to be confirmed by the causal attributions teachers give in response to children's performances (see Dweck *et al.*, 1978 on feedback patterns of teachers which favour 'learned helplessness' attributions in girls).

Education is an area where research on sex differences in achievement attributions could be of demonstrable practical relevance. Educational psychologists and teachers could be trained to perceive the practical consequences of achievement attributions and their dependence on sex role stereotypes. Modification programmes (see Dweck, 1975; Krug and Hagel 1976) for children with disadvantageous attribution patterns could be developed, but will only have lasting effects if teachers' attributions are changed at the same time.

Following from the foregoing, three major lines of future research are regarded as necessary. First, longitudinal studies should be set up in order to separate general cognitive developmental changes from the development of sex differences. Secondly, observational studies should be carried out in order to investigate how socialisation agents transmit stereotypical sex role expectations by the way they attribute causes to children's behaviour. Finally, an attempt should be made to develop and test modification strategies which could be applied in educational settings.

## Notes

1. This is an example of a sexist bias in psychological research which assumes the male to stand for the general, compared with which the female is a deviation (see Weinreich and Chetwynd, 1976).
2. This may be seen as a realistic estimate of the fact that women have to overcome more difficulties and barriers in a masculine profession, and therefore must be more motivated and show more effort to obtain the same results as men.
3. In the actual experiment two more dependent variables were included. The question 'Do you think you will be able to do that?' was asked before the task started (initial expectancy). Following failure subjects responded to the question 'Do you think you could do it if you tried harder?' (expectancy of success after failure, given effort).

   The data on these variables will not be reported in this chapter but interested readers may obtain them from the author.

4.  Readers interested in definitions and examples for all the categories may obtain
    them from the author.
5.  As can be seen from the results, not all the differences found reached the
    conventional level of statistical significance. This could possibly be overcome by
    future research controlling the following variables:
    1. perception of sex-type of task; 2. social class of subjects, and 3. subjects' level of
    cognitive development.

# Part III

# Social Attribution

# 8

# Social Attribution

Jean-Claude Deschamps

*Translated by* Miles Hewstone

## Introduction

Work on attribution in social psychology was made possible when an explicit cognitive psychology like Heider's (1958a) accorded an important place to the 'subject'. Behaviourism, to some extent, allowed the birth of contemporary social psychology by going beyond the study of the rigid organism to consider also the milieu in which this organism lives. However, it gives the subject a severely limited place by considering the individual only as the locus of a response to a stimulus. The reinforcement function of stimuli in learning theory makes man 'une machine à répondre'[1], passively reacting to stimuli (Moscovici, 1972). But contrary to the claims of reinforcement or conditioning theorists the subject is not passive but actively organises her/his goal(s) and is motivated by the search for cognitive equilibrium. For example, it is clear that to account for the celebrated research of Orne (1962), the individual must also be seen as 'une machine à inférer'[2] (Moscovici, 1972). We only understand why the subjects in the experiments carried out tasks which were meaningless, boring, rather disagreeable, apparently useless and without justification, if we assume that they made some sense of the situation and attributed some meaning to them (by, for example, thinking that they were taking part in an endurance test).

A few decades ago the subject began to be seen as an 'inference machine' and an actor, the perpetrator of a behaviour and not simply a reacting organism. This view had important consequences because a subject cannot be held responsible for his or her acts unless s/he is perceived as the source, or the cause, of this behaviour. However, an individual is not perceived as the source of an action unless s/he can choose – or give the impression of choosing – the behaviour. In other words, the individual becomes a subject when one can attribute to him or her the cause of, and then the responsibility for, personal acts; if this is not possible the individual remains dependent on the physical and social environment. In the first case, we are talking about internal causality where the individual as subject is autonomous or relatively autonomous. In the second case, we are talking of external causality: here the individual acts under the pressure of events, and is heteronomous.

The notion of attribution is very general and the extent of the domain covered by the idea of attribution leaves out almost nothing. As Da Gloria and Pagès (1974–1975) argue, this notion of attribution could be seemingly extended to the totality of mental activity. In this chapter, however, attention is directed primarily to one particular aspect of attribution, that of perceiving the causes of behaviour. Our aim will be to explore the implications of the prevailing notion of attribution and to see to what extent it is perhaps still an obstacle to the development of a really social psychological theory. In order to do this we will analyse the publications from which attribution theory grew, namely Heider's (1958a) monograph and the work of Jones and Davis (1965) and of Kelley (1967). An exhaustive discussion of these texts is not intended, nor do we claim to cover the multitude of recent developments brought about by the work of these authors. Instead, we focus on those aspects which will allow us to lay the foundations, or basic premises, of what might be called a theory of 'social attribution'.

## Attribution theory: A critical examination

Heider (1944, 1958a), but perhaps above all Jones (1979; Jones and Davis, 1965; Jones and Harris, 1967; Jones and Nisbett, 1972; Jones, Kanouse, Kelley, Nisbett, Valins and Weiner, 1972) and Kelley (1967, 1971, 1972a, 1973) are certainly the authors whose contributions to the study of attribution processes are the most important for social psychology. It is from a discussion of these works that we can lay the foundations of a study of the mechanisms of inference which goes beyond the level of interindividual relations, and which no longer unfolds in an empty social context in which personal 'involvement' is negligible. First of all we would like to point out that for Jones and Davis differentiation between individuals is most important. Kelley, on the other hand, tries to explain how a subject eliminates all actor differentiation of this sort in order to attain an 'objective' reality which is not tied to a particular individual. For Heider, attribution results from the individual's need to organise the environment in a coherent manner and permits the search for its invariant features. He considers behaviour from a purely cognitive point of view (the same is true for Kelley as we shall see later), but insists that the object, or 'distal stimulus', has a reality of its own: 'whatever its designation, it [the distal stimulus or initial focus], refers to the environmental reality, an objective stimulus defined by properties perceivable by everyone' (Heider, 1958a, p. 23, parentheses added). It seems then that, according to Heider, for whom naive perception is already pre-scientific, the search for the stable is linked with the search for 'reality' (or for the 'truth'), the object having intrinsic properties that all 'subjects' can perceive.

In their paper Jones and Davis (1965) concentrate on the perception of others. They seek to understand how a subject attains a specific truth about an observed individual and attempt to isolate the conditions for attributing stable personal dispositions to another on the basis of observed actions. The subject makes inferences about the actor's intentions which permit the attribution of a personal disposition to the individual. It is thus the specific effect of an act, generally low in social desirability (and thus 'deviant' according to the social norm), which reveals the stable, personal characteristics of the actor. What is 'real' about a subject is identified by Jones and Davis with the personal; the true person resides in idiosyncrasy and is opposed to what might seem like a simple social role. We would argue, however, that the assumption of a role can be individualised (for example by the interpretation of a role, by a personal style of behaviour, etc.) without necessarily being deviant. Jones and Davis' model has been summarised as follows: '. . . l'attribution de caractéristiques individuelles s'identifie donc à l'attribution de caractéristiques déviantes: la théorie ne permettant aucune inférence face aux autres types de comportements (Apfelbaum and Herzlich, 1970–1971, p. 963).[3]

But if finding a personal disposition is confounded with deviant characteristics, deviance becomes an individual disposition opposed to the norm which is culturally determined and socially shared. Thus Jones and Davis see deviance as freely chosen and uncommon. This notion of deviance can be defined minimally as a collection of behaviours involving transgression of powerful norms and enforced rules within a society. Take as an example the establishment of a new group with a new set of norms. The norms of such a group are deviant with respect to society and thus deviance is much more the norm of this group than an individual characteristic. In this case, contrary to Jones and Davis, the deviant character of an act need not imply that its origin is personal. It might even be argued that, in the case of deviance, group characteristics rather than personal characteristics will be attributed to individuals. This might occur in the case where individuals refer to their group membership, or where such membership is inferred. In this manner even the most bizarre behaviour need not be seen as individualistic. Thus we might for example, attribute an instance of abnormal behaviour not to personal dispositions, but to the actor's membership of a particular group, that is, a group of mental patients. Steiner and Field's (1960) results support this line of reasoning. Contrary to the propositions of Jones and Davis, the variable freedom of choice was not found to influence attributions. Steiner and Field argue that it is the attitude of the confederate (who defends a segregationist position and so in relation to anti-segregationist subjects represents a social category) which has the greatest effect on the attributions made by subject observers.

As we have just mentioned, it is the dichotomy between the personal and the social (or, for Jones and Davis, between on the one hand the non-common, the deviant, the freely chosen and on the other hand what is assimilated to the norm, the general, the imposed) which we find debatable in this model. Nothing is less certain than the claim that it is the personal pole which is more informative than the social pole. As the research of Steiner and Field indicates, the social nature of an act seems able, in many cases, to be at least as informative as the personal or the freely chosen.

For Kelley (1967), attribution is an inferential process which enables the individual to 'know' the environment. According to Kelley, subjects are assumed to behave like statisticians, devoting themselves to objective information processing. This processing of information consists of an analysis of variance integrating information coming simultaneously from objects in the environment (entities), persons interacting with these objects and the consistency of behaviour (both in time and as a function of the circumstances of the interactions with the objects). However, it is quite clear that nothing proves that 'naive' subjects behave like statisticians. As Lemaine, Desportes and Louarn (1969) remarked, it seems to be: '. . . une erreur épistémologique de croire qu'un agent social, dans la vie quotidienne, *cherche* à avoir une vue "objective" ou "scientifique" du monde dans lequel it doit se comporter . . .' (Lemaine *et al.*, 1969, p. 242).[4]

We might also question whether subjects discern Kelley's dimensions and furthermore classify them as sources of variation corresponding to persons, entities and time/modalities. It should be acknowledged that these four factors already constitute an initial form of cognitive organisation. These factors are, therefore, to some extent, the products of, rather than the input to, an attribution process. On this matter Da Gloria and Pagès note that: 'En dehors d'une illusion naturaliste, les choses, les personnes et leurs propriétés utilisables par le sujet dans un but classificatoire, sont difficilement concevables autrement que comme des produits des attributions' (Da Gloria and Pagès, 1974–1975, p. 231).[5]

Kelley also postulates, as we have seen above, that the individual is driven by the search for the real, the 'real' being an intrinsic property of the object. Moreover, the fact that Heider had already emphasised attributional errors illustrates the fact that, in this view, inferential processes have the clear aim of leading to a 'real' knowledge of the properties of objects, 'properties perceived by everyone'. As Apfelbaum and Herzlich write, to aspire to this objective knowledge:

Pour le sujet, attribuer, rechercher le vrai, s'identifie à enregistrer passivement l'environnement. Passif dans sa recherche d'objectivité, l'individu ne peut être que neutre vis-à-vis de l'objet, et non impliqué dans sa propre action. (Apfelbaum and Herzlich, 1970–1971, p. 973)[6]

This theory of attribution seems to apply to an isolated subject, detached from the social context, passive with regard to the world which surrounds him or her. The social dimension of attribution is not envisaged. At one and the same time this model is both too simple and too complex. As Moscovici and Faucheux (1972) demonstrated in their studies on social influence, if there is attribution of stable properties to the environment, this attribution does not involve simple information processing, but should be defined in terms of exchange or of negotiation between the self and others. Subjects do not seek an objective view of reality at all costs. In order to understand subjects' attributions one has to take into account the influence processes at work in both inter- and intragroup relations. For Kelley, socially constructed reality is opposed to the conception of a physical reality. Kelley includes consensus in his model, but he seems to assert that physical and social reality are independent and that, in the last resort, it is physical reality (a constant reality of which one can have a veridical picture) which is more important for the subject. However, contrary to this view, it appears that sometimes, in perceiving the causal structure of the environment, attributions are made much more as a function of social phenomena (e.g., intergroup differentiation), than as a function of real, objective characteristics of the situation. This leads us to take up the distinction, often asserted in social psychology (e.g. Festinger, 1950) between physical and social reality. Social reality has for a long time been conceived of as a distorted substitute for physical reality, but, as Tajfel remarked: 'La réalité sociale peut être aussi "objective" que la réalité non sociale et inversement, l'"objectivité" peut être aussi sociale qu'elle est physique' (Tajfel, 1972, p. 294).[7]

In the first place 'objective' non-social reality only acquires meaning in a given social context and in addition the so-called 'objective' means available are often not used, because of the social (or consensual) reality of the nature of a phenomenon. In these conditions, social reality is as objective as physical reality and there may be a greater range of situations in which social criteria are used in attribution processes, than in which 'objective' non-social criteria are utilised. Not only can we think that: 'Le caractère d'"objectivité" ne peut avoir pour base une classification de phénomènes en "sociaux" et "non sociaux" ' (Tajfel, 1972, p. 294),[8] but the problem is also that of knowing whether social reality, as Moscovici and Faucheux (1972) suggested, is one of the factors constituting physical reality, rather than one of its substitutes. In our view, social reality should no longer be considered as a distortion of 'objective' physical reality, but as the real basis of human activity.

Taking account of these criticisms, it can be argued that the 'pioneering' works on attribution tend to forget the role of the social context in inference processes, in order to emphasise personal factors or the intrinsic properties of objects. In particular we assert that individuals are also invariably members of various social groups, and frequently act as a function of their membership of these social groups. The thesis which we defend here is that these multigroup memberships of collectivities, categories and social classes influence attributions. The basic criticism which we level at the original attribution studies is that these works concern only interindividual relations which take place in a context where reference to group membership has been carefully eliminated, or in an intragroup context. However, these interindividual and intragroup relations depend to some extent on the relations between groups, if only for the reason that no group exists, is conscious of itself or has an individuality, except in relation to other groups and in an intergroup context. We might even question whether intergroup and interpersonal relations are of a different 'nature' and whether, in most cases, interindividual relations are not already, at least potentially or symbolically, relations between groups.

Certain studies seem to indicate that an analysis of attribution in terms of the relations between groups is well founded. We review here a number of these studies which will allow us to discuss in more detail the social nature of attribution processes.

## Attribution and intergroup relations

In the abovementioned study by Steiner and Field (1960), the notion of choice within a role is introduced. More precisely, the central variable in this research is that the role taken up in a discussion by a confederate appears to be either freely chosen or assigned by the experimenter. We saw that the freedom of choice dimension had no influence on attributions, but that it was the confederate's attitude (his segregationist stance representing a different social category for the non-segregationist subjects) which had the greatest impact on the attributions of the subjects. In other words, this study can be reinterpreted within the framework of intergroup or intercategory relations.

The problem which Thibaut and Riecken (1955) attempted to resolve was somewhat different. These authors hypothesised that an individual would perceive the source of the 'compliant' behaviour of another (an experimental confederate) as internal in the case of a high status, powerful person, and as external when the person was of low status and powerless. The results demonstrated that the manipulation of the confederate's status did induce in the subjects a different perception of the confederate's ability to resist influence: the high status confederate, before the experiment proper, is perceived as less susceptible to influence than the low status confederate. In the post-experimental discussions, the subjects located the source of causality as external for the low status confederate and internal for the high status person. In other words, the subjects think that the low status confederate has been influenced by their communication, thus attributing his compliant behaviour to an external cause, whereas they believe that the high status confederate has not been influenced by their communication, and that the cause of his behaviour is internal.

In the experiment by Thibaut and Riecken (1955), as in that by Steiner and Field (1960), the results seem above all due to the fact that the stimulus persons were defined by their belonging to different categories. However, these studies certainly do not provide serious empirical support for our assertion that category membership influences attribution, as this variable is not explicitly examined in these studies. We will now deal with attribution more strictly within the framework of intergroup relations.

A first experiment, carried out by Taylor and Jaggi (1974) in southern India allows us to demonstrate the importance of category memberships for attribution. In an initial phase of this study, the authors show that the subjects (all of the Hindu religion) evaluate their own group more favourably than they evaluate the Muslim religious sect (an antagonistic group in the Indian context). In the second part of this study, the subjects were confronted with a series of passages describing the behaviour of an actor in a social context. The actor was either Hindu or Muslim and his behaviour was either socially desirable or socially undesirable. Following each passage four or five possible reasons for the actor's behaviour in this situation were presented. One of these reasons reflected an internal attribution of causality to the actor for his behaviour and the other alternatives referred to external attributions of causality for the actor's behaviour. The subjects had to indicate which of the possible alternatives, in their opinion, explained the actor's behaviour. It was predicted that the attribution of causality for a desirable behaviour would be more internal for stimulus persons belonging to the same group as the subjects (thus, for the Hindus), and more external for stimulus persons from the other group (the Muslims). For the undesirable act, the authors expected inverse attributions of causality, that is to say, more external for ingroup members (Hindus) and more internal for outgroup members (Muslims). The results verified these predictions.

In another study (Duncan, 1976), white American students watched a videotaped interaction between a black person and a white person, and then had to describe the behaviour of the protagonists. The same act perpetrated by the black protagonist was more often characterised as violent than when it was perpetrated by the white protagonist. Furthermore, when the aggressor was black, the subjects perceived his behaviour as due to a personal disposition (they attributed causality internally) whereas when the aggressor was white, his behaviour was attributed more to the situation, or to external constraints.

Although Taylor and Jaggi (1974), and Duncan (1976), explicitly introduce intergroup relations into their studies, they only focus on attributions to the ingroup and to the outgroup from the point of view of members of a single group. Other studies examine the reciprocal attributions between groups.

One study (Deschamps, 1972–1973) allows us to demonstrate the influence of category membership on reciprocal attributions. This experiment was carried out at 'wolf cub' camp (a division of the 'boy scout' movement) in France. Groups of 12 children were made up, within which there were multiple divisions (known to each other/not known to each other; membership of the same 'six' at camp/ membership of a different 'six' at camp). Within these groups, each child completed a number of pencil and paper games in the presence of others. Each group was placed in competition with another group and the winning group was the one whose members completed the greatest total number of tasks. In fact, winning and losing were determined according to the experimental design. The subjects then had to attribute a particular level of competence to each member of their group (by individually writing down their estimations of how well each member of their group performed). The results show that the competence attributed to another is greater when this person belongs to the same categories as the subject (knowledge or same six) than when he is not part of these categories (no knowledge or other six). However, there is no difference between the success and failure conditions with regard to favouring the ingroup. In the case of failure, the cause of the behaviour is attributed internally to members of the categories to which the subjects do not belong (they are perceived as performing poorly and as being responsible for the group's failure). The cause of failure for members of the categories to which the subjects do belong is externally attributed (they are seen as more competent and cannot be seen, in these conditions, as being responsible for the group's failure). The inverse would be true for the case of success – the cause of the behaviour being internally attributed for members of the same category as the subjects (these members having more ability and being held responsible for the group's success). The cause of the behaviour would be externally attributed for members of the categories to which the subjects did not belong.

However, we should be wary of believing that internal causation of a positive effect is always attributed to the ingroup, and that internal causation for a negative effect is systematically attributed to the outgroup. The existence of 'ethnocentric' phenomena, demonstrated in the experiments of Taylor and Jaggi (1974), Duncan (1976) and Deschamps (1972–1973), is indisputable. However, such results, concealing as they do a part of reality, run the risk of leading only to an incomplete model, one which assumes the universality of ethnocentric responses. Such a model risks making co-existing groups into 'equals' or, at the least, interchangeables and it tends to overlook the fact that at a given moment one category or group is ideologically dominant in society.

Some authors are preoccupied with the influence of the relative status of co-existing categories on attributions. This is true, for example, of Mann and Taylor (1974) who, in a study using French Canadian and English Canadian subjects, were able to show that the factors which play a role in the attribution of causality to different cultural groups (English Canadians or French Canadians) or to different social classes (middle-class or working-class, the subjects themselves being middle-class) depend on the relative socio-cultural positions of the subjects.

In a study bearing on the explanation of success on a task, Deaux and Emswiller (1974) demonstrate that what is attributed to ability for a man is attributed to luck for a woman. Subjects, male and female students, had to evaluate the same achievement of a male or female stimulus person in a task specified as masculine or feminine. The two types of task presented, masculine and feminine, were indeed perceived as such by subjects of both sexes and the performance of male and female stimulus persons was perceived similarly by subjects. The results show, as the authors predicted, that the performance of the male stimulus person is attributed to internal causes (competence) when the task is masculine and that, in the same tasks, an identical performance by a female stimulus person is attributed to external causes (luck), results which are valid both for male and female subjects. On the other hand, and contrary to the authors' predictions, the inverse is not true for a feminine task in which a male stimulus person is perceived as being as competent as a female stimulus person, a result which again held for both male and female subjects. If one considers each stimulus person as representing his or her sexual category, this experiment shows that the position of social groups or categories in a social structure plays a role in the internal or external attribution of causality to individuals belonging to these groups or categories. Other studies (see Deschamps, 1977a; Deschamps and Doise, 1978; Deschamps, Doise, Meyer and Sinclair, 1976; Doise, Deschamps and Meyer, 1978) also seem to show clearly that attributions between groups depend on the relative positions which the groups occupy in the social context.

To summarise this short review of relevant research, internal or external causal attribution appears to be a function of a person's belonging to certain social categories which have a specific value in the eyes of the observing subjects. Stated slightly differently, in a great number of situations we do not attribute to another personal or intrinsic qualities reflecting individual intentions, but rather characteristics of the group to which s/he belongs or to which s/he has been assigned. This is done as a function of the respective positions which the categories occupy and the relations between groups.

## Towards a theory of social attribution

In several texts (Deschamps, 1973–1974, 1977a, 1978; Hewstone and

Jaspars, 1982a,c), the social nature of attributional phenomena has already been discussed and the foundations of an alternative perspective laid. This has involved, initially, a critique of earlier work. We have seen that, for Jones and Davis (1965), the social is assimilated to the norm, to the general, and is not therefore informative of another's personal dispositions. Thus the social is opposed to the individual or personal which manifests itself in deviance. Given their emphasis on dispositional attributions these authors are then interested only in the attribution of internal causes. As for Kelley, he seems to affirm the primacy of 'physical reality' (consistency) over 'social reality' (consensus) in attribution processes. Thus Kelley concentrates on external attribution, in opposition to internal, or self, attribution. This alone, he argues, allows the subject to attain the stable properties of the environment. In addition, Kelley's theoretical approach to attribution is limited to social situations in which, as we have remarked, subjects are neutral and passive.

Attribution has not been considered, from a social psychological viewpoint, except as the act of an isolated subject, and it has only been studied in the perspective of interindividual relations. However, one might ask whether, at least from the perspective of the observer, the personal is really more informative than the social. The social perspective adopted here introduces the fact that individuals belong to different social groups which are important to them, which define them in a certain way and in terms of which they act. We can then ask whether, in the case of intergroup relations, we still attribute behaviour to individual characteristics, or to social group membership (see Apfelbaum and Herzlich, 1970–1971). Indeed, such an attribution process has been illustrated by studies reported in the previous section (e.g. Deaux and Emswiller, 1974; Deschamps, 1972–1973; Duncan, 1976; Taylor and Jaggi, 1974). A closely related question is whether, even in the case of interindividual relations, individuals characterise each other in terms of their respective group memberships. Even if this were true, one would still have a case of intergroup relations, at least at the symbolic level. We are led to think in these terms by the studies of both Steiner and Field (1960) and Thibaut and Riecken (1955). Both studies emphasise that social category memberships, rather than personal characteristics, may be important determinants of attribution. A meeting between individuals belonging to different groups can, at least in certain cases, make the difference of group membership salient and cause these individuals to see themselves and each other as representatives of their respective groups.

Our basic premise, based on the empirical evidence presented, is that attribution is not independent of the various networks of groups within which individuals are, at one and the same time, the sources and targets of multiple attributions. We will thus try to reconsider attribution, within the framework of a social psychology concerned with the relations between groups, and not only, as has so often been the case, within the framework of interindividual or intragroup relations. For this purpose, it is argued that there is no real difference in 'nature' between interindividual and intergroup relations and that, in most cases, interindividual relations are already, at least potentially and at the symbolic level, relations between groups.

Our central theoretical problem lies, however, beyond the questions raised in the preceding paragraphs. This is the question of whether inferential behaviour relies on an 'objective' knowledge of the environment (knowledge itself based on 'simple' information processing) or whether this activity draws on a 'social reality' which would be the product of groups, their interaction and their differentiation. It seems legitimate to start from the proposition that 'reality' is always socially constructed, through the interaction of individuals marked by their group and category memberships, and is not a given fact, worked out by isolated individuals. From this perspective, it is difficult to envisage the study of attribution processes without taking cognizance of research on intergroup relations, on interactions between individuals belonging to different social categories. Attribution, in one way or another, seems to be tied up with the different group allegiances of individuals. It can therefore be maintained that an understanding of such mechanisms of inference can only be achieved through the integration of these processes with the study of intergroup relations. For this reason intergroup research is drawn on in the attempt to elucidate attribution processes.

Research on categorisation suggests a number of important propositions for investigations of social attribution. Following Moscovici (1972) we conceptualise attribution, in the first place, as a process of putting representations into operation. Representation refers to both content and process. The content of a representation is part of the universe of opinions about an object, these opinions implying an underlying positive or negative attitude with regard to the object. As far as the processes at the core of a social representation are concerned, we single out here the process of categorisation. Indeed, categorisation supplies the system which allows for the concrete identification of situations, objects, persons and so on to which the practical norms of behaviour which are governed by a representation will be applied. In other words, a representation, as Moscovici (1961) mentions, not only orients conduct and behaviour by the nature of the social norms which it controls, but a representation also identifies circumstances where the norms it directs are applicable and at the same time provides a system of categories. A representation thus structures perception by obeying certain cognitive laws, in particular those of the categorisation process.

Studies on categorisation owe much to the work of Bruner (for example, 1957a, b, 1958). The notion of categorisation has been developed by Bruner in his theory of perception, perception for him being close to cognition. Thus, all perception is seen to involve an act of categorisation since perception:

... dépend de la construction d'un système de catégories en fonction desquelles on classe les stimuli (on) leur donne une identité et une signification plus complexe que dans une classification . . . (et) . . . dépend de la construction de tels systèmes de catégories, construites sur l'inférence de l'identité à partir d'indices ou de signes.   (Bruner, 1958, p. 42)[9]

A perceptual stimulus is placed in a category of items by the subject, on the basis of its similarities with and differences from items of different possible categories. Categorisation is therefore not different from the attribution of a stimulus to a class of stimuli. This is what has been called the inductive aspect of categorisation. Once these categories are made up, an item's membership in a category is used to associate with this item the characteristics of the category: this is the deductive aspect of categorisation. These categorisation processes allow for the explanation of inferences made about category member-ships, as well as for those made from these same category memberships. We may illustrate these attribution processes in the domain of the perception of physical stimuli by means of a study by Tajfel and Wilkes (1963) (see also Deschamps, 1977b; Marchand, 1970) which shows the effect of categorisation of physical stimuli on quantitative judgements. In certain conditions of this experiment, where subjects were asked to estimate the length of lines of different size, a classification in terms of a characteristic other than the physical dimension which subjects were asked to estimate was superimposed on this series of stimuli (a letter 'A' was added to the shorter lines and a letter 'B' to the longer lines). Thus the position of these stimuli on a physical dimension (length) was connected to the membership of a category superimposed on the stimuli. The results show that it is only in the conditions where a categorisation is superimposed onto the physical dimension that the differences between the shortest and the longest lines (classified as lines A and B respectively) are overestimated and that the differences between lines belonging to the same category ('A' for the shortest and 'B' for the longest) are underestimated. We can interpret the results of this study in the following manner; the subjects connected the stimuli presented to them with the characteristics of the category to which they belonged or were associated (the 'longer' lines or the 'shorter' lines), that is, they ascribed certain characteristics to the stimuli they judged, based on their belonging to two distinct categories. The difference between the characteristics of stimuli belonging to two categories was exaggerated when the most similar characteristics were attributed to stimuli within the same category. In this study of the perception of physical stimuli it can be said that the subjects inferred the characteristics of an object from the properties of the category to which it belonged. One of the effects of this process would be to minimise the differences between stimuli within the same category and to exaggerate the differences between stimuli belonging to two different categories.

The problem now is to ascertain what happens when one is interested in the perception of persons, and not in the classification of physical objects. The first point is that the perception of objects and related attributions are often anthropomorphic. In his research on the perception of causality Michotte found that subjects in his experiment involving the shape and movements of small geometric surfaces: '. . . ont, une propension étonnante à utiliser (pour décrire les éxperiences) des comparaisons avec l'activité humaine et animal' (Michotte, 1946, p. 277).[10]

Such a process concerns the projection of human intentions from interpersonal relations onto the physical world. One might then be tempted to assert that there is no fundamental difference between the apprehension of the physical world and the social world. There would be a homology between the attribution processes applying to 'objects' and to 'subjects' and both sets of inferential mechanisms would be founded on a system of categories.

However, when it is no longer physical stimuli which are divided into two categories, but individuals, subjects' behaviour with regard to the other category or group becomes systematically discriminatory (see for example Tajfel, Flament, Billig and Bundy, 1971). One then discovers that subjects have a tendency to favour the ingroup and to derogate the outgroup. Rather than an intergroup differentiation, it is really a differential treatment between and within the groups present. In other words, in the case of investigations into social causality, the inferring subject is situated within a network of categories as a function of which s/he makes attributions. We have seen above that categorisation involves an exaggeration of similarities between elements of the same category and an increase in the differences between elements of distinct categories. But, in addition, this exaggeration of intercategory differences and intracategory similarities is evaluative in the case of social categorisation and involves a positive evaluation of the membership of the ingroup in relation to the other group(s). This is what we denote by the term 'sociocentrism' (or 'ethnocentrism') to account for the finding that members of a group establish a distinction between themselves and the members of other groups at the behavioural, evaluative and representational levels. (For a full discussion of social categorisation, see Tajfel, 1972, 1978, and of the extension of this process to what we have called category differentiation, see Deschamps, 1979; Deschamps *et al.* 1976; and Doise, 1973, 1976.)

In relation to this sketchy discussion of sociocentrism, we are led to wonder about the generality of such a phenomenon. This leads to a consideration of what is meant by this notion of a group. Definitions of the group which one finds in the literature comprise a common core as the group is defined by the interaction and interdependence of its members (see the work of Cartwright and Zander, 1953; also Bales, 1950; Homans, 1950; Lewin, 1948; Thibaut and Kelley, 1959). Thus the group is defined 'from within', that is to say there is a preoccupation with certain intragroup processes, as if the relations with the other social entities have no influence on the internal structure, or even on the existence of these groups. However, these elements are not sufficient to define a group (nor, moreover, a category of physical objects) because a group only has meaning in relation to other groups. As Tajfel argued:

Les caractéristiques de son propre groupe (son statut, sa richesse ou sa pauvreté, sa couleur de peau, sa capacité à atteindre ses buts) n'acquièrent de signification qu'en liaison avec les différences perçues avec les autres groupes ou les différences évaluatives ... la définition d'un groupe (national, racial ou tout autre) n'a de sens que par rapport aux autres groupes. Un groupe devient un groupe en ce sens qu'il est perçu comme ayant des caractéristiques communes ou un devenir commun, que si d'autres groupes sont présents dans l'environnement. (Tajfel, 1972, p. 295)[11]

We should note, however, that relations between groups, even at the the symbolic level, are often asymmetrical. Groups such as 'children' or 'old people', 'women', 'blacks', 'manual workers' or 'workers' and so on are not equivalent or interchangeable with groups such as 'adults' 'males', 'whites', 'the bourgeoisie'. Age, sex, race and social position assign these groups a specific place in the social relations of production. Power relations will then emerge in this context of interdependence between groups. Dominant groups will maintain their dominant position over these other groups. This is important for attribution, because the all round positive evaluation of the ingroup will, in the case of 'dominated' groups, be difficult because the devalued image reflected by society (or at least by a dominant model) sets itself against the 'sociocentric' tendency.


## Conclusion

We are now ready to advance, by way of a conclusion, several propositions concerning social attribution. The first point is to consider man (the inference machine) no longer as an isolated entity, but as an individual located within a network of groups or social categories, in terms of which he acts. We can then say that *the attribution process is a function of the category memberships (both real and symbolic) of an individual.*

Next, we return briefly to the very definition of attribution. For Heider (1958a) and perhaps even more for Jones and Davis (1965) and Kelley (1967), attribution is the process by which the subject infers a cause from an effect. Their accounts of causal inference rely upon a restricted model of attribution (e.g. in the case of Heider, factor analysis, or according to Kelley, analysis of variance). We believe that a wider, less restricted definition of attribution can be given in that attribution is seen as a process of organising the universe of the subject (both internal and external) and the environment (both physical and social). *Thus attribution is a process of putting representations into operation.*

We must add that social representations structure perception by obeying certain cognitive laws, in particular the processes of categorisation. As far as the process underlying intergroup representations is concerned, social representations structure the relations between groups. *Social categorisation is then one of the processes at the core of social attribution.*

These propositions, together with the preceding discussion, give rise to several predictions about social attribution. Amongst other things we can hypothesise that:

(1) Rather than an individual differentiation, a differentiation at the group level will be salient and subjects will infer the characteristics of another as a function of the perceived properties of the category (categories) or group(s) to which the other belongs (this allegiance may be claimed by the other or simply inferred by the subjects);

(2) Within the same category, individuals will, to some extent, be considered as 'carbon copies'. In other words, individuals will have a tendency to minimise the differences between characteristics attributed to members of the same group or category;

(3) The attribution of properties or characteristics to groups will be effected in such a way as to value the ingroup, that is, as a function of a 'sociocentric' dimension which leads to a systematic discrimination in favour of ingroups, *vis-à-vis* outgroups;

(4) On the other hand, when a group is socially subordinated by another group, the attribution process will turn out to be slightly different. In these conditions, the 'sociocentric' dimension (whose major effect is discrimination in favour of the ingroup in relation to other groups) will be thwarted by the negative image this 'dominated' group is given in intergroup relations. The 'sociocentric' dimension cannot then manifest itself in this condition.

To summarise, this chapter has argued that attribution theory can be made more social in a number of ways. First, we have pointed to the importance of intergroup variables as determinants of attribution. Closely linked to the first point, we have emphasised that the attribution process is based on beliefs about the social world – social representations. The final theoretical point has been to integrate the processes of social categorisation with attribution theory and to make a number of predictions for future research. All three of these additions to the theory make it a more adequate theory of causal attribution in the social world.

## Acknowledgements

This chapter was written within the framework of the research project No. 1.339-0.81 sponsored by the *Fonds National Suisse de la Racherché Scientifique* (FNRS).

## Notes – Translations

1   A response machine.
2.   An inference machine.
3.   . . . the attribution of individual characteristics is identified with the attribution of deviant characteristics: the theory permits no inference with respect to other types of behaviour.
4.   . . . an epistemological error to believe that a social agent, in everyday life, seeks an 'objective' or 'scientific' view of the world in which he must act. . .
5.   Outside of a naturalistic illusion, the objects, the persons and their properties of use to the subject for a classificatory purpose, are difficult to conceive of except as products of attributions.
6.   For the subject, to attribute, to search for the real, is identified with passive recording of the environment. Passive in his search for objectivity, the individual can only be neutral in relation to the object, and not involved in his own action.

7.  Social reality can be as 'objective' as non-social reality and inversely, 'objectivity' can be as social as it is physical.

8.  The character of 'objectivity' cannot have as its basis a classification of phenomena into 'social' and 'non-social'.

9.  . . . depends on the construction of a system of categories as a function of which one classifies stimuli, (one) gives them an identity and a meaning which is more complicated than in a classification, . . . (and) . . . depends on the construction of such systems of categories, constructed by inferring identity from cues or signs.

10.  . . . had a surprising propensity to use (to describe the experiments) comparisons with human and animal activity.

11.  Ingroup characteristics (status, wealth or poverty, colour of skin, ability to achieve goals) only acquire significance in connection with the perception of, and value attached to, outgroup differences. . . . The definition of a group (national, racial or any other) only has meaning in relation to other groups. A group becomes a group in the sense that it is perceived as having common characteristics or a common origin and only if there exist other groups in the environment.

# 9

# The Role of Language in Attribution Processes

## Miles Hewstone

### Introduction

In a typical attribution experiment a subject is presented with a brief, written vignette describing an action or segment of behaviour. The subject's task is to read the vignette and then ascribe the described behaviour to a cause (e.g. McArthur, 1972). Alternatively, the subject may listen to another person, reading an essay perhaps (e.g. Jones and Harris, 1967), and then have to attribute that behaviour to a given cause. As a final example, the subject may observe and listen to someone on a videotape and then have to make a number of attributional judgements concerning the other (e.g. Storms, 1973). In all three types of experiment (and possibly in other attributional experiments, for these three do not exhaust all possibilities) language will play a role. On the one hand, there is what this chapter will refer to as *stimulus language*, such as the type of syntax the vignette contains, or the speech rate, volume and so on adopted by the essay reader or videotape actor. Just what effect such features may have on the attribution process has received scant attention, a fact that this chapter aims to rectify. On the other hand, there is *response language*. In each of the three experiments outlined subjects are asked to make some sort of rating, on *a priori* response scales. But what effect might the labelling of the end-points of such scales have on the ensuing attributions? Would the subject have responded differently with differently labelled scales, or with a free-response format?

Both aspects of the role of language will be explored in this chapter. First, however, some conceptual clarification is required. A number of contributions to this volume (e.g. see chapters 1 and 2) have posed the question: 'What gets attributed in attributional research?' Studies reviewed in this chapter are varied in this respect. Sometimes researchers have examined the *traits* attributed to a speaker on the basis of his or her speech style, sometimes *causes* are ascribed, sometimes *responsibility* is attributed. Whilst reluctant to ignore the clarification of attributional concepts in these chapters, the present chapter is hamstrung by a meagre pool of research on which to draw. Thus it is sometimes general inferences on the basis of language which are discussed, while at other times specifically attributional research is available. This state of affairs is not desirable, but the author will make clear the nature of the social judgement wherever research is discussed.

Stimulus language is dealt with first, spanning from micro-linguistic work on syntax to macro-linguistic work on speech styles. This section concludes with a discussion of the implications of this work for attribution studies. The second major section of the chapter is concerned with response language and again spells out the implications of this work for attribution. Taken together these two strands of theory and research make a strong claim for a future concern with the linguistic aspects of attribution research.

## Stimulus language

In their attributional analysis of moral judgements Ross and DiTecco (1975) provide a useful analysis of the attribution process. They refer specifically to the attribution of responsibility, but it can be argued that their analysis applies to attribution in general. They note that two separate phases of the process have been specified (by Jones and Thibaut, 1958 and Shrauger and Altrocchi, 1964), namely, the selection of cues from available information and the drawing of inferences from these cues. This two-phase process assumes that there is too much information in an experimental situation (probably in any situation) for observers completely to assimilate and their response to this overloading is to categorise and simplify. Where there is very little evidence available there is obviously not the same overloading problem, but subjects may still focus on a particular aspect of the stimulus material and in this chapter we draw attention to their focus on linguistic cues. Where there is more information available we have to explain why subjects focus on language, but this problem is considered below, when dealing with interpersonal attributions. First we outline the micro-linguistic studies which have concentrated on the influence of very minor linguistic details.

MICRO-LINGUISTIC STUDIES

The micro-linguistic approach to the relationship between language

and attribution is typified by the work of Kanouse (1972). This approach
is crystallised in his statement that:

The way in which a given phenomenon is described is almost certain to affect the
way in which it is explained. There are at least two ways in which labeling can
affect causal attribution. First, the language used to describe events and actions
frequently contains implicit attributions in itself. Second, the level of generality
used in describing a given phenomenon is likely to influence the level of
generality at which the phenomenon is explained. (Kanouse, 1972, p. 133)

Although Kanouse's approach is explicitly psycholinguistic, as
examples from his work make clear, his arguments have important
implications for *social* psychology. In addition, he was the first researcher
to draw attention to the link between language and attribution.

Kanouse demonstrates this first point by referring to work on 'implicit
quantification' (e.g. Abelson and Kanouse, 1966). This attempts to
specify the minimal amount of evidence required to justify an assertion.
Consider Kanouse's example, 'Artists buy magazines'. What criteria
are set by the subject for the justification of this assertion? Does s/he
require that 'all', 'most', 'many' or 'a few' artists buy magazines? And
how many magazines must be purchased – 'a few', 'many' etc? In their
experiment Abelson and Kanouse provided subjects with a number of
such assertions and had them mark on an 'implicit quantifier scale'
(choosing from 'a few', 'many' etc.) what information they required
before accepting the statement. Thus, if a subject accepted the above
assertion, on the basis that 'Some artists buy a few magazines', the
relevant quantifiers ('some' and 'a few') were indicated on the scale. The
quantifier chosen was found to vary with the sentence verb. Thus, the
two types of verb identified by Gilson and Abelson (1965), 'manifest' and
'subjective' verbs, were found to require different quantifiers. Subjective
verbs (verbs that denote feelings) required more evidence prior to
justifying the assertion than manifest verbs (verbs that denote actions).

These same verb types had implications for another type of implicit
attribution – the extent to which the subject agreed with a generalisation. Inferences about generality were examined by providing
subjects with the following kind of problem:

Altogether there are three kinds of tribes:
Southern tribes, Northern tribes and Central tribes.
Northern tribes buy bees.
Southern tribes do not buy bees.
Central tribes do not buy bees.
Do tribes buy bees? (Kanouse, 1972, p. 122)

Manifest verbs (like buy in the above example) were found to produce greater rates of agreement to generalisation (or inductive inference) than subjective verbs. Such studies show that subjects respond quite differently to similar evidence expressed in terms of different verbs.

We can now move to Kanouse's second point, concerning the relation between the level of generality at which a phenomenon is described and the level of generality at which it is explained. Kanouse makes clear the link between this point and Jones and Davis' (1965) discussion of correspondent inferences. Thus the kind of question at issue is: How do we move from the description of behaviour (e.g. 'John hit Peter') to its explanation (e.g. 'John hit Peter because John is aggressive')? To answer this question Kanouse draws on a study by Kanouse and Gross (1970) which investigated how the individual moves from a certain piece of evidence to a conclusion. Kanouse takes as an example the piece of evidence 'O destroys *Reader's Digests*' and the conclusion 'O hates magazines'. He argues that one could move from the evidence to the conclusion either directly, or via one of two intermediate steps. First, one could infer that 'O destroys magazines'. This inference process can be represented as follows:

(1)      O destroys *Reader's*          Therefore O destroys          Therefore O hates
              *Digests*→                           magazines→                        magazines
                 (a)                                       (b)                                   (c)

Secondly, one could infer that 'O hates *Reader's Digests*' and then move to the conclusion. This process can be represented similarly:

(2)      O destroys *Reader's*          O hates *Reader's*             Therefore O hates
              *Digests*→                           *Digests*→                        magazines
                 (a)                                       (b)                                   (c)

Although paths (1) and (2) look very similar, Kanouse argues, on the basis of Abelson and Kanouse's (1966) results, that the path taken is most important. He reiterates the earlier made point that it is easier to make inductive inferences on the basis of manifest verbs than on the basis of subjective verbs. In other words, step $(a) \rightarrow (b)$ in (1) is easier than step $(b) \rightarrow (c)$ in (2). Assuming that the leap from destroy to hate is similar for both paths, then path (1) should be faster. This prediction was corroborated by Kanouse and Gross (1970).

Details of further experiments in this vein are given in Kanouse's (1972) work. These lead him to conclude that, 'path differences occur when the intermediate inferences in the two paths differ with respect to their ability to explain or account for the initial evidence sentence' (p. 130). This point is most clear-cut when one verb is manifest and the other subjective; as Kanouse demonstrates, hating *Reader's Digests* 'explains' destroying them, while the same is not true of destroying magazines.

This second of Kanouse's main points has clear implications for attribution research. The ease of making certain inferences will be determined by the particular verb type involved. Once again we are led to the conclusion that the language used in simple descriptions has an important, if subtle, influence on attributions.

Although Kanouse's work bears on attributional phenomena and appears in a volume on this topic (Jones, Kanouse, Kelley, Nisbett, Valins and Weiner, 1972) its implications are perhaps more evident in McArthur's (1972) well-known study. This experiment is generally cited for its examination of Kelley's (1967) informational criteria – consensus, consistency and distinctiveness. However, it also invest-igated a number of psycholinguistic issues and only results relating to these issues are presented here. McArthur presented to subjects a 16-item questionnaire which reported responses made by actors, for example, 'John laughs at the comedian'. The 16 different responses represented four verb categories – emotions, accomplishments, opinions and actions. Subjects in the control condition received a straightforward written description, or vignette, of each response with no additional information. Experimental subjects received the same descriptions followed by some combination of consensus, consistency and distinctiveness information, such as: 'John laughs at the comedian. Almost everyone who hears the comedian laughs at him. John does not laugh at almost any other comedian. In the past John has almost always laughed at the same comedian' (*Adapted* from McArthur, 1972, p. 174).

In all cases the subject's task was to attribute the described response to one of a number of causal factors – something about the person, the stimulus, the circumstances or some combination of these factors.

The results for verb categories are perhaps best dealt with in terms of each of the above causal factors, but results will only be reported in detail for person and stimulus attributions.[1] For subjects in the experimental condition person attributions were found more for accomplishments and actions than for emotions and opinions. How-ever, this result did not emerge from an analysis of variance on the frequency of person attributions, but from a one-degree-of-freedom test contrasting emotions and opinions with actions and accomplishments. For subjects in the control condition a significant verb category main effect emerged from the analysis of variance. This revealed the following descending order of person attributions: accomplishments > actions > opinions > emotions. For stimulus attributions a significant verb category main effect emerged from the analysis of variance for subjects in both conditions. The following descending order of stimulus attributions was obtained: emotions > opinions > accomplishments > actions.

McArthur concluded that the nature of the response affects its causal attribution. She also drew attention to the consistent pattern of verb category effects: accomplishments and actions leading to significantly more person attributions and less stimulus attributions than emotions and opinions. These verb effects were discussed in terms of Gilson and Abelson's (1965) manifest – subjective verb dimension. McArthur also cites Heider's (1958a) suggestion that we tend to attribute enjoyment to the object (i.e. the stimulus), rather than the person. She goes on to argue that this tendency applies to other emotions and to opinions; thus we see emotions and opinions as being *elicited by stimuli*. In contrast, accomplishments and actions tend to be perceived as being *emitted* by persons.

It is interesting to compare the relative importance of verb category in the experimental and control conditions. It is certainly not surprising that in the absence of information pertaining to consensus, consistency and distinctiveness subjects' causal attributions are strongly influenced by the nature of the verb type used to describe the response. This is clear from the vastly different role of the verb category for experimental and control subjects (see Table I). However, the comparatively minor importance of verb category for experimental subjects should not be taken as insignificant. Referring to table 2 in McArthur (1972) the reader will note that the percentage of variance accounted for by consensus information is of a similar order.[2]

TABLE I   Percentage of total variance in causal attributions accounted for by verb category. (From McArthur, 1972, Table 2)

| Condition | Causal attribution | | | |
|---|---|---|---|---|
| | Overall | Person | Stimulus | Circumstance |
| Experimental | 1.02 | 0.97 | 2.85 | 0.17 |
| Control | 45.03 | 57.46 | 51.02 | 68.68 |

Despite the significant results of this study there is a problem in assuming that it is the verb type that is responsible for the obtained results. It may be that if one were to show on a videotape both actions and emotions, they would receive person and stimulus attributions respectively. To summarise, McArthur's study shows that in a vignette-type attribution experiment the stimulus language may significantly influence the emerging pattern of causal attributions. Although there is some doubt as to whether the verb category represents a purely linguistic effect, the difference between the experimental and control conditions makes an important point. The more limited and simplistic the material is, the greater the effect of the stimulus language may be.

## MACRO-LINGUISTIC STUDIES

The studies of Kanouse and McArthur demonstrate the role of language in the absence of almost all other variables. Where the situation is more complex, however, we must look for reasons to explain the influence of language. This question has been faced in a number of recent social psychological writings on language (e.g. Giles, 1979a; Giles, Scherer and Taylor, 1979; Giles, Robinson and Smith, 1980; Smith, Giles and Hewstone, 1979). Giles et al. (1979) acknowledge that there are many cues to interpersonal judgements other than language. Style of dress and personal appearance spring readily to mind, but there are occasions on which speech markers are especially important – for example, when other cues are not available. In addition, certain kinds of speech markers (level 1 markers) categorise individuals in broad terms (e.g. age, sex and ethnic group membership) which the individual is often not at liberty to control or obscure. Thus they may be taken as relatively accurate indicators. In addition to these reasons why linguistic variables may be important in social interaction and may affect attributions, Giles et al. (1979) draw attention to the two main functions served by speech markers. The first is called the 'cognitive organisational' function and refers to the activity of making sense of the world, by categorising others and 'filtering' social information. According to these authors the use of speech markers in this manner provides knowledge about how to behave, generates predictions concerning the outcome of an interaction and so on. The second function, the 'identity maintenance' function, refers to the manner in which speech markers provide a speaker with the opportunity for self-definition in a chosen manner. Thus an individual who is proud of, for example, her/his ethnic group membership may emphasise this aspect when interacting with others. In addition, group markers in another's speech may be processed preferentially, to maintain one's own positive identity. This function becomes more relevant in a later section (see below).

*The role of language in interpersonal attribution processes*

In recent years the role played by language in social processes has received considerable attention and we know that the way we speak and how listeners interpret this speech has important consequences for our interactions with others (see Giles and Powesland, 1975 for a review). Most of these studies have been concerned with *trait* attribution, but the experiments reported in this section have gone beyond some of the earlier approaches and are of considerable relevance to attribution researchers. The two studies reported below examined the role of language in a legal setting where attributional notions were of considerable importance.

Erickson, Lind, Johnson and O'Barr (1978) began by carrying out a large-scale analysis of the language used in (North American) courts of law. This analysis identified a cluster of linguistic features which varied as a function of speakers' social power and status. This cluster is referred to as a 'powerless' speech style when the speaker is low on the above two characteristics and is characterised by such forms as 'hesitation' ('uh', 'well', 'you know'), 'hedges' ('Kinda', 'I think', 'I guess') and especially formal grammar.[3] A full discussion of the potential and actual influence of such a speech style is included in their article. For example, the 'powerful' style (characterised by the absence of the above features) may lead to the speaker's being seen as more difficult to communicate with, more credible etc. Insofar as the study looks at certain social judgements of this type it is still concerned with trait attribution and impression-formation. However, the court setting and the particular dependent variables used in this study justify its inclusion in this chapter.

Erickson *et al.* (1978) presented audiotapes of the witness (for the plaintiff) speaking with a powerful or powerless speech style, in a dialogue with a lawyer.[4] Dependent variables included a series of scales measuring listeners' impressions of the witness; how responsible and how negligent the defendants were; and what amount of damages the defendants should pay the plaintiffs. Summarising and selecting from the results there are a number of important findings. First, as expected, the powerful speakers were seen as more credible and more attractive. However, speech style of the witness had no effect on beliefs about the defendants' responsibility for an accident, or their negligence. Speech style did have an effect on the amount of damages recommended, as subjects recommended higher damages if the witness' speech style were powerful. Thus this particular speech style was shown to have interesting and significant effects on a number of social judgements.

The effect of speech style on the damages index might well be expected to be closely linked to attributions (see discussion of the 'entailment' model in chapter 5 and Fincham and Jaspars, 1980).

The second study, by Lind, Erickson, Conley and O'Barr (1978), concerns language and attribution in a more direct manner. Their experiment tested the proposition that 'listeners use dyadic conversational style to generate social attributions concerning the relationship between two speakers as well as to form impressions of the individual speakers' (Lind *et al.*, 1978, p. 1559). Once again the focus of the study was an exchange between a witness and a lawyer, in the course of a criminal trial. The speech styles of interest were named 'narrative' and 'fragmented'. The former label is given to testimony conversation in which relatively infrequent questions by the lawyer receive extensive, narrative answers from the witness; the latter style is characterised by frequent questions on the part of the lawyer, which receive only brief, fragmented answers from the witness.

The importance of these speech styles for the generation of social attributions was introduced by these authors via a discussion of the adversary system of legal procedure; specifically, they draw attention to the fact that this system allows the lawyer to control the content, and to some extent the style, of the delivered testimony. The lawyer controls explicitly when s/he imposes the fragmented style on the witness and thus directs the latter's testimony. When the narrative style is used, Lind *et al.* (1978) suggest that the lawyer may be seen to concede authority, or tight control. It is here that listeners' attributions become relevant. It is argued that listeners will search for the cause of this latter, control-transferring behaviour. For example, they may attribute the lawyer's loosened grip over the proceedings to a greater trust in, or evaluation of, the witness. In addition, Jones and Davis' (1965) correspondent inference theory may be relevant, because of its concern with attributions for normative violations. If a lawyer unexpectedly allows a witness to use the narrative style, Lind *et al.* (1978) argue that the effect will be even stronger when the witness is female (and the lawyer is male). This prediction is based on sociolinguistic work which suggests that males are more assertive linguistically, than females (e.g. Key, 1975; Lakoff, 1975). Lind *et al.* (1978) suggest therefore that the lawyer will be seen as more 'controlling' when he imposes a fragmented style on a male witness, rather than a female witness. By the same reasoning, a female witness' use of the narrative style may be seen as a counter-normative transfer of control and a male witness' use of the fragmented style may be attributed to strong control exerted by the lawyer. Lind *et al.* (1978) propose that listeners will locate the cause of such non-normative speech in the lawyer's evaluation of the witness. The study tests the following basic predictions: (1) Liking or trust of the witness will only be attributed to the lawyer in the case of the female witness – narrative style combination. (2) Dislike or distrust of the witness will only be attributed to the lawyer in the case of the male witness – fragmented style combination. In addition Lind *et al.* (1978) examined whether these attributions of trust would affect listeners' own attributions concerning the witness.

The interaction of speech style and sex of witness referred to in predictions (1) and (2) above was qualified by the background of the subjects. For a sample of law students prediction (1) was upheld: they attributed the lawyer's transfer of control to the witness to his positive evaluation of her. For undergraduates hearing this tape there were no effects of speech style. On the other hand prediction (2) was only upheld for a sample of undergraduates: they attributed the 'controlling' behaviour of the lawyer to his negative evaluation of the (male) witness. For law students in this condition there were significant main effects for style of testimony on subjects' attitudes regarding the lawyer's evaluation of the witness, their own evaluation of the witness and perceived control by the lawyer. Subjects who heard the testimony delivered in a narrative style perceived the lawyer's evaluation of the witness to be higher, themselves had a higher evaluation of the witness and perceived the lawyer to be exerting less control. With regard to the sex-of-witness main effect, subjects hearing the female witness evaluated her more highly and saw her as more credible, than did subjects hearing the male witness. In addition subjects perceived the female witness to be more highly evaluated, and less controlled, by the lawyer than the male witness.

Finally, Lind *et al.* (1978) were able to examine the causal sequence of subjects' evaluations of the witness. It was predicted that subjects' own evaluations of the witness would parallel their attributions concerning the lawyer's perceived evaluations. Path analyses confirmed this hypothesis. Thus it was shown that subtle stylistic characteristics of dyadic conversation are used to generate complex attributions. Furthermore, these stylistic variables were related to a distinction between 'first-order' and 'second-order' attributions. First-order attributions are based on the personal characteristics of speakers, while second-order attributions are based on the nature of the relationship between the speakers heard in conversation. In other words, when we hear two persons A and B conversing, we may use the stylistic nature of A's speech to B (and *vice versa*) to generate attributions concerning what each thinks of the other.

Other areas in which the relationship between language and interpersonal attribution processes has been explored include persuasive communication (see Eagly and Chaikin, 1975; Eagly, Wood and Chaikin, 1978) the development of interpersonal relationships (Berger, 1979) and the interrelations between language forms and social situations (see Giles and Hewstone, 1983; Price and Bouffard, 1974). Further discussion of these areas is not possible in this chapter and we turn now to an examination of the importance of stimulus language for intergroup, rather than interpersonal, attributions.

*The role of language in intergroup attribution processes*

The research reviewed above demonstrates that variables at the macro-linguistic level can and do influence attributions. Thus far, however, the studies cited have been concerned with interpersonal attribution. This author has recently argued (Hewstone and Jaspars, 1982a; Jaspars and Hewstone, 1982) that traditional attribution theory has been too individualistic and has neglected the importance of attribution processes at the level of intergroup relations. Attribution theory has not completely ignored the importance of social categories (see Jones and McGillis, 1976; Thibaut and Riecken, 1955) but it has tended to focus on explaining the behaviour of the individual *qua* individual, rather than the individual as a representative of a social group. In this alternative perspective an observer attributes the behaviour of an actor, not simply on the basis of individual characteristics, but on the basis of the group or social category to which the actor belongs and to which the observer belongs (for a review of intergroup attribution research see Hewstone and Jaspars, 1982a; Pettigrew, 1979; see also chapter 8). The importance of language in relation to this intergroup level of attribution is now considered.

The significance of language in intergroup relations has been spelled out recently in a number of publications (see Giles, 1978, 1979b; Giles, Bourhis and Taylor, 1977; Giles and Johnson, 1981; Giles and Taylor, 1979; Lambert, 1979; Ryan, 1979) and need not be repeated here. What is important for this chapter is that individuals may be perceived in intergroup terms (see Tajfel and Turner, 1979) because of the language they speak. It is in this way that social categorisation via language becomes important in attribution.

The importance of attribution processes in explaining and giving meaning to intergroup encounters (e.g. Simard, Taylor and Giles, 1976) has been explored, but the attributional implications of categorising an actor on the basis of linguistic cues have not been looked at.

What happens when we categorise someone in this way? Do we simply use language as an index of social category? This is what Robinson (1972) argues, in proposing a two-stage model of inference. Speech characteristics are seen as enabling the judge to apply an 'identifying label', which in turn has certain traits associated with it. Thus the sequence is:

Accent ──────────→ Identity ──────────────→ Personality

This simple model has been criticised by a number of researchers (e.g. Ryan and Carranza, 1975) and recently revised (Robinson, 1979) but these changes do not explain the role of language in attributions. An interesting line of speculation that may be of use is suggested by the notions of category 'accessibility' (Bruner, 1957a), the 'availability' heuristic (Tversky and Kahneman, 1974) and *a priori* causal categories (Kelley, 1972b).

Bruner suggests that under certain circumstances particular categories may be more accessible to the perceiver than other categories and he makes three points concerning the accessibility of categories for use in social perception:

The greater the accessibility of a category,
(*a*) the less the input necessary for categorisation to occur in terms of this category,
(*b*) the wider the range of input characteristics that will be 'accepted' as fitting the category in question,
(*c*) the more likely that categories that provide a better or equally good fit for the input will be masked.    (Bruner, 1957a, p. 129–130)

Thus accessible categories would tend to preclude the selection of other categories. An example of the process is given by Duncan (1976) who found that the category *violence* was more accessible when white American students viewed a black person on a videotape, than when they viewed a white person. If language has the capacity to trigger stereotyped judgements (which is what many of the above-cited references indicate) then some of these traits which make up the stereotype may be utilised as causal categories and may prevent the use of other explanatory categories. A similar line of reasoning is suggested by Tversky and Kahneman's availability heuristic, the major attributional implications of which are spelled out elsewhere in this volume (chapter 3). These notions may be linked with Kelley's ideas on causal preconceptions if we allow for some sort of cognitive link between categories and these preconceptions. Kelley argues that prior beliefs about causation have an effect on information-intake and it can easily be shown that these link with categories. Take Duncan's study as an example. If the observer holds prior beliefs about black people causing harm to others, then we might assume that the category *violence* would be more accessible to this observer. It is suggested that future research on language and intergroup attribution processes should examine whether language makes certain categories available, how it does so and what effect this has on attribution.

SUMMARY AND IMPLICATIONS OF THE ROLE OF STIMULUS LANGUAGE

In this section we have concentrated on the effects that various kinds of linguistic presentation can have on attributions. From Kanouse's studies we learned that stimulus language at a micro-linguistic level can contain implicit attributions. These studies have important implications made clear in the discussion of McArthur's study. In particular, the results of her study suggest that the effects induced by stimulus language (in this case verb categories again) may be most significant when the stimulus material is most simplistic. Moving on to macro-linguistic variables in stimulus language, Erickson *et al.* (1978) demonstrated that particular speech styles (powerful–powerless) may have a direct influence on trait attribution and an indirect effect on responsibility attribution. The study by Lind *et al.* (1978) demonstrated similar effects, drawing attention to the reciprocal language used by interactants as a potent source of attributions. Finally, the role of stimulus language at the level of intergroup attributions was discussed. The most exciting prospect to emerge from this analysis was that language may serve to suggest categories in terms of which attributions are made.

In summary, stimulus language at both micro- and macro-linguistic levels has an effect. We now turn to consider the other side of the coin, the language with which subjects make their attributions – response language.

## Response language

In considering response language in attribution studies we are dealing not with the way stimulus information is presented to the attributor, but with the language in terms of which the attributor is able to respond. Ross and DiTecco (1975) have discussed some of the effects of language on responsibility attributions and their conclusions appear relevant to all kinds of attributional judgements: 'Language implicity forms the basis by which we interpret events in the world. . . . Consequently, the language we learn to use can influence and indeed determine our attributions' (Ross and DiTecco, 1975, p. 100).

Despite this recognition of the importance of language for attribution theory, this area has received barely any attention from researchers. Response language has, however, been examined in a number of attitude studies and these are discussed below as a preliminary to an examination of response language biases in attributional studies.

RESPONSE LANGUAGE IN ATTITUDE STUDIES

A number of recent studies by Eiser and colleagues (Eiser, 1975; Eiser and Mower-White, 1974a, b, 1975; Eiser and Pancer, 1979; Eiser and Ross, 1977) have been concerned, in part, with the distinction between the descriptive and evaluative aspects of language. The problem, for attributional experiments as well as other types of social psychological experiments, is that these two aspects are often confounded in the methodology we use. Eiser (1975) takes the example of an attributional experiment in which one subject rates another on a number of bipolar rating scales (e.g. 'friendly–unfriendly', 'clever–stupid', 'selfish–unselfish'). As he points out, the end-points of such scales, and the ratings made on such scales, are both evaluative and descriptive. In order to unconfound the effects a rather complex procedure suggested by Peabody (1968, 1970) is required. The subject should be presented with two scales for each of the traits of interest, one should be worded positively, the other negatively. Only then can we tease apart the evaluative and descriptive aspects of language.

Eiser goes on to discuss a number of issues relating language and attitudes, including the fact that differences in polarisation on attitude scales can be explained in terms of the judges' attitudes and the value connotations of the language with which they have to respond (Eiser and Mower-White, 1974a, 1975). More specifically, when discriminating between different attitude statements, subjects seem to prefer to use response language which is 'evaluatively consistent' with their own opinion. In fact, Eiser suggests, such language may be as much a determinant of attitudes as an effect. This leads him to the interesting question of whether an individual will sometimes adopt an attitude to fit in with the language s/he uses.

There have been a number of studies which have looked at how the use of evaluatively biased language may be a medium of social influence in a rather indirect way. First, Eiser and Mower White (1974b) attempted to change subjects' attitudes by providing them with, and inducing them to make us of, certain kinds of evaluative labels. Subjects had to indicate their agreement/disagreement with 10 attitude statements. Preceding this task one of three sets of experimental instructions was presented. These were *control*, *pro-bias* and *anti-bias*. The experimental instructions implicitly ascribed a positive value to the pro position in the *pro-bias* condition, and to the anti position in the *anti-bias* condition. Subjects shifted their attitudes in accordance with these manipulations, indicating that language can be a subtle source of influence through experimental instructions. Secondly, the influence of evaluative language on attitudes has been examined by asking subjects to write essays on a topic and to include evaluatively biased words implying a preference for either the pro- or anti-standpoint on the issue (Eiser and Pancer, 1979; Eiser and Ross, 1977). Subjects' attitudes were found to become more consistent with the language they had been using. Thus attitudes may be adopted so as to fit with the language which has previously been applied to an issue.

These studies show some of the effects that can be generated by manipulations in response language. Thus far the research reviewed has concerned language and attitudes, but van der Pligt (1981), has recently applied some of the same reasoning to attribution research.

RESPONSE LANGUAGE IN ATTRIBUTION STUDIES

Van der Pligt (1981) argues that attribution research, just as attitude research, has failed to distinguish between descriptive and evaluative aspects of judgements. Referring to the work on descriptive and evaluative aspects of traits (e.g. Felipe, 1970; Peabody, 1968, 1970; Selby, 1976) he suggests that such work has implications for attribution research too. In this section we will concentrate on the language in terms of which subjects are to respond and the response format; finally, some methodological criticisms will be offered.

First, we might consider response format, what explanatory categories subjects are provided with in attribution experiments. Often these are *a priori* response scales (5-, 7-, 9- and 11-point scales) which constrain the subject's range of responses. As an example van der Pligt cites Taylor and Koivumaki's (1976) study on actor–observer differences in attribution. These authors had subjects rate behaviours on an 11-point scale where 1 indicated situational causality and 11 dispositional causality. As van der Pligt points out, this approach may force the experimenter's frame of reference upon the subject, implying that the two factors are mutually exclusive (see chapter 12 for further discussion of this methodological point).

Another type of response format is that utilised by McArthur (1972). After reading a short vignette reporting an actor's response to a stimulus or entity subjects were asked what probably caused the event to occur. They were given four response alternatives, one of which was to be selected:

(*a*) Something about *the stimulus*
(*b*) Something about *the particular circumstances*
(*c*) Something about *the person*
(*d*) Some combination of (*a*), (*b*), and (*c*) above.  (see McArthur, 1972, p. 175)

Once again it is clear that subjects' responses are limited. The subject may not even perceive the situation in terms of these response categories, but is still forced to respond in terms of them.

The manner in which response language (rather than response format) may bias subjects' attributions emerges from a reconsideration of the descriptive–evaluative distinction discussed earlier. Van der Pligt (1981) refers to a number of studies (e.g. Nisbett, Caputo, Legant and Maracek, 1973; Taylor and Koivumaki, 1976) which have attempted to disentangle evaluations and (purely descriptive) attributions. The latter study showed favourability of the presented adjectives to be an important determinant of attributions. The importance of adjectives selected for response-scales may be illustrated with reference to an example from Le Vine and Campbell (1972). These authors were interested in intergroup relations and, in part, in the question of how groups describe themselves and other groups. Table II shows how the Americans and English describe themselves and each other on traits related to the dimension introversion–extraversion.

TABLE II  Auto- and hetero-descriptions of English and Americans. (From Le Vine and Campbell, 1972, p. 172, fig. 10.3)

| | Descriptions of | |
| --- | --- | --- |
| Descriptions by | English | American |
| English | + Reserved<br>+ Respect privacy<br>   of others | − Intrusive<br>− Forward<br>− Pushing |
| Americans | − Snobbish<br>− Cold<br>− Unfriendly | + Friendly<br>+ Outgoing<br>+ Open-hearted |

According to Table II introversion is characteristic of English people, a fact accepted by both groups. However, the trait is evaluated differently by the two groups. Whereas the English rate it positively and interpret it in terms of reserve and respect for privacy, the

Americans rate it negatively and label it as snobbishness, coldness or unfriendliness. Similarly, both the Americans and English seem to agree that the former are extraverted although the evaluations of this trait are again quite different.

Let us now suppose, by way of an example, that an experiment has been designed to examine the behaviour of interactors in a 'getting acquainted situation' (cf. Storms, 1973). In addition, let us assume that we are interested in the extent to which behaviours in this situation are *caused* by the interactors' being introverted/extraverted. Finally, let us assume that each pair of interactors consists of one American and one English person, that the judges are of both nationalities and that the relations between the two countries are at an all time low. We would have to predict that ratings of the causal role of the traits introversion/extraversion would vary greatly as a function of the labels attached to the rating scales.

We are left now in some doubt as to which, if any, of these methodologies we should utilise. Or, indeed, whether we should eschew such dependent variables completely and use some sort of 'think aloud' procedure (see Newell and Simon, 1972) to escape the vagaries of response language. The obvious solution to this problem might seem to be to do away with structured response formats and to use open-ended measures. Indeed this alternative has been explored (see Nisbett *et al.*, 1973, study 2, and chapter 6 in this volume). However, such techniques bring their own problems (see van der Pligt, 1981) and no obvious solution is apparent. It is not, in any case, the place of this chapter to resolve such issues. We would, however, suggest a multimethod approach, with particular attention being paid to the examination of differences between research using different approaches.

SUMMARY AND IMPLICATIONS OF THE ROLE OF RESPONSE LANGUAGE

By integrating the work of Eiser and colleagues on language and attitudes with van der Pligt's critique of attribution studies we have drawn attention to a number of ways in which the language an individual uses can influence social judgements. Eiser's studies, of course, are primarily concerned with attitudinal responses, but an intriguing question exists as to whether these results would generalise to other social judgements. Take, for example, the change of attitude induced by forcing subjects to use particular language (Eiser and Pancer, 1979; Eiser and Ross, 1977). It would be interesting to know whether such a manipulation had similar carry-over effects on attributional judgements.

Van der Pligt's contribution is to demonstrate that response language biases vitiate many of the methodologies adopted in attribution research. Researchers should now take note of the dangers and limitations of whichever approach they adopt and future effort should be expended on finding solutions to some of these problems.

## Conclusion

The central argument of this chapter has been that language plays an important role in attributional processes. Ross and DiTecco (1975) have also discussed some of the implications of linguistic variables for attributional work and their views are shared by this author:

> The attribution process appears to be far more complex and subtle than might have been previously supposed. From a methodological point of view it is apparent that research must be carefully examined with respect to the evaluative connotations and implicit attributional biases in the language presented to the subjects. Minor differences in wording may have major attributional implications. (Ross and DiTecco, 1975, p. 101–102)

Ross and DiTecco do not, however, draw a distinction between stimulus and response language, an omission which prevents them from more clearly elucidating the influence of language on attributions.

On the one hand, we have argued, this influence is expressed via the material from which attributions are to be made – the stimulus language. Whether presented as written vignettes or tape recordings linguistic material has been shown to affect attributions. On the other hand, attributions may be influenced by the response language made available to subjects. This response language may exclude certain categories from the subject's response repertoire or may suggest other categories which the subject had been previously unaware of. This chapter has attempted to draw researchers' attention to the pervasive influence of language at both levels. Future research should concentrate on outlining what kinds of language can bias the attribution process, how they do so and why they have this effect.

In his original exposition of attribution theory Kelley (1967) drew attention, albeit in passing, to 'the interplay between language and attribution' (p. 235) as a significant aspect of the theory. This chapter has tried to underline the importance of this relationship as one which deserves greater attention in the future.

## Acknowledgements

The author would like to thank the Social Science Research Council for a doctoral research grant and the following for their most valuable comments: Michael Argyle, Richard Eiser, Howard Giles, Jos Jaspars and Peter Robinson.

## Notes

1.  Stimulus is the term McArthur uses to refer to the entity, or object. In the example given the stimulus is the comedian.
2.  This chapter is not the place to discuss the importance of consensus information, but the reader is referred to Ruble and Feldman (1976) for a critique of McArthur's (1972) study and an alternative set of data.
3.  The nature of this speech style is elaborated in Erickson *et al.* (1978, p. 267).
4.  For the purposes of this discussion we focus on one independent variable, the powerless v. powerful speech style.

# 10

# Attributions of Cause and Responsibility as Social Phenomena

Sally Lloyd-Bostock

## Introduction

Perhaps the most obvious and dramatic instances of 'real world' attributions of responsibility are those that occur in legal contexts. This chapter aims to show that such contexts, taken together with the extensive legal literature that relates to them, suggest dimensions of attribution processes not satisfactorily dealt with in attribution theory and not confronted in the bulk of attribution studies. In particular, it becomes clear that current attribution theory is insufficiently social in emphasis to cope with explanation of attribution of cause and responsibility outside the laboratory.

The legal literature contains a wealth of material which could help provide a much-needed clarification and elaboration of the concepts used in attribution research. Attributions of responsibility in legal contexts are by their nature explicit and often permanently recorded. Moreover, the grounds on which the attribution has been made must often be set out and defended, and legal concepts of cause and responsibility are extensively explained, analysed and argued over in the legal literature. While questions about responsibility and related concepts arise in all branches of the law, one area where legal discussion is most clearly of relevance to current attribution research is the law of torts (that branch of the law which is concerned with civil wrongs, such as injury and defamation), and in particular, the tort of negligence. The first section of the chapter therefore outlines how legal material in this area relates to psychologists' questions about responsibility, suggesting possibilities for drawing on this material as a resource.

At the same time, it is important not to draw on legal material uncritically or overenthusiastically. While psychologists have much to gain from familiarising themselves with legal material, I do not wish to imply that lawyers' theories, definitions, distinctions and models can be lifted directly and used by psychologists. The main concern of the chapter is to argue that both the law and psychological theory have often worked with an over-simple model of attribution processes. In particular, lawyers and psychologists have both proceeded as if it makes sense to talk about attributions of cause and responsibility without reference to why the judgement is being made. Both are also often unclear or undecided about what it means to talk about error, bias or irrationality in such attributions. The second section of the chapter proposes a more complex model of attribution processes which places emphasis on the social context as a source of variance, and illustrates its application with examples from legal contexts and data from interviews with accident victims. The third section discusses the notions of error, bias and irrationality in judgements of cause and responsibility.

## The legal literature as a resource for psychologists

POSSIBILITIES

Much of the existing psychological research on responsibility attribution has used an oversimplified, narrow notion of responsibility, and of attribution processes. An ambiguous and usually undefined concept of 'responsibility' often not distinguished from 'cause' is used in many experiments. It is not surprising that findings are frequently contradictory, not replicable, and difficult to interpret. Since legal writers and practising lawyers have grappled with questions about responsibility for many years, it seems sensible for psychologists to take advantage of their thinking. To some extent attribution researchers have begun to exploit the legal, especially jurisprudential literature, and have done so with some enthusiasm (e.g. Darley, Klosson and Zanna, 1978; Fincham and Jaspars, 1980; Hamilton, 1978; Shultz, Schleifer and Altman, 1979; also see chapter 2). Failure to draw on this resource to any great extent may result largely from the fact that the relevant material is not readily accessible to psychologists. It may also be that psychologists working on attribution do not expect to find much common ground in the types of questions responsibility raises for the law.

Lawyers and psychologists do, of course, have very different reasons for their interests in how responsibility is attributed. Psychologists have been trying to make empirical generalisations about how and why people in fact assign causes and responsibility, not develop tests or criteria for deciding on responsibility under the law. Sometimes the fine distinctions, elaborate definitions, and answers to questions about borderlines which need to be worked out in relation to the law are simply not of the same relevance for the psychologist. But their concerns may be closer than at first appears. Although legal writing is predominantly concerned with the conceptual structure of the law, law is essentially a practical art, where decisions have to be made. As Hart (1951) writes, 'rules of law . . . are not linguistic or logical rules, but to a great extent, rules for deciding' (p. 156). Legal definitions of responsibility are definitions which have to work in practice. In the area of tort law they are, moreover, definitions which purport to accord with common sense, non-legal notions of cause and responsibility. Although there is now much statute law in the tort area, the law of torts is basically common law, formed by actual legal decisions of the courts. The claim that judicial decisions should, and do, accord with common sense recurs in court pronouncements. (Hart and Honoré, 1959 cite several examples; the judgement in Barty-King v. Ministry of Defence, 1979[1], gives recent confirmation of the prevalence of this view.)

Justifications of the tort system as a whole also often involve an appeal to common sense. This is clear in the arguments which are put forward for and against retaining the tort system of compensation for personal injury. Arguments in this debate often implicitly rest on the idea that it is somehow a matter of common justice that fault provides grounds for demanding payment of compensation. Thus, for example, Atiyah (1975) suggests that the ultimate justification for embodying the 'fault principle' in law must be that it is a moral principle generally accepted in society today, and this view of the fault principle recurs repeatedly in various forms in legal writings (e.g. Linden, 1977; Pearson Commission, 1978; Williams and Hepple, 1976).

The tort system is thus one which purports, both at the level of general principle and at the level of particular definitions of fault and their application, to accord with common sense. Whether or not this is a justified, or even meaningful, claim is another question (cf. Lloyd-Bostock, 1979a). The point here is that both lawyers and psychologists are interested in how ordinary people attribute responsibility in non-legal, everyday settings. Lawyers' questions about ordinary people's common sense notions of cause and responsibility, and how these correspond to the law and legal decisions, are in this respect close to psychologists' questions of empirical fact about how people perceive causality, what factors determine how they will attribute responsibility, and what they see as just.

This means that legal analyses such as Hart and Honoré's (1959) analysis of common sense notions of cause and responsibility (see further below) are directly related to the substance of at least some attribution research. In addition to works of this kind, textbooks on tort law, justifications for decisions in written court judgements, law reports, and casebooks, are all potential goldmines for the attribution researcher, setting out what are held to be the legal rules for deciding cause and responsibility and illustrating their application in practice, as well as offering insights and observations on how we in fact react to and deal with events.

Discussion throughout this literature of such legal concepts as 'reasonableness', 'foreseeability', 'remoteness of damage' and 'duty of care', suggest many new hypotheses, and new classes of variables to be explored. Moreover, casebooks provide an endless supply of accounts of 'real events' which might be used as stimulus materials in experiments, conveniently classified according to the legal issue (e.g. 'What is reasonable?') which they exemplify together with a legal solution which may suggest a lay solution to the problem of responsibility attribution. The special legal importance of difficult borderline cases means that it is easy to find reports of cases in which there is some uncertainty regarding attribution of responsibility. This uncertainty means that if such cases are used as the basis for psychology experiments, some variance in subjects' attributions can be hoped for, and experimental manipulations can be expected to have a maximum impact.

SOME CAUTIONARY REMARKS

An almost unlimited programme of experiments could be devised simply by browsing through this material. However, a piecemeal 'browsing' approach could easily yield little more than a catalogue of discrete and probably contradictory findings to complicate still further an already confused body of literature. For one thing, the number of 'useful ideas' quickly becomes overwhelming. Two cases picked almost at random from a casebook (Weir, 1979) will illustrate this point.

The first, Cuttress v. Scaffolding (Great Britain) Ltd (1953)[2] raised the issue of the effects on judgements of causation of an intervening act by a third party. The facts of the case are summarised in a footnote with little discussion, but in itself the case suggests several possible hypotheses and experimental manipulations. The defendants in the case were repairing a bombed house, and constructed for that purpose a scaffold which was perfectly stable, but not supported against lateral stress. Before leaving for a weekend, the defendants' workmen had coiled the pulley-rope at the top of the scaffolding. During the weekend a boy climbed the scaffolding, uncoiled the rope and threw it down to his companions below. Then about a dozen of them swung on the rope, and rocked the scaffolding to and fro until it fell on the plaintiff who was crossing public land nearby. The trial judge held that all this was foreseeable, but the Court of Appeal 'had no difficulty in reversing him and entering judgement for the defendants' (Weir, 1979, p. 186).

It is not difficult to envisage how these 'facts' might be used as stimulus material to explore several questions besides the influence of an 'intervening act'. What difference does it make that the act was by children? Would subjects hold the company rather than the workmen responsible? What difference does it make what the plaintiff was doing? – and so on.

A second, this time very famous, case on the question of foreseeability and the directness of causation is *The Wagon Mound* (1961).[3] The facts of this case are summarised in Weir (1979) as follows:

A large quantity of oil was carelessly allowed to spill from *The Wagon Mound*, a ship under the defendant's control, during bunkering operations in Sydney Harbour on October 30th, 1951. This oil spread to the plaintiff's wharf about 200 yards away, where a ship, *The Corrimal*, was being repaired. The plaintiff asked whether it was safe to continue welding, and was assured (in accordance with the best scientific opinion) that the oil could not be ignited when spread on water. On November 1st, a drop of molten metal fell on a piece of floating waste; this ignited the oil, and the plaintiff's wharf was consumed by fire.   (Weir, 1979, p. 167)

The question was whether the destruction of the wharf was the direct and foreseeable consequence of the carelessness of the defendant in spilling the oil. The case is an important one in terms of legal doctrine, and very widely discussed. The defendants won this case on appeal, but when they were also sued by the owners of the ships berthed at the wharf the Judicial Committee held on appeal that the damage was after all reasonably foreseeable, and they lost that case. Heuston (1977) comments that 'Nobody has yet produced a satisfactory reconciliation of the two decisions' (p. 223).

Discussion of this case suggests many hypotheses as to how people attribute causes and responsibility. For example, it raises the question of what it is that has to be foreseeable – the *specific* damage that materialises, or harm of the *general type* that occurred. Did the precise set of circumstances leading to damage by fire have to be foreseeable? That damage by fire might somehow occur as a result of the discharge of oil? Or that some type of harm, by fire or otherwise, might result?

Many more such cases and discussions are readily found. Further

examples will arise in the course of this chapter, but first a broader
theoretical framework is needed within which both legal and non-legal
contexts can be considered, and both the legal material and psychological research and theory can be understood.

Before turning to this in the next section, three further caveats need
brief mention. First, legal material in the tort field often does not relate
to 'common sense' as a psychologist might use the term. Legal
decisions, legal writings, and the present structure of the law of torts
can often only be understood with reference to its own history, to
specifically legal problems, and to matters of legal policy. This may
seem too obvious to be worth saying, but it does mean that legal
concepts and distinctions can relate rather strangely to common sense
after all, and legal discussion can often reflect struggles to shuffle off old
ideas in response to social change rather than difficulties inherent in
newer ones. In the two *Wagon Mound* cases cited above, for instance, an
additional complicating factor was the fact that one action was brought
for negligence and the other for nuisance – a distinction with its roots in
legal history and strictly speaking superfluous even in law. Secondly, it
is most important not to lose sight of the fact that there are internal
disagreements and confusions at every level within the law and
amongst lawyers. If legal ideas are imported uncritically into
psychology, confusions and contradictions are likely to be imported
along with them. Tort law is perhaps one of the most confused and
fluctuating branches of the law, to the extent that exposition of the law
is frequently hedged about with reservations. Thus, Street, in the fifth
edition of his student text on the law of torts, prefaces his discussion of
the concept of 'Duty' with the warning that

What follows is to be regarded as one person's attempt to reconcile the need for
logic and orderliness in legal presentation with the paramount obligation of
stating the law in the terminology commonly employed by English courts, and
at the same time to explain the several techniques applied by the courts to the
solution of problems in negligence. In negligence alone of the torts (though
perhaps to a much slighter extent in nuisance) do the constituent elements
lack reasonably clear definition.   (Street, 1972, p. 102)

Coutts (1960), referring to the confusion surrounding legal use of
causal language, writes

. . . one has a sneaking sympathy for the Irish High Court Judge who evaded
the task of explaining the tangled rules of 'last opportunity' to the jury in a
running down action by asking them to answer 'the simple question: Which
car hit the other first'.   (p. 708)

Similar sentiments were expressed by the judge in the case of

Barty-King v. Ministry of Defence (1979), who quoted earlier judgements making the same point. In this case, a man who had sustained a war wound in 1944 died of cancer in 1967. His executors applied to the Defence Council for a certificate that the man 'died from a wound inflicted' while on active service, since such a certificate would give exemption from estate duty. The Council accepted that recurrent attacks of septicaemia resulting from the wound had reduced the man's resistance to cancer, and hastened his death. The question for the court was whether this causal link was such as to constitute a cause. The judgement (that it was) emphasised somewhat scathingly that the task of finding legal answers to questions of causation such as this one is not much helped by 'the use of Latin tags such as *causa causans* and *sine qua non*, through English metaphors such as chains of causation and breaks in their links, and back to Latin phrases such as *novus actus interveniens*' (p. 89). The question was rather to be answered on the basis of common sense (which, interestingly, is here seen as in contrast with attempts to analyse and codify common sense). Psychologists need to ensure that they are in a position to decide for themselves whether their tasks can be helped by such analyses. In the following sections I hope to show how they sometimes can be.

It is important for psychologists to understand not only how they can and cannot benefit from legal material, but also what help psychological research can and cannot offer to legal concerns. If legal references to common sense, the ordinary man, and so on do indeed involve empirical statements of some kind, it would seem that psychologists might try to 'test the law'. This is not the concern of this chapter, and will not be discussed further than a final caveat here, that this is by no means a straightforward matter. Since questions about how ordinary people attribute cause and responsibility interest psychologists as well as lawyers and philosophers, legal thinking should at least take account of the kinds of empirical findings and explanations offered by psychology. But a great deal of ground work is still needed before psychologists can be sure of their position here (cf. Lloyd-Bostock, 1979a).

## Attribution of causes and responsibility as a function of the social context

SOCIAL CONTEXT AS DEFINING 'RESPONSIBILITY'

*Two types of attribution*

The use of the term 'attribution' in the psychological literature is probably determined more by the fact that it has been adopted as the label for a body of theory and research in a certain tradition than by any idea of a particular process which can be clearly defined. It could be used even more generally to refer to the process of organising and interpreting a set of information. Although attribution theory focuses on causal interpretation, many basic features of causal attributions are likely to be of very general application. Conversely, many areas of psychology are likely to be potentially relevant to attribution research. For example, it is generally agreed that the visual perception of physical objects, like causal attribution, is an active constructive process which goes beyond the immediate information, is subject to error, is affected by our expectations, attitudes, past experience, the way we attend selectively to stimuli, and is influenced by the structure of our language.

However, it is of some importance here to distinguish between two types of attribution. On the one hand there is the attribution of causes as a relatively unreflective, rapid processing of information going on inside a person's head and unobservable (probably) even to her/himself. On the other there is attribution as a form of social act, most often verbal, and probably what J. L. Austin describes as a performative utterance (Austin, 1965). Contrast for example, a motorist processing and causally interpreting complex information as an integral part of his driving skill, and the same motorist explaining how his accident happened to the police, or attributing responsibility to another driver in order to support a claim to compensation. As Ginsburg (1976) points out, it seems that the latter, much rarer type of attribution occurs following events which are puzzling or violate some kind of norm and require explanation, excusing, justifying, or otherwise accounting for. Social rules will govern what, in a particular context calls for such an attribution; what constitutes an adequate explanation or account; how it is made or negotiated; and what further action may be implied – such as the imposition of rewards or sanctions. The law itself can be seen as a cluster of rules of this sort.

These two types of attribution are quite obviously not totally different, independent phenomena. Nor are they neat categories. Attributions can be in varying degrees reflective, made with reference to social rules, and so on, without being communicated to others. Nonetheless, at the two extremes attributions as social acts and attributions as unobservable causal inferences raise very different sorts of question which need to be approached with differing theoretical emphases. For example, if one is concerned with the social act of explaining events to others and attributing responsibility, then a question of primary importance is 'How does the individual select *the* cause (or even *a* cause) from a range of conditions and complex causal connections?' Indeed, this is the central question posed by Hart and Honoré (1959) in their discussion of common sense concepts of cause, and must be answered with reference to the social context in which the attribution occurs. However, if one is concerned with continuous, rapid causal inferences, the question may make no sense since such a choice may simply not need to be made for an adequate execution of the task at hand. The legal literature outlined above is thus of close relevance to attribution theory insofar as the theory is concerned with attributions of the first, social type. Where this legal material contains empirical claims these are probably claims about everyday social rules governing such attributions, as compared with the legal rules.

The origins of attribution theory in questions about the causal inference tasks facing the naive psychologist would seem to place it as concerned more with the second, continuous, unspoken type of attribution. Many studies are cited by Kelley (1972a) as relevant to attribution theory in that assumed causal attributions link stimulus and observed behaviour. But at the same time explicit causal statements and/or judgements of responsibility have been widely regarded as providing an appropriate measure of such attributions. Indeed, Kelley (1972a, p. 2) implies that such statements would be the most appropriate and direct measure. This involves seeing the relationship between causal statements and causal inferences as direct and unproblematic – a view which as Nisbett and Wilson (1972) show is highly questionable. Whatever the original focus of attribution theory may have been, by adopting explicit attributions as dependent variables research has *de facto* moved into questions about the much rarer social acts of causal explanation and responsibility attribution.

*Two types of responsibility*

Ambiguity over which of these two types of attribution is the primary concern has been compounded by a further ambiguity in the use of the term 'responsibility'. Hart and Honoré (1959) point out that two uses of the term need to be carefully distinguished if confusion is to be avoided. First, the term may be used to mean something like 'answerable', 'liable', or 'accountable'. There is no implication that a person held responsible for harm in this sense actually did, or caused the harm. It could refer for instance, to the responsibility of a parent for the harmful actions of his children, or of a guarantor for the debts of another person. In the second use, however, the expression does mean that the person did or caused the harm, usually with the implication that it is permissible to blame, punish, or exact compensation. Hart and Honoré (1959) write

This double use of the expression no doubt arises from the important fact that doing or causing harm constitutes not only the most usual but the primary type of ground for holding people responsible in the first sense. We still speak of inanimate or natural causes such as storms, floods, germs, or the failure of electricity supply as 'responsible for' disasters; this mode of expression, now taken only to mean that they caused the disasters, no doubt originated in the belief that all that happens is the work of spirits when it is not that of men.   (p. 61)

Without making this distinction explicit, attribution research has extended from questions where there need be no implication of blame to questions regarding responsibility where cause may not even be a factor.

*Attributions and social expectations*

The questions raised by attributions as social phenomena need to be approached within a much more social theory of attribution. At a very general level, tort doctrine provides a starting point for such a theory. Although 'cause' and 'responsibility' are obviously closely linked, research on attribution of responsibility in the sense of 'answerable' may often be better framed in terms of standards of behaviour as it affects others rather than anything like degrees of causal contribution to an outcome. The criteria of responsibility which evolve in a society reflect the standards of behaviour which members of the society expect (or demand) of each other. Deviations from these standards provide grounds for attributing responsibility and thence imposing social sanctions or rewards. Much explanation of the law of negligence is framed in such terms as 'standards of care' and 'reasonableness'. The law's 'reasonable man' embodies the notion of a standard against which actual behaviour can be judged, and the social nature of responsibility is reflected in the legal concept of 'duty of care'. The following much-quoted passage from a judgement by Lord Atkin is generally seen as the original formulation of the 'neighbour principle' which attempts to clarify the limits on to whom the 'duty of care' is owed;

the rule that you are to love your neighbour becomes in the law, you must not injure your neighbour; and the lawyer's question Who is my neighbour? receives a restricted reply. You must take reasonable care to avoid acts or omissions which you can reasonably foresee would be likely to injure your neighbour . . . [i.e.] . . . persons who are so closely and directly affected by my act that I ought reasonably to have them in contemplation as being so affected when I am directing my mind to the acts or omissions which are called in question. (Donoghue v. Stevenson, 1932, p. 561)[4]

A broad principle of this kind (and it is regarded by most lawyers as over-broad) accommodates many more partial theories than, say, Heider's 'levels' model.

If the central notions of 'standards' and 'duty' are used to provide a very broad framework for approaching attribution questions, then discussion in legal writing at a more detailed level can be drawn on in a coherent and useful way. For instance, the notion of standards of care is often discussed in legal writing in terms of risk, a discussion which shows that there are several aspects of risk which should be considered in experiments manipulating seriousness of damage. In particular, three elements of risk are normally distinguished, which together determine the reasonableness of risk taking: (1) the probability of harm, (2) the magnitude of the harm that would occur, and (3) the cost of avoiding the risky activity. For instance, the case of Paris v. Stepney Borough Council (1951)[5] concerned an injury to a garage hand's only good eye. It was held that the fact that he had only one eye increased the seriousness of such an injury, and was therefore relevant to the precautions his employer should have taken. If such a formulation, made for legal purposes, is to be drawn on in attribution research, then it is necessary to be clear about how it is integrated into *psychological* theory. It would fit naturally into theory conceived in terms of standards of care, as suggested above.

*The social consequences of attributions*

Because attribution research has neglected the social dimensions of attribution processes it has failed to see attribution of causes and responsibility as a function of the *social* reasons why these questions arise. In particular psychological research has paid scant attention to the fact that an attribution of responsibility can carry the most serious social and/or material consequences both for the person held responsible, and for the victim of her/his negligence. As Morris (1961) writes, questions about responsibility and blame are 'quite literally . . . philosophical questions which touch the purse strings' (p. iii). This aspect of attribution processes is missing from responsibility judgements elicited in laboratory experiments.

Of course, the relationship between responsibility judgements and further social consequences has been recognised, but the implications of this relationship have been almost totally missed. The possibility of social sanctions or rewards is ignored in the central idea, that an attribution of responsibility is a judgement based on information about the circumstances in which the act occurs. This judgement may then in turn provide grounds for further judgements about the appropriateness of further consequences such as compensation, punishment, or revision of safety rules, but this is apparently thought of as a later step in the sequence which need not concern the attribution researcher, since the responsibility judgement is based on a consideration of the causes and other circumstances of the accident (cf. the 'entailment' model recently examined by, e.g. Fincham and Jaspars, 1980; Fincham and Shultz, 1981, see also chapter 2). In many experiments subjects are supplied with outline information about an event and asked to make a responsibility judgement on this basis. A similar model underlies legal ideas about how common sense attributions are made.

An immediate problem with this is of course that the information or 'facts' about an event are going to be potentially infinite. Anyone who has carried out experiments using vignettes as stimuli, and then discussed the task with subjects, is likely to have found that they complain about the inadequacy of the information provided (see chapter 12). More important, the basis on which such 'facts' are selectively sought out and presented already implies some sort of criterion of relevance. Someone describing or investigating an accident can be expected to do so in a way geared to the reason why s/he is describing or investigating. This applies *a fortiori* to the way in which responsibility is attributed. That is to say, whether, and how, responsibility is attributed can be expected to be geared to why it is being made, which must include its potential *sequelae*. Thus Collingwood (1961) suggests that we can expect different contributory factors to the same accident to be cited as causes by the driver (her/his driving), the county surveyor (the road) and the vehicle manufacturer (the car design), because these are the factors each could prevent. When each is threatened with sanctions, however, one might expect a defensive shift in the factors selected. The victim interested in compensation might causally interpret what has happened in a way which provides grounds for attributing responsibility to the most likely source which will satisfy this need.

This may look like no more than the familiar idea of motivational bias in responsibility attribution which has been the object of much research. However, this research has emphasised *psychological* reasons and sources of motivation, such as the need to understand and hence feel in control of events, or in some way psychologically comfortable about what has happened. It has therefore focused on such factors as the seriousness of the accident, or similarity between the subject and characters in the 'story'. The responsibility judgement elicited in such experiments is seen as a function of the information about the event in the story and of the relevant characteristics of the individual attributor. If one accepts that attribution needs to be understood as a social act it is necessary to consider two further sources of variance. First, the social rules governing the attribution of responsibility may differ according to why the judgement is being made. Second, the possibility of social rewards/sanctions following the attribution of responsibility means that it is necessary to allow for social and material, as well as psychological, costs and payoffs, as motives for the judgement.

These two possible sources of variance, the influence of rules on the one hand, and of motives for appying rules on the other, are hard to disentangle both conceptually and empirically. But a distinction is implicit in the idea outlined above, of attribution of responsibility as a rule-governed social act. Even it if were possible to identify the very large cluster of rules about when and how an attribution of responsibility in everyday life may be made, what form it may take, and its consequences, these rules would not in themselves, predict the rest of an episode from the initial event, any more than legal rules and conventions predict whether a potential case will reach the courts, how it will be made, or its outcome. Rules may be used, bent, broken, interpreted, or ignored. Even within a specific social context, the appropriate rules may leave alternatives open, so the 'correct' common sense attributions are as difficult to pin down as the correct solution to a legal case may be.

A distinction of this kind is also implicit in the labelling of some attributions as erroneous, biased, etc. The legal notion of correct solutions to cases has its counterpart in psychological research which works with such ideas as motivational bias, error, irrational tendencies, and so on (e.g. Ross, 1977) implying that some unbiased, accurate, rational criterion judgements can be arrived at – presumably intuitively by the experimenter, perhaps with the help of a calculator. This cluster of ideas needs also to be understood in terms of the context of the judgement, and is discussed in more detail below. First, the rest of this section develops further the idea that the social functions and consequences of an attribution of responsibility can both define what is meant by responsibility and be a source of motivation for the individual attributor, affecting how he perceives and feels about events.

SOCIAL CONSEQUENCES AS A SOURCE OF INDIVIDUAL MOTIVATION

Heider's five levels (Heider, 1958a) imply that there are different grounds for an attribution of responsibility (see chapter 5), which range from being associated with an event to being unjustified in one's actions. Although Heider suggests that the level at which a judgement is made is a function of the respondent's sophistication, it is evident that response level may be determined by a number of actors, including the form of question asked and the anticipated consequences. The effect of the context of the judgement is not only on whether responsibility is assigned, and how much, but also on what is meant by responsibility.

We do not need experiments to make this point. Everyday experience is sufficient, and it is clearly seen in law where responsibility judgements are made within elaborate frameworks of definition which may define response level, and which are closely tied to some form of consequence. Legal rules sometimes prescribe the response level, so that classification according to contextual level leads automatically to a responsibility judgement (e.g. manslaughter, murder, justified homicide). Legal liability to compensate is often assigned at a lower level, in Heider's terms, than would provide grounds for a criminal charge carrying a different sort of penalty. Thus, damage to property must be intended if it is to form the basis of a criminal charge of malicious damage, but not necessarily if it is the basis of liability to compensate. Hart and Honoré (1961) recognise this kind of interdependence between what constitutes an adequate attribution and its implied consequences when they write that moral and legal responsibility do and probably should differ because very different consequences are attached to them.

It is not a new observation that various 'levels' of responsibility are used in law in this way, but the wider implications seem to have been missed. Rules, legal or otherwise, about what constitutes grounds for an attribution of responsibility cannot be seen in isolation from rules about the consequences which may follow if one has been successfully made. Someone may attribute responsibility in order to exact compensation, and s/he may do this by pointing to causal connections between another's actions and her/his own harm. These causal claims will in turn rest on shared beliefs about causes, and may themselves be open to negotiation. The rule governing whether or not agreement on a particular causal connection entitles someone to make an attribution of responsibility can be distinguished from those governing what future action may be implied. This does not mean, however, that they are independent. An acceptable attribution paving the way to compensation might look very different from one anticipating some other consequence (e.g. striking someone off a professional register, modifying safety rules or simply demonstrating public disapproval of careless behaviour).

This means that the act of attributing responsibility has a two-sided Janus-like quality looking both to the definition of an event and to the further social consequences which depend on, or are implied by a particular definition. This two-sidedness is reflected in what actually happens when an attribution of responsibility is being made or negotiated. To ask whether someone caused harm could, in certain contexts, be equivalent to asking whether s/he is morally to blame, should pay or should be punished. Similarly, agreement on certain causal connections could be tantamount to admission of guilt, liability, etc. Indeed, in some contexts it can be very difficult to ask about causes without sounding accusing. This rests on understandings (or suspicions) about where, given the context, the whole episode is leading, and what rules govern further steps along the way. Questions which ostensibly seek simply to establish what happened so that responsibility can appropriately be allocated may be answered in ways which show that they have been taken as questions about responsibility, or at least as threatening to lead up to an attribution of responsibility. Excuses and justifications may be offered at this stage, for example, and a version of events negotiated which minimises or denies moral responsibility, of liability to pay or be punished, even if these are irrelevant to the question taken at its face value. Knowledge that one's judgement will have certain sorts of consequences, as is the case for a jury or judge, may mean that the attribution becomes a judgement of the appropriateness of these consequences. (See Hester and Smith, 1973; Vidmar, 1972.) A jury may be unwilling to find fault or guilt if it is aware that the sentence or other sanction would be in its view too severe.

Newspaper reports often provide clear examples of how attributions of responsibility in one context can be quite inappropriate in another. For example, a *Sunday Times* article (April, 1977) after describing at some length the circumstances surrounding the collision between two jumbo jets at Santa Cruz airport in Tenerife, concluded by attributing responsibility: 'Blame for the world's worst aviation tragedy will no doubt be apportioned in time. One name will certainly not feature in any official inquest, however: Antonio Cubillo. It is he who, no matter how indirectly, must shoulder responsibility for what happened at Santa Cruz'. (Cubillo was leader of the movement which claimed responsibility for a bomb at Las Palmas airport. As a result of the bomb, aircraft, including those in the accident, were diverted to Santa Cruz, overloading the airport.) This is clearly not *the* everyday answer to the question 'who is responsible for the crash?' and would be quite inappropriate in the context of an official inquiry.

Much of Hart and Honoré's (1959) discussion of causation attacks the viewpoint that the anticipated legal consequences of attributing responsibility are the real concern of the law. According to this view, legal questions about cause may look like questions of fact, but this is illusion. They are to be answered 'only by inquiring what limit on liability or responsibility is required by "the scope", "the purpose", or "the policy" of specific legal rules involved in the particular case' (p. 4). They quote N. St. J. Green as putting forcibly a variant of this doctrine in 1874: 'Where a court says the damage is remote, it does not follow naturally, it is proximate, all they mean and can mean is that they think that in all the circumstances the plaintiff *should* not recover,' (Hart and Honoré, 1959, p. 4).

There are certainly problems about taking the connection between attributions of responsibility and their consequences, or the purposes behind making them, to these extremes. Hart and Honoré (1959) point out, for example, that Collingwood was forced into a position of having 'heroically to accept the conclusion that it is logically impossible to speak of discovering the cause of a disease unless we can use our knowledge to cure it' (p. 270). They point to a number of similarly awkward corollaries of attempts to by-pass or assimilate the notion of cause to purpose, scope, or policy, or to claim that statements that someone caused harm are a disguised way of saying something else. Thus they reject certain policy theories on the grounds that they:

fail to do justice to the conviction, deeply ingrained in the very moral notions they invoke, that one ground for holding it just to exact compensation or punish the wrongdoer is that he caused harm. How can this be so if, as these theories claim, to assert that one has caused harm presupposes, because it includes in it its meaning the conclusion that it is just to punish or exact compensation?' (p. 269)

This kind of criticism does not, however, demolish the less extreme idea, that what constitutes grounds for responsibility can vary according to the potential social consequences of the judgement, consequences which may well, in legal contexts, follow automatically.

These social consequences must include the wider functions and justifications of rules as well as the consequences for the individuals in a particular case. Legal decisions especially may have important legal policy implications. Judges may, for instance, be worried about opening the floodgates to litigation because they are aware that their judgements may make or change the law. Sometimes the policy reasons for a decision are made explicit (for example, a reason of policy was given in Shaw Savill and Albion Co. Ltd v. The Commonwealth

$(1940)^6$ for the decision that H.M. ships during operations of war owe no duty of care to other ships). The latter possibility in particular means that a rather large proportion of the legal literature is devoted to apparently trivial cases with sometimes comical results. A case may be trivial in the sense that no-one has suffered greatly, and yet be of great legal significance because it sets a precedent or because the judgement explains a legal principle. Weir notes in the introduction to his book, *A Casebook on Tort*, that the cases (all obviously important for the student of law) cover situations from the very tragic, to 'a policeman riled by criticism, a credulous advertising agent, and a television mogul miffed at being photographed' (1979, p. 3).

Probably the most notable example of the lack of correspondence between the seriousness of the case in itself and its legal significance is Donoghue v. Stevenson (1932). This case is enormously important in the law of negligence because it established that manufacturers can be sued by the consumers of their products. In addition, it was in his judgement in this case that Lord Atkin set out the 'neighbour principle' (see above) finally establishing negligence as a tort in its own right, rather than an element in other torts. Yet the harm alleged to have been suffered by the plaintiff, though not trivial, hardly amounts to anything extremely serious. A friend of Mrs Donoghue bought her a bottle of ginger-beer in a cafe. The waiter poured her some; she drank some. When her friend refilled the glass from the bottle there floated out the decomposed remains of a snail. She suffered from shock and severe gastro-enteritis as a result of the nauseating sight and of the impurities she had already consumed. Mrs Donoghue claimed that it was the duty of the manufacturer (Stevenson) to provide a system in his business which would prevent snails entering his ginger-beer bottles, and to provide an efficient system of inspection of bottles prior to their being filled with ginger-beer, and that his failure in both duties caused the accident. Such cases provide lawyers with the opportunity to ask seriously such questions as 'Would it make any difference if the label on the bottle had said "Ginger-Beer with Snails In"?'.

This attention to trivial or odd cases for peculiarly legal reasons may seem to mark off legal from non-legal attributions of responsibility. In everyday life we simply would not agonise for years over responsibility for shock and illness suffered at finding snails in ginger-beer and still be talking about it fifty years later. However, non-legal decisions are very often concerned with precedent. Legal systems may also seem to be separated from other social systems in aiming to serve a range of functions. The tort system is supposed to serve such functions as deterrence of dangerous behaviour, equitable apportionment of the cost of risky activities, provision of a public forum of enquiry into the cases of disasters; upholding standards, and so on. The cases brought against Distillers on behalf of victims of the 'Thalidomide tragedy' can be seen to have had all sorts of social consequences beyond the individual awards made, consequences which would not have followed if deciding on awards had not entailed enquiring closely into the effects of the drug, its marketing, etc., in order to attribute responsibility under the law. More recently cases on behalf of children whose mothers took the drug Debendox during pregnancy, or who have suffered as a result of high lead levels, are aimed not so much at securing awards as at getting the drug off the market, or forcing oil companies to stop putting lead in petrol.

Lawyers have probably been led to look for the social functions of legal systems rather than psychological reasons why we attribute causes and responsibility, because legal decisions and legal systems have to be justified in these terms. Again, however, the same considerations apply to non-legal decisions which are often concerned with example, convenience, deterrence, and the practical feasibility of enforcing sanctions. These considerations can be expected to govern the attribution of responsibility in everyday contexts.

SOCIAL CONSEQUENCES AS A SOURCE OF INDIVIDUAL MOTIVATION

The above section has tried to show that what constitutes an acceptable attribution of responsibility depends on the context in which it is made, and that the anticipated consequences of the attribution, both for the individual involved and for society, are an essential part of the context to be taken into account. This section aims to show that there can be considerable leeway within this, and that the way in which responsibility is in fact attributed is influenced by the anticipated social and material consequences for the individual making the attribution. It aims also to show that the way in which an individual perceives an event is influenced by the social context, and by social rules governing who might be held responsible, even if s/he in fact holds no-one responsible. Similar ideas have been proposed by equity theorists (e.g. Austin, Walster, E. and Utne, 1976; Walster, E., Berscheid, E. and Walster, G. W., 1979). An example is the notion of 'psychological equity' whereby an individual may distort the 'facts' to justify what has happened and make any adjustment (such as compensation) irrelevant. The converse of this would be to distort events so as to justify punishing, obtaining compensation, etc. However, the suggestion in the present chapter is not that 'reality' is distorted but rather that alternative definitions of events may be possible, so that it is open to the individual to make the preferred norms applicable without distortion. Perhaps closer than equity theory are the ideas discussed by Schwartz (1975), that humanitarian norms may be held in a general sense (such as 'be kind'), but neutralised or not activated in a particular setting. The individual's definition of the situation must be such as to make them relevant, and their scope must be sufficiently specific to that kind of setting to generate expectations and hence to influence behaviour. Where a general norm exists which could be applied but which is not specific in scope, it must be crystallised. The process he proposes of crystallisation and activation, and the possibility of neutralisation would allow for a considerable amount of leeway.

A range of alternative interpretations of an event may thus be available, and hence a range of potential justifications and responsibility attributions. Having arrived at a definition, and attribution, the individual may defend it vigorously in terms of fairness, moral beliefs, or just rights. However, her/his motives in applying the rule or norm may lie elsewhere. Data obtained in interviews with victims of serious accidents illustrate this[7]. Amongst questions on a variety of topics (such as the financial consequences of their accident) accident victims were asked a set of questions about whether they thought the accident was anyone else's fault and if so in what way; whether they thought anyone should pay them compensation; and any legal *sequelae*. More detailed presentation of the results are given in Lloyd-Bostock (1979b, 1983). Selected findings are summarised here. It is of course very difficult to draw firm conclusions about the factors influencing responses to such questions, but there are some clear indications in the pattern of attributions of fault (the question was phrased in terms of fault rather than responsibility) that three major influences lie in the social context, namely, the prospect of damages, the impact of blaming on personal relationships and, more generally, the impact of legal structures. These factors may be articulated by the accident victims in answer to further questions asked about their perspective on the accident, reasons for not taking legal action, and so on. However, the data are consistent with the hypothesis that these factors influence responsibility attributions in a very fundamental way which is not consciously thought out by the accident victim.

*The prospect of damages*

This is perhaps the hardest influence of all to demonstrate since it involves assuming a direction of causal influence contrary to that one might suppose. The data are consistent with the hypothesis that fault is a justification rather than a reason for seeking damages. In other words, the attribution of fault does not necessarily come first and the idea that the person at fault is therefore liable to compensate follow from that. Rather, where there is a prospect of compensation, the victim attributes fault in a way which justifies her/his claim.

It is possible to infer this from the data because the prospects of compensation, and the likelihood that the victim will be aware of the possibility, differ widely according to the type of accident. Drivers and employers are both covered by compulsory liability insurance, and road and work accidents account for the vast majority of legal claims to damages. Table I shows that fault is attributed most often for these types of accident where the possibility of compensation is most likely to occur to the victim, and where it can be attributed to someone likely to be insured (the employer or a workmate for whose acts the employer is vicariously liable, in work accidents, and the other driver in road accidents). In contrast, it is rare for anyone to be blamed for domestic accidents, the other main category.

TABLE I   Type of accident by whether anyone else was at fault

| Type of accident | Someone else at fault | Total no. of accidents |
|---|---|---|
| Road | 165 (67%) | 246 |
| Industrial (including road/ industrial combined) | 155 (37%) | 409 |
| Domestic | 7 (4%) | 142 |
| Other accidents* | 44 (24%) | 184 |
| *Totals* | *371* | *981* |

*Mostly leisure and sports, including, e.g. tripping on pavements.

A further indication of this lies in the ways in which people were said to be at fault. There were very striking differences between reasons given by victims of road and work accidents. Table II shows the results

TABLE II   Type of fault by type of accident (work and road only)

| Type of fault | Accident | |
|---|---|---|
| | Road | Work |
| Careless/negligent act at the time | 149 (90%) | 31 (20%) |
| Negligence at another time or place: background conditions | 12 (7%) | 122 (79%) |
| Not stated/not codeable | 4 | 2 |
| *Total* where someone else at fault | *165* | *155* |

obtained when responses were sorted into two categories: those cases where fault was attributed in terms of the immediate causes of the accident (e.g. he dropped a hammer on my foot; he pulled out in front of me without looking) and those where fault was in terms of more remote or background factors (e.g. they sent two men to do a three-man job; the handrail had not been fixed). In road accidents, fault was almost always attributed with reference to immediate causes, whereas in work accidents it was the less proximate, more background type of cause which predominated.

It is true, of course, that road accidents are often caused by someone doing something careless at the time. Work accidents are often caused by poor management and safety standards, and home and leisure accidents often are 'just accidents'. But this is an inadequate explanation of the very marked differences found. It seems to be a question of which, if any, out of a range of possible causes and conditions, gets the label 'fault' attached. The example given earlier of the boys swinging from scaffolding illustrates the point that there can be several potential candidates for an attribution of fault – the boys, the workmen, the employers, and perhaps yet others. In the present data this narrowing down from a range of possibilities again seems to be influenced by the prospect of damages. The insured other driver's causal contribution is likely to be an immediate one while the insured employer's is likely to be more remote.

*The relationship between victim and harm-doer*

Attributing fault, blame, or responsibility brings with it potential conflict which people may prefer to avoid altogether rather than resolve. Holding someone else responsible for one's injuries will obviously have different sorts of impact on relationships between friends, family members, employer and employee, fellow employees and strangers. In domestic accidents a person who might be blamed is likely to be a family member or friend, and the prospects of benefit in the form of compensation remote. As Table I shows, these tend to be seen as 'just accidents'. Burman, Genn and Lyons (1977) show that victims of domestic accidents very rarely sue the person they blame. The present data sugggest that most potential legal cases arising from such accidents are filtered out at an earlier stage, since the victim does not attribute fault in the first place. Even accidents at work are seen far more often as the fault of the employer than of a fellow employee, although either could provide grounds for a claim against the insured employer because s/he would be vicariously liable. The importance of the social connotations of blaming are evident in the reasons given by accident victims for stating that the person at fault should not pay them compensation and for not pursuing what they thought might be a legal claim. The victim often acknowledged that the person s/he named as being at fault could be thought of as liable, but preferred not to take this view because s/he was a friend, neighbour or family member. Taking legal action is seen as a rather nasty vindictive thing to do. As one victim put it, 'I don't want blood money'. Another said she 'would not do something like that – though an American probably would'. A number were worried about causing trouble with their employers. In fact there were several cases where employers were obstructive and even threatened to sack or blacklist employees who sued them. It is probably here that the most real difference between legal and non-legal attribution processes arise. Invoking the law is in itself a potent social act which changes the nature of the relationship between, in this case, victim and harm-doer, and introduces the need for particular types of negotiating skill, as well as new characters on the scene and new sources of costs and benefits to be weighed up.

The data also confirm that there may be different senses in which someone is said to be 'responsible', 'to blame', 'at fault', as suggested in the last section. Fault, even where attributed, does not necessarily create a relationship where the payment of compensation is an appropriate consequence. Thus, out of the 393 victims who said their accident was someone else's fault, only about half (202) thought that the person should pay them compensation. Reasons given for this difference by the remaining 192 victims indicate that fault and liability to compensate simply do not always coincide. Sometimes payment of money is inappropriate because there was no financial loss. Or the other person may have 'paid' in some other way (s/he may have been very upset, prosecuted or tried to help). Punishing the person or making sure it does not happen again can be seen as more appropriate than compensation. Sometimes replies indicated that the type of fault was not of the appropriate kind. For example, 'He couldn't really help it', 'You couldn't blame him', 'He didn't mean to do it' or even 'It was just an accident'. This apparent ambivalence over fault and blame need not mean that the respondents, or the principles they are applying, are confused, but rather that these principles are complex and flexible, depending on the context, and anticipated consequences. When the issue of compensation is specifically raised, some respondents find they wish to revise an attribution made earlier (usually about half an hour earlier) in the interview.

*The impact of legal structures*

A direct impact of the law on victims' accounts of their accidents is seen in cases where someone has suggested to the victim that s/he might get compensation and s/he has relied on others to interpret what has happened and what s/he is entitled to receive. This is not just a matter of obtaining information on legal rights. What the victim *feels* seems often to be largely the results of what a lawyer, trade union, friends, or the police have suggested since the accident. The very fact that these results were obtained in interviews which took place some time after the event (at least six months) and were clearly not connected with any legal case which may have arisen, suggests that the process of defining and interpreting the accident in legal terms had a lasting effect on the victims' interpretation of the event. Moreover, the questions about fault were asked before, and quite separately from any questions mentioning legal matters.

A much less direct, and more pervasive, impact of legal rules governing responsibility and liability is also evident. The way in which the victim of an accident attributes responsibility for it will be a function of the rules or norms s/he is used to applying in that sort of context. A second factor of importance, especially where there is uncertainty or ambiguity, is likely to be the acceptability to others with whom s/he has contact, of a particular account (cf. the factors proposed in equity theory as optimising the possibility of opting for 'psychological equity'). The norms available to accident victims, particularly road and work accidents, are very likely to be legal norms of some kind or another. Thus driving is governed by all kinds of legal

rules about speed, right of way, and so on, which provide a guideline for
establishing who was in the wrong. The police are likely to be called
and the account they are looking for will be in terms of who, if anyone,
has broken the criminal law, which is likely to be determined by the
person's actions at the time of the accident. At work on the other hand,
there is a variety of rule systems putting responsibility on the employer
for ensuring safety and compensating the injured, moving the emphasis
away from 'fault' in the more immediate sense. There are statutory
duties, strict and vicarious liability, and other compensation systems,
such as industrial accident compensation, where fault is irrelevant
anyway. Thus in 80% of work accidents where someone was said to be
at fault, it was in the sense of responsibility for safety, good management, and other remote causes and conditions. Both the social
norms available to the victim of an accident and the social outcomes
which affect her/him are likely to have their origins in the law and
legal procedures. When these accident victims attributed fault or liability, it was in terms which clearly reflected legal rules and existing compensation systems, rather than some separate extra-legal
moral system.

## Error and bias in attributions of responsibility

This chapter has emphasised throughout the importance of taking into
consideration the context – especially the social context – of attributions of cause and responsibility. Such an emphasis has implications
for the notions of error, bias, and rationality in judgements, which are
widely used in the attribution literature. In particular, it has implications for the thorny issue of what might constitute criteria for correct,
unbiased, rational judgements. Attribution researchers have generally
made the assumption that something like scientific method would
ultimately provide the most rational basis for causal claims. Statistical
models of objective probability have been drawn on, not only as models
of the cognitive processes involved in the perception of causes and
responsibility, but also as criteria of rationality. If attributions of cause
and responsibility are viewed as social phenomena, this entails a need
for a more social definition of 'error' and 'bias' in terms of social rules
and the social context.

In practice, an implicit notion of 'acceptability' or 'appropriateness'
which reflects the social nature of attributions, has frequently been
interwoven with more explicit formal criteria. For example, a classification of sources of variance into 'appropriate' and 'inappropriate'

grounds for responsibility is implicit in research on motivational bias. One might hold a man responsible for an accident on the grounds that he acted carelessly; but one would not get far in persuading others if one argued that he was responsible because he was insured against personal injury claims, or because the accident had a certain hedonic relevance to oneself. If factors of this latter sort are found to relate to attributions of responsibility they are counted as sources of motivational bias. There is certainly a distinction to be drawn here, but it needs to be drawn carefully and explicitly – especially since it rests on an intuitive judgement by the researcher about what constitute acceptable or appropriate grounds for holding someone responsible. The researcher's judgement will be hard to challenge empirically, since any contrary evidence can be classified as rule-breaking; and the extent to which her/his theory or research report is found convincing is liable to be influenced by the researcher's own sociolinguistic skills.

While it is evidently part of what we understand by attributions that they can be based on inappropriate grounds, it is very difficult to derive from this satisfactory criteria for categorising attributions as correct or incorrect for research purposes. In addition to the problem of circularity indicated above, there is the fact that the same event may call for several different attributions of cause or responsibility, each of which in context would be correct. It is important therefore that any implication that an attribution is correct in this sense specify the context in which it is made. Moreover, where, for example, there is the possibility of gaining compensation, judgements can be determined by what is rational from the individual's perspective, while at the same time being perfectly legitimate, and acceptable to others. A single attribution can thus be appropriate and acceptable in this sense, and involve no deception or distortion; and yet at the same time, in another sense, be biased.

Clearly, a range of social and psychological factors interact to determine when an attribution of cause or responsibility will be made and the form it will take, and distinctions between these various factors need to be drawn. But it is surely misleading to label those factors which seem inappropriate as sources of error, bias, prejudice, and so on. These terms are heavily evaluative in their import and imply distortion of some kind. For example, it could lead one to view the accident victims' perspectives discussed above as distorted by a selfish quest for money. It is difficult, but important, to resist a feeling of having caught subjects (or judges) out in some way, or uncovered a failing, when one discovers that their responses appear to be influenced by factors which would not support the case if explicitly put forward as grounds for responsibility. That would be to enter, rather than study, the argument.

The idea of 'appropriateness' would seem to be most relevant to attributions of responsibility and cause as social acts. When one is concerned with rapid, unspoken and unobservable causal inferences, quasi-scientific criteria would seem to become more appropriate. But here too it is necessary to take very much fuller account of the context and purposes of the attributions, and resist misleading terminology. The concepts of objective probability and logic are clearly central and useful in attribution theory, and provide a basis for comparison with actual causal judgements which has yielded some provocative and revealing research findings. It is important, however, not to be led by the use of evaluative terminology (such as 'error', 'bias', 'short-comings', 'irrational') to treat statistical models as providing criteria which attributions of cause or responsibility in everyday life should ideally meet. There is no *a priori* reason to prefer a particular kind of 'scientific' solution to causal questions and indeed it seems rather rash to assume that a model such as analysis of variance or Bayesian statistics is adequate and appropriate and that the subject is biased or making an error. A model appropriate to scientific enquiry, tied to a Humean notion of 'cause', may not be at all appropriate in other contexts. Moreover, the use of such models tends to focus research excessively narrowly on one aspect of attribution processes – namely the use of a given, and already at least partially processed set of information to arrive at a causal attribution. This, of course, leaves open such crucial questions as what information will be sought and taken into account? how do we cope with incomplete information and the burden of starting from scratch with every judgement? and when and for what purposes do we attribute causes and responsibility at all?

A far more promising approach to the explanation (as distinct from evaluation) of causal attributions abandons the idea that people carry out an analysis analogous to, say, an analysis of variance, and instead postulates causal schemata (e.g. Kelley, 1972b). This approach recognises the fact that causal judgements are made in accordance with assumptions, pre-conceptions, experiment and/or teaching about causal effects. Though rational in that they are a 'best guess', attributions go beyond the information given, and gaps are filled by expectations and assumptions. Judgements which are a 'best guess' in this sense cannot be simply categorised as irrational or mistaken, using criteria derived from the more formal idealised models and estimates of objective probablity. All judgements of cause and responsibility rest in some degree on assumptions, and talking about them on shared assumptions. As Hart and Honoré (1959) point out, those of interest to lawyers are those open to negotiation, and not such basics as the effects of blows, impacts, etc., which provide the raw material for further interpretation of what has happened. The problem of drawing the line between what can and cannot rationally be assumed none-theless remains.

The answer probably includes seeing the line as variable, depending on the *context*. The 'rational' attribution of causes is a function not only of the formal objective probability that A caused B, but also of the rewards and costs attached to being laborious but accurate v. quick but approximate. The efforts put into seeking specific new information rather than relying on assumptions should thus relate to the context and the reasons why the question of cause or responsibility is raised. Relying heavily on assumptions most of the time is necessary as well as time saving, and indeed it would for many purposes be looked on as irrational to insist on high levels of probability or precision.

It is here that we we may find the answer to the question why legal processes of attribution can be so lengthy, reflective and laborious compared with attributions in extra-legal contexts, while still having essential features in common. Even where the type of consequences attached to each is similar (e.g. punishment, making amends, public censure) the seriousness of legal consequences for the defendant and other costs attached to legal decisions are likely to be considerably greater than for everyday decisions. Methods of establishing and categorising facts, controlling the interpretation put on them, seg-menting and making public the process of deciding, and probably too of distinguishing between varieties of responsibility, which are appro-priate in legal contexts would be pedantic (or irrational) and un-necessarily costly in most non-legal ones. Even in legal contexts a line must be drawn beyond which it becomes irrational to pursue things further. Hart and Honoré (1959) observe that: 'The law is satisfied, in deciding whether the negligence of a motorist caused a collision with another vehicle, with a description of the position of the two vehicles which would not be accurate enough for the purpose of atomic physics' (1959, p. 418).

Attributions of cause and responsibility cannot easily be categorised as correct, reasonable, rational, unbiased, etc. on the one hand, or as prejudiced, irrational, mistaken, etc. on the other. Much finer dis-tinctions in the use of these terms are needed, and a much stronger sense of the context and purpose of attributions. All judgements are in a sense biased and subject to error, and two people can rationally arrive at conflicting interpretations of the same event. There can be rational error and bias; and irrational insistence on accuracy. Differing perceptions and accounts of cause and responsibility arise from differences in context, motive and experience, and hence in information sought, interpretation and levels of certainty required. Rather than reasonable v. unreasonable; biased v. unbiased; correct v. in error etc., it might be more appropriate and less emotive to describe attribution judgements as more or less adaptive to their purpose.

## Conclusion

There is some consensus among social psychologists that attribution research needs re-evaluation. Both the basic model of the naive psychologist as scientist/statistician, and the ways in which the central concepts of cause and responsibility have been used, have come in for criticism. This chapter has attempted to clarify the nature and source of some of the difficulties and has proposed a speculative new framework.

Approaching questions about the attribution of cause and responsibility through questions about the workings and structure of the law throws into relief important aspects of these processes which are easily overlooked in laboratory studies. Legal analyses can also suggest where conceptual difficulties have arisen. Many tentative suggestions have been made in this chapter which will not be repeated here, but the two main general conclusions can be summarised as follows. First, if attribution research is to continue to explore the attribution of the causes of social behaviour and ask questions about responsibility in the sense of 'answerable', a new and broader theoretical base is needed which recognises the essentially social nature of the phenomena under study. In particular, the social context of an attribution is a crucial source of variance which has been overlooked. The social context can determine when an attribution is called for, what form it will take, and the way in which it will be argued or negotiated. Moreover, the further anticipated social consequences of making an attribution at all, or one rather than another, can be at least as important a source of motivation as, say, identification with a similar other.

A general framework to take account of such factors was suggested. The attribution of causes and responsibility is seen as a complex function of psychological and social processes. Emphasis is placed on accounting for attributions as observable rule-governed social acts rather than as continuous cognitive processes, but this does not imply independent types of attribution, nor empirically separable aspects of attribution processes which could form separate fields of research. On the contrary, they are closely interwoven. The way in which an individual continuously causally interprets the social world, and how s/he feels about events, is structured at least partly by social (including legal) rules, norms and expectations. Theory concerned with rapid unspoken inferences about the causes of behaviour, or causes of events which might form grounds for an attribution of responsibility, still needs to take account of this fact.

Secondly, attribution research has run into difficulties because the field has grown rather unsystematically around a cluster of ill-defined concepts. Because the exact phenomena under study have not been clearly delineated it can also be unclear what models and questions are appropriate. Indeed some lines of research, because they have been conceived and interpreted in the context of attribution theory, have probably impaired rather than advanced our understanding of attribution processes. Phenomena better understood in terms of social sequences, standards of behaviour, learned social norms and their violation, and so on, have been approached in more limited terms of the determinants of causal inference. Much has been made of the notions of 'error' and 'bias', thought of in a quasi-scientific way, where it might have been more appropriate to talk of maladaptive or incompetent attributions.

The attribution of causes and responsibility involves immensely complex processes and concepts. Against this, attribution theory appears limited and narrow in emphasis and to have been outgrown by the research it has generated. It is necessary to take stock and do some fundamental re-thinking, and perhaps reformulate some of the questions which are being addressed in attribution research.

## Notes

1. Barty-King v. Ministry of Defence [1979] 2 ALL ER 88.
2. Cuttress v. Scaffolding (GB) Ltd [1953] 2 ALL ER 1075.
3. *The Wagon Mound*: Mounts Dock and Engineering Co. Ltd v. Overseas Tankship (UK) Ltd [1961] AC 388.
4. Donoghue v. Stevenson [1932] AC 562.
5. Paris v. Stepney B.C. [1951] 1 ALL ER 42.
6. Shaw Savill and Albion Co. Ltd v. The Commonwealth [1940] 66 CLR 344.
7. The data were collected as part of a national household survey of victims of injury and illness carried out by the SSRC Centre for Socio-legal Studies, Oxford, and funded by the Social Science Research Council.

# Part IV

# Attribution Theory and Personality Research

# 11

# Implications of the Traits v. Situations Controversy for Differences in the Attributions of Actors and Observers

Thomas C. Monson

## Introduction

The main aim of attribution theory and research is to define the means by which individuals understand and explain behavior. Most investigators of the attribution process have assumed that the major question a perceiver asks is whether a particular behavior can be better explained by some enduring internal ability, personality trait, or attitude that the person possesses (dispositional attribution) or by some external characteristic of the particular situation in which the person is momentarily located (situational attribution). As a result of extensive research and theorising, a number of basic rules or principles have been postulated to elucidate the processes by which perceivers arrive at these inferences (e.g. Bem, 1967, 1972; Harvey, Ickes and Kidd, 1976, 1978a; Heider, 1958a; Jones and Davis, 1965; Jones, Kanouse, Kelley, Nisbett, Valins and Weiner, 1972).

## Attribution rules

Kelley (1973) divides these attributional principles into two convenient categories: those cases in which the attributor has information from multiple observations of behavior and those where there is information relating to only a single observation of behavior. In the former case, the attributor is hypothesised to operate according to the 'covariation' principle. If a behavior occurs often (high consistency), occurs only in the presence of a particular situation (high distinctiveness), and occurs for many people (high consensus), then the cause of behavior will be attributed to characteristics of the situation (Kelley,

1967; McArthur, 1972). On the other hand, if a behavior occurs often (high consistency), occurs in the presence of varied situations (low distinctiveness), occurs uniquely for a particular person (low consensus), then the cause of the behavior will be attributed to characteristics of the person.

If the attributor does not have access to the multiple observations of behavior necessary to apply the covariation principle then he or she is likely to apply the 'discounting' principle. Again research (e.g. Jones, Davis and Gergen, 1961; Jones and Harris, 1967; Strickland, 1958; Thibaut and Riecken, 1955) indicates that acts which are easily justified, have a high base rate of occurrence, or occur in the context of sufficient situational causes are unlikely to be attributed to dispositional causes. Furthermore, Kelley (1972b) has specified the role of 'facilitative' and 'inhibitory' situational cues in the discounting process. If the situational cues encourage or are 'facilitative' of the behavior performed, then dispositional causation is likely to be discounted. On the other hand, dispositional causation is not discounted if the situational cues are neutral to the behavior performed and is even augmented if the situational cues discourage or are 'inhibitory' to the behavior performed.

## Differences in the attributions of actors and observers

Although actors' explanations of their own behavior (self-attributions) and observers' explanations for the behavior of others (interpersonal attributions) have been assumed to operate on the same attributional principles (cf. Bem, 1967, 1972), it has been suggested that actors' and observers' attributions may often diverge because of differences in the information that is normally available to them (e.g. Bem, 1972; Jones and Nisbett, 1972). For example, Bem (1972) has cited three informational differences and one motivational difference between actors and observers that may be responsible for divergent attributions.

The *Intimate v. Stranger* distinction refers to the greater role of historical information in determining the attributions of actors as compared with observers. Actors usually have more knowledge about their own behavior in other situations and at other times. This implies that actors should have more and better evidence upon which to judge covariation (Kelley, 1972a) between their own behavior and possible situational and dispositional causes. To the extent that they recall cross-situational consistency in their behavior, actors have excellent evidence on which to base a dispositional attribution. Similarly, they also have excellent evidence on which to base a situational attribution when they recall high situational distinctiveness in their behavior. Observers, not having access to this historical information, must rely on other more subtle rules of inference (e.g. Kelley's discounting principle).

Bem's *Actor v. Observer* distinction refers to Jones and Nisbett's (1972) observation that the actor's environment is differentially salient for actors and observers. For the observer, behavior constitutes the figural stimulus whereas situational cues are foremost in the perceptual field of the actor. Since the environment receives more attention from actors than from observers, it would seem that actors are in a better position to assess whether situational cues are facilitative, neutral, or inhibitory to the behavior performed by them.

The *Insider v. Outsider* difference refers to the potential stimuli (e.g. cognitions, attitudes, intentions, emotions, etc.) inside the body of the actor that are relatively unavailable to the observer. Actor's knowledge of their inner states should allow them to compare the importance of these inner states with situational cues in their immediate environment. Thus, actors should be in a better position than observers to discount the role of less plausible causes.

The *Self v. Other* difference refers to the possible role of motivational variables in the attribution of causality. For instance, an actor's self-attributions are more likely to be influenced by the motive to maintain or enhance one's self-esteem than would an observer's interpersonal attributions. Actors should be more concerned than observers with making dispositional attributions for praiseworthy behavior and situational attributions for blameworthy behavior.

Although the motivational difference suggested by Bem (1972) may occasionally undermine the actor's advantageous position, the three informational differences discussed by Bem seem to imply that actors should often be in a better position than observers to identify accurately the causes of their own behavior (e.g. Kelley, 1972a; Monson and Snyder, 1977). Such an implication depends, however, on one's assumptions concerning what type of attribution is most likely to be correct.

JONES AND NISBETT'S DIVERGENT PERSPECTIVES HYPOTHESIS

Jones and Nisbett (1972) have assumed that dispositional attributions are, more often than situational attributions, incorrect attributions. This assumption has been given credence by the lack of cross-situational consistency found in relation to personality traits and other dispositions. Empirical reviews have suggested that the relationship between attitudes and behavior (Wicker, 1969) and traits and behavior (Mischel, 1968) rarely produce correlations above +0.30. Mischel (1968) has interpreted this failure of dispositions to account for more than 10% of the variance in social behavior as evidence for it being specific to the situation and controlled by the situation. Accordingly, if behavior is predictable from a knowledge of an individual's situation rather than from a knowledge of her/his dispositions, then dispositional attributions are not warranted (cf. Jones and Nisbett, 1972). According to the informational differences between actors and observers, actors should not make incorrect dispositional attributions. Thus, it is not surprising that Jones and Nisbett (1972) have proposed that 'there is a pervasive tendency for actors to attribute their actions to situational requirements, whereas observers tend to attribute the same actions to stable personal dispositions' (p. 80).

If behavior is more likely to be determined by situational factors, then it is clear how the informational distinctions offered by Bem (1972) should lead actors to offer relatively more situational attributions than observers. For example, in the prior discussion of Bem's *Intimate v. Stranger* distinction, it was suggested that actors should be more aware of how distinctive their behavior is, depending on whether it is consistent or inconsistent across situations. However, based upon Mischel's (1968) review, Jones and Nisbett (1972) suggested that the latter case occurs more frequently. In other words, they proposed that actors' intimate knowledge of the considerable variability of their behaviors at different times and in different situations should induce them to perceive greater distinctiveness and lower consistency in their behavior than would be perceived by observers (cf. Eisen, 1979). Thus, as a consequence of the employment of Kelley's (1972b) covariation principle, one would expect actors to offer causal explanations which are relatively more situational than those offered by observers.

Similarly, in discussing Bem's *Actor v. Observer* distinction, it was suggested that the visual perspective of actors should better enable them to ascertain whether the situational cues are facilitative, neutral, or inhibitory to the behaviors that they exhibit. Given the assumption that behavior is more frequently determined by situational factors, the first case in which the situational cues are facilitative to the behavior performed should occur more frequently. As a consequence of the actor's being in a better position to use this information in the employment of Kelley's (1972) discounting principle, one would expect attributions to be more situational from the actor's than the observer's perspective.

Although there exists considerable empirical research which is consistent with Jones and Nisbett's (1972) proposition, the evidence is far from unequivocal (for a review, see Monson and Snyder, 1977). In a number of the studies reviewed, the attributions offered by actors were more situational than those offered by observers. However, there were also investigations in which there were no differences in the attributions of actors and observers and investigations in which the attributions offered by actors were more dispositional than those offered by observers.

Rather than questioning the assumption that informational differences may often lead actors to more accurate perceptions than observers, Monson and Snyder (1977) suggested that the crucial issue is whether it can be assumed that situational attributions are more likely to be accurate than dispositional attributions. In order to evaluate whether situational attributions are any more likely to be valid than dispositional attributions, it is necessary to examine in more detail research investigating the extent to which behavior can be predicted by knowledge of a person's traits or by the characteristics of the situation in which that person is momentarily located.

## The traits v. situations controversy

In his survey Mischel (1968) found very little evidence for the temporal stability and cross-situational consistency in behavior that would be expected if traits were useful in predicting behavior. However, other personality theorists have argued that personality traits can be used to predict behavior in some circumstances much more effectively than was suggested by Mischel's (1968) brief review of the literature (cf. Block, 1977; Hogan, DeSoto and Solano, 1977). Block (1977) has also suggested that the poor empirical support is not due to inadequacies inherent in the trait model but rather to a number of methodological inadequacies in much of the personality research conducted (see chapter 12). In addition, other personality researchers have suggested that even though they may not always be useful in predicting single act criteria, traits may often be highly correlated with multiple act criteria (e.g. Epstein, 1977; Jaccard, 1974; McGowan and Gormly, 1976).

### INTERACTION BETWEEN PERSONS AND SITUATIONS

Mischel (1968) interpreted the failure of personality traits strongly to predict behavior as evidence for the situational control and situational specificity of behaviour. This view is not shared by Bowers (1973) who has offered an important critique of the situationist position. His review of the literature indicated that the average variance in behavior due to situational variables was no higher than that due to person variables. Instead, much more variance in behavior was accounted for by examining the interaction between person variables and situation variables. Thus, most of the recent discussion on the 'traits v. situations' controversy has emphasised that one must know the characteristics of both the person and the situation to predict behavior (e.g. Endler and Magnussen, 1976; Magnussen and Endler, 1977).

Despite the considerable evidence that has been reported concerning the existence of person × situation interactions, the use of such interactions to predict behavior is not without its problems. If one needs to know how the characteristics of each person interact with the characteristics of each situation in order to predict behavior, one is left with an almost hopeless task. However, if one can specify in advance more generalised interactions which allow for the prediction of behavior in a broader range of situations or for a broader group of individuals, than the interactionist perspective becomes much more useful.

*Predictability for some people.* One form that a generalised person × situation interaction can take is when personality traits are useful in predicting the behaviors of some individuals but relatively unhelpful in predicting the behaviors of other people. The most frequently cited study demonstrating this pattern was conducted by Bem and Allen (1974). Based upon a self-report measure, individuals were divided into two groups, namely, those who reported that they exhibited considerable cross-situational consistency in their friendliness and conscientiousness and those who reported that they exhibited con-siderable variability in their behaviors. The research revealed a strong relationship between the individuals' traits and behaviors in a variety of settings for the former group but the more customary, weak relationship for the latter group.

In contrast to research by Bem and Allen (1974) which examined the specific trait dimensions of friendliness and conscientiousness, Snyder (1979) has proposed that there may be more generalised tendencies for the behavior of some individuals to be predicted by traits. Snyder (1974) developed a 25-item personality scale called the Self-Monitor-ing Scale which aims to discriminate between individuals who exhibit the cross-situational consistency predicted by traits (low self-monitoring individuals) and individuals whose situational specificity and variability in their behaviors make it very difficult to predict their behavior from dispositional measures (high self-monitoring indi-viduals).

Snyder's (1974) research has indicated that individuals who are known to have the ability to exhibit considerable variability in their behaviors (e.g. actors) have higher than average self-monitoring scores. In addition, Moos (1968) has indicated that hospitalised psychiatric patients typically exhibit less variability in their behavior than do normals. Research has also indicated that hospitalised psychiatric patients score lower than average on the Self-Monitoring Scale (Snyder, 1974). Other more direct evidence suggests that high self-monitoring (HSM) are more able than low self-monitoring (LSM) individuals effectively to change their behavior from one situation to another (e.g. Lippa, 1976; Snyder, 1974). Furthermore, HSM individuals are more likely than LSM individuals to report high cross-situational variability in their behavior in such diverse domains as altruism, honesty, and self-restraint (Snyder and Monson, 1975). Thus, it is not surprising to find that the relationship between dispositional measures and behavior is higher for LSM individuals than for HSM individuals (e.g. Snyder and Swann, 1976; Snyder and Tanke, 1976).

*Predictability in some situations.* If it is possible to specify persons for whom traits can or cannot be used to predict behavior then it may also be possible to specify situations in which traits can or cannot be used to predict behavior. Softening somewhat his earlier social learning or social behavior theory, Mischel (1973, 1977) has proposed a cognitive social learning formulation which reaffirms the importance of person variables which interact with situational factors to determine behavior. Mischel's (1977) discussion of 'when do individual differences make a difference' (p. 346) suggests another generalised form a person × situation interaction can take. Research by Price and Bouffard (1974) indicates that there are settings (e.g. 'in church' or 'at a job interview') in which there is a considerable 'situational constraint' and few behaviors are considered appropriate. Mischel (1977) suggests that in such settings where situational pressures are strong, there should be a few individual differences in the stimulus meaning that is assigned to the situation. As a consequence, there should be little variance in the behavior exhibited by different individuals, and a knowledge of individuals' relative positions on trait dimensions should be of minimal benefit in predicting their behavior.

Price and Bouffard (1974) also found that there are other settings (e.g. 'in the park' or 'in one's own room') in which there is little 'situational constraint' and a wide range of behaviors are considered appropriate. Situations that are ambiguously structured are more likely to have relatively different psychological meanings for different individuals (cf. Mischel, 1977). As a consequence, there should be considerable variance in the behavior exhibited by different individuals, and a knowledge of individuals' relative positions on trait dimensions should be of considerable benefit in predicting their behavior.

Monson, Hesley and Chernick (1980b) conducted several studies to investigate Mischel's assertions. In a questionnaire study, extraverts and introverts were asked to report the probability that (*i*) they would choose a telephone sales job over a library research job, (*ii*) would go to a college-sponsored 'getting acquainted' party, (*iii*) would choose to give a speech rather than write a research paper, and (*iv*) would go to a company party sponsored by their employer. In addition, participants were asked to assume that there were strong situational pressures to exhibit the extraverted behaviors (e.g. the sales job paid $5.00 per hour and the research job paid $2.65 per hour), or intraverted behaviors (e.g. sales job = $2.65 and the research job = $5.00), moderate situational pressures to exhibit the extraverted behaviors (e.g. sales job = $3.25 and research job = $2.65), or introverted behaviors (e.g. sales job = $2.65 and the research job = $3.25), or relatively weak situational pressures to exhibit either the extraverted or introverted behaviors (e.g. both jobs paid $2.65 per hour). As expected, the average correlation between the participants' relative position on the introversion–extraversion dimension and their predicted behaviors was the highest when situational pressures were weakest ($r = +0.42$) and conversely was lowest when the situational pressures were strongest ($r = +0.13$). In a conceptual replication conducted in the laboratory, the participants' trait scores on introversion–extraversion predicted behavior better when situational pressures were weak ($r = +0.63$) than when they strongly encouraged either extraverted ($r = +0.25$) or introverted ($r = +0.36$) behavior.

## Implications for actor–observer differences

Based upon Mischel's (1968) review and conclusion that personality traits are inadequate as predictors of behavior, Jones and Nisbett (1972) assumed that situational attributions would more frequently be valid than dispositional attributions. However, in the time since Jones and Nisbett's paper was published, there has been a sufficient number of research and theoretical developments in the 'traits v. situations' controversy which suggest that this assumption may be wrong. It appears that if personality traits and other dispositional measures can predict behavior for some people and in some situations, then dispositional attributions may in some specifiable instances be more appropriate than situational attributions. Furthermore, if traits cannot predict behavior for some people and in some situations, then situational attributions may in some specifiable instances be more appropriate than dispositional attributions.

If the informational differences between actors and observers tend to give an advantage to the actor in offering a valid attribution, then some of the evidence inconsistent with Jones and Nisbett's (1972) proposal may possibly be explained by the fact that dispositional attributions may have been more appropriate in those instances. In fact, Monson and Snyder (1977) have tried to explain most of the research by proposing that 'actors should make more situational attributions than should observers about behavioral acts that are under situational control; by contrast, actors' perceptions of behaviors that are under dispositional control ought to be more dispositional than the perceptions of observers' (p. 96).

Although Monson and Snyder's proposal provided an adequate *post hoc* explanation for some of the inconsistent research on actor–observer differences, a proposition of this nature is best judged by its ability to predict and specify in advance what differences might be expected between actor and observer attributions.

ACTOR–OBSERVER DIFFERENCES FOR DIFFERENT PEOPLE

If HSM individuals are relatively more influenced by situational factors and LSM individuals by dispositions, then one might expect differences in the attributions that would be offered for behaviors from the actor's and observer's perspectives. Some indirect evidence for these predictions comes from several sources. For example, Snyder and Tanke (1976) presented research which indicates that LSM individuals are more likely than HSM individuals to make correspondent dispositional self-attributions for counter-attitudinal behaviors. In contrast, research has suggested that HSM individuals are more likely to offer attributions from the observer's perspective that are more dispositional than those offered by LSM individuals (Berscheid, Graziano, Monson and Dermer, 1976). More direct evidence has indicated that HSM individuals perceive greater cross-situational variability in their own behaviors (Snyder and Monson, 1975) and offer more situational attributions for their own behaviors (Brockner and Eckenrode, 1979) than they do for others. In contrast, LSM individuals perceive greater cross-situational consistency in their own behaviors (Snyder and Monson, 1975) and offer more dispositional attributions for their own behaviors (Brockner and Eckenrode, 1979) than they do for others.

ACTOR–OBSERVER DIFFERENCES IN DIFFERENT SITUATIONS

It was mentioned in a previous section that research by Monson *et al.* (1980a) indicated that individuals' introversion–extraversion scores predicted behavioral intentions fairly well when situational pressures were weak, but very poorly when situational pressures were strong. As a follow-up to this study, Monson and Hesley (1980) asked the participants to complete an additional questionnaire in which they were asked to offer attributions based upon the assumption that they (the actor's perspective) or someone they did not know (the observer's perspective) had exhibited the extraverted behaviors in settings which weakly, moderately, or strongly encouraged the extraverted behaviors. In addition, the participants were asked to offer attributions based upon the assumption that they or someone else had exhibited the introverted behaviors in settings which weakly, moderately, or stongly encouraged the introverted behaviors. The means for the attributions are presented in Table I.

Overall, attributions for behaviors consistent with the actor's traits

TABLE I   Attributions as a function of perspective, consistency with traits, and situational pressure. (Larger numbers indicate that relatively more dispositional attribitions were offered)

|  | Behavior consistent with actor's trait | Behavior inconsistent with actor's trait |
|---|---|---|
| *Weak situational pressure:* | | |
| Actor's perspective | 5.38 | 4.00 |
| Observer's perspective | 4.60 | 4.53 |
|  | +0.78 | −0.53 |
| *Moderate situational pressure:* | | |
| Actor's perspective | 3.47 | 3.00 |
| Observer's perspective | 3.14 | 3.34 |
|  | +0.33 | −0.34 |
| *Strong situational pressure:* | | |
| Actor's perspective | 2.54 | 1.85 |
| Observer's perspective | 2.37 | 2.21 |
|  | +0.17 | −0.36 |

tended to be more dispositional when offered from the actor's perspective than from the observer's perspective. In contrast, more situational attributions tended to be given for behaviors inconsistent with the actor's traits when offered from the actor's perspective.[1]

In addition, there was an interaction which indicated that these effects were strongest when the situational pressures were weak and were less marked when the situational pressures were moderate or strong. Probably the most reasonable interpretation of this interaction is that the differential knowledge actors and observers possess about the actor's traits will produce the largest differences in attributions when there is little other useful information upon which to base the attributions. However, when there exists other useful information (e.g. information that the behavior was performed in the context of moderately facilitative or strongly facilitative situational cues) that is shared in common by actors and observers, than the attributions of actors and observers should be more similar.

A RE-EXAMINATION OF INFORMATIONAL DIFFERENCES

A clearer picture of why Jones and Nisbett's (1972) proposition has not received unequivocal support is emerging. In many settings, particularly in laboratory studies (cf. Monson and Snyder, 1977), the behavior of actors can be best predicted by a knowledge of the situation in which they are momentarily located. In such settings the attributions offered by actors are likely to be more situational than those offered by observers. However, in other circumstances the behavior of actors can be best predicted by a knowledge of their dispositions. In such circumstances the attributions offered by actors may be more dispositional than those offered by observers.

However, these conclusions are predicated upon the same informational differences between actors and observers that were suggested by Jones and Nisbett (1972) to explain their proposition. A re-examination of several of these informational differences may enable us to better specify the direction of actor–observer differences in attributions.

*The intimate v. stranger distinction.* One of the most important information differences between actors and observers is the information that actors possess about their behavioral histories. Actors have more knowledge of their past actions and are in a better position to evaluate the distinctiveness and consistency of a present behavior with past behaviors. In fact, research conducted by Hansen and Lowe (1976) has indicated that actors tend to rely more upon distinctiveness and consistency information in forming their attributions, whereas observers tend to rely more upon consensus information.

As a consequence of their suggestion that actors would perceive high distinctiveness in their behavior, Jones and Nisbett (1972) hypothesised that individuals are less likely to ascribe traits to themselves than to others. This has been supported by recent research (e.g. Goldberg, 1978; Nisbett, Caputo, Legant and Marecek, 1973). Nisbett *et al.* developed a measure of trait ascription that consisted of 20 bipolar adjective pairs (e.g. cautious–bold) each with the option 'depends on the situation'. When asked to check one of the three alternatives for each trait category that best described themselves and others, participants were more likely to choose 'depends on the situation' for themselves than for others.

In subsequent research, Monson *et al.* (1980b) replicated the results of Nisbett *et al.* (1973) when they used the same format for the trait ascription questionnaire. However, when the 'depends on the situation' alternative was deleted and the participants were asked to choose which of the 40 trait adjectives (listed in random order) could be used to describe the target, a different pattern of results emerged. The participants reported that a greater number of traits could be used to describe themselves than their acquaintances.[2] In addition, on a different set of 6-point bipolar trait scales, the participants rated themselves more extremely and confidently than they did their acquaintances. Furthermore, Monson *et al.* (1980b) reported that the participants ascribed a greater number of personality traits and offered more extreme and confident dispositional inferences to acquaintances with whom they were relatively familiar than to acquaintances with whom they were less familiar.[3]

Why would individuals respond with 'depends on the situation' more frequently for themselves on one trait ascription questionnaire, but yet appear to attribute more traits to themselves on others? One possible explanation is suggested by the previously mentioned research that indicates that traits may predict behavior in some settings but not in others. Having a greater knowledge of their behavioral histories than do observers, actors have a much better basis upon which to judge whether or not they exhibit sufficient cross-situational consistency in their behavior in order to warrant a trait ascription. For example, Monson *et al.* (1980a) found extraverts to report that they would generally exhibit extraverted behaviors when situational pressures encouraging extraversion were weak, moderate or strong. However, the extraverts reported a strong likelihood of exhibiting introverted behaviors when there were situational pressures which moderately or strongly encouraged introversion. Despite this latter finding it is clear that the extraverts thought they exhibited extraverted behaviors frequently enough to describe themselves as such.

Furthermore, although Jones and Nisbett (1972) suggested that actors' knowledge of their inconsistent behavior should divert them from perceiving themselves to possess personality traits, both theory and research indicate otherwise. Allport (1966) has proposed that 'acts and even habits, that are inconsistent with a trait are not proof of the nonexistence of the trait' (p. 1). Likewise, Regan, Straus and Fazio (1974) have reported research to support their conclusion that 'behavior which is consistent with prior trait ascriptions is attributed internally and provides additional evidence for the trait ascription; behavior inconsistent with trait ascriptions is attributed externally, to situational factors, and thus does not disconfirm the trait ascription' (p. 397).

In fact, the countless experiments conducted to investigate cognitive dissonance (Festinger, 1957) and self-perception processes (Bem, 1967, 1972) support this conclusion. The lesson to be learned from these studies is that actors will change their attitudes and dispositions to be consistent with their counter-attitudinal behaviors when the behaviors are performed under conditions of low external justification. However, what is often ignored or under-emphasised is that there is no tendency for the actors to change their perceptions of their dispositions when they perform the inconsistent behaviors under conditions of high external justification.

Since actors are most likely to exhibit behaviors that are consistent with their traits when situational pressures are weak and *vice versa*, it would appear that actors are likely to have considerable data upon which to base a trait ascription but little data upon which to disconfirm that ascription. Thus, when provided with the opportunity to choose the traits that describe themselves (Monson *et al.*, 1980b; Turner, 1978), actors have much more behavioral history information than observers which allows them to infer that they have personality traits. However, when the question includes an option of the type 'depends on the situation' (Nisbett *et al.*, 1973), knowledge of their behavioral history allows actors to state that their behavior is occasionally inconsistent with their traits and as a consequence does depend on the situation.

Research indicates that people often (when not constrained by options like 'depends on the situation') report themselves as having more personality traits than other people. This differential tendency in attributing personality traits should also have certain implications for causal attributions of particular behaviors. If behaviors consistent with prior trait ascriptions are attributed more situationally (cf. Regan *et al.*, 1974), then this should produce differences in the attributions of actors and observers. Actors should be more aware than unacquainted observers of whether a given behavior is consistent or inconsistent with a prior trait ascription. Monson *et al.* (1980b) have concluded that the attributions of actors should be more dispositional than those of observers when the actors exhibit behaviors consistent with their traits but that the attributions of actors should be more situational than those of observers when the actors exhibit behaviors inconsistent with their traits.

The research reported by Monson and Hesley (1980a), is consistent with this proposal, but it does not actually demonstrate that the difference is due to the differential knowledge that actors and observers have of the actors' traits or behavioral histories. Some substantiating support has been provided by several attempts to simulate actor–observer differences (Smith, Monson, Hesley and Graziano, 1979a).

In one of the studies, participants were asked to make attributions after viewing a videotape of an interaction in which the target person exhibited either extraverted behavior or introverted behavior. In addition, participants were provided with information on how the target person or one of the other participants had completed the introversion–extraversion scale of the Eysenck Personality Inventory (H. J. Eysenck and S. B. G. Eysenck, 1964). The information provided made it appear that the person completing the scale was either extraverted or introverted. Those participants having no information about the target person could be regarded as uninformed observers' whereas those with such information might be regarded as simulating the informed actors' perspective.

The data indicated that the participants offered attributions that were more dispositional when they possessed information that the target had a trait that was consistent with the behaviors than when they possessed no information. In contrast, participants offered attributions that were more situational when they possessed information that the target had a trait that was inconsistent with the behaviors than when they possessed no information.

In a second study reported by Smith *et al.* (1979a) essentially the same results were produced when information about the target's traits was conveyed by means of behavioral histories. These behavioral histories consisted of a series of six videotaped episodes in which the target acted consistently in either an extraverted or an introverted manner with six different people.

Further evidence for the role of distinctiveness and consistency information in producing differences in the attributions of actors and observers was reported by Eisen (1979). Contrary to Jones and Nisbett's (1972) prediction, she found no general tendency for actors to think that their behavior was more distinctive and less consistent than observers thought it was. Instead, Eisen (1979) concluded that 'actors reported their desirable behavior to be less distinctive and more consistent than observers thought it was, whereas undesirable behavior was seen as more distinctive and less consistent than observers believed it to be' (p. 270). Consistent with these differences in perceptions of distinctiveness and consistency, Eisen reported that positive behaviors tended to be explained more dispositionally and negative behaviors to be explained more situationally by actors than by observers. Furthermore, the strong role of the informational differences was revealed by the disappearance of these differences in the attributions of actors and observers when the observers were provided with the same information possessed by the actors.

*The actor v. observer distinction.* The effects of visual perspective on the attributions of actors and observers has been cited as the area of research which has provided the strongest support for Jones and Nisbett's (1972) proposition (e.g. Jones, 1976; Taylor and Fiske, 1978). There has been a great deal of research that has indicated that greater causality is attributed to those features that are most salient to the perceiver (for a review, see Taylor and Fiske, 1978). Furthermore, since the environment is most visually salient to the actor and the actor is most visually salient to the observer, the common consensus is that this should produce attributions that are more situational when offered from the actor's perspective than when offered from the observers's perspective.

The study that has been most frequently cited to support this conclusion was conducted by Storms (1973). Participants in pairs served as actors by engaging in a 'getting acquainted' conversation and participants in pairs served as observers with each of the observers focusing on a different actor. Following the interactions, some of the participants viewed a videotape of the interaction from the same or from a different perspective than they had the first time. The other participants viewed no videotape. In all these conditions, the participants were asked to offer attributions for the actors' behaviors. When the videotape allowed the actors to see the interaction from the observer's perspective, their attributions became more dispositional. In addition, when the videotape allowed the observers to see the interaction from the actor's perspective, their attributions became more situational. Thus, this research and many other studies (cf. Taylor and Fiske, 1978) suggest that visual perspective or anything else that makes something salient can influence causal explanations for behavior.

However, there remain some important issues that need to be examined in evaluating the visual perspective and salience studies. First of all, it is interesting that there was no significant difference between the attributions of actors and observers in the control condition of Storms' (1973) experiment. Furthermore, most of the salience studies have not actually compared the attributions of actors and observers, but rather have compared the attributions of different observers having different perspectives. Probably the most crucial issue to be considered is whether salience will lead to different actor–observer attributions when the type or usefulness of the situational information is allowed to vary. In fact, Jones and Nisbett's (1972) conclusion that differences in visual perspective would lead actors to offer more situational attributions than observers might be mediated by two different possible processes. The first process assumes a fairly unsophisticated perceiver who attributes causality to the actor if s/he is the observer and is focusing on the actor. This process assumes that it is unimportant whether those situational cues are facilitative, neutral, or inhibitory to the behavior performed by the actor.

Taylor and Fiske (1978) have acknowledged the possibility that salience may only have an effect on attributions when the situational cues are informationally irrelevant. In attempts to dismiss this reservation, several studies have been reported which demonstrate the generalisability of salience effects (McArthur and Solomon, 1978; Taylor, Crocker, Fiske, Sprinzen and Winkler, 1979). However, in neither study was there an attempt to examine the effects of varying salience and information value at the same time. In fact, the only salience study that examined the effects of salience and information at the same time was conducted by Pryor and Kriss (1977). Although they reported that salience had a significant effect, it is interesting to note that the $F$ value for the information main effect ($F = 286.06$) was over 40 times higher than the $F$ value for the salience main effect ($F = 6.84$). This suggests that it is erroneous merely to examine the effects of salience on attributions without taking into consideration the possible effects of situational context information.

A second possible process by which visual perspective may influence the attributions of actors and observers assumes more sophistication on the part of the actor as an attributor. In fact, this process is based upon the assumption that the actor as an attributor will rely very strongly on informational cues in assessing causality. Due to his or her visual perspective, the actor is assumed to be in a good position to assess whether the environmental cues are facilitative, neutral, or inhibitory to the behaviour exhibited. However, given Jones and Nisbett's (1972) assumption that behaviour is most frequently situationally caused, one would then expect that most behaviors of actors would be performed in the presence of facilitative situational cues. Being more aware than observers of facilitative situational cues, actors should be more likely to offer situational attributions.

It should be clear that this second possible process produces different conclusions if one does not accept the assumption that most behaviour is situationally determined. In fact, if one accepts the assumption that there are many circumstances in which behavior is predictable by traits and other dispositions, one must also assume that there are many circumstances in which behavior is performed in the presence of neutral or inhibitory situational cues. As a consequence, one might expect that the visual perspective of actors would lead them to offer more situational attributions than observers only when the situational cues facilitate the behaviors exhibited. In contrast, more dispositional attributions should be offered by actors when the situational cues are inhibitory.

Some evidence for this proposal has been reported by Smith, Monson and Graziano (1979b). Subjects in this research were asked to listen to the audio track of two videotapes in which the target person exhibited extraverted behaviors while engaging in a 'getting acquainted' conversation with two other people. In the facilitative videotape, one of the other participants in the conversation exhibited behaviors that strongly encouraged the target to act in an extraverted manner, whereas the other participants in the conversation exhibited behaviors that weakly encouraged the target to act in an extraverted manner

Although the target was perceived as exhibiting extraverted behaviors in both conditions, the target was seen to act in a relatively more extraverted manner in the inhibitory videotape than in the facilitative videotape. Furthermore, the initial explanations for the target's extraverted behaviors were more dispositional for the inhibitory videotape than for the facilitative videotape. Whereas the subjects offered these initial ratings on the basis of only listening to the videotape (the television monitor was covered), they were provided with an additional opportunity to evalute the videotapes under one of three information conditions. In the first condition which could be construed as simulating the observer's perspective, the subjects were asked to again listen to the interaction and to focus their visual attention on a photograph of the target that was placed over part of the cardboard screen that covered the television. The remaining two conditions could be construed as simulating the actor's perspective. In the strong situational information condition, the subjects were allowed to view on the television monitor only the behaviors of the individual who strongly encouraged (facilitative videotape) or who strongly discouraged (inhibitory videotape) the target from acting in an extraverted fashion. In the weak situational information condition, the subjects viewed the individual who weakly discouraged (facilitative videotape) or who weakly encouraged (inhibitory videotape) the target to act in an extraverted way.

The effect of the different visual perspectives on the causal attributions offered for the target's extraverted behaviors are presented in Table II.

TABLE II    Changes in causal attributions for the target's extraverted behaviors as a function of salience and contextual information*

| Videotape | Focus on strong situational information | Focus on the actor | Focus on weak situational information |
|---|---|---|---|
| Facilitative | −0.41 | +0.81 | +1.00 |
| Inhibitory | +1.38 | +0.19 | −0.88 |

*Positive numbers indicate that the attributions offered the second time under different focus of attention conditions were relatively more dispositional than those offered the first time under the same listening-only condition. Negative numbers indicate that the attributions offered the second time were relatively more situational than those offered the first time.

The interaction between visual focus and type of videotape was statistically significant, $F(2186) = 10.75$, $p<0.001$. Examination of simple effects revealed that visual focus influenced attributions both for the facilitative videotape, $F(2186) = 3.63$, $p<0.05$, and for the inhibitory videotape, $F(2186) = 7.89$, $p<0.001$. In the facilitative videotape condition, focus of visual attention on situational cues that strongly encouraged the actor's behavior resulted in attributions that were significantly more situational than those offered when attention was focused on the actor. In contrast, in the inhibitory videotape condition, focus of visual attention on situational cues that strongly discouraged the actor's behavior resulted in attributions that were significantly more dispositional than those offered when attention was focused on the actor.

## Summary and conclusions

The task confronting the naive psychologist is very similar to the task confronting the professional psychologist. Psychologists, whether they be professional or naive, are interested in explaining current behavior in order better to predict and control subsequent behavior. Because of the similarities of the tasks confronting these two types of psychologist it is proposed that considerable insight can be gained about the attribution process employed by the naive psychologist by determining the current theory and research employed by the professional psychologist.

There have been a number of recent developments in the 'traits v. situations' controversy. Whereas earlier research questioned the wisdom of using personality traits and other dispositions to predict behavior, recent work has provided a promising indication that under certain specifiable circumstances traits can be used to predict behavior. As a consequence, there is much less reason to assume that attributors are wrong when they offer dispositional attributions than when they offer situational attributions. Instead, dispositional attributions would seem to be more appropriate than situational attributions in those circumstances in which individuals' behaviors correlate highly with their traits and *vice versa*. In contrast, situational attributions would seem to be more appropriate when individuals' behaviors do not correlate highly with their traits.

A number of informational differences between actors and observers have been suggested which imply that the attributions offered by actors may often be more valid than those offered by observers. Thus, attributions offered from the actor's perspective can generally be expected to be more situational than those offered from the observer's perspective when the actor's behavior can be best predicted by a knowledge of the characteristics of the situation in which the actor is momentarily located. In contrast, attributions offered from the actor's perspective can generally be expected to be more dispositional than those offered from the observer's perspective when the actor's behavior can best be predicted by a knowledge of the actor's personality traits and other dispositions.

In addition, it may be possible to predict actor–observer differences

in attributions with more precision by examining the specific informational differences existing between actors and observers and by
examining in more detail whether the behaviors of the actors are
performed in the presence of facilitative, neutral, or inhibitory
situational cues. As previously noted, the visual perspective of actors
should enable them to perceive more accurately whether the situational cues are facilitative, neutral, or inhibitory to their behavior. In
addition, depending upon whether the behaviors are performed in the
presence of facilitative, neutral, or inhibitory situational cues, there are
different likelihoods that the actors would be exhibiting behaviors that
are consistent or inconsistent with their personality traits.

For example, if an actor exhibits a behavior that is strongly
discouraged or inhibited by his or her immediate environment, or in
the presence of neutral situational cues, one would expect that there
would be a high probability that the behavior would be consistent,
rather than inconsistent, with his or her personality traits. However, if
the behavior exhibited is strongly encouraged or facilitated by his or
her immediate environment, one would expect moderate and approximately equal probabilities that the behaviors would be consistent or
inconsistent with her or his personality traits.

Since actors are more likely than observers to be aware of the
consistency or inconsistency of a behavior with their personality traits
and since actors are more likely than observers to be aware of whether
situational cues are facilitative, neutral, or inhibitory, the following
predictions can be made:

BEHAVIOR IN THE PRESENCE OF INHIBITORY SITUATIONAL CUES

Actors are better able to notice the inhibitory nature of their immediate
environment. As a consequence of employing Kelley's (1972b)
augmentation principle, they should therefore offer relatively more
dispositional attributions than observers. The intimate knowledge of
their behavioral histories should better enable actors to notice the
consistency of their behavior with their personality traits. As a
consequence of employing Kelley's (1972a) covariation principle, they
should offer relatively more dispositional attributions than observers.
(Overall, the attributions of actors should be more dispositional.)

BEHAVIOUR IN THE PRESENCE OF NEUTRAL SITUATIONAL CUES

Since the the situational cues neither encourage nor discourage the
behavior, the different perspectives of actors and observers should do
little to produce differences in attributions. The intimate knowledge of
their behavioral histories should better enable actors to notice the

consistency of their behavior with their personality traits. As a consequence of employing Kelley's covariation principle, actors should offer relatively more dispositional attributions than observers. (Overall, the attributions of actors should be more dispositional.)

BEHAVIOUR IN THE PRESENCE OF FACILITATIVE SITUATIONAL CUES

Actors are more able to judge the facilitative nature of their immediate environment. As a consequence of employing Kelley's (1972b) discounting principle, they should offer relatively more situational attributions than observers. The intimate knowledge of their behavioral histories should better enable actors to notice the consistency or inconsistency of their behavior with their personality traits. As a consequence of employing Kelley's covariation principle, actors who exhibit behavior which is inconsistent with their personality traits should offer relatively more situational attributions than observers. Similarly, those who exhibit behavior consistent with their personality traits should offer relatively more dispositional attributions than observers. (Overall, actors who exhibit behavior inconsistent with their personality traits should offer more situational attributions. It is difficult to predict whether actors who exhibit behavior consistent with their personality traits should offer more situational, more dispositional, or similar attributions to observers. However, averaging all actors, the attributions should be more situational than when offered by observers.)

## Notes

1.  These conclusions apparently are not dependent upon a questionnaire format; similar findings have been reported in a laboratory study conducted by Small and Peterson (1980).
2.  Similarly, Turner (1978) reported that when subjects were asked to construct their own lists of personality traits they were likely to list more for themselves than for others.
3.  Monson et al. (1980b) also reported data that were suggestive of the validity of these attributions.

# 12

# Professional and Naive Psychology: Two Approaches to the Explanation of Social Behaviour

## Adrian Furnham, Jos Jaspars and Frank D. Fincham

### Introduction

Social psychologists have found themselves in the unique position of both offering a professional 'scientific' explanation of social behaviour and studying the layman's explanations and attributions for the same behaviour. Despite this unique advantage to compare and contrast these explanations, the two research areas have developed independently of each other. The historical, theoretical and methodological similarities between them are as striking as their differences, yet no attempt has been made to integrate or compare both fields. The present chapter rectifies this omission by examining attribution theory and interactional psychology. The former is the sophisticated successor of social perception research and attempts to offer a theory of the cognitive processes which individuals use to explain and interpret behaviour of people and events. The latter is an attempt to revitalise a very old debate in personality theory, which explains in intra- and interpersonal terms how people represent and respond to their social environment. Since Heider (1958a) attribution theorists have referred to the layman's view as naive, perhaps implying that the psychologist's view is somehow informed or sophisticated. Appealing and complimentary though this assumption is, it is misplaced. Like Mischel (1979) we shall attempt to show that the professional psychologist is as fallible to errors as the intuitive psychologist.

## The origins and development of interactional psychology and attribution theory

INTERACTIONAL PSYCHOLOGY

Parallelling the growth of interest in attribution theory over the past twenty years has been a major debate in personality theory which has spilled over into social psychology. The debate, which has revived interest in personality theory and measurement, has been said (e.g. Endler and Magnusson, 1976; Mischel, 1968) to have brought personality research to the cross-roads and caused yet another crisis in modern experimental psychology. It resurrects the perennial issue of internal v. external causes of behaviour and takes place on an old philosophic battle ground where professional psychologists have long jousted in their endless quest for the (true and only) explanation of social behaviour. Three different approaches are common in personality theory. They are the trait approach, the situationist approach and the interactional approach and each is considered briefly below.

The trait approach suggests that individuals differ on continuous stable trait dimensions which are the prime determinants of behaviour (Endler and Magnusson, 1976). According to Bowers (1973): 'The classic trait view (a) employs correlational techniques (b) suggests that an individual's behaviour should be relatively constant from one situation to the next and (c) suggests that in the same situation individual differences should emerge' (p. 316). However, this is something of an oversimplification as a number of trait theorists (e.g. Cattell, 1965) take situational factors into account in their formulae. The issue of stability or consistency of behaviour over time and across situations has been central to this approach (Alker, 1972; Block, 1977; Olweus, 1977). Epstein (1979) has listed seven empirical reasons why low stability coefficients have been found for the same behaviour over time, and suggests that if a large number of measures of behaviour over a number of events are collected then stability coefficients increase to fairly high significance levels for most kinds of behaviour. However the trait approach does attempt to explain various aspects of social behaviour as the function of one or more specified and measurable internal traits or dispositions (Allport, 1966). This tendency invariably to attribute acts to internal (person) sources even when incorrect, was first noted by Heider (1944) and has been called the 'fundamental attribution error' (Ross, 1977).

The situationist approach on the other hand suggests that social behaviour is a function of external situational constraints. In the words of Bowers (1973): 'Situationalism (a) leads to experimental (or operant) techniques, (b) suggests that an individual's behaviour should change from one situation to another and (c) regards individual differences in behaviour within the same situation as something of an embarrassment – to be conceptualized as the result of past experiences or simply as error variance' (p. 138). Situationists base their evidence on three major sources of empirical evidence: low correlations between the same behaviour in different situations, the smaller variance attributable to individual differences rather than situations or interactions in analysis of variance designs, and the finding that observers tend to attribute more stability to individuals across situations than is objectively warranted (Epstein, 1979). Although proponents of this approach are for the most part social learning theorists (Mischel, 1973) they have no conceptual objection to the existence of traits but prefer to support their argument empirically. They are, moreover, particularly interested in the interface of personality and cognition, and especially behaviour-outcome, and stimulus-outcome expectations (Mischel, 1973, 1979; Rotter, 1954). However, there is no clear attempt to spell out which situational stimuli determine social behaviour or how they might do so.

Recently, an attempt has been made to reconcile these two disparate approaches stemming primarily from the studies of Endler and coworkers. It has been known as interactional psychology because of its emphasis on the statistical interaction between person and situation in ANOVA studies. Ekehammar (1974) in a historical review of the interactional ideas pointed out that this perspective is by no means new, though he did predict with some accuracy the present interest in interactionism. According to Endler and Magnusson (1976) interactionism has four basic tenets. These are that behaviour is a function of a continuous process or multidirectional interaction (feedback) between the individual and the situation he or she encounters; that behaviour is the purposive goal-directed activity of an intentional active agent; cognitive and to a lesser extent emotional factors are the essential person determinants of behaviour whereas the psychological meaning of the situation is the essential situational determinant. Thus interactionism maintains that the person–situation debate is meaningless since behaviour is always a joint function of the person and the situation which are interdependent. Further as behaviour never takes place in a vacuum, but always in a situational context, it is meaningless to consider characteristics of an individual's behaviour without specifying the situation in which the behaviour occurs. However, interactional psychology has been bedevilled by a number of problems that are historical, empirical or theoretical. Historically interactional psychologists have not been fair in their criticism of other approaches notably the trait model (Golding, 1975; Jaspars and Furnham, 1980). Empirically, much of the earlier work seems to have used inappropriate statistics (Endler, 1966; Olweus, 1977) or incorrectly interpreted results. More importantly, the numerous ANOVA studies do not reveal the clear importance of the person–situation interaction effect which rarely accounts for more than 30% of the variance (Sarason, Smith and Diener, 1975). Theoretically, there has been little conceptual advance over and above the eminently reasonable posits of early interactionism which reflect in any case current thinking in many areas of psychology. In fact there has been a considerable conceptual problem surrounding the very concept of interaction (Buss, 1977; Howard, 1979; Krauskopf, 1978) which is sometimes used in a purely statistical sense and sometimes refers to reciprocal causation.

One might well ask where the popular debate has led professional psychologists in their study of the determinants of social behaviour. Firstly, it has resulted in disillusionment with simple conceptual attempts to resolve the trait-situation issue by using complex, statistical techniques and in 'how' and 'when', rather than 'how much', questions. Secondly, there is a realisation that there are important motivational issues such as when and why person and situational variables interact (Furnham, 1981). This involves studying both cognitive and affective variables. There is also a renewed interest in behavioural consistency and stability across time and situations and the effect of measurement on results. A further noticeable emphasis is on the situation-specific nature of many behavioural processes such as assertiveness and altruism that have hitherto been investigated *in vacuo* (Ginsberg, 1979). Finally, and perhaps most important for social psychology, there is now a focus on the immediate psychophysical situation in which behaviour occurs and how this affects the behaviour (Argyle, Furnham and Graham, 1981; Magnusson, 1979). The settings in which behaviour occurs have long been studied (Barker, 1968) but there is now a concern to describe both the elements in and the dimensions along which social situations or social episodes may be described (Forgas, 1979).

A review of the P × S debate and interactional psychology may lead one to question who is being naive about the causal explanations of behaviour – the layman or the professional psychologist. Interactional psychology has at least provided a middle ground whereby narrow and zealous schools of thought may openly debate and experiment. However, recent developments in, or perhaps serendipitous results of, the P × S debate seem much more promising.

ATTRIBUTION THEORY

In many ways the growth of attribution theory seems to have developed along similar lines to interactional psychology. Although primarily interested in the layman's analysis of behavioural causation, attribution theorists have been concerned with much the same methodological and theoretical questions as interaction theorists. Attribution theory is historically a development of the work on social and person perception in general. The starting point is usually taken to be the work of Heider (1944, 1958a, b) who was concerned with how the naive psychologist came to know and understand the causes of action in order that he could make his world more predictable and hence controllable. Apart from Heider's (1958a) theory two other major theories have stimulated research in this area – those of Jones and Davis (1965) and that of Kelley (1967). The similarities and differences between these theories are considered by Jones and McGillis (1976).

Although experimental work in attribution theory has ranged widely from developmental aspects of attribution (see chapter 5) to intergroup attributions (e.g. Hewstone and Jaspars, 1980a; see also chapter 8), the issue that seemed to dominate attribution theory in the early- and mid-1970s was in fact remarkably similar to the P × S debate (Jones, Kanouse, Kelley, Nisbett, Valins and Weiner, 1972) and concerned the divergent perceptions of actors and observers in the explanation of behaviour. The work of Jones and Nisbett (1972) proved to be as much a catalyst for attribution experiments, as the work of Endler and colleagues (1962, 1968, 1969) on personality measurement was for P × S experiments. Jones and Nisbett (1972) summarised their findings:

Actors tend to attribute the causes of their behaviour to stimuli inherent in the situation while observers tend to attribute behaviour to stable dispositions of the actor. This is due in part to the actor's more detailed knowledge of his circumstances, history, motives and experiences. Perhaps more importantly, the tendency is a result of the differential salience of the information available to both actor and observer. For the observer behaviour is figural against the ground of the situation. For the actor it is the situational cues that are figural and that are seen to elicit behaviour. Moreover, the actor is inclined to think of his judgments about the situational cues as being perceptions or accurate readings of them. (p. 51)

The actor–observer literature flourished and gave rise to considerable controversy (Monson and Snyder, 1977; see also chapter 11).

However, the work on causal attribution led to methodological problems, especially in determining whether attributions were situational or dispositional. This problem is most apparent if free response answers are subject to a content analysis (Lalljee, 1981). Mischel, Jeffrey and Patterson (1974) demonstrated, as others have done subsequently, that people use both types of information in their attributions, predictions etc. Snyder and Swann (1976) in fact maintain that the dispositional-situational dichotomy is not really a dichotomy at all in that it is more of a linguistic than a conceptual distinction. Ross (1977) makes a similar point maintaining that some content analyses have gone wrong in coding in terms of linguistic form rather than actual content. The fundamental error which is found in attribution processes, namely the overestimation of personality or dispositional factors, might even be an artifact of such procedures.

What are the present developments in attribution theory? First, less interest in pure actor/observer, person/situation differences in attribution with a resultant interest in the integration of the two factors by specifying under what conditions salient information of the person and the situation is perceived and interpreted (Ross, 1977). Second, a less extensive interest in purely causal judgements and more interest in other judgements such as the prediction of behaviour, the amount and type of punishment/retribution to be made, and the number, range and type of free attributions/explanations offered. Third, there is an emphasis on the social functions of attributions and explanations – that is the reasons why, when, how, and for which purpose they are made as well as interpersonal, intergroup and possibly even cultural differences in attributions. As Jones and Nisbett (1972) remarked: 'The individual, whether he is an actor or an observer, is a self-esteem enhancer, a balance maintainer, a dissonance-reducer, a reactance believer, a seeker after truth, and more' (p. 51).

There thus appear to be some historical and theoretical similarities between attribution and interactional theories (experienced and naive psychologisms). Both began by asking crude dichotomous questions about the person and the situation which proved to be inadequate and distorting, and have recently begun taking a more interactional approach. In addition, both had serious methodological problems, often as a result of their theoretical stances, that have done injustice to their subjects' cognitive complexities. The two are also similar in that they have overemphasised personality/individual factors, rather than situational factors, to which they are now belatedly turning, and have neglected the social and motivational basis of the processes they are investigating.

Despite these similarities there are naturally differences in emphases and interests, two of which are particularly noteworthy. Whereas interactional psychologists present subjects with hypothetical situations and ask them to report on how *they* would act (i.e. the probability of them acting in various ways), attribution theorists usually present a subject with the situation and various other people's behaviour and ask for an explanation of that behaviour. Another striking difference between the two approaches may help to account for the 'fundamental attribution error'. The difference lies in the emphasis of the questions asked. Interactional psychologists asked subjects to rate their own (though occasionally others') behaviour in specific situations – thus the constraints, difficulties and parameters of each situation are in the forefront of their minds. Attribution theorists, however, ask subjects to infer the causes of other *people's* actions in a limited number of situations, so focusing on the person. It seems to be tacitly assumed that by asking how much *a person* is the cause of an act we can decide or calculate the extent to which the *situation* in which he acted was the cause, i.e. that the one is the mirror image of the other (they add up to one, so to speak). This might not be the case at all. If in fact we ask a subject to rate the extent to which the *situation*, and not the person, is causally relevant we might find that it is at least, if not more, important a determinant of the person's action. That is, by asking exclusively intra- or interpersonal questions we might be contributing to the fundamental error that we so often find.

## The methodology of both approaches

Psychologists are fortunate in having a number of well tried and proven methods at their disposal. These include laboratory experiments, field studies, observational techniques, role-playing questionnaires, computer simulation etc. Each has its strengths and weaknesses which have been well documented (Orne, 1962; Westland, 1978). Attribution theory and interactional psychology have both been very conservative in the extensive use of questionnaires and multivariate statistics. In fact it has been suggested by many researchers in interactional psychology that psychologists' inability to demonstrate cross-situational consistency of behaviour is due to empirical and methodological rather than theoretical considerations (Argyle, 1976; Block, 1977a, b; Epstein, 1979). There is always a danger in using one methodology exclusively, that certain epiphenomenal results occur while important processes which the methodology does not reveal are overlooked. Similarities and differences in the two predominantly used methods of questionnaire and observational studies in both research areas are considered briefly.

Interactional psychology has relied very heavily on one particular questionnaire format called the S–R (Situation–Response) Inventory devised by Endler *et al.* (1962). It consists of a set of brief descriptions of everyday social situations and a range of possible responses in them requiring subjects to rate how likely they are to respond in the specified ways. This format allows a three way ANOVA to be done which may be used to apportion variance to person, situation and response factors. Over thirty studies have been done using this format and nearly twenty S–R Inventories exist (Jaspars and Furnham, 1980). However, these have been criticised on constructional (Cartwright, 1975; Lanzarini, Cox and Mackay, 1979) and statistical grounds (Golding, 1975; Olweus, 1977). Apart from the S–R Inventories, free response formats (Pervin, 1976), Q-sort tasks (Bem and Funder, 1978) and similarity judgements (Forgas, 1976; Magnusson and Endler, 1977) have also been used by interactional psychologists.

Attribution psychologists use a similar method. Usually a number of vignettes (stories) are carefully prepared to test specific hypotheses. These vary considerably and may contain more or less 'situational' information. Further, the stories also specify the people present who are usually named, and the subject is required to make a number of attributions (e.g. dispositional, situational). Once again the questions are usually the same for each vignette which allows the experimenter to determine which factors are influencing the subject's attributions (e.g. Fincham and Jaspars, 1979).

The major differences between the use of questionnaires in these two traditions are three-fold. In attribution experiments the stimulus vignettes are extremely carefully prepared and balanced to test specific hypotheses (e.g. McArthur, 1972), whereas in interactional psychology the situations are chosen 'more or less at random, from some universe, albeit unspecified' (Dworkin and Kihlstrom, 1978, p. 52) and inconsistently described in terms of length and specific details such as the people present (Endler and Hunt, 1968). Rarely are situations defined by Pervin's (1978) three basic criteria of who is involved, where the action is taking place and what type of actions or activities are occurring. Further the situations are considered to be typical everyday social episodes (Forgas, 1976) rather than specific unique events. Secondly, subjects in attribution experiments are asked to answer specific and important questions because of their possible consequences, about a specific incident, whereas subjects in interactional psychology experiments are required to give probabilistic answers about a type or category of social situations and responses. Thus in attribution theory experimenters are interested in different perceptions of the same act given differences in situation or person variables, whereas interactional psychology experimenters are interested in the variation in the perception of, and reported responses to, a wide range of social situations. Thirdly, attribution experiments usually involve subjects rating others' specific, if hypothetical, behaviour whereas interactional experiments involve subjects rating their own actually experienced or imagined behaviour.

Interactional psychologists and attribution theorists have also done a limited number of observational studies though quite differently. The former have observed behaviour over different situations and calculated the systematic differences in social behaviour, avoiding all self-reports (Moos, 1969, 1970). On the other hand, attribution theorists have used video equipment or role playing techniques to provide stimulus material which was rated by subjects or participants (Storms, 1973; Taylor and Fiske, 1975). In fact, interactional studies comparing observational and questionnaire measurement produced systematically different results. In the studies of Moos (1969, 1970) there appeared to be more variation in both person and situation factors in the observational as opposed to questionnaire studies (Jaspars and Furnham, 1980). However, the comparability of these results is difficult to evaluate as varying behaviours are being assessed at different levels, a different number of observations are being made, and the behaviour is analysed by different methods. Observational studies have consistently found a higher cross-situational consistency in various forms of behaviour than self-report studies, a result in accordance with attribution theory (Jones and Nisbett, 1972). This has been true of aggressive behaviours (Olweus, 1977), honesty (Hartshorne and May, 1928) and emotional expression (Epstein, 1979).

Observational studies in attribution theory have revealed that given the opportunity of observing one's own behaviour from a different perspective (Taylor and Fiske, 1975) or having a different focus of attention on the same behaviour, the attribution of actors and observers change considerably (Storms, 1973). These results are however not in conflict with self-report studies (Nisbett et al., 1973) though not all studies have revealed differences in attribution between actors and observers (Taylor and Koivumaki, 1976).

## Problems with research

A subjects' eye view of an attribution and interactional experiment reveals some of the difficulties encountered by using these traditional methods. It is not until professional psychologists adopt the role of one of their 'naive' subjects that they will begin to appreciate some of the frustrations of the subjects. These subjects are often coerced into providing data that they are unhappy with, not confident about and which do not tap their abilities, cognitions or relevant processes. Four problems are particularly apparent.

PAUCITY OF INFORMATION

For respondents to report accurately and fully on how they would respond to or explain a particular type of social situation they would require a full and sufficient description of that situation and its relevant parameters and constraints. Interactional psychology questionnaires, particularly those not carefully piloted, often present subjects with situational stimuli that are extremely brief and ambiguous and hence there may be wide individual differences in the cognitive represent- ations that different subjects respond to. That is, interaction between person and situation might occur intitially in the cognitive structuring of the stimuli by subjects as well as in their reported reactions to different situations. There have been attempts to overcome this by using diaries to decide on stimulus situations (Forgas, 1976), by exploring idiographic free response approaches (Pervin, 1976) by using the Repertory Grid technique with individual subjects providing their own constructs (Furnham, 1980) and using longer, fuller decriptions (Bishop and Witt, 1970).

The problem is worse in attribution experiments. Before being asked to give any judgement, particularly of blame or responsibility for an act with serious consequences, it is natural to seek as much relevant information as possible. The more important or complex the judge- ment in its consequences, the more information a person might want. One has only to read two newspaper reports of the same episode, a two paragraph v. a three column report, to notice the very different impressions that one might get, and hence the differences in attri- butions that one might offer. Warr and Knapper (1966) have demonstrated changes in person perception through adding further information. Consider also the amount and type of additional infor- mation that is sought and digested in a court room with various parties trying to attribute causality and blame to different sources. Often minimal information presents a highly biased picture which may lead an observer to be very insecure and unconfident about his or her attributions and explanations of behaviour. Epiphenomenal results may occur as a function of the type, brevity and restricted nature of vignettes. Thus in under-using subjects' ability and potential their performance may be no indication of their competence or habitual patterns of making attributions. This problem is apparent even in the most celebrated attribution experiments (e.g. McArthur, 1972).

There seem to be a number of possible solutions to these problems. These include using longer, more realistic and representative stimulus materials (situations or stories) and checking that subjects are similarly familiar with them, as well as asking subjects to rate the confidence of their responses, omitting or weighting judgements with ratings below a certain point. More importantly, subjects might be allowed to request more information should they require it before making attributions. Further requested pieces of information could be content analysed and used as data for experimental analysis (see Experiment 1).

NEGLECT OF MOTIVATIONAL CRITERIA

Both interactional psychology and attribution theory have neglected important aspects of the motivational and social functions of, on the one hand, seeking out certain social situations and, on the other hand, of making certain characteristic attributions. Interactional psychologists in their attempt to understand personality and situational determinants of behaviour have not sufficiently taken into consideration the fact that people seek out and avoid certain situations as a function of their personality (Furnham, 1981; Mehrabian, 1977; Zuckerman, 1978), or change situations in which they find themselves to achieve certain goals or satisfy different needs (Wachtel, 1973) or to maintain social relationships (Harré, 1979). Many institutionalised social situations exist in a culture to fulfil various needs and hence can be sought out deliberately when these needs arise (Graham, Argyle and Furnham, 1981). Thus the personality variables operate twice, both before the situation, in that they partially determine whether a person will enter that situation, and during the situation in determining how he or she will behave. Thus asking people how they would respond to various social situations does not take into consideration whether or why they have experience of these situations.

Similarly, attribution theorists have not taken cognisance of the fact that some events, and not others, are felt to be worthy of attributions and explanations. Some people are motivated for various reasons to seek out, offer or share explanations for certain events and at certain times while others are not. The fact that people make attributions in certain situations may be determined by cultural, sub-cultural and individual factors. Studies have shown that attributions serve numerous social functions such as to condemn, explicate, illustrate, exonerate and justify (Antaki, 1978). Thus the reasons for and the situations in which attributions are offered provide very useful information on the nature of the attributions themselves. However, few experiments have looked at whether the task for the subjects is considered meaningful and worthwhile, or why an attribution or explanation is required.

Consequently, it seems necessary to ask subjects about their experience and patterns of approach and avoidance of social situations, in addition to response questions, and to explain the act they are presented with and to indicate to whom they would offer their attribution. More naturalistic observational studies also seem to be needed. Finally, more extensive pre- and postexperimental briefing may indicate hitherto unsuspected difficulties and areas for investigation.

RESTRICTIVE ANSWERING SET

Another related methodological problem is the nature of the responses that a subject is able to provide. These are often restricted to a particular category which is unclear to the subjects and may not allow them to express their predominant or natural response.

Consider, for example, any of the S–R Inventories for anxiety. Subjects are required to rate the likelihood of their own responses on 10–15 scales measuring behavioural, affective and physiological reactions related to, say, anxiety (Cartwright, 1975). However, it is quite possible that some people experience none of these reactions, being predominantly bored. Zuckerman (1978) has shown for instance that sensation-seekers actively seek out dangerous threatening situations, in which to participate, as this exhilarates and excites them. Subjects are, however, not able to report their actual responses but only state whether the specified reactions are extremely unlikely. This radically affects the utility of any data collected.

Similarly, in attribution experiments subjects are often asked very direct and structured questions concerning attribution of responsibility, cause or blame. Although some experiments ask subjects to give confidence ratings to their judgements, they rarely allow subjects to respond freely, possibly because of the problems of content analysis (Lalljee, 1981).

A more phenomenological analysis might be useful such as that suggested by Marsh, Harré and Rosser (1978) who elicited unstructured 'accounts' from participants in football and classroom violence and reconstructed their perspective on this behaviour which differed significantly from that of the authorities and the media.

INATTENTION TO INDIVIDUAL DIFFERENCES

One of the most curious aspects of the person–situation debate is the neglect on the part of the experimenters of individual differences relating to social behaviour in different situations. Notable exceptions are the studies on self-monitoring (Snyder, 1974; 1979), locus of control (Rotter, 1954) and sensation-seeking (Zuckerman, 1978) which demonstrated individual differences in the choice of, and behaviour in, everyday social situations. In their eagerness to demonstrate interaction effects (Endler and Hunt, 1968, 1969) interactional psychologists have neglected nearly 50 years' work on individual differences. A few studies have however demonstrated the importance of personality differences such as authoritarianism (Endler and Shedletsky, 1973), and dominance (Dworkin and Kihlstrom, 1977). Demographic variables have been neglected to a lesser extent. Sex and age have been considered fairly extensively (Endler and Hunt, 1968; Magnusson and Ekehammar, 1973) while there has been some work on cultural differences (Magnusson and Stattin, 1978). However, such variables as social class and marital status which the social skills literature have suggested are important determinants of social anxiety (Trower, Bryant and Argyle, 1978) have been largely neglected.

Attribution theory has also neglected individual differences, though both Heider (1958a) and Kelley (1967) mentioned that personality factors influence the biases and errors in attribution. It is quite possible that people have characteristic ways or styles of attribution based on personality factors. These might be very similar to defence mechanisms (Freud, 1935) which are internal dynamic processes that operate to protect the person against feelings of anxiety, guilt and anger. Some of the more common defence mechanisms are easily translatable in attribution terms (e.g. projection in which individuals refuse to recognise or accept their faults and deficiencies and consistently blame them on somebody else; or reaction formation in which an individual might offer false attributions in order to deny certain drives or needs which are socially unacceptable). Studies on depression and neurosis have shown that people with different needs perceive behaviour in quite unique ways. Young (1979) found that neurotics attend to different types of information from normals and hence offer a different pattern of attributions. Similarly, Lewinsohn, Mischel, Chaplin and Barton (1980) showed that depressed subjects were more realistic in their self-perceptions than were controls who perceived themselves more positively than others saw them. Further, as Lalljee (1981) has pointed out, there may be cultural and sub-cultural differences in the range and type of attributions made.

## Situational variables in attribution experiments

One of the most important consequences of the person–situation debate has been that it has encouraged personality and social psychologists to conceptualise the salient variables of the situation in which social behaviour occurs (Argyle *et al.*, 1981; Magnusson, 1979; London, 1978; Pervin, 1978b). There have been essentially two approaches to this problem. Most experimenters have adopted the dimensional approach attempting to find the major descriptive factors along which subjects characteristically perceive social situations (Forgas, 1976; Magnusson, 1971; Wish and Kaplan, 1977). Others favour the structural or componential approach and have attempted to specify the major components in all social situations and indicate how they relate to one another (Argyle *et al.*, 1981; Harré and Secord, 1972). The latter has led to the development of models or analogues of social situations being developed – the 'game' analogy in the case of Argyle *et al.*, and the 'theatre' analogy in the case of Harré and Secord. Both approaches have revealed that different persons perceive social situations differently in terms of their socialisation and expectations of behaviour in those situations. The expectations which they bring to these situations inevitably affect their attributions.

Attribution researchers on the other hand have not paid very much attention to conceptualising situational factors though they recognise their importance in determining attributions (Sagatuin and Knudsen, 1977; Teglasi, 1977). Where situational variables have been compared these are usually along broad dimensions such as constrained–unconstrained (Price and Bouffard, 1974) and inhibitory–facilitatory (see chapter 11). Previous research would suggest that other important dimensions affecting people's attributions are evaluative (pleasant–unpleasant, involved–uninvolved), emotional (stressful–non-stressful) and cognitive (know how to behave–don't, ambiguous–non-ambiguous).

There are, however, two quite distinct, though equally important situational variables in the attribution process. These are the parameters of the social situation *in which* attributions are offered and *about which* attributions are made.

These may be very similar or even identical if the attributor offers an explanation of another person's behaviour while the two are together in the same situation (sports game, cocktail party) or very different if the attributor offers an explanation about another person's social behaviour in a different situation (courtroom, hospital). There is thus usually, though not necessarily, a temporal factor involved as situations in which attributions are made often occur after the behaviour about which attributions are made and are thus influenced by other factors such as memory (Woll and Yopp, 1978). Furthermore, because social rules and conventions of situations partly determine the length, form and even content of an attribution it is possible that attributions made in situations which have occurred in another (later) context are considerably different from attributions made in situations at the time. This implies that people are able to offer a range of attributions which differ in style, form and content depending on their perception of situational constraints. Finally, where subjects are required to make attributions about behaviour in situations that they themselves have not been in, the definition as well as the range and type of information they have of the situation, are not of their own construction but are usually provided by an experimenter. As Alexander and Sagatuin (1973) have shown, subjects' experimental responses are often determined by their perception and expectations of the experimenter and the experimental norms and demands.

But what social situational parameters are likely to be important in determining the nature of the attributional process? Argyle *et al.*(1981) have proposed that a number of components or elements make up social situations forming a dynamic Gestalt. Many of these situational elements seem directly relevant to the attributional process and are thus considered briefly:

### The goal structure of the situation

Most social situations have a complex goal structure, which may be both implicit and explicit, and developed within a sub-culture to satisfy certain needs (Graham *et al.*, 1980). The goal of the situation in a court of law, for example, or in a doctor's consultation, may be specifically to obtain certain types and styles of attributions and prohibit others. Where the goals of two people in a situation are in conflict attributions are likely to be disputed or negotiated (Berger and Luckmann, 1973).

### The rules of the situation

Formal and informal situations are rule-bound to the extent that people are aware of the appropriateness of certain types of behaviour (Collett, 1977). Situational rules may determine the length or content of an attribution such as in a confessional or after a display of aggression (Marsh *et al.*, 1978). Argyle *et al.* (1979) proposed a functional theory of rules which are seen as created in order to attain situational goals. These rules which include answering truthfully, being polite, not embarrassing or being unfriendly to others may be seen as relevant to others.

### The role relationships in the situation

The nature of the role relationship and status difference between people can greatly affect the type of attributions made. Attributions of self-blame from a low status to a high status group member are likely to be quantitatively and qualitatively different from those of a high to a low status member. Numerous other demographic variables which are salient to the social situation in which attributions are made might effect these attributions. Hinde (1979) has suggested such factors as intimacy and commitments in social relationships affect the nature of the attributions within those relationships.

*Situational concepts and constructs*

Certain concepts or constructs for describing and explaining behaviour are very clearly situationally specific. Identical actions with similar outcomes, but in different social situations, may be quite differently explained because of different situationally relevant and appropriate concepts associated with each.

Other relevant situational variables which may affect the quality and quantity of the attributions include aspects of the physical environment (e.g. the arrangement of spaces and territories in the situation, the intensity of modifiers such as heat, light and sound, the presence of certain symbolic objects or props) and certain factors such as the sequence of behavioural acts and the duration of the activity in the situation.

Further, whether attributions are offered spontaneously or not may largely be determined by situational factors such as the appropriateness of seeking or offering explanations, and the amount of the information a situation provides. The fact that attributions are offered or shared at all is perhaps as interesting as the nature of the attributions themselves. Because people appear to use covariation information provided in experiments does not mean that they seek out or use this information in spontaneously making attributions.

Two areas of research that throw light on situational determinants of explanations and attributions are self-disclosure and altruism or helping behaviour. Self-disclosure is the process whereby one lets oneself be known to another person by revealing one's thoughts, feelings, ideas and attributions of one's own or mutually shared behaviour. Three situational factors affecting how disclosed information is accepted, understood and explained have been pinpointed. Situational goals might affect self-disclosure either by encouraging it in situations where the express purpose is to initiate friendships or discouraging it in situations where anonymity or confidentiality is important. Various studies have revealed how the norms or social rules in a sub-culture often dictate aspects of disclosure: what amount and degree, at what time and in what place etc. (Jourard, 1964; Luft, 1969).

Finally the role relationship between people also affects their mutual self-disclosure. Some role relationships institutionalise and even demand self-disclosure (e.g. therapist–client) while others make it negligible and undesirable (e.g. customer–assistant) (Chaiken and Derlega, 1976).

Similarly, with respect to altruism research, a number of studies have revealed the importance of situational factors which will determine the extent to which people assume personal responsibility for helping others. Situational variables which have been shown to affect helping include the number and actions of bystanders (Bryan and Test, 1967), the ambiguity of the situation (Clark and Word, 1972) and the 'cost' of helping (Walster and Piliavin, 1972). Altruism research points clearly to the importance of specific concepts in the determining of behaviour.

One of the most celebrated and contentious findings in attribution theory is that actors tend to attribute their behaviour to stable dispositions of the actor (Nisbett, Caputo, Legant and Maracek, 1973). As Monson (chapter 11) has suggested, some of the controversy regarding this finding may be resolved by concentrating on *which* situational variables affect the actors' behaviour, and *what* distinctions are made between them or weights given to them by the observer. Also distinctions in the nature of the behaviour itself suggest that actions are attributed more to person factors and emotions more to the situation (McArthur, 1972). It seems therefore that some of the inconsistencies in the research findings might be resolved if more careful attention were given to situational factors and their effect on attributions.

### Differences in the results and conclusions in both fields

Attribution theory as developed by Heider (1958a) Kelley (1973) suggests that lay persons interpret social behaviour mainly as a simple additive function of person and situation factors, and that a consistent error occurs in the attribution of one's own, as opposed to others', behaviour. Interactional psychologists such as Endler and Magnusson (1976) and Argyle (1976), on the other hand, suggest that social behaviour is a function of the interaction between person and situation factors, and that self reports are relatively free of systematic bias. This theoretical difference has naturally led to important empirical differences.

THE USE OF RATING SCALES

There are a number of dangers associated with rating scales (Eiser and

Mower-White, 1974a; Oppenheim, 1966). In order to ensure high inter-rater reliability it is important that rating scales are clearly defined and understood by the subject. Pendleton and Wakeford (1980) found considerably higher inter-rater reliability when using specific skill rating scales than using overall or general impression scales in a task requiring subjects to rate videotaped interactions. This implies that the use of global behavioural or extremely vague rating scales should be avoided (see Experiment 2). Comparing interactional psychology and attribution theory, it seems that the former tends to use more global scales (e.g. lose patience, become tense) while the latter uses specific, direct questions. The nature of the questions in the two approaches are however quite different. Interactional studies attempt to establish to what extent situational factors affect behaviour by calculating the variance accounted for by the situation factor and the interactions, over various situations. In attribution theory a direct question is asked about the effect of person and situation factors in each specific stimulus story. Furthermore, the subjects' confidence and reactance associated with ratings of cause and responsibility of another's behaviour in a specific situation is likely to be different from rating the likelihood of an emotional or cognitive response in oneself.

ACTOR AND OBSERVER DIFFERENCES

Much of the work in attribution theory investigates the divergent perceptions of actor and observer (Jones and Nisbett, 1972). This distinction is consistently confounded in interactional studies because of the use of self-report methods. That is, in interactional experiments the subject is both actor and observer in that they report as an observer on how they would probably behave as an actor in various situations. Experiments in interactional psychology which have not confounded actor and observer have obtained conflicting results from observational and self-report studies (Moos, 1969, 1970). Despite the variability in results across scales it appears that observational studies produce a higher percentage of person and person × situations variance, and self-report studies produce a higher percentage of situation variance (Jaspars and Furnham, 1980).

Although subjects in interactional experiments are not asked actually to attribute their own behaviour to stimuli inherent in the situations, one would predict from attribution theory, that they would rate their own behaviour as less consistent over situations and more situation specific than the behaviour of others. van Heck and van der Leeuw (1975) demonstrated this in an experiment using a standard

S–R Inventory for aggression in which subjects completed it with respect to both their own behaviour and that of their best friend. As predicted, the percentage of variance accounted for by persons (high cross-situational consistency) was greater for judgements of others, than for self-judgements, while the percentage of variance accounted for by person × situation interaction (high cross-situational variability) was smaller for judgements of others than for self-judgements.

## MEASURING PERSON AND SITUATIONAL ATTRIBUTIONS

Because attribution theory has suggested that observers interpret social behaviour as a simple additive function of person and situational factors whereas interactional psychologists believe that social behaviour is a function of the interaction between person and situation, the two approaches have measured person and situational attributions differently. Although attribution theorists have employed at least three procedures in measuring person and situational attributes, they all assume that there is a direct inverse relationship between person and situation attributions (Soloman, 1978). However, in experiments which have shown changes in the actors' and observers' person and situational attributions, the two have not varied inversely (Arkin and Duval, 1975; Sherrod and Farber, 1975). Taylor and Koivumaki (1976) in fact found a non-significant negative correlation of −0.14 between person and situational attributions. If there is a consistent low correlation between these two factors it implies that the process is not entirely additive but interactional and that the statistical and empirical assessment of person and situation attributions and the conclusions drawn therefrom have been largely incorrect (see Experiment 1). That is, the layman is to some extent perhaps an interactionist, a fact that has been concealed by this methodology.

## AVERAGING ACROSS SUBJECTS

Both attribution and interactionist experiments average across subjects and it is thus possible that certain artifacts may occur. In interactional experiments subjects are required to imagine a type or category of situation and then rate the likelihood of their response in that situation. The situations subjects rate are not actually the same, but are considered to be functionally equivalent. However, as subjects' experiences of situations vary considerably, a large amount of the person × situation interaction may occur because of the differences in the imagined stimuli. Unless subjects are drawn from a closely homogeneous group, or the situations are fully described or shown on video equipment, this problem will continue to occur. Attribution theory on the other hand, does not empirically allow for possible differences between the ratings of observers, thus obscuring variation that might exist between observers.

These numerous methodological differences suggest why different conclusions have been reached. Further, they suggest that the lay person is to some extent an interactionist and that interactional psychologists' findings are perhaps inflated because of methodological weaknesses.

## Two illustrative studies

The following two studies were designed to test a number of the hypotheses derived from the methodological criticisms already mentioned.

### MEASURING PERSON AND SITUATION ATTRIBUTIONS

In a two stage experiment concerned primarily with situational factors in attribution we were interested in a number of hypotheses, two of which will be reported here. Eighty subjects read stimulus stories involving minor accidents and assigned blame, cause and responsibility to person and to situation; they also gave confidence ratings for each judgement. They were asked to specify what additional information they would like on each story, if any, before completing the rating scale. This information was in fact not supplied.

First we were interested in the quantity and quality of the further information subjects would have liked to have had before making their attributions. The requested information from all subjects over all the stimulus stories was content analysed by three post-graduates and a reliability coefficient of 0.76 was obtained, which is significant at the 0.01 level. Twenty-three categories were derived from the literature and an inspection of the data. Three groups of categories were formed, namely, personality, interpersonal and situational factors (See Table I). Nearly 800 additional pieces of information were requested; an average of just under one per subject per story, implying that in nearly all experiments of this kind subjects would like to have more information before making attributions.

Furthermore, nearly half of the information requests concerned a variety of situation factors, a sixth concerned personality factors, while nearly a third concerned the nature of the relationship between the two people. Although these results may not be generalisable to other populations or to different stimulus material it seems that subjects by

TABLE I  Content analysis of the requested information

| | Categories | Number | % | Total (%) |
|---|---|---|---|---|
| **A** | ***Personality factors*** | | | |
| 1 | Personality trait of the agent | 32 | 4.0 | |
| 2 | Personality trait of the recipient | 36 | 4.5 | |
| 3 | Personality state of the agent | 12 | 1.6 | 13.7 |
| 4 | Personality state of the subject | 11 | 1.3 | |
| 5 | Perception of the situation by agent | 11 | 1.3 | |
| 6 | Perception of the situation by recipient | 8 | 1.0 | |
| **B** | ***Interpersonal factors*** | | | |
| 7 | Relationship between the 2 people: formal | 26 | 3.2 | |
| 8 | Relationship between the 2 people: informal | 156 | 19.6 | |
| 9 | Reaction to agent by recipient | 8 | 1.0 | 35.8 |
| 10 | Reaction to recipient by agent | 11 | 1.3 | |
| 11 | Past interpersonal behaviour of the agent | 30 | 3.8 | |
| 12 | Past interpersonal behaviour of the recipient | 55 | 6.9 | |
| **C** | ***Situational factors*** | | | |
| 13 | Other reasons for agent's behaviour | 51 | 6.4 | |
| 14 | Recognition by the subject of the agent's action | 1 | 0.1 | |
| 15 | Deliberateness/awareness of the act by the agent | 46 | 5.7 | |
| 16 | Truth/accuracy/justifiability of agent's statement | 58 | 7.2 | |
| 17 | Background/immediate previous happenings in the situation | 31 | 3.8 | |
| 18 | Nature/extent of the physical forces | 12 | 1.5 | 49.9 |
| 19 | Prediction of the consequences of the act by the agent | 18 | 2.2 | |
| 20 | Specific situational information to the story | 129 | 16.2 | |
| 21 | Awareness by subject of the act | 11 | 1.3 | |
| 22 | Feelings of the agent and the subject | 30 | 3.7 | |
| 23 | Reaction of the agent to the subject and *vice versa* afterwards | 13 | 1.6 | |
| | *Total* | *796* | *100* | |

and large require more information particularly about the situation in which behaviour occurs. Not only does this indicate the limitations of the stimulus material, it also provides useful data that could be used in investigating attributional processes.

Secondly, we were interested in the relationship between person and situational attributions as it was suggested that these may not be perfectly correlated. In each story subjects were requested to give ratings of person and situation responsibility, cause and blame. The correlations between person and situation judgements are presented in Table II.

TABLE II    Correlations between person and situation attributions

|  | Person responsibility | Person cause | Person blame |
|---|---|---|---|
| Situation responsibility | −0.345† | −0.175 | −0.417* |
| Situation cause | −0.285†† | −0.482* | −0.329† |
| Situation blame | −0.389* | −0.198 | −0.514* |

*p<0.001    †p<0.01    ††p<0.05

As expected, all the correlations are negative and although most are significant, they are not particularly high. Indeed the correlation between person and situation responsibility is only −0.345 which accounts for 21% of the variance. Because person and situational attributions do not correlate perfectly, experimenters should measure both separately and report the results of each measure. This would allow attribution theorists to test fully an interactional hypothesis (Soloman, 1978).

OBSERVATIONAL EFFECTS IN THE GENERALISABILITY OF SOCIAL BEHAVIOUR ACROSS SITUATIONS

In this study it was hypothesised that in a number of everyday situations fairly strong constraints are placed upon people because of role expectations. Attribution theory would predict that under those circumstances behaviour is mainly attributed to the situation. However, because attribution studies usually have only one stimulus person, the situation factor also contains the possibility of a confounding with a stimulus × person interaction. If one allows for different stimulus persons in the same situation the effect of the stimulus person (the actor) and the situation can be separated from the observational effects. It is suggested that the vaguer or more global the observational scales, the stronger are the observational effects.

In the study nine under-graduates rated videotaped, natural consultations of three doctors, each interacting with three patients.

TABLE III Results of the analysis of variance of verbal and non-verbal specific rating scales. (Calculated according to the formula in Gleser, Cronbach and Rajuratnam, 1965)

| | Verbal behaviour | | | | | | | |
|---|---|---|---|---|---|---|---|---|
| | Positive socio-emotional | | Negative socio-emotional | | Questions | | Answers | |
| Sources of variance | F | % Var | F | % Var | F | % Var | F | % Var |
| Doctors | 5.2* | −15.9 | 2.4 | 6.6 | 32.6 | 33.9 | 20.7 | 30.4 |
| Patients | 8.6* | 31.3 | 0.8 | 4.7 | 10.4 | 48.7 | 6.2 | 39.5 |
| Observers | 33.1* | 21.8 | 0.0 | 12.2 | 1.7 | 1.1 | 5.3 | 3.1 |
| Doctors × Observers | 9.2* | 22.6 | 1.9 | 17.9 | 2.8 | 6.1 | 3.3 | 11.7 |
| Error | | 8.2 | | 58.4 | | 10.0 | | 15.0 |

| | Non-verbal behaviour | | | | | | | | | | | |
|---|---|---|---|---|---|---|---|---|---|---|---|---|
| | Hand/arm | | Foot/leg | | Gen. movement | | Scratch | | Nodding yes | | Smiling | |
| Sources of variance | F | % Var | F | % Var | F | % Var | F | % Var | F | % Var | F | % Var |
| Doctors | 16.4* | 38.5 | 0.6 | −51.6 | 60.5* | 49.5 | 7.7* | 27.1 | 52.4* | 30.9 | 21.6* | 19.0 |
| Patients | 4.9† | 38.8 | 3.4 | 25.8 | 13.5* | 43.0 | 1.9 | 12.3 | 37.2* | 17.4 | 10.0* | 50.0 |
| Observers | 0.1 | −1.2 | 0.1 | 0.6 | 2.5 | 0.5 | 4.2* | 14.8 | 6.4* | 33.3 | 6.5* | 7.3 |
| Doctors × Observers | 0.7 | −1.6 | 0.6 | −1.6 | 1.4 | 1.0 | 1.0 | 3.7 | 1.0 | 0.0 | 2.3 | 7.3 |
| Error | | 19.6 | | 20.9 | | 6.5 | | 41.9 | | 18.5 | | 17.0 |

*p<0.01  †p<0.05

Each doctor was rated on thirteen scales divided into the three categories of verbal and non-verbal behaviour (specific) and impression scales (global) derived from Bales (1953), Moos (1969) and Pendleton and Wakeford (1980). For each observation category and each rating scale separate analyses of variance were conducted. A nested design was employed because each doctor (person factor) treats different patients (situation factor) and the situational factor is nested within the person factor.

TABLE IV   Results of the analysis of variance of overall impression ratings scales. (Calculated according to the formula in Gleser *et al.* 1965)

|  | Tension | | Skill | | Satisfaction | |
|---|---|---|---|---|---|---|
| Sources of variance | F | % Var | F | % Var | F | % Var |
| Doctors | 0.3 | 3.4 | 1.1 | −0.4 | 2.9 | 2.5 |
| Patients | 1.2 | 0.7 | 0.8 | −0.4 | 1.0 | 0.3 |
| Observers | 12.1* | 38.0 | 14.8* | 52.8 | 8.9† | 40.4 |
| Doctors × Observers | 2.7* | 21.1 | 1.6 | 8.0 | 1.5 | 8.0 |
| Error | | 36.5 | | 38.0 | | 48.8 |

*p<0.001   †p<0.05

Comparing Tables III and IV, it is apparent that the largest variance component in overall impressions is due to the difference between observers, whereas in specific ratings it is due primarily to the difference between patients and to some extent between doctors, particularly in measures of non-verbal communication. This partly confirms our hypothesis that social behaviour in a professional setting is largely determined by situational demands and role expectations. However, the most interesting finding is that when using global *post hoc* ratings the differences between observers explains most of the variance. This finding is highlighted by a correlational analysis of the agreement between the raters: the average correlation was +0.60 for verbal behaviour, +0.81 for non-verbal behaviour and +0.20 for overall rating scales. Further, the correlation between verbal and non-verbal behaviour is +0.58, whereas the correlation between verbal behaviour and the global ratings is −0.39 which is non-significant.

Thus even though we are to a large extent measuring the same social behaviour, the results appear to be quite different depending upon the method of observation. Because most person–situation studies use the most unreliable method of observation and confound actor–observer effects, the ubiquitous person–situation interaction could be the result of a simple observer effect in situations which involve mainly role specific behaviour. These results have implications for both person–situation interactions and attribution theory. In interactional psychology one should make use of observation data by others in addition to self report. If interested in personality traits, rather than role-related behaviour, one should collect data in situations that do not involve strong role expectations and constraints. Attribution theory, on the other hand, should explicitly allow for differences between observers and between actors by averaging observations with respect to only one, rather than across all, actors. These implications make possible a partial resolution of at least three of the problems pointed out above, namely the confounding of actor/observer differences, the averaging across subjects and the use of specific v. global rating scales.

## Summary and conclusion

In this chapter we have concentrated primarily on the historical and empirical differences between interactional psychology and attribution theory. We have argued that because these two areas of research have had different historical antecedents (the former in theoretical psychology and correlation theory, and the latter in experimental social psychology), they have conceptualised the same problem regarding the explanation of behaviour somewhat differently. These theoretical or conceptual differences have led to the development of different empirical procedures, which have influenced the results and conclusions in each field.

We have attempted to compare the methodology of both fields, highlighting some common weaknesses. These problems, which mainly concern inattention to salient motivational and demographic differences between subjects and the inadequacy of stimulus material, have implications for future research. Specifically, consideration of situational variables in attribution theory might help resolve conflicting results. We have also suggested that various distinctions such as that between parameters of the situation in which and about which attributions are made may be important in understanding the social attribution process.

Detailed comparisons of the experimental techniques in both fields helped to account for the differences in the results and conclusions which have been reached in each. Four special issues which included the use of different rating scales, confounding actor and observer differences, measuring person and situation attributions and averaging across subjects were examined and empirically tested in two experiments.

These results have implications for both interactional psychology and attribution theory. Interactional psychology has not taken sufficient cognisance of the consistent and systematic biases in social perception (Mischel, 1979) and more particularly of actor/observer differences leading to the fundamental attribution error (Ross, 1977). These biases in social perception are as apparent in the professional psychologist's formulation of hypotheses and design of experiments as they are in the naive subjects who take part in them. Secondly, it seems important to determine when and which person–situation factors interact and the quality and quantity of that interaction rather than presuming that this interaction is constant across all persons, situations and social behaviours. On the other hand, attribution theory has not taken sufficient cognisance of the fact that subjects make interactional as well as dispositional and situational attributions for certain events and under certain circumstances. It is important to determine in which situations and for which behaviours people make interactional attributions. Finally, as a measure of external validity, is it important to determine when and how attributions are spontaneously offered and what psychological functions they fulfil for different people.

# Epilogue

# Perceived Causal Structures

## Harold H. Kelley

### Introduction

The chapters in this book raise a number of important issues. Among them are the question of *accuracy* of attributions, the effect on the attribution process of the *content* (the particular type of cause and/or effect), the relative importance of *social* and *physical* 'reality', and the relation between categorisation, especially social categorisation, and attribution. This chapter will not consider further these and similar issues. Each of them has received attention in prior writings, not only in this book but elsewhere. Instead, the present chapter will develop a theme that runs as an undercurrent thoughout this book, but that has not been explicitly developed in the way it deserves. This theme concerns the way people perceive the temporal flow of life's events to be structured causally.

There are many indications in the preceding chapters that people often think in terms of chains and networks of causes. One cause is seen to lead to an effect which itself becomes the cause for a further effect, several causes are seen jointly to determine a single effect, a given cause gives rise to several different effects, two factors affect each other in a circular causal relationship, and so on. These are obvious features of the common person's causal understanding, and they were described in Heider's original writings on 'the naive analysis of action' (1958a), but their implications have not yet been fully appreciated in current attributional thought. This chapter will be devoted to speculation about the properties of the perceived causal structures constituted by chains and networks and to describing some of the implications of the analysis of these structures.

The general point is this: *The common person's understanding of a particular event is based on the perceived location of that event within a temporally ordered network of interconnected causes and effects.* I will refer to this temporally ordered network as a causal structure, with the understanding that the term always pertains to a *perceived* structure.

### Examples of causal structures

It will be useful to begin with some concrete examples of causal structures.

We may note first that such structures are implicit in people's unprompted accounts of important events in their lives. Some illustrations are found in Fletcher's report (1981) of his research on people's explanations for separations from their marriage partners. Although Fletcher's results support the importance placed by attribution theorists on personal dispositions, he found that many respondents went beyond dispositions to background factors, as in this example:

Background and upbringing come into it as well. I was very strictly brought up by an old army man. Dad said you did something you did it *now*. Whereas Gary was brought up by his parents who were very busy earning money and didn't really have any time to bring up the children at all. They didn't have any discipline or affection and that shows through his attitudes. (p. 62)

In addition to the succession of causal factors implicit in this example (upbringing → attitudes → separation), many accounts described converging and interacting causal connections, as in the following statement of a woman who, after thirty years of marriage, had been left by her husband:

He wasn't well. He was on the wrong tablets from the doctor. That caused his depression. . . . The trouble happened at a bad time. It was the time of my change of life, and my son's growing up stage, when he wanted to find out the facts of life. I had various conversations with him but he didn't talk with his father. I tried to get his father to talk to him, but he was a shift-worker and didn't have the same contact with him. . . . Once she [the other woman] got out of the hospital she rang him up here and promised to look after him. She demanded that he come and live with her. He is flattered and having a lovely time now. If it wasn't for her, he would still be here. . . . The death of our daughter may have had a delayed reaction with him. . . . With him working on shift-work we could not have a normal relationship. . . The people at the post office [his workplace] are all a loose living lot, living with each other. . . . Perhaps the war affected him. . . . Life may have just been too humdrum for him.   (p. 64)

Here, distant events (death of daughter, the war) are seen to cause present ones, and various concurrent causes (the wife's change of life, the son's needs, the wrong prescription, the example of coworkers) are seen to converge to make the husband vulnerable (depressed, bored) to the other woman's invitation that triggers the separation.

Some accounts imply that the sequence of events might have been different, had certain crucial causes been different. In the following example, the cause that made the difference is the wife's attitude:

Grog was a problem insofar as my wife had something against it. Mind you,

I was not drinking more than my friends. O.K., I used to come home about 7.30. Lots of my friends used to come home at 1 or 2 o'clock in the morning. Their wives would abuse them in the morning, and then it was over. My wife is very quiet . . . she wouldn't row. . . . My wife knew my life style (including my drinking) before I got married. . . . I would argue that if drinking causes you to bash your wife or your children, then fair enough . . . but that never happened. (p. 67)

Not surprisingly, the causal structures for a particular effect may be viewed differently by husband and wife. Fletcher describes that one wife attributed her husband's impotence to guilt feelings he suffered after stealing money. The husband's explanation for his impotence was in terms of his wife's loss of sexual attractiveness resulting from gaining weight.

In an entirely different domain of important life events, Cowie (1976) provides evidence about cardiac patients' perceptions of the causes for their heart attacks. He reports that '. . . patients, in responding to my general question "Why are you in [the] hospital?", did not begin with the event itself, but always placed it in a historical context of anything from a few hours to one year' (p. 87). A limited context is illustrated by the example of Mr X and a more extended one, covering both immediate and more distant causes, by Mr L, as follows:

*Mr X*: I think I'd just overdone it. I was working on Thursday night up until 11 o'clock and on Friday and all day Saturday until 8 o'clock. And it just seemed to come to me on Monday. I think I'd just worked a bit too much. I think it was the strain of too much work over a period. And then we've had a bit of trouble with the lad as well. Everything just built up and came to a head.

*Mr L*: I was just asking the doctor the other day why I had a heart attack at the particular time I had it. Because I wasn't doing anything strenuous at the time like on occasions before, *many* occasions before when I've been working physically hard . . . the times you'd think it was the correct background for it to happen. And then the holiday weekend, having a lazy weekend, it came on.
*Cowie*: Any ideas yourself why it happened?
*Mr L*: Well I'm inclined to think . . . I had an operation 2 or 3 years back for varicose veins, and about 10 years ago I had piles. Well, as you grow older . . . I mean why did my varicose vein reach a stage when it had to be stripped, or my piles became so bad that I had to get them operated on? So I suppose the heart condition . . . just as we're getting older . . . plus smoking doesn't help. The physical and mental strain of my particular job. It gives both. Plenty of problems, plenty of worries, stress and strain, chasing about . . . so you reach a point when some things, like a safety valve or a fuse has to blow.

In both of these accounts, as in the earlier ones for marital separation, there is implied a causal structure in which earlier causes lead to later ones and causes converge and interact to produce the final focal effect.

And again, as the first part of Mr L's comments show, the thinking includes references to causal links that might have been present but were not. It is important to note that in some cases, a patient is not able to provide a causal account of the heart attack because he cannot locate in his own biography what he assumes to be plausible causes. We should not be surprised if people do not possess causal structures for all the significant events in their lives, although we might suspect that the greater an event's importance, the more strenuous will be the efforts to formulate its causal context.

Axelrod and his colleagues (1976) derive perceived causal structures (referring to them as 'cognitive maps') from the arguments that policy makers present in their advocacy of various governmental actions. That causal structures are latent in such arguments is not surprising inasmuch as they consist largely of explanations of how things link together causally and the implications of the alleged linkages for the effects to be expected of various policy decisions and for making certain decisions rather than others. It should be noted, of course, that the structure presented in the course of policy debate may not reflect the advocate's true perceived structure, but rather one that, for his own purposes, he wishes other people to accept.

Axelrod illustrates the construction of a causal structure by a fragment from the transcript of a December, 1918, meeting of the Eastern Committee of the British Imperial War Cabinet, in which the members discussed how active a role Britain should play in a post-war Persia (now, Iran). Lord Cecil, deputy to the foreign secretary, explains a position he had held at an earlier time, when he favored little intervention in Persia's affairs. Axelrod quotes the following text (1976, p. 83):

*Cecil*: I was very much attracted at one time by the suggestion that it was not really justifiable for us to go on spending this amount of money in Persia, that we had very little interest in the place, that it was not at all certain that the good government of Persia really mattered to us, and further that apparently our interference had not so far, for various reasons, conduced to the improvement of the government of Persia, but that, on the contrary, the government had become decidedly worse than it was when we had relatively less to do with them. Therefore I was disposed to think that there was a good deal to be said for the 'stewing in their own juice' policy.

Within that text, Axelrod identifies four 'concept variables': A, Amount of money spent in Persia by Britain; B, British utility (the interests of Britain); C, Quality of government in Persia; and D, Existence of British interference in Persia. Lord Cecil's text is analysed as asserting that A does not promote B ('. . . not really justifiable for us . . .'), that C has no relation to B ('. . . not at all certain . . . really mattered to us, . . .'), that D has not promoted C ('. . . our interference has not conduced . . . to improvement . . .') and, in fact, that D has inhibited C ('. . . had become worse . . .'). The entire statement implies that interference requires spending money, so D requires A. This analysis can be summarised by the causal structure shown in Fig. 1. The 'variables' are shown as points and the causal assertions, by arrows. The signs associated with the arrows indicate the net effect of one variable upon another, whether positive (the first variable augments the second), negative (the first inhibits the second), or zero (the first has no causal relevance to the second). Lord Cecil's last sentence ('Therefore, I . . .') is a summary of the implications of the causal structure: there is a good deal to be said for non-interference, i.e. letting the Persians 'stew in their own juice'. This implication can be derived formally from the structure by using the rule from the theory of signed digraphs (Harary, Norman and Cartwright, 1965) that the sign of a path is determined by multiplying the signs of its component parts. Thus, the D–A–B path is negative: Interference requires spending money and spending money in Persia does not promote British interests; therefore, interference does not promote British interests.

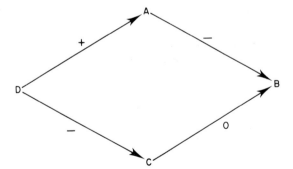

Fig. 1   Causal structure for Lord Cecil's text. (After Axelrod, 1976)

A great deal might be said about the many ways in which Axelrod's work is important to the study of causal structures. He and his colleagues deal not only with the methodological details of coding the structures implied in policy argumentation but also with the conceptual problems of indexing and summarising the properties of such structures. Perhaps the most provocative implication for an attribution researcher is that causal assertions comprise the basic content of the thoughts and arguments involved in group decision-making. This point, though obvious once one thinks about it, emphasises the necessity of locating our studies of attributions in the broad context of interpersonal communication. This emphasis is wholly consistent with one of the main themes in the preceding chapters of this book, especially those by Deschamps, Eiser, Hewstone, and Lloyd-Bostock, that attribution must be studied in relation to social interaction phenomena. Axelrod's work also opens up new materials for attribution researchers. We need no longer rely on answers to our explicit 'why?' questions as our sole source of information about people's causal thinking. With suitable adjustments made for what is asserted v. what is believed (no small problem!), naturally occurring arguments can provide useful information about the attribution process.

A final example of causal structures is provided by Bowerman (1978, 1981). Anticipating the present paper, Bowerman assumes that people locate the significant events of daily life within 'subjective competence structures'. These are perceived causal structures in which the self (or some other actor) is perceived to be linked causally to certain consequences that are good or bad. For example, Fig. 2 summarises the perceptions that self smokes cigarettes which, along with air pollution, causes lung disease, which in turn causes intense pain. In this structure, the causal path from self to pain links self positively with a negative consequence. This kind of linkage is assumed to have negative implications for one's sense of self-competence. As described later, threats to self-competence may lead to certain modifications in the perceived structure which reduce its negative implications for the self. In the example in Fig. 2, the existence of another cause of lung disease reduces the threat somewhat, and it would be reduced further if the

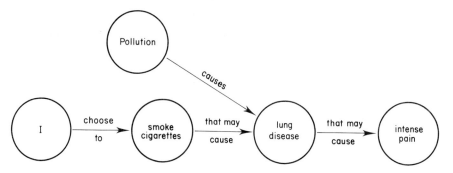

Fig. 2    Possible causal structure for a smoker. (Adapted from Bowerman, 1981)

perceived causal link between smoking and disease could be broken, or if smoking could be seen to have other consequences that are very positive in nature. Bowerman uses the notion of causal structure, combined with the motivational assumption of a tendency to maximise one's own subjective competence, in a very fruitful way to derive the various tendencies people display in selecting a line of action, carrying it out, and reacting to a past, irrevocable action.

## Properties of causal structures

Research on causal structures will require describing them in terms of their most important properties. The preceding examples suggest some of these properties and further ideas are provided by the causal distinctions that exist in the language, the structural concepts incorporated in current attribution theories, and evidence from studies of lay concepts. A selective review of these sources will indicate how structural distinctions are latent in current attribution research and suggest the major structural properties to be distinguished, see below.

### SIMPLE–COMPLEX

In the common person's causal structure, simple one-to-one connections (one cause leads to one effect) are distinguished from complex, multiple connections (several causes converge to produce an effect; one cause has many effects). This distinction is shown in several ways. In the dictionary (Webster's *New Collegiate Dictionary*, 1977), 'cause' refers to anything, such as an event, circumstance, or condition, that brings about or helps bring about an effect. Under this broad rubric, there are distinguished 'determinants' which play a powerful role in fixing the effect and 'occasions' or 'circumstances' which serve as precipitating causes in conjunction with other underlying causes of long standing. A determinant may be the single cause of an effect but a precipitating cause is usually one of several causes contributing to an effect. Both simple and complex causation figure prominently in McArthur's (1972) and Pruitt and Insko's (1980) studies of explanations given for events imbedded in various configurations of information. Certain patterns are interpreted largely in terms of simple causation (e.g. person or stimulus) but some are interpreted as reflecting complex causation (e.g. something about both the person and the stimulus). The common person's awareness of multiple effects of a given cause is an inherent feature of Jones and Davis' theory of correspondent inference (1965). An actor is understood by a perceiver to be aware of the various consequences of his alternative actions. Once a particular course of action is chosen, the perceiver gains information about the underlying intention by identifying the consequences unique to that line of behavior. The meaning of the choice is clearest when there is only one such unique consequence. The assumption that people distinguish between simple and complex causation is also at the basis of Kelley's theory of causal schemata (1972b). It is assumed that some phenomena are interpreted in terms of multiple sufficient causes (any of several causes acting singly can produce the observed effect) and other phenomena, in terms of multiple necessary causes (several causes must operate jointly to produce the observed effect).

A recent factor analytic study (Wimer and Kelley, 1982) identifies a simple–complex dimension in students' causal ascriptions. At the 'simple' pole of the dimension there is only one cause, it produces only the one effect, and it is sufficient to do so whenever it is present. At the 'complex' pole are causes that are not sufficient always to produce the effect and that produce other effects besides the particular one. To illustrate, rated as simple were laughing at a clown because of 'something about the clown' and shoplifting an ashtray from a store because of 'being a kleptomaniac'. Rated as complex were applauding heartily after a concert because of 'being in a good mood' and doing something that displeases one's spouse because of 'pressure of one's friends'. As the authors describe the difference, '. . . simple causes are those which are more complete explanations and are sufficient to account for the event's occurrence, whereas complex causes are those which are partial explanations and are embedded in a more intricate web of causality'.

PROXIMAL–DISTAL

Data presented by Löchel (chapter 7) in this book show that common people distinguish causes that are close to the focal event from those distant from it. In their explanations for success or failure, her four-year-olds often mentioned the proximal factors of ability (can, know) and task difficulty. However, they also mentioned the more distal factor of 'learned', referring to previous experience and instruction. Thus, a given event can be explained by an earlier process (during which knowledge and skill are acquired) or by the end products of that process as they exist concurrently with the event (current ability). The notion of intermediary events, which children seem to learn rather early (chapter 5), also implies that causes are perceived to be located at various distances from a focal event, distance being describable in terms of number of intervening causal links.

In their explanations for success and failure, adult respondents mention not only the proximal factors such as mood and effort, but also distal ones, such as the teacher's style of instruction or choice of test questions, which are responsible for the student's performance. Distal v. proximal causes are also given by adults for negative behavior in close interpersonal relations (Orvis, Kelley and Butler, 1976). The actor's current state or characteristics (proximal) are sometimes explained by reference to antecedent causes such as background, upbringing, present family or peer pressure, and the partner's provocations. Activities are seen as undertaken because they are enjoyable *per se*, i.e. because of their immediate consequences, or because of their more remote consequences (e.g. in order to make a certain impression on other persons or to elicit a desired response from them). A closely related theoretical distinction is that drawn by Kruglanski (1975) between endogenous and exogenous attributions, that is, between action perceived to be undertaken as an end in itself and action perceived to serve as a means to some distal end.

PAST–FUTURE

The common person shares the scientist's view that the temporal order of things constrains what can be considered to be cause and effect. This is apparent in research on the role of temporal order in children's causal judgements (Kun, 1978) and in adults' perceptions of causality (Michotte, 1963). Given the importance of this cue, the temporal flow of life's events is not experienced as a simple ordering, like St Patrick's Day parade or a succession of newsreel shots, but as reflecting an underlying causal organisation.

Given the constraint that temporal order imposes on the perception of causation, the perceived causal structure is ordered temporally, from the past, through the present, and into the future. In most instances a focal event is seen to be both the resultant of one or more pre-existing causes and one of the antecedents for real or potential subsequent effects. As a consequence, focal events located in the past often draw their meaning as much from their perceived consequences as from their perceived antecedents. This is particularly true for the behavior of persons and other purposeful systems which are thought to act out of anticipation and assessment of the consequences of action. This is at the basis of Anscombe's observation (quoted in chapter 4) that what a person actually does usually provides a basis for understanding that person's intentions.

The interpretation of behavior is sometimes oriented to its anticipated consequences ('He did it in order to . . .') and sometimes, to its

antecedents ('He did it because . . .'). This is clearly indicated by the
evidence in the earlier chapter by Lalljee, Watson and White. They
were able to classify the explanations given by their young respondents
in categories arranged along the temporal dimension: past events, the
current situation, and future states (goals). The first two types of
explanation were given most often for emotional behavior (feeling
happy or angry) and the last type was given most often for actions
(tidying, painting, lying). More generally, as the authors suggest, the
data imply that behavior seen to be under the person's control tends to
be explained in terms of goals. This is in contrast to behavior that is
seen to be reactive or impulsive, which is explained in terms of past or
present causal factors.

STABLE–UNSTABLE

The causal structure of the common person includes both causes that
are stable and lasting and ones that are variable or fleeting. This
distinction is a familiar one in current attribution research, particularly
in the writings of Weiner (e.g. 1979) who shows that in their
interpretations of success and failure, subjects distinguish the stable
causes of ability and task difficulty from the unstable causes of effort
and luck. Beyond the notion of unchanging v. changing, which is at the
core of Weiner's distinction, a number of other temporal distinctions
are made. Certain perceived causes change slowly and systematically,
some doing so inexorably (as illustrated by the factor of 'age' which was
given by some of Löchel's child subjects as an explanation for success
or failure) and others doing so as a function of other identifiable causes
('learned' which is presumably the result of certain opportunities for
experience). Some unstable causes fluctuate unpredictably, as implied
by the concept of 'luck', but others are understood to fluctuate in a
systematic and predictable way, for example, female menstrual periods
(Ruble, 1977).

   The perceived causal structure also incorporates various conceptions of the interplay between stable and unstable causes. For
example, brief precipitating or inciting causes are seen to set in motion
or give expression to underlying causes that have existed for some time.
The dictionary example describes a trivial international incident that
occasions a war because of a long time antipathy between two peoples.

ACTUAL–POTENTIAL

The perceived causal structure includes conceptions both of *actual* or
real causes and causal links and of *potential* causes and causal links. The
person has ideas about what has actually led to what, but also ideas

about what, in the past, might have led to what and about what, in the future, might lead to what. To be clear, 'actual' here refers to the reality as understood by the perceiver, that is, the perceiver's beliefs about what were and are the actual causes and interconnections. 'Potential' refers to the perceiver's conception or imagination of past, present, and future, i.e. the beliefs about the causes and interconnections as they might have been, as they might be now, and as they might be in the future. The causal structure of the future is, of course, wholly potential, constructed by and existing in the perceiver's imagination. The causal structure of the past and present includes in parallel the conceptions of what was and is and the imaginations of what might have been and what might now be. It is the comparison of these that produces feelings of relief (when the potential represents dangers avoided) or regret (when the potential represents opportunities lost). An error of commission is identified when a person's causal intervention generates an actual causal course less good than the ones that, with no intervention or with a more appropriate one, were potential. An error of omission is identified when the actual causal course is less good than one that was potential had the person intervened.

The prospective notions of where the causal connections might lead form the basis for attempts to manipulate causes and for choices about the parts of the causal structure in which to locate oneself. When another person is observed to manipulate causes or make choices, an understanding of what he perceives to be the potential causal structure affords a basis for inferring his goals or values. This meta-attributional basis of intention inference is incorporated in Jones and Davis' theory of correspondent inferences (1965). The inference about an actor's goals is based on the observer's perceptions of the actor's understanding of what might have been the consequences had he made different choices.

## Some problems for research

The central proposition here is that focal events are interpreted – understood, explained, and evaluated – in terms of their location within a perceived causal structure. As the preceding comments suggest, this structure has direction (past to future), extent (proximal–distal), patterning (simple–complex), components of varying stability–instability, and features some of which are actual and others of which are potential. Beyond these properties, the perceived causal structure includes various types of causes, such as those associated with persons (e.g. traits, states), with the physical and social environment (e.g. problems, opportunities, role prescriptions), and with particular entities and stimuli (e.g. goal objects, barriers, tools, personal provocations). The perceived causal linkages also vary, for example, in whether a cause is believed to promote or inhibit a given effect and in whether the joint action of several causes is understood to be additive, multiplicative, or such. Depending upon the number of causal factors seen to be relevant to any focal event, the causal structure may (independently of its extensity and patterning) be a sparse one, with only a few causes being identified, or a dense one, with many causes being distinguished.[1]

To propose that common people organise events within a perceived causal structure is to suggest a number of general problems for attribution research. It is of first importance to develop procedures for identifying and characterising these structures. This requires learning the terms in which causal analysis is represented in thought, whether in verbal statements, visual imagery, or whatever. Such procedures will permit a characterisation of the form and complexity of causal thought that common people typically bring to bear upon various types of problems.

The preceding analysis suggests the terms in which to characterise the quality of people's causal thought. An extensive, differentiated, and complex causal analysis is possible only for persons of considerable intellectual development and then, only under optimal conditions in which adequate information is available, interest is high, and sense of urgency and emotional arousal are stimulating but not interfering. These, of course, are the conditions usually considered requisite for productive scientific causal analysis. They are not the usual conditions of everyday thought. However, it seems important not to prejudge the quality of common thought. As Furnham, Jaspars and Fincham note, in our reliance upon research procedures using restricted information, we may underuse our subjects' attributional abilities and underestimate the level of competence they customarily exhibit. Efforts to assess perceived causal structures will provide a more realistic view of common persons' potentialities and even perhaps suggest ways in which more useful causal analyses can be encouraged.

It would seem fruitful to compare adults' and children's causal thinking in terms of properties of their causal structures rather than, as is common in recent research, in terms of whether specific conceptions are or are not present. Certain structural features have been the subject of developmental research on causal schemata (e.g. Kun, 1977) and mediated causation (Piaget, 1974), but there remain other properties and characteristics of entire structures to be examined from a developmental perspective (cf. Kelley, 1980b).

One problem basic to the study of perceived causal structures concerns the extent to which successions of life events are organised in causal terms rather than in other ways. This chapter assumes the organisation to be a causal one. However, there are other possible bases of organisation (e.g. sequential: what follows what; categorical: types and frequencies of events), and the actual basis is a matter for empirical determination.

If, as assumed here, life's events are organised in causal terms, the nature of the perceived causal structure may or may not correspond to what scientists understand to be the objective one. Thus, it is uncertain how the scripts of plans that scientists find to characterise the organisation or action are represented in common people's thinking. For example, a line of action may commonly be thought of merely as a succession of causal links, each event leading to the next one. The governing 'plan' that imposes that overarching organisation upon the sequence may not always be part of the phenomenology of causal systems of this type. Alternatively, the perceiver of a sequence of actions may impose more organisation upon it than can be demonstrated objectively. Nothing here should be taken to imply that the perceived causal structure always, or even usually, corresponds to the objective one. Indeed, certain known interaction practices have the consequence of producing erroneous perceived structures. The procedures employed by professional magicians are directed deliberately at producing discrepancies between a real causal sequence and the sequence as it appears to an observer (Kelley, 1980c). The latter's sense of witnessing 'magic' requires that the apparent causal sequence include a supernatural cause–effect linkage. Similar discrepancies between real and apparent sequence are managed in everyday settings, though usually in less self-conscious ways. Fascinating examples are provided by Pollner and Wikler's (1981) account of the practices by which a family made their severely retarded five-year-old daughter appear to act intelligently. One practice consisted of 'commanding the already done', in which 'family members observed the beginnings of possible actions and then ordered their completion'. Done skilfully, this created an apparent causal sequence in which the temporal order of command and action was reversed from that in the real sequence. By this means, it was made to appear that the child was able to follow instructions far better than she actually could.

That example reminds us of the basic problem of the relation between the successive portions of the causal structure. The present

conception emphasises the continuity between the person's conceptions of past, present and future. However, it is an empirical matter
to determine the connectedness and consistency between the several
temporal segments and, indeed, the degree to which they are distinguished at all. The past and present portion of the structure are
generated by the processes of attribution (causal perception and
inference) and represent the person's causal understanding of past
events and of what is currently unfolding. The future portions of the
structure reflect the person's predictions and expectations about the
future course of events. One wonders about the relations among these
processes and the consequent nature of the boundaries between the
temporal segments, e.g. whether there may not be considerable
vagueness about where one leaves off and the next one begins.

The few studies that have encompassed both past and future yield
indications as to possible discrepancies. Anderson and Butzin (1974)
found differences between, on one hand, the thought models involved
in predictions of performance from various combinations of ability and
motivation and, on the other hand, those involved in attributional
inferences of motivation from various combinations of performance
and ability (or of ability from various combinations of performance and
motivation). This finding may reflect logical problems in the research
designs employed, but taken at face value, it points to a possible source
of discrepancy between peoples' view of the future and their interpretation of the past. Fischoff's (1975) work has a similar implication.
It suggests that, relative to a future that is seen to be highly uncertain,
the past may seem to be rather strongly determined. This implies that
perceivers' perceptions of the potential courses of causality in the past
will be quite sparse relative to their conceptions of the future
potentialities. It may be a human tendency to have a sense that what
has happened was fated to happen.

The attributions made for past behavior have been compared with
those made for present behavior, in studies by Lenauer, Sameth and
Shaver (1976) and Moore, Sherrod, Liu and Underwood (1979). Both
indicate that our explanations for our own actions may become less
situational and more dispositional as the actions recede into the past.
This result brings to mind the evidence about goal gradients, that
external incentives have less effect on behavior the more distant they
are, either temporally or spatially (cf. Kelley, 1980b). In contrast to the
above, Miller and Porter (1980) find evidence that as one's behavior
recedes into the past, one tends to interpret it in *more* situational terms.
These investigations present evidence that one possible reason for this
shift is a diminution, with the passage of time, in the need to see one's

self in control of situations. These several studies suggest that the effects of the passage of time are probably quite complex, the past being viewed with different information and with different motives than the present. Also relevant to differences between cognitive processes as they are past-oriented v. present- or future-oriented is research on decision making. A distinction has been made (e.g. Festinger, 1964) between pre-decision scanning of alternatives, which enables the person to make an informed confident choice, and post-decision processes, which serve to restructure the perception of the alternatives in ways that support the choice.

As tomorrow inexorably becomes today and today becomes yesterday, our expectations are confirmed or disconfirmed. In his chapter, Eiser makes the pregnant suggestion that attribution comes to play when expectations fail. When events unfold as expected, no question is raised about their causal dynamics. This view leads one to wonder about how the nature of the resulting attribution process might be affected by the nature of the expectations and the nature of the disconfirmation. An interesting though perhaps rather extreme case is one in which a great deal of thought went into predicting the course of events and the disconfirmation is unequivocal. We might suppose that the resulting attribution inquiry will not only reexamine the relevant information but will also involve a meta-cognitive component, in which questions are raised about one's information gathering and processing methods.

## Implications

### MULTIPLE EXPLANATIONS

Both Lalljee and his colleagues (chapter 6) and Furnham (chapter 12) emphasise that people can provide a variety of explanations for a given event. This important notion is implicit in the conception of a perceived causal structure. Given a structure of any complexity, its possessor will have difficulty communicating his full understanding of the event's causes and will be able to provide a number of rather different partial answers to the question 'Why?'. These answers will vary in the number of steps through which the causal linkage is traced back, in whether the person chooses to mention actual factors that explain the event through their occurrence or potential factors that explain it through their non-occurrence, in whether important but well-known factors or less important but uncommon ones are mentioned, and in other similar ways.

This point has an important implication for measurement procedures used to assess the person's attributions. How is a respondent to be expected to encode a complex causal understanding into choices between alternative causes, or into ratings or rankings of a given list of causes? How is importance to be allocated between a precipitating cause and the underlying one it sets in motion (the triggering 'incident' v. the latent hostility)? How is a question of internality v. externality to be answered when both are thought to be involved proximally (both the temptation and the person's weakness led to the embezzlement)? And how is it to be answered when an internal and an external cause are seen to be successive elements in the causal chain leading to the event (e.g. the person's failure reflects the bad situation he was in but the person had gotten himself into that situation in the first place). It was once assumed that internal and external (or disposition and situation) attribution ratings would be inversely related, inasmuch as these terms seemed to represent opposite poles of explanation. The conception of perceived causal structures,in which effects are often multiply determined, makes this assumption seem quaintly simple.

PURPOSES OF THE ATTRIBUTION INQUIRY

One probable way I decide how to communicate about my complex causal understanding to another person is by making a meta-attributional inquiry, asking myself (or the other person) why the other might wish and/or need to know about my causal perceptions. There are many answers to this question but the one noted by Lalljee and his co-authors is obviously of great general relevance: the other person could need to know only what I know that he doesn't know. Therefore, my answer should first of all be informative. As Lalljee has commented (1981), different assumptions about the questioner's knowledge can result in references either to the person (if the questioner is assumed to be familiar with the situation) or to the situation (if the questioner is assumed to be familiar with the person). Thus, 'He chose chemistry because he wants to make a lot of money' and 'He chose chemistry because it is a high paying field' may reflect the same causal structure (the intersection of a person's motives and an occupation's opportunities) as it is reported to two third parties assumed to have different prior knowledge.

More generally (and as Lalljee *et al.*, chapter 6, describe), the attribution a person reports for a given event will depend in part upon the purposes to be served by the report. According to the present view, this reflects the common circumstance that the person's causal understanding is complex and, in brief interactions, must be reported selectively. Rarely is the structure simple enough that questions about which factors caused an event or about the relative importance of several factors are fitting. From this perspective, improved attribution measurement requires not only less restrictive answering sets (cf. Furnham, Jaspars and Fincham) but means of describing such structural features as chains and networks.

Research subjects must often be puzzled about the purposes to be served by their attributional reports. They must often wonder what it is about which the researcher is uncertain and needs information. Consider a subject in a study of the effects of freedom of choice on attributions. She (or he) is given a choice among several tasks, works on the chosen one, succeeds or fails in its solution, and is then asked to explain this outcome. In answering the question, how far back in the sequence of events is she expected to go? Should she focus on the relevant proximal factors (ability, effort, task difficulty) or is it appropriate to refer back to the quality of her choice, the information available to her at the time of choice, and the resulting fortunate or unfortunate matching between her abilities and those required by the task? If more distal accounts are acceptable, should she go even further back, to the set of tasks the researcher presented, the researcher's possible reasons for doing so, the course of events by which she arrived at the laboratory in the first place, etc. Of course, the subject is not completely free to decide which kind of account to provide and the researcher's questions will guide this decision to some degree. The problem is that we know very little about the implicit constraints upon this process. The preceding chapters (e.g. Furnham, Jaspars and Fincham; Lloyd-Bostock) are quite correct in emphasising the need to identify the social rules and conventions that constrain the attributions offered in various inquiry contexts, including our research settings.

## PRESERVING FAVORABLE SELF-EVALUATIONS

If, with differing focus and emphasis, a complex perceived causal structure lends itself to a variety of reports, then the selection among the various possibilities can be guided by the person's interests in the evaluation that he himself and others are likely to make of the central event. In both their own thoughts and their public accounts, actors can selectively emphasise factors that are most favorable to themselves in their evaluative implications. Bowerman's important work on subjective competence structures (1978) illustrates the value of structural analysis of this phenomenon. He describes the case in which a student's present low grade on a test is seen to be causally linked to such prior events as (proximally) the curve the teacher used in assigning grades and the nature of the test the teacher gave, and (distally) the fact that his parents made the student go to school. The low grade itself is seen to serve as a cause for such subsequent events as negative affect, motivation to study for the next test, and possible flunking out of school (with its own potential distal consequences). Bowerman's theory is that (1) self-evaluations depend upon the consequences to which the self is perceived to be linked causally and (2) people act and think in ways to make their self-evaluations as positive as possible. The latter entails not only trying actively to promote good things and to prevent bad ones but also, after the fact, changing one's perceptions of the relevant causal links. Thus, when there is evidence that through a specific act the self has contributed to a negative consequence, the person may restore a positive self-evaluation by (a) identifying positive consequences of the same act, perhaps more distal ones and/or (b) identifying other causes for the negative consequence (perhaps more distal ones or convergent ones) which overshadow one's own causal role. In brief, favorable self-evaluation is promoted by selectively identifying and highlighting certain causes and effects that constitute the causal structure within which the crucial self-to-consequence sequence is located. Bowerman also identifies other cognitive strategies for maintaining a positive self-evaluation such as changing the evaluation of a consequence. His theory deals solely with the elements in the 'subjective competence structure', these consisting of actors, actions, events, and affective consequences, all of which are perceived to be interlinked causally. The 'subjective competence structure' is a special case of the perceived causal structure described in the present chapter. The distinguishing feature is the particular sequence around which the structure is organised, this being a causal link between one's own actions and a consequence of considerable affective importance.

## LEGAL RULES AND PROCEDURES

In addition to those discussed above, a variety of situational and social factors determine the portion of a perceived causal structure to which we give most thought. The effect of our current concerns can be illustrated by Eiser's example of different persons' thoughts about a large warehouse fire. A person working there or driving nearby will think prospectively about the fire's consequences; a person owning a similar building will think retrospectively about the fire's causes and about measures that might have prevented it (potential causal sequences with better consequences). Culturally shared beliefs about causality affect not only the particular contents of the perceived causal structure (e.g. what factors are seen to cause illness) but also the properties of the structure. Such as its distality and interconnectedness. For example, in 10th century Japan, the flow of events was often seen as having been set by fate (alternative potential courses were not very salient) and current interpersonal relations were felt to have been affected (distally) by events in a prior life.

In some domains of life, rules specify the aspects of the causal structure upon which the person should focus. Each scientific discipline defines a set of focal events and various aspects of the relevant causal structure (types of causes, distality and complexity of analysis, etc.) upon which researchers are supposed to focus their efforts. The most elaborate rules are those incorporated in the law as it relates to problems of personal responsibility. These rules are perceptively discussed in earlier chapters by Lloyd-Bostock and by Shultz and Schleifer, so they will be reviewed only briefly here.

A first important feature of the legal rules pertaining to responsibility is that they set *quality standards* for the subjective causal structure. These standards imply not only extensity, complexity, potentialities, and such, but also accuracy, i.e. conformity of the subjective structure to some 'objective' one. A second important aspect of legal rules is that they address two rather different but complementary attributional problems. The first concerns defining responsibility *prospectively* for actors and the second concerns eliciting responsibility judgements *retrospectively* from observers. These correspond roughly to the two uses of 'responsibility' that Lloyd-Bostock notes to be distinguished by Hart and Honoré (1959).

Actors are supposed to recognise their present 'responsibilities', that is, their potential causal roles in relation to important current and future events. They are supposed to hold themselves to high standards of causal understanding, such as are possible for an intelligent person acting under good informational and motivational conditions. The perceived causal structure is supposed to be extensive in its look into the future and complex in its awareness of potentialities for preventing harm. The most important domain of responsibility is the social one as defined by Lord Aitkin's 'neighbour principle' (quoted by Lloyd-Bostock): the actor must consider actions and omissions that potentially harm other persons who are 'closely and directly affected' by the actor. And in all these respects, the perceived causal structure is supposed to be accurate.

The second attributional problem of the law pertaining to responsibility concerns an observer (e.g. a jury member or judge) who has the task of assessing the responsibility of an actor for past injury or harm. The observer is asked to make judgements about the actor's relevant causal structure and about the causal structure that might reasonably have been expected of the actor. What did the actor know, foresee, and consider? What should the actor, being a responsible person, have known, foreseen, and considered? Was the actor's causal understanding adequate or should he have 'known better'? If the actor's causal understanding is viewed as inadequate or inaccurate, questions may be raised about the causes for the understanding itself. In this case, the observer's task becomes meta-attributional, that is, to provide an explanation for the actor's attributions. For example, it may be asked whether the actor might not have foreseen the potential distal consequences of an action if he had taken the trouble to find out more about the situation, had given the problem more thought, or have been less influenced in his analysis by self interest.

In their everyday roles as observers of their fellows, common people make the kinds of judgements required of them in their official capacities within the legal system. However, the system is not satisfied to let them continue in their everyday ways. As jurors, judges, etc., they become actors whose actions have important consequences and, therefore, they are held to the high standards of accountability that the law applies to actors in general. The observers' meta-attributions, their causal understanding of the original actor's causal structure, must be of high quality – extensive, complex, accurate, etc.

How are the problems of adequacy and accuracy of perceived causal structure, as they occur above, dealt with? In general, the two approaches seem to be (1) assessment of a structure through comparing it with other persons' causal understandings, and (2) evaluation of the quality of the attributional process on the basis of meta-attribution principles. These are readily illustrated by legal procedures relating to observers' judgements of responsibility. First, provisions are made to have a number of people form, more or less independently, their understandings of what the actor knew and should have known. The multiplicity of jury members and of stages in the judicial review process enables various understandings to be placed in contention. Second, provisions are made to ensure that the understandings will be of high quality in the first place. These provisions take account of meta-attribution theories about the causes of attributions. Observers are selected so as to insure their intellectual competence and the irrelevance of their personal interests. They are exhorted to bring their full capabilities to bear upon the problem and are provided complete information and unrestricted time for processing it. These are the goals of the procedure, at least. As numerous critiques of the jury system attest, these conditions may not be fully satisfied. For example, subtle personal biases may be brought to the case, the information may constitute an overload on the observer's processing capabilities, and strong time pressures may exist for a quick decision.

Most pertinent to our consideration of causal structures is that the observers are given various rules and criteria that are intended to focus and improve their causal analysis as it relates to the focal event. They are told what to look at, what information to seek, what causal ideas to consider, and how to assess them. For example, the *but for* rule (see Shultz and Schleifer: the actor is responsible if the harm would not have occurred but for his action or omission) directs the observers' attention to the set of potential non-harmful sequences in which the actual sequence was embedded and asks the question of whether the actor either provided a necessary link in the actual sequence or failed to provide a necessary link to the non-harmful set. The notion of 'unforeseeable intervening cause' focuses the analysis upon links in the causal sequence subsequent to the actor's action and raises the meta-attributional question of whether they should have been a part of the actor's perceived potential links at the time of the action. Depending on the situation, the observers are instructed to focus on proximal causes, as in most auto accidents, or on distal causes, as in industrial accident cases where safety rules have explicitly defined the employer's distal responsibilities. The latter instance illustrates how rules that have defined the actor's responsibility are brought to observers' attention so that the causal structure expected of the actor can form part of their judgement. In the absence of rules, what was common practice (as in maintaining equipment, exercising foresight) plays a similar role in enabling observers to define what structure the actor should have known and acted upon.

STRUCTURAL ANALYSIS OF SPECIFIC PROBLEMS

A number of problems have arisen in attribution research that may be clarified through analysis of perceived causal structures. To conclude our considerations of the implications of this approach, it is appropriate to mention a few such matters. A first one concerns the relations among enduring, stable causes and the more short-lived, unstable ones. In his critique of Jones and Davis' correspondent inference theory (1965), Eiser raises questions about the perceived causal links among behavior, intentions, and traits. Jones and Davis specify a set of conditions that permits an observer to identify the intention behind a particular behavior and a further set of conditions that permits the intention to be traced back to a more stable and general trait. As Eiser observes, this certainly does not preclude the inference of traits on other grounds inasmuch as traits have other causal links to behavior than through the person's intentions. One doubts that Jones and Davis would disagree, but it does seem probable that a close analysis of subjects' perceived linkages among these various factors would make clear the particular parts of the causal structure to which the Jones and Davis argument applies and would suggest the different attribution rules applicable to the other parts. For example, these would be the rules by which observers infer traits from an actor's non-voluntary behavior.

Passer, Kelley and Michela (1978) commented about the lack of knowledge about perceived connections between general achievement motivation, on one hand, and more specific proximal factors, such as ability, effort, and task difficulty, on the other hand. One possible pattern is suggested by Kun's (1977) evidence for what she describes as a 'halo scheme'. Some of her young respondents perceived there to be a positive relation between ability and effort. This might well reflect their beliefs that both ability and effort are affected by general achievement motivation. Earlier, Kelley (1972b) had noted that there are many instances in which it is reasonable for a person to assume that causes covary. As his examples suggested, one possible basis for perceived covariance is in the relation of a general causal factor to more specific ones. Degree of interest in school may be seen to give rise to both a student's ability level and the effort he puts into his school work. Similarly, a general concern about maintenance of self-esteem, seen to be widespread among actors, may be understood to induce them to select tasks with difficulty levels consistent with their respective abilities.

Perceived correlations between factors permit one to be inferred from the other in ways not envisioned by the typical attribution hypothesis. For example, attribution hypotheses deal with the problem of inferring ability from information about task difficulty and level of performance. It is assumed that ability and effort are seen to be independent of each other and to act jointly to produce the observed performance. Accordingly, ability will be inferred by taking account (by means of an augmentation or discounting principle) of both the known level of performance and the known task difficulty. In contrast, perceived correlation between ability and difficulty, as for any of the reasons described above, affords the person a more direct means of estimating the first from the second.

An interesting question arises as to the nature of the inference process in cases where A and B are seen to be separate effects of a third (usually more general and stable) factor, C. If A and B are understood to be correlated by virtue of their common origin, is the value of A directly estimated from the known value of B? Or does the inference process follow the underlying perceived causal structure, going back from the known value of B to a value of the underlying factor, C, and then going forward to the value of A that C is expected to generate? An example is provided in Hewstone's chapter by research on inferences of actors' personalities from their speech accents. Robinson's two-stage model (described by Hewstone) seems to assume that the inference process follows a perceived causal structure in which both accent and personality are seen to be consequences of a person's social category. Thus, an actor's accent is used as a basis for inferring its cause (group membership) and the latter is used as a basis for expectations about the actor's personality.

As the preceding example suggests, it is important to maintain a clear distinction between the structure of the inferential process and that of the perceived causal sequence on which the inferential process is based. Thus, the inferential sequence 'accent to category to personality' is described above as reflecting a simple causal structure in which a single cause (category) generates two separate effects (accent and personality). On the assumption that inference processes always reflect the relevant underlying causal structure, the nature of the process will be determined jointly by the nature of the inference task (what is known and what is unknown) and the perceived causal relations among the relevant items.

Tversky and Kahneman (1980) identify situations in which the perceived correlation between events will be positive if they are seen to be consequences of the same third factor but negative if one is seen to cause the other. In the case mentioned by Eiser, home heating by solar energy and fuel rationing will be seen as positively covariant if both are attributed to the cost of fossil fuels but as negatively covariant if solar energy usage is seen to affect the need for rationing. The evidence suggests that most subjects view this problem in terms of the latter causal structure. It is not obvious that conclusions can be drawn from this fact, as Eiser does, about the greater ease of answering questions requiring prediction than questions requiring explanations. It seems more likely to the present author that the possible role of third causes in this type of situation is not likely to be salient for persons who are not familiar with it. The opposite result would be likely for retiring college professors asked to judge the relation between the outside post-retirement employment they will seek and the degree to which they will use up their savings. The third factor that contributes to both effects, namely inflation, will be highly salient for these respondents.

Some of Tversky and Kahneman's most provocative examples concern cases in which a given effect is commonly seen to result from several separate causes. For example, a child's eye color or height is probably seen by the common person as causally linked (in some manner) to properties of both parents and to various historical factors (diet, disease, etc). According to the principles of regression, if the Pearson product-moment index (across child-parent pairs) provides an apt summary of the correlation, it is as easy to predict a property of the parent from a property of the child as *vice versa*. However, Tversky and Kahneman find that more respondents feel justified in making the parent-to-child prediction than the reverse one. This is taken by the authors as evidence that 'causal data have greater impact than other data of equal informativeness' (Tversky and Kahneman, 1980, p. 50) and by Eiser as another indication that prediction is easier than explanation.

A sharply different interpretation assumes that a respondent's judgement is, in every case, based on the relevant perceived causal structure, but that the reasoning is idiographic rather than nomothetic. That is, the respondent tends to think about a specific parent and child rather than, as the normative analyst does, about the relation over many parent-child pairs. Given a perceived causal structure in which the child's properties are multiply determined, a particular property of one parent suggests something about what the child's property will be, but a particular property of the child is ambiguous in its implications for any single parent. For example, a short father suggests that the son may be short, but the son's shortness tells little about the father. It may come from the mother's side of the family, from faulty diet, from childhood illness, etc. The purpose of this interpretation of this example is not to recommend idiographic reasoning, but rather to suggest that thought about such problems is generally, perhaps always, based on an underlying perceived causal structure. What Tversky and Kahneman describe as diagnostic reasoning is also, in the present view, causal reasoning. Explanation of the past events and prediction of future ones are both parts of the same fabric of thought which is, at bottom, an understanding of the causal linkages between and among successive phenomena and events.

The preceding examples involve perceptions of the multiple consequences of a single cause and of the multiple causes of a single effect. One problem discussed by several authors in this book (Fincham; Lalljee, Watson and White) involves the distal elements in causal chains. The relevant research has to do with the effects of an extrinsic cause (reward or pressure) upon perceptions of an actor's intrinsic interest in an activity he is undertaking. The scenario (e.g. Karniol and Ross, 1979) describes a first child who, in the absence of any special incentive, plays with a particular one of two toys and a second child who does the same after its mother offers it a piece of cake for doing so. Most adult respondents judge the first child to be the one who really likes the particular toy. However, many young respondents (kindergarten children) say that it's the second child who really likes the played-with toy. In explaining this phenomenon, Karniol and Ross present evidence that the adult judgement, which discounts intrinsic interest when external reward is present, requires that the respondent understand that the mother's intention in offering the cake was to get the child to play with the particular toy. In terms of perceived causal structures, this result suggests that the meaning of a particular event (the mother's offer of reward) depends upon *its* perceived cause. It becomes seen as a possible cause of the child's choice (independent of its own interests) only when it is understood to originate from her intention to influence him. As noted earlier, events derive their meaning in part from their perceived causes. In this case, the causal properties of a particular event seem to be understood in terms of its perceived cause.

Karniol and Ross' result identifies one feature of the perceived causal structure that promotes the 'discounting' judgement made by most adult respondents (intrinsic interest is seen to be lower when the extrinsic incentive is present). However, there remains the question of why the very young respondents sometimes come to the opposite conclusion, that intrinsic interest is higher with the extrinsic incentive. Fincham describes a number of possible explanations for this. Among them is one based on assumptions about the children's causal structures, namely, that the child-respondent sees the offer of cake as increasing the desirability of playing with the designated toy. This explanation becomes quite plausible when we remember that children's causal structures are generally less differentiated than those of adults. Thus, children are less likely to distinguish extrinsic from intrinsic factors on the causal side and 'fun with the toy' from 'enjoying the cake' on the effect side. Moreover, such distinctions are not always clear for adults. As indicated by some of the research that Fincham summarises, the intrinsic and extrinsic can become quite indistinguishable when one undertakes an enjoyable activity in order to attain an enjoyable end (e.g. going to a party to see an old friend).

A different interpretation of the young childrens' judgements (presented in slight variants by Fincham and by Lalljee, Watson and White) assumes that the mother's offer of the reward is itself seen to be

368                                                    ATTRIBUTION THEORY AND RESEARCH

caused by her assessment of the attractiveness of the particular toy for her child. Thus, the child's interest in the toy is high because the mother's action somehow defines the toy as desirable. The meta-attributional processes assumed by this interpretation are mind-boggling. In one version the child–respondent must perceive that the child–actor perceives that the mother believes the toy to be one the latter will find attractive. Minimally, the child–respondent must perceive that the mother perceives the toy to be one her child finds attractive. One must doubt how many of these Langian cycles a kindergartener can manage. And yet, at some degree of mental maturity such complex reasoning probably becomes a part of our explanatory repertoires. The research by Lind, Erickson, Conley and O'Barr (1978) (described in Hewstone's chapter) indicates exactly this. Respondents listening to a lawyer questioning a witness, infer from the style of questioning how the lawyer perceives the witness. Thus, the respondents make judgements about the lawyer's attri-butions. Conceivably this process even involves a perception of the lawyer's understanding of the witness's causal structure. A lawyer would be presumed willing to relinquish control of the course of the interaction only to a witness whose testimony the lawyer understands to be controlled by a proper understanding of the consequences of various statements.


## Conclusion

This chapter proposes that people's causal understanding of important events be studied in terms of the perceived causal structures in which those events are embedded. This requires determining such things as (1) the prior causes, in their chains and interconnections, that are antecedent to the focal event, (2) the potential courses of causation that might have led to alternative events or, via alternative routes, to the observed event, and (3) the subsequent events seen to be conditioned (made more or less likely) by the observed event. A description of the causal context of a focal event in these terms is in sharp contrast to most current attributional analysis. The latter focuses almost exclusively on the antecedent perceived to be proximal to an event and attempts to specify the basis on which the person decides which of such antecedents are most important or whether a specific one played a noteworthy causal role. A re-reading of Heider (1958a) suggests to the author that recent attributional work has adopted a much narrower analysis of causal perception than Heider had envisioned and that a consideration of causal structures is more in keeping with his original analysis. Structures comprising chains and networks of causes are illustrated repeatedly in Heider's naive analysis of action, for example, in the comparison of the perceived causal networks in personal and impersonal causality, in the alternative but convergent lines of causality that characterise the equifinality of personal causality, in the subjective framework of causality in which personal responsibility is judged, and in the perceived influence of the person's reasons and 'can' upon her/his intentions.

This chapter attempts to identify some of the consequences of analysing attributional problems in terms of perceived causal structures. The structural analysis suggests the source of some of the problems encountered in assessing attributions (e.g. the relative independence of judgements of person- and situation-attributions) and provides a framework within which to examine variations in communicated attributions due to shifts in the reporting context. It has also been shown how the structural analysis illuminates certain practical problems (the legal principles relating to the encouragement and judgement of personal responsibility) and clarifies various current research questions (e.g. judgements of intrinsic motivation under conditions of extrinsic incentives).

## Acknowledgement

The preparation of this chapter was made possible, in part, by Grant BNS-76-20490 from the National Science Foundation.

## Note

1. Here or earlier the reader may have noted a resemblance of these concepts to those proposed by Lewin (1936) for characterising the life space, e.g. time perspective, degree of differentiation and connectedness. The life space was proposed by Lewin as a means of representing the psychological field as it exists for a person at the time of action. The present conception is essentially an adaptation of Lewin's life space that takes account of subsequent research and thought about the perception of causation.

# References

Abelson, R. P. and Kanouse, D. E. (1966). Subjective acceptance of verbal generalizations. *In* S. Feldman (ed.) *Cognitive consistency: Motivational antecedents and behavioural consequents.* New York: Academic Press

Ajzen, I. (1977). Intuitive theories of events and the effects of base rate information on prediction. *Journal of Personality and Social Psychology* **35**, 303–314

Ajzen, I. and Fishbein, M. (1975). A Bayesian analysis of attribution processes. *Psychological Bulletin* **82**, 261–277

Ajzen, I. and Fishbein, M. (1978). Use and misuse of Bayes' theorem in causal attribution: Don't attribute it to Ajzen and Fishbein either. *Psychological Bulletin* **85**, 244–246

Ajzen, I. and Holmes, W. H. (1976). Uniqueness of behavioral effects in causal attribution. *Journal of Personality* **44**, 98–108

Ajzen, I., Dalto, C. A. and Blyth, D. P. (1979). Consistency and bias in attribution of attitudes. *Journal of Personality and Social Psychology* **37**, 1871–1876

Alexander, C. and Sagatuin, I. (1973). An attributional analysis of experimental norms. *Sociometry* **36**, 127–142

Alker, H. (1972). Is personality situationally specific or intrapsychically consistent? *Journal of Personality* **40**, 1–16

Allport, F. H. (1955). *Theories of perception and the concept of structure.* New York: Wiley

Allport, G. W. (1937). *Personality: A psychological interpretation.* New York: Holt

Allport, G. W. (1966). Traits revisited. *American Psychologist* **21**, 1–10

Allport, G. W. and Odbert, H. S. (1936). Trait-names: A psycho-lexical study. *Psychological Monographs* **47** (Whole No. 211)

Alston, W. (1976). Traits, consistency and conceptual alternatives for personality theory. *In* R. Harré (ed.) *Personality.* Oxford: Blackwell

Amir, Y. (1969). Contact hypothesis in ethnic relations. *Psychological Bulletin* **71**, 319–342

Anderson, N. H. (1974). Cognitive algebra: Integration theory applied to social attribution. *In* L. Berkowitz (ed.) *Advances in experimental social psychology* Vol. 7. New York: Academic Press

Anderson, N. H. (1978). Progress in cognitive algebra. *In* L. Berkowitz (ed.) *Cognitive theories in social psychology.* New York: Academic Press

Anderson, N. H. and Butzin, C. A. (1974). Performance = motivation × ability: An integration – theoretical analysis. *Journal of Personality and Social Psychology* **30**, 598–604

Anscombe, G. E. M. (1957). *Intention.* Oxford: Blackwell

Anscombe, G. E. M. (1963). *Intention* (2nd edn). Oxford: Blackwell

Antaki, C. (1978). Self-serving explanations and attribution theory. Paper presented at the Annual Meeting of the British Psychological Society, London

Apfelbaum, E. and Herzlich, C. (1970/71). La théorie de l'attribution en psychologie sociale. *Bulletin de Psychologie* **24**, 961–976

Argyle, M. (1975). *Bodily communication.* London: Methuen

Argyle, M. (1976). Personality and social behavior. *In* R. Harré (ed.) *Personality.* Oxford: Blackwell

371

Argyle, M., Graham, J., Campbell, A. and White, P. (1979). The rules of different situations. *New Zealand Psychologist* **8**, 13–22

Argyle, M., Furnham, A. and Graham, J. (1981). *Social situations*. Cambridge: Cambridge University Press

Arkin, R. and Duval, S. (1975). Focus of attention and causal attributions of actors and observers. *Journal of Experimental Social Psychology* **11**, 427–438

Armsby, R. E. (1971). A reexamination of the development of moral judgements in children. *Child Development* **42**, 1241–1248

Atiyah, P. S. (1975). *Accidents, compensation and the law* (2nd edn). London: Weidenfeld and Nicolson

Atkinson, J. M. and Drew, P. (1979). *Order in court: The organisation of verbal interaction in judicial settings*. London: Macmillan

Atkinson, J. W. (ed.). (1958). *Motives in fantasy, action, and society*. Princeton, N.J.: Van Nostrand

Ausbel, D. P. and Schiff, H. M. (1954). The effect of incidental and experimentally induced experience in the learning of relevant and irrelevant causal relationships by children. *Journal of Genetic Psychology* **84**, 109–123

Austin, J. L. (1965). How to do things with words. In J. O. Urmsa and G. Wornoch (eds) *Philosophical Papers*. Oxford: Oxford University Press

Austin, W., Walster, E. and Utne, M. (1976). Equity and the law: The effects of a harmdoer's "suffering in the act" on liking an assigned punishment. In L. Berkowitz and E. Walster (eds) *Advances in experimental social psychology* Vol. 9. New York: Academic Press

Averill, J. R. (1974). An analysis of psychophysical symbolism and its influence on theories of emotion. *Journal for the Theory of Social Behaviour* **4**, 147–190

Averill, J. R., DeWitte, G. W. and Zimmer, M. (1978). The self attribution of emotion as a function of success and failure. *Journal of Personality* **46**, 323–347

Axelrod, R. (ed.) (1976). *Structure of decision: The cognitive maps of political elites*. Princeton: Princeton University Press

Baldwin, C. P. and Baldwin, A. L. (1970). Children's judgements of kindness. *Child Development* **41**, 29–47

Bales, R. (1953). *Interaction process analysis: A method for the study of small groups*. Cambridge, Mass.: Addison-Wesley

Bar-Hillel, M. (1980). The base-rate fallacy in probability judgements. *Acta Psychologica* **44**, 211–233

Barker, R. (1968) *Ecological psychology*. Stanford: Stanford University Press

Beckman, L. (1970). Effects of students' performance on teachers' and observers' attributions of causality. *Journal of Educational Psychology* **61**, 75–82

Bell, N. Contarello, A., Daniël, H.-D., Debuschere, M., Jaspars, J., Jonas, K., Lorenzi, F. and Velthuijsen, A. (1981). Common sense explanations of failure in 'A'-level examinations. Unpublished manuscript, 5th Summer School of the European Association of Experimental Social Psychology, Aix-en-Provence, France

Bem, D. J. (1965). An experimental analysis of self-persuasion. *Journal of Experimental Social Psychology* **1**, 199–218

Bem, D. J. (1967). Self-perception: An alternative interpretation of cognitive dissonance phenomena. *Psychological Review* **74**, 183–200

Bem, D. J. (1972). Self-perception theory. In L. Berkowitz (ed.) *Advances in experimental social psychology* Vol. 6. New York: Academic Press

Bem, D. J. and Allen, A. (1974). On predicting some of the people some of the time: The search for cross-situational consistencies in behaviour. *Psychological Review* **81**, 506–520

Bem, D. J. and Funder, D. (1978) Predicting more of the people more of the time: Assessing the personality of situations. *Psychological Review* **85**, 485–501

Bentham, J. (1948). *An introduction to the principles of morals and legislation*. New York: Hafner. (Originally published in 1789)

Berg-Cross, L. G. (1975). Intentionality, degree of damage, and moral judgements. *Child Development* **46**, 970–974

Berger, C. R. (1979). Beyond initial interaction: Uncertainty, understanding and the development of interpersonal relationships. *In* H. Giles and R. St. Clair (eds) *Language and social psychology*. Oxford: Blackwell

Berger, P. and Luckmann, R. (1973). *The social construction of reality*. Harmondsworth: Penguin

Berndt, T. J. (1977). The effect of reciprocity norms on moral and causal attribution. *Child Development* **48**, 1322–1330

Berscheid, E. and Walster, E. (1970). Physical Attractiveness. *In* L. Berkowitz (ed.), *Advances in experimental social psychology* Vol. 7. New York: Academic Press

Berscheid, E., Graziano, W., Monson, T. and Dermer, M. (1976). Outcome dependency: Attention, attribution and attraction. *Journal of Personality and Social Psychology* **34**, 978–989

Berzonsky, M. (1971). The role of familiarity in children's explanations of physical causality. *Child Development* **42**, 705–715

Bierhoff-Alfermann, D. (1977). *Psychologie der Geschlechtsunterschiede*. Köln: Kiepenheuer und Witsch

Bindra, D., Clarke, K. and Shultz, T. R. (1980). Understanding predictive relations of necessity and sufficiency in formally equivalent 'causal' and 'logical' problems. *Journal of Experimental Psychology: General* **109**, 422–443

Bishop, D. and Witt, P. (1970). Sources of behavioural variance during leisure time. *Journal of Personality and Social Psychology* **16**, 352–360

Block, J. (1977a) Advancing the psychology of personality: Paradigmatic shift or improving the quality of research. *In* D. Magnusson and N. Endler (eds) *Personality at the crossroads: Current issues in interactional psychology*. New York: Wiley

Block, J. (1977b) Recognising the coherence of personality. *In* D. Magnusson and N. Endler (eds) *Personality at the crossroads: Current issues in interactional psychology*. New York: Wiley

Boehm, L. (1962). The development of conscience: A comparison of American children of different mental and socioeconomic levels. *Child Development* **33**, 575–590

Boehm, L. and Nass, M. L. (1962). Social class differences in conscience development. *Child Development* **33**, 565–574

Bonoma, T. V. (1977). Business decision making: Marketing implications. *In* M. F. Kaplan and S. Schwartz (eds) *Human judgement and decision processes in applied settings*. New York: Academic Press

Borgida, E. and Brekke, N. (1981). The base rate fallacy in attribution and prediction. *In* J. H. Harvey, W. J. Ickes and R. F. Kidd (eds) *New directions in attribution research* Vol. 3. Hillsdale, N.J.: Erlbaum

Bower, G. H. (1972). Mental imagery and associate learning. *In* L. Gregg (ed.) *Cognition in learning and memory*. New York: Wiley

Bowerman, W. R. (1978). Subjective competence: The structure, process and function of self-referent causal attributions. *Journal for the Theory of Social Behaviour* **8**, 45–75

Bowerman, W. R. (1981). Applications of a social psychological theory of motivation to the language of defensiveness and self-justification. In M. M. T. Henderson (ed.) *1980 Mid-America Linguistics Conference Papers*. Lawrence: University of Kansas Linguistics Department

Bowers, K. (1973). Situationism in psychology: An analysis and a critique. *Psychological Review* **80**, 307–336

Brainerd, C. J. (1978). *Piaget's theory of intelligence*. Englewood Cliffs, N.J.: Prentice-Hall

Brainerd, C. J. (1979). Commentary. In L. Hood and L. Bloom, What, when, and how about why: A longitudinal study of early expressions of causality. *Monographs of the Society for Research in Child Development* **44**, 1–47

Brewer, M. B. (1977). An information-processing approach to attribution of responsibility. *Journal of Experimental Social Psychology* **13**, 58–69

Brickman, P. (1978). Is it real? In J. H. Harvey, W. J. Ickes and R. F. Kidd, (eds) *New directions in attribution research* Vol. 2. Hillsdale, N.J.: Erlbaum

Brockner, J. and Eckenrode, J. (1979). Self-monitoring and the actor-observer bias. *Representative Research in Social Psychology* **9**, 81–88

Brooks-Gunn, J. and Lewis, M. (1978). Early social knowledge: The development of knowledge about others. In H. McGurk (ed) *Issues in childhood social development*. London: Methuen

Broverman, I., Broverman, D., Clarksen, F., Rosenkrantz, P. and Vogel, S. (1970). Sex-role stereotypes and clinical judgements of mental health. *Journal of Consulting and Clinical Psychology* **34**, 1–7

Brown, A. and French, L. (1976). Construction and regeneration of logical sequences using causes or consequences as the point of departure. *Child Development* **47**, 930–940

Brown, G. and Desforges, C. (1977). Piagetian psychology and education: Time for revision. *British Journal of Educational Psychology* **47**, 7–17

Brown, L. and Lalljee, M. (1981). Young persons' conceptions of criminal events. *Journal of Moral Education* **10**, No. 3, 165–172

Bruner, J. S. (1957a). On perceptual readiness. *Psychological Review* **64**, 123–152.

Bruner, J. S. (1957b). On going beyond the information given. In H. E. Gruber, K. R. Hammon and R. Jesser (eds) *Contemporary approaches to cognition*. Cambridge, Mass.: Harvard University Press

Bruner, J. S. (1958). Les processus de préparation à la perception. In J. S. Bruner, F. Bresson, A. Morf and J. Piaget (eds) *Logique et perception*. Paris: P.U.F.

Bryan, J. and Test, M. (1967). Models and helping. *Journal of Personality and Social Psychology* **6**, 400–407

Bryant, P. E. (1977). Logical inferences and development. In B. A. Geber (ed.) *Piaget and knowing: studies in genetic epistemology* pp. 53–65. London: Routledge

Bullock, M. and Gelman, R. (1979). Preschool children's assumptions about cause and effect: Temporal ordering. *Child Development* **50**, 89–96

Bunge, M. (1959). *Causality: the place of the causal principle in modern science*. Cambridge, Mass.: Harvard University Press

Bunge, M. (1973). Review of P. Suppes' *Probabilistic theory of causality*. *British Journal for the Philosophy of Science* **24**, 409–410

Burman, S. B., Genn, H. G. and Lyons, J. (1977). Pilot study of the use of legal services by victims of accidents in the home. *Modern Law Review* **XL**, 47–57

Buss, A. R. (1977). The trait-situation controversy and the concept of interaction. *Personality and Social Psychology Bulletin* **3**, 196–201

Buss, A. R. (1978). Causes and reasons in attribution theory: A conceptual critique. *Journal of Personality and Social Psychology* **36**, 1311–1321

Buss, A. R. (1979). On the relationship between causes and reasons. *Journal of Personality and Social Psychology* **37**, 1458–1461

Campbell, D. T. (1963). Social attitudes and other acquired behavioral dispositions. *In* S. Koch (ed.) *Psychology: A study of a science* Vol. 6. New York: McGraw-Hill

Cantor, N. and Mischel, W. (1977). Traits as prototypes: Effects on recognition memory. *Journal of Personality and Social Psychology* **35**, 38–49

Cartwright, D. (1975). Trait and other sources of variance in the S–R inventory of anxiousness. *Journal of Personality and Social Psychology* **32**, 408–414

Cartwright, D. and Zander, A. (1953). *Group dynamics: Research and theory*. Evanston: Row, Peterson

Cattell, R. (1965). *The scientific analysis of personality*. Harmondsworth: Penguin

Chaikin, A. and Darley, T. (1973). Victim or perpetrator: Defensive attribution of responsibility and the need for order and justice. *Journal of Personality and Social Psychology* **25**, 268–275

Chaikin, A. and Derlega, V. (1976). Self disclosure. *In* J. Thibaut, J. Spence and R. Carsen (eds) *Contemporary topics in social psychology*. Morristown, N.J.: General Learning Press

Chandler, M. J. (1977). Social cognition. *In* W. F. Overton and J. M. Gallagher (eds) *Knowledge and development* Vol. 1. New York: Plenum Press

Chetwynd, J. and Hartnett, O. (eds) (1978). *The sex role system: Psychological and sociological perspectives*. London: Routledge

Clark, R. and Word, L. (1972). Why don't bystanders help? Because of ambiguity? *Journal of Personality and Social Psychology* **24**, 392–400

Cohen, E. A., Gelfand, D. M., Hartmann, D. P., Partlow, M. E., Montemayor, R. and Shigetomi, C. C. (1979). Children's causal reasoning. Paper presented at the biennial meeting, Society for Research in Child Development, San Francisco, California

Collett, P. (1977). *Social rules and social behaviour*. Oxford: Blackwell

Collingwood, R. G. (1961). On the so-called idea of causation. *In* H. Morris (ed.) *Freedom and responsibility*. Stanford: Stanford University Press

Coombs, C. H. (1964) *A theory of data*. New York: Wiley

Cooper, J., Jones, E. E. and Tuller, S. M. (1972). Attribution, dissonance and the illusion of uniqueness. *Journal of Experimental Social Psychology* **8**, 45–47

Corrigan, R. (1975). A scalogram analysis of the development of the use and comprehension of 'because' in children. *Child Development* **46**, 195–201

Costanzo, P. R., Coie, J. D., Grumet, J. F. and Farnhill, R. (1973). A reexamination of the effects of intent and consequence on children's moral judgement. *Child Development* **44**, 154–161

Costanzo, P. R., Grumet, J. F. and Brehm, S. S. (1974). The effects of choice and source of constraint on children's attributions of preference. *Journal of Experimental Social Psychology* **10**, 352–364.

Coutts, J. A. (1960). Review of causation in the law. *Modern Law Review* **23**, 708–709

Cowie, B. (1976). The cardiac patient's perception of his heart attack. *Social Science and Medicine* **10**, 87–96

Crandall, V. C. (1969). Sex differences in expectancy of intellectual and academic reinforcement. *In* C. P. Smith (ed.) *Achievement-related motives in children*. New York: Russell Sage

Crandall, V. C., Katkovsky, W. and Crandall, V. J. (1965). Children's beliefs in their control of reinforcements in intellectual-academic achievement situations. *Child Development* **36**, 91–109

Cronbach, L. J. (1955). Processes affecting scores on 'understanding of others' and 'assumed similarity'. *Psychological Bulletin* **52**, 177–193

Cross, R. and Jones, P. A. (1964). *An introduction to criminal law*. London: Butterworth

Da Gloria, J. and Pagès, R. (1974–1975). Problèmes et exigences d'une théorie de l'attribution. *Bulletin de Psychologie* **28**, 229–235

D'Arcy, E. (1963). *Human acts: An essay in their moral evaluation*. Oxford: Clarendon

Darley, M. J., Klosson, E. D. and Zanna, M. P. (1978). Intentions and their contexts in the moral judgements of children and adults. *Child Development* **49**, 66–74

Davidson, D. (1963). Actions, reasons, and causes. *The Journal of Philosophy* **60**, 685–700

Deaux, K. (1976). Sex: A perspective on the attribution process. *In* J. H. Harvey, W. J. Ickes and R. F. Kidd (eds) *New directions in attribution research*. Vol. 1. Hillsdale, N.J.: Erlbaum

Deaux, E. and Emswiller, T. (1974). Explanations of successful performance on sex-linked tasks. What is skill for the male is luck for the female. *Journal of Personality and Social Psychology* **29**, 80–85

Deci, E. L. (1975). *Intrinsic motivation*. New York: Plenum Press

DeJong, W., Morris, W. N. and Hastorf, A. H. (1976). Effect of an escaped accomplice on the punishment assigned to a criminal defendant. *Journal of Personality and Social Psychology* **33**, 192–198

De Ridder, R. (1980). *Agressie in sociale interactie: Waarneming en reactie*. Unpublished doctoral dissertation, University of Tilburg

Deschamps, J.-C. (1972–1973). Imputation de la responsabilité de l'échec (ou de la réussite) et catégorisation sociale. *Bulletin de Psychologie* **26**, 794–806

Deschamps, J.-C. (1973–1974). L'attribution, la catégorisation sociale et les représentations intergroupes. *Bulletin de Psychologie* **27**, 710–721

Deschamps, J.-C. (1977a). *L'attribution et la catégorisation sociale*. Berne: Peter Lang

Deschamps, J.-C. (1977b). Effect of crossing category memberships on quantitative judgement. *European Journal of Social Psychology* **7**, 517–521

Deschamps, J.-C. (1978). La perception des causes du comportement. *In* W. Doise, J.-C. Deschamps and G. Mugny (eds) *Psychologie sociale expérimentale*. Paris: Armand Colin

Deschamps, J.-C. (1979). Psychosociologie des relations entre groupes et différenciation catégorielle. *Schweizerische Zeitschrift für Soziologie* **5**, 177–199

Deschamps, J.-C. and Doise, W. (1978). Crossed category memberships in intergroup relations. *In* H. Tajfel (ed.) *Differentiation between social groups*. London: Academic

Deschamps, J.-C., Doise, W., Meyer, G. and Sinclair, A. (1976). Le sociocentrisme selon Piaget et la différenciation catégorielle. *Archives de Psychologie* **44**, 31–44

Dienstbier, R. A. (1978). Attribution, socialization, and moral decision making. *In* J. H. Harvey, W. J. Ickes and R. F. Kidd (eds) *New directions in attribution research* Vol. 2. Hillsdale, N.J.: Erlbaum

Dion, K. K. (1972). Physical attractiveness and evaluations of children's transgressions. *Journal of Personality and Social Psychology* **24**, 207–213

Di Vitto, B. and McArthur, L. Z. (1978). Developmental differences in the use of distinctiveness, consensus, and consistency information for making causal attributions. *Developmental Psychology* **14**, 474–482

Doise, W. (1973). Relations et représentations intergroupes. *In* S. Moscovici (ed.) *Introduction à la psychologie sociale* Vol. 2. Paris: Larousse

Doise, W. (1976). *L'articulation psychosociologique et les relations entre groupes*. Bruxelles: De Boeck

Doise, W., Deschamps, J.-C. and Meyer, G. (1978). The accentuation of intra-category similarities. *In* H. Tajfel (ed.) *Differentiation between social groups.* London: Academic Press

Doob, A. (1979). Police discretion in the handling of juvenile offenders. Paper presented at the meeting of the Social Science Research Council Law and Psychology Seminar Group, University of Oxford

Duncan, B. L. (1976). Differential social perception and attribution of intergroup violence: Testing the lower limits of stereotyping of Blacks. *Journal of Personality and Social Psychology* **34**, 590–598

Duval, S. and Wicklund, R. A. (1972). *A theory of objective self-awareness.* New York: Academic Press

Dweck, C. S. (1975). The role of expectations and attributions in the alleviation of learned helplessness. *Journal of Personality and Social Psychology* **31**, 674–685

Dweck, C. S. and Bush, E. S. (1976). Sex differences in learned helplessness: I. Differential debilitation with peer and adult evaluators. *Developmental Psychology* **12**, 147–156

Dweck, C. S. and Gilliard, D. (1975). Expectancy statements as determinants of reactions to failure: Sex differences in persistence and expectancy change. *Journal of Personality and Social Psychology* **32**, 1077–1084

Dweck, C. S. and Goetz, T. E. (1978) Attributions and learned helplessness. *In* J. H. Harvey, W. J. Ickes and R. F. Kidd (eds) *New directions in attribution research* Vol. 2. Hillsdale, N.J.: Erlbaum

Dweck, C. S. and Repucci, N. D. (1973). Learned helplessness and reinforcement responsibility in children. *Journal of Personality and Social Psychology* **25**, 109–116

Dweck, C. S., Davidson, W., Nelson, S. and Enna, B. (1978). Sex differences in learned helplessness: II. The contingencies of evaluative feedback in the classroom and III. An experimental analysis. *Developmental Psychology* **14**, 268–276

Dworkin, R. and Kihlstrom, J. (1978). An S–R inventory of dominance for research on the nature of person situation interaction. *Journal of Personality* **46**, 43–56

Eagly, A. H. and Chaikin, S. (1975). An attribution analysis of the effect of communicator characteristics on opinion change: The case of communicator attractiveness. *Journal of Personality and Social Psychology* **32**, 136–144

Eagly, A. H., Wood, W. and Chaikin, S. (1978). Causal inferences about com-municators and their effect on opinion change. *Journal of Personality and Social Psychology* **36**, 424–435

Edwards, W., Lindman, H. and Savage, L. J. (1963). Bayesian statistical inference for psychological research. *Psychological Review* **70**, 193–242

Eisen, S. U. (1979). Actor-observer differences in information inference and causal attribution. *Journal of Personality and Social Psychology* **37**, 261–272

Eisenberg-Berg, N. (1979). Development of children's prosocial moral judgement. *Developmental Psychology* **15**, 128–137

Eiser, J. R. (1971). Enhancement of contrast in the absolute judgment of attitude statements. *Journal of Personality and Social Psychology* **17**, 1–10

Eiser, J. R. (1975). Attitudes and the use of evaluative language: A two-way process. *Journal for the Theory of Social Behaviour* **5**, 235–248

Eiser, J. R. (1980). *Cognitive social psychology.* Maidenhead: McGraw-Hill

Eiser, J. R. and Mower White, C. J. (1974a). Evaluative consistency and social judgement. *Journal of Personality and Social Psychology* **30**, 349–359

Eiser, J. R., and Mower White, C. J. (1974b). The persuasiveness of labels: Attitude change produced through definition of the attitude continuum. *European Journal of Social Psychology* **4**, 89–92

Eiser, J. R. and Mower White, C. J. (1975). Categorization and congruity in attitudinal judgement. *Journal of Personality and Social Psychology* **31**, 769–775

Eiser, J. R. and Pancer, S. M. (1979). Attitudinal effects of the use of evaluatively biased language. *European Journal of Social Psychology* **9**, 39–47

Eiser, J. R. and Ross, M. (1977). Partisan language, immediacy, and attitude change. *European Journal of Social Psychology* **7**, 477–489

Eiser, J. R. and Stroebe, W. (1972). *Categorization and social judgement.* London: Academic Press

Ekehammar, B. (1974). Interactionism in personality from a historical perspective. *Psychological Bulletin* **81**, 1026–1048

Ekman, P., Friesen, W. V. and Ellsworth, P. (1972). *Emotion in the human face.* New York: Pergamon

Endler, N. (1966). Estimating variance components from mean squares for random and mixed effects analysis variance models. *Perceptual and Motor Skills* **2**, 559–570

Endler, N. and Hunt, J. (1966). Sources of behavioural variance as measured by the S–R inventory of anxiousness. *Psychological Bulletin* **65**, 336–346

Endler, N. and Hunt, J. (1968). S–R variations of hostility and comparison of the properties of variance from persons, response and situation for hostility and anxiousness. *Journal of Personality and Social Psychology* **9**, 309–315

Endler, N. and Hunt, J. (1969). Generalizability of contributions from sources of variance in the S–R inventory of anxiousness. *Journal of Personality* **37**, 1–24

Endler, N. and Magnusson, D. (1976). *Interactional psychology and personality.* Washington, D.C.: Hemisphere Publishing

Endler, N. and Shedletsky, R. (1973). Trait v. state anxiety, authoritarianism and ego threat and physical threat. *Canadian Journal of Behavioural Science* **5**, 347–361

Endler, N., Hunt, J. and Rosenstein, A. (1962). An S–R inventory of anxiousness. *Psychological Monographs* **76**, 1–33

Epstein, S. (1973). The self-concept revisited. Or a theory of a theory. *American Psychologist* **28**, 404–416

Epstein, S. (1977). Traits are alive and well. *In* D. Magnusson and N. S. Endler (eds) *Personality at the crossroads: Current issues in interactional Psychology.* Hillsdale, N.J.: Erlbaum

Epstein, S. (1979). The stability of behaviour: I. On predicting most of the people most of the time. *Journal of Personality and Social Psychology* **37**, 1097–1127

Erickson, B., Lind, E. A., Johnson, B. C. and O'Barr, W. (1978). Speech style and impression formation in a court setting: The effects of 'powerful' and 'powerless' speech. *Journal of Experimental Social Psychology* **14**, 266–279

Erwin, J. and Kuhn, D. (1979). Development of children's understanding of the multiple determination underlying human behaviour. *Developmental Psychology* **5**, 352–353

Eysenck, H. J. and Eysenck, S. B. G. (1964). *Manual of the Eysenck Personality Inventory.* London: University of London Press

Falbo, T. (1975). Achievement attributions of kindergarteners. *Developmental Psychology* **11**, 529–530

Feather, N. T. (1968). Change in confidence following success or failure as a predictor of subsequent performance. *Journal of Personality and Social Psychology* **9**, 38–46

Feather, N. T. (1969). Attribution of responsibility and valence of success and failure in relation to initial confidence and task performance. *Journal of Personality and Social Psychology* **13**, 129–144

Feather, N. T. and Raphelson, A. C. (1974). Fear of success in Australian and American student groups: Motive or sex-role stereotype? *Journal of Personality* **42**, 190–201

Feather, N. T. and Simon, J. G. (1971a). Attribution of responsibility and valence of outcome in relation to initial confidence and success and failure of self and other. *Journal of Personality and Social Psychology* **18**, 173–188

Feather, N. T. and Simon, J. G. (1971b). Causal attribution for success and failure in relation to expectations of success based upon selective or manipulative control. *Journal of Personality* **39**, 527–541

Feather, N. T. and Simon, J. G. (1973). Fear of success and causal attribution for outcome. *Journal of Personality* **41**, 525–542

Feather, N. T. and Simon, J. G. (1975). Reactions to male and female success and failure in sex-linked occupations: Impressions of personality, causal attributions, and perceived likelihood of different consequences. *Journal of Personality and Social Psychology* **31**, 20–31

Fein, D. A. (1973). Judgements of causality to physical and social picture sequences. *Developmental Psychology* **8**, 147

Feinberg, J. (1968). Action and responsibility. *In* A. R. White (ed.) *The philosophy of action.* Oxford: Oxford University Press

Feldman-Summers, S. and Kiesler, S. B. (1974). Those who are number two try harder: The effect of sex on attributions of causality. *Journal of Personality and Social Psychology* **30**, 846–855

Felipe, A. I. (1970). Evaluative and descriptive consistency in trait inferences. *Journal of Personality and Social Psychology* **16**, 627–638

Festinger, L. (1950). Informal social communication. *Psychological Review* **57**, 271–282

Festinger, L. (1957). *A theory of cognitive dissonance.* New York: Peterson

Festinger, L. (1964). *Conflict, decision and dissonance.* Stanford: Stanford University Press

Fincham, F. D. (1979). Outcome valence and situational constraints in the evaluation of intentional acts. Paper presented at the British Psychological Society Conference. London

Fincham, F. D. (1980). *Attribution of responsibility.* Unpublished doctoral dissertation, University of Oxford

Fincham, F. D. (1981). Perception and moral evaluation in young children. *British Journal of Social Psychology* **20**, 265–270

Fincham, F. D. (1982a). Piagetian theory and the learning disabled: A critical analysis. *In* S. Modgil and C. Modgil (eds) *Piaget at the crossroads.* London: Holt

Fincham, F. D. (1982b). Responsibility attribution in the culturally deprived. *Journal of Genetic Psychology* **140**, 229–235

Fincham, F. D. and Hewstone, M. (1982). Social categorisation and personal similarity: A test of defensive attribution. *British Journal of Social Psychology* **21**, 51–56

Fincham, F. D. and Jaspars, J. (1979). Attribution of responsibility to the self and other in children and adults. *Journal of Personality and Social Psychology* **37**, 1589–1602

Fincham, F. D. and Jaspars, J. (1980) Attribution of responsibility: From man the scientist to man-as-lawyer. *In* L. Berkowitz (ed.) *Advances in experimental social psychology* Vol. 13. New York: Academic Press

Fincham, F. D. and Jaspars, J. (1983). A subjective probability approach to attribution of responsibility. *British Journal of Social Psychology* (in press)

Fincham, F. D. and Shultz, T. R. (1981). Intervening causation and the mitigation of responsibility for harm. *British Journal of Social and Clinical Psychology* **20**, 113–120

Fischoff, B. (1975). Hindsight = foresight: The effect of outcome knowledge on judgement under uncertainty. *Journal of Experimental Psychology: Human Perception and Performance* 1, 288–299

Fischhoff, B. and Lichtenstein, S. (1978). Don't attribute this to Reverend Bayes. *Psychological Bulletin* 85, 239–243

Fischhoff, B., Slovic, P. and Lichtenstein, S. (1979). Improving intuitive judgement by subjective sensitivity analysis. *Organizational Behavior and Human Performance* 23, 339–359

Fishbein, M. and Ajzen, I. (1973) Attribution of responsibility: A theoretical note. *Journal of Experimental Social Psychology* 9, 148–153

Fishbein, M. and Ajzen, I. (1975) *Belief, attitude, intention and behaviour: An introduction to theory and research.* London: Addison Wesley

Fitzgerald, P. J. (1961). Voluntary and involuntary acts. *In* A. G. Guest (ed.) *Oxford essays in jurisprudence.* Oxford: Clarendon

Flavell, J. H. (1963). *The developmental psychology of Jean Piaget.* Princeton, N.J. : Van Nostrand

Flavell, J. H. (1971). Stage-related properties of cognitive development. *Cognitive Psychology* 2, 421–453

Flavell, J. H. (1974). The development of inferences about others. *In* T. Mischel (ed.) *Understanding other persons.* Oxford: Blackwell

Flavell, J. H. (1977). *Cognitive development.* New Jersey: Prentice Hall

Fletcher, G. J. O. (1981). *Causal attributions for marital separation.* Unpublished doctoral dissertation, University of Waikato, New Zealand

Forgas, J. (1976). The perception of social episodes: Categorical and dimensional representations in two different social milieus. *Journal of Personality and Social Psychology* 32, 199–209

Forgas, J. (1979). *Social episodes: The study of interaction routines.* London: Academic Press

Fransella, F. and Frost. K. (1977) *On being a woman: A review of research on how women see themselves.* London: Tavistock Publications

Freud, A. (1935). *The ego and mechanisms of defence.* London: The Hogarth Press

Friend, P., Kalin, R. and Giles, H. (1979). Sex bias in the evaluation of journal articles: Sexism in England. *British Journal of Social and Clinical Psychology* 18, 77–78

Frieze, I. and Weiner, B. (1971). Cue utilisation and attributional judgements for success and failure. *Journal of Personality* 39, 591–605

Furnham, A. (1980). Constructing social situations: A Repertory Grid analysis of person-situation interaction. Unpublished paper. Oxford University

Furnham, A. (1981). Personality and activity preference. *British Journal of Social and Clinical Psychology* 20, 57–68

Furnham, A. (1982). Why are the poor always with us? Explanations for poverty in Britain. *British Journal of Social Psychology* (in press)

Garbarino, J. and Bronfenbrenner, U. (1976). The socialisation of moral judgement and behavior in cross-cultural perspective. *In* T. Lickona (ed) *Moral development and behaviour.* New York: Holt

Garcia-Esteve, J. and Shaw, M. E. (1968). Rural and urban patterns of responsibility attribution in Puerto Rico. *Journal of Social Psychology* 74, 143–149

Giles, H. (1978). Linguistic differentiation in ethnic groups. *In* H. Tajfel (ed.) *Social differentiation between groups.* London: Academic Press

Giles, H. (1979a). Sociolinguistics and social psychology: An introductory essay. *In* H. Giles and R. St. Clair (eds). *Language and social psychology.* Oxford: Blackwell

Giles, H. (1979b) Ethnicity markers in speech. *In* K. R. Scherer and H. Giles (eds) *Social markers in speech.* Cambridge: Cambridge University Press

Giles, H. and Hewstone, M. (1983). Cognitive structures, speech and social situations: Two integrative models. *Language and Science* (in press)

Giles, H. and Johnson, P. (1981). The role of language in inter-ethnic behaviour. *In* J. C. Turner and H. Giles (eds) *Intergroup behaviour.* Oxford: Blackwell

Giles, H. and Powesland, P. F. (1975). *Speech style and social evaluation.* London: Academic Press

Giles, H. and Taylor, D. M. (1979). At the crossroads of research into language and ethnic relations. *In* H. Giles and B. Saint-Jacques (eds.) *Language and ethnic relations.* Oxford: Pergamon

Giles, H., Bourhis, R. Y. and Taylor, D. M. (1977). Towards a theory of language in ethnic group relations. *In* H. Giles (ed.) *Language, ethnicity and intergroup relations.* London: Academic Press

Giles, H., Scherer, K. and Taylor, D. M. (1979). Speech markers in social interaction. *In* K. Scherer and H. Giles (eds.) *Social markers in speech.* Cambridge: Cambridge University Press

Giles, H., Robinson, W. P., and Smith, P. (1980a) *Language: Social psychological perspectives.* Oxford: Pergamon

Gilson, C. and Abelson, R. P. (1965). The subjective use of inductive evidence. *Journal of Personality and Social Psychology* **2**, 301–310

Ginosar, Z. and Trope, Y. (1980). The effects of base rates and individuating information on judgements about another person. *Journal of Experimental Social Psychology* **16**, 228–242

Ginsburg, G. (1976). Unpublished Lecture Notes I and II. Lectures given at the Oxford Summer School in Social Psychology

Ginsburg, G. (ed.) (1979). *Emerging strategies in social psychology.* Chichester: Wiley

Gleser, G., Cronbach, L. and Rajaratram, N. (1965). Generalisability of scores influenced by multiple sources of variance. *Psychometrica* **30**, 395–418

Goffman, E. (1955). On face-work. *Psychiatry* **18**, 213–231

Goldberg, L. R. (1978). Differential attribution of trait-descriptive terms to oneself as compared to well-liked, neutral, and disliked others: A psychometric analysis. *Journal of Personality and Social Psychology* **36**, 1012–1028

Goldberg, P. A. (1968). Are women prejudiced against women? *Transaction* **5**, 28–30

Golding, S. (1978). Flies in the ointment: Methodological problems in the analysis of variance due to persons and situations. *Psychological Bulletin* **82**, 278–288

Gorovitz, S. (1965). Causal judgements and causal explanations. *The Journal of Philosophy* **62**, 695–711

Graham, J., Argyle, M. and Furnham, A. (1980). The goal structure of situations. *European Journal of Social Psychology* **10**, 345–376

Grice, H. P. (1975). Logic and conversation. *In* P. Cole and J. L. Morgan (eds.) *Syntax and semantics* Vol. 3. New York: Academic Press

Gutkin, D. C. (1972). The effect of systematic story changes on intentionality in children's moral judgement. *Child Development* **43**, 187–195

Guttentag, M. and Longfellow, C. (1977). Children's social attributions: Development and change. *In* C. B. Keasey (ed.) *Nebraska symposium on motivation.* Lincoln: University of Nebraska Press

Hamilton, V. L. (1978). Who is responsible? Toward a *social* psychology of responsibility attribution. *Social Psychology* **41**, 316–328

Hansen, R. D. and Donoghue, J. M. (1977). The power of consensus: Information derived from one's own and others' behavior. *Journal of Personality and Social Psychology* **35**, 294–302

Hansen, R. D. and Lowe, C. A. (1976). Distinctiveness and consensus: The influence of behavioral information on actors' and observers' attributions. *Journal of Personality and Social Psychology* **34**, 425–434

Harary, F., Norman, R. Z. and Cartwright, D. (1965). *Structural models: An introduction to the theory of directed graphs*. New York: Wiley

Harper, F. V. and James, F. (1956). *The law of torts* Vol. 2. Boston: Little, Brown

Harré, R. (1977). The ethogenic approach: Theory and practice. *In* L. Berkowitz (ed.) *Advances in Experimental Social Psychology* Vol. 10. New York: Academic Press

Harré, R. (1979). *Social being*. Oxford: Blackwell

Harré, R. and Madden, E. H. (1975). *Causal powers: A theory of natural necessity*. Oxford: Blackwell

Harré, R. and Secord, P. (1972). *The explanation of social behaviour*. Oxford: Blackwell

Harris, B. (1977). Developmental differences in the attribution of responsibility. *Developmental Psychology* **13**, 257–265

Hart, H. L. A. (1968). *Punishment and responsibility*. Oxford: Clarendon Press

Hart, H. L. A. and Honoré, A. M. (1959). *Causation in the law*. Oxford: Clarendon Press

Hart, H. L. A. (1978). The ascription of responsibility and rights. *In* H. Flew (ed.) *Logic and language*. Oxford: Blackwell

Hart, H. L. A. and Honoré, A. M. (1961). Causation in the law. *In* H. Morris (ed.) *Freedom and responsibility*. Stanford: Stanford University Press

Hartshorne, H. and May, M. (1928). *Studies in the nature of character: Studies in deceit*. New York: Macmillan

Harvey, J. H. and Tucker, J. A. (1979). On problems with the cause-reason distinction in attribution theory. *Journal of Personality and Social Psychology* **37**, 1441–1446

Harvey, J. H., Ickes, W. J. and Kidd, R. F. (eds) (1976). *New directions in attribution research* Vol. 1. Hillsdale, N.J.: Erlbaum

Harvey, J. H., Ickes, W. J. and Kidd, R. F. (eds) (1978a) *New directions in attribution research* Vol. 2. Hillsdale, N.J.: Erlbaum

Harvey, J. H. Wells, G. L. and Alvarez, M. D. (1978b) Attribution in the context of conflict and separation in close relationships. *In* J. H. Harvey, W. J. Ickes and R. F. Kidd (eds) *New directions in attribution research* Vol. 2. Hillsdale, N.J.: Erlbaum

Harvey, M. D. and Rule, B. G. (1978). Moral evaluations and judgements of responsibility. *Personality and Social Psychology Bulletin* **4**, 583–588

Hebble, P. W. (1971). The development of elementary school children's judgement of intent. *Child Development* **42**, 1202–1215

Heckhausen, H. (1972). Die Interaktion der Sozialisationsvariablen in der Genese des Leistungsmotivs. *In* C. F. Graumann (ed.) *Handbuch der Psychologie* Vol. 7/2. Göttingen: Hogrefe

Heckhausen, H. (1973). Die Entwicklung des Erlebens von Erfolg und Misserfolg. *In* C. F. Graumann and H. Heckhausen (eds) *Pädagogische Psychologie Entwicklung und Sozialisation*. Frankfurt: Fischer-Taschenbuch

Heckhausen, H. (1977). Achievement motivation and its constructs: A cognitive model. *Motivation and Emotion* **1**, 283–329

Heckhausen, H. (1978). Kognitive Grundlagen in der Entwicklung der Leistungs-motivation, Vorlaufige Fassung. *In* W. W. Hartup (ed.) *Review of Child Development Research* Vol. 6. Chicago: University of Chicago Press

Heider, F. (1944) Social perception and phenomenal causality. *Psychological Review* **51**, 358–384

Heider, F. (1946). Attitudes and cognitive organization. *Journal of Psychology* **21**, 107–112

Heider, F. (1958a). *The psychology of interpersonal relations*. New York: Wiley

Heider, F. (1958b) Perceiving the other person. *In* R. Tagiuri and L. Petrullo (eds) *Person perception and interpersonal behavior*. Stanford: Stanford University Press

Heider, F. and Simmel, A. (1944). An experimental study of apparent behavior. *American Journal of Psychology* **57**, 243–249

Hester, R. K. and Smith, R. E. (1973). Effects of a mandatory death penalty on the decisions of simulated jurors. *Journal of Criminal Justice* **1**, 319–326

Heuston, R. V. F. (1977). *Salmond on the law of torts* (17th edn). London: Sweet and Maxwell

Hewstone, M. (1981). *Social dimensions of attribution*. Unpublished doctoral dissertation. University of Oxford

Hewstone, M. and Jaspars, J. (1982a) Intergroup relations and attribution processes. *In* H. Tajfel (ed.) *Social identity and intergroup relations*. Cambridge/Paris: Cambridge University Press/Maison des Sciences de l'Homme

Hewstone, M. and Jaspars, J. (1982b). Re-considering the roles of consensus, consistency and distinctiveness: Kelley's cube re-visited. *British Journal of Social Psychology*

Hewstone, M. and Jaspars, J. (1982c). Explanations for racial discrimination. The effect of group discussion on intergroup attributions. *European Journal of Social Psychology* **12**, 1–16

Hewstone, M., Jaspars, J. and Lalljee, M. (1982). Social representations, social attribution and social identity: The intergroup images of 'Public' and 'Comprehensive' schoolboys. *European Journal of Social Psychology* **12**, 241–269

Higgins, E. T., Rholes, W. J. and Jones, C. R. (1977). Category accessibility and impression formation. *Journal of Experimental Social Psychology* **13**, 141–154

Hilton, D., Jaspars, J., Lalljee, M., Lamb, R. and Smith, C. (1981). Causal attribution and common sense explanations. Paper presented at Annual Conference of The British Psychological Society (Social Psychology Section), University of Oxford

Hinde, R. (1979). *Towards understanding relationships*. London: Academic Press

Hoffmann, L. W. (1974). Fear of success imagery in males and females: 1965 to 1971. *Journal of Consulting and Clinical Psychology* **42**, 353–358

Hoffmann, N. (1970). Moral development. *In* P. H. Mussen (ed.) *Carmichael's manual of child psychology* Vol. 2. New York: Wiley

Hoffmann, N. (ed.) (1976). *Depressives Verhalten. Psychologische Modelle der Atiolonie und der Therapie*. Salzburg: Otto Muller Verlag

Hogan, R., DeSoto, C. B. and Solano, C. (1977). Traits, tests, and personality research. *American Psychologist* **32**, 255–264

Homans, G. C. (1950). *The human group*. New York: Harcourt, Brace

Hood, L. and Bloom, L. (1979). What, when, and how about why: A longitudinal study of early expressions of causality. *Monographs of the Society for Research in Child Development* **44**, 1–47

Horner, M. S. (1972). Toward an understanding of achievement-related conflicts in women. *Journal of Social Issues* **28**, 157–175

Howard, J. (1979). Person-situation interaction models. *Personality and Social Psychology Bulletin* **5**, 191–195

Hume, D. (1960). *A treatise of human nature*. Oxford: Clarendon Press. (Originally published, 1739)

Imamoglu, E. O. (1975). Children's awareness and usage of intention cues. *Child Development* **46**, 39–45

Jaccard, J. J. (1974). Predicting social behavior from personality traits. *Journal of Research into Personality* **7**, 358–367

Jamison, W. and Dansky, J. L. (1979). Identifying developmental prerequisites of cognitive acquisitions. *Child Development* **50**, 449–454

Janis, I. L. (1972). *Victims of groupthink*. Boston: Houghton Mifflin

Jaspars, B., Jaspars, J., King, J., Pendleton, D. and Rowe, K. (1981). A functional approach to attribution theory. Paper presented at Annual Conference of the British Psychological Society (Social Psychology Section), University of Oxford

Jaspars, J. (1965) *On social perception*. Unpublished Ph.D. Thesis. University of Leiden

Jaspars, J. (1968). De waarde van het psychologisch advies. *Nederlands Tijdschrift voor Psychologie* **23**, 295–331

Jaspars, J. and Furnham, A. (1980). Interactionism in psychology or the person revisited. Unpublished paper, Oxford University

Jaspars, J. and Hewstone, M. (1982). Cross-cultural interaction, social attribution and intergroup relations. *In* S. Bochner (ed.) *Cultures in contact: Studies in cross-cultural interaction*. Oxford: Pergamon

Johnson, R. C. (1962). A study of children's moral judgements. *Child Development* **33**, 327–354

Johnson, T. J., Feigenbaum, R. and Weiby, M. (1964). Some determinants and consequences of the teacher's perception of causation. *Journal of Educational Psychology* **55**, 237–246

Jones, E. E. (1976). How do people perceive the causes of behavior? *American Scientist* **64**, 300–305

Jones, E. E. (1978). A conversation with Edward E. Jones and Harold H. Kelley. *In* J. Harvey, W. J. Ickes and R. F. Kidd (eds) *New directions in attribution research* Vol. 2. Hillsdale, N. J.: Erlbaum

Jones, E. E. (1979). The rocky road from acts to dispositions. *American Psychologist* **34**, 107–117

Jones, E. E. and Davis, K. E. (1965). From acts to dispositions: The attribution process in person perception. *In* L. Berkowitz (ed.) *Advances in experimental social psychology* Vol. 2. New York: Academic Press

Jones, E. E. and DeCharms, R. (1967). Changes in social perception as a function of the personal relevance of behavior. *Sociometry* **20**, 75–85

Jones, E. E. and Harris, V. A. (1967). The attribution of attitudes. *Journal of Experimental Social Psychology* **3**, 1–24

Jones, E. E. and McGillis, D. (1976). Correspondent inferences and the attribution cube: A comparative reappraisal. *In* J. Harvey, W. Ickes and R. F. Kidd (eds) *New directions in attribution research* Vol. 1. Hillsdale, N. J.: Erlbaum

Jones, E. E. and Nisbett, R. E. (1972). The actor and observer: Divergent perceptions of the causes of behaviour. *In* E. E. Jones, D. Kanouse, H. H. Kelley, R. E. Nisbett, S. Valins and B. Weiner (eds) *Attribution: Perceiving the causes of behavior*. Morristown, N. J.: General Learning Press

Jones, E. E. and Thibaut, J. W. (1958). Interaction goals as bases of inference in interpersonal perception. *In* R. Tagiuri and L. Petrullo (eds) *Person perception and interpersonal behaviour*. Stanford: Stanford University Press

Jones, E. E., Davis, K. E. and Gergen, K. J. (1961). Role playing variations and their informational value for person perception. *Journal of Abnormal and Social Psychology* **63**, 302–310

Jones, E. E., Rock, L., Shaver, K. G., Goethals, G. R. and Ward, L. M. (1968). Pattern of performance and ability attribution: An unexpected primacy effect. *Journal of Personality and Social Psychology* **10**, 317–340

Jones, E. E., Worchel, S., Goethals, G. R. and Grumet, J. F. (1971) Prior expectancy and behavioral extremity as determinants of attitude attribution. *Journal of Experimental Social Psychology* **7**, 59–80

Jones, E. E., Kanouse, D. E., Kelley, H. H., Nisbett, R. E., Valins, S. and Weiner, B. (1972). *Attribution: Perceiving the causes of behavior.* Morristown, N. J.: General Learning Press

Jones, R. A., Linder, E. E., Kiesler, C. A., Zanna, M. and Brehm, J. W. (1968). Internal states or external stimuli: Observers' attitude judgements and the dissonance-theory self-persuasion controversy. *Journal of Experimental Social Psychology* **4**, 247–269

Jourard, S. (1964). *The transparent self.* New York: Van Nostrand

Kahneman, D. and Tversky, A. (1972). Subjective probability: A judgement of representativness. *Cognitive Psychology* **3**, 430–454

Kahneman, D. and Tversky, A. (1973). On the psychology of prediction. *Psychological Review* **80**, 237–251

Kalven, H. and Zeisel, H. (1966). *The American jury.* Boston: Little, Brown

Kanouse, D. E. (1972). Language, labeling, and attribution. *In* E. E. Jones *et al.* (eds) *Attribution: Perceiving the causes of behaviour.* Morristown, N.J.: General Learning Press

Kanouse, D. E. and Gross, D. (1970). From specific acts to general dispositions. Unpublished manuscript, University of California at Los Angeles

Karniol, R. (1978). Children's use of intention cues in evaluating behavior. *Psychological Bulletin* **85**, 76–85

Karniol, R. and Ross, M. (1976). The development of causal attributions in social perception. *Journal of Personality and Social Psychology* **34**, 455–464

Karniol, R. and Ross, M. (1979). Children's use of a causal attribution schema and the inference of manipulative intentions. *Child Development* **50**, 463–468

Kassin, S. M. (1979). Consensus information, prediction, and causal attribution: A review of the literature and issues. *Journal of Personality and Social Psychology* **37**, 1966–1981

Kassin, S. M. (1981). From laychild to "layman": Developmental causal attribution. *In* S. S. Brehm, S. M. Kassin and F. X. Gibbons (eds) *Developmental social psychology.* New York: Oxford University Press

Kassin, S. M. and Lowe, C. A. (1979). On the development of the augmentation principle: A perceptual approach. *Child Development* **50**, 728–734

Kassin, S. M., Lowe, C. A. and Gibbons, F. X. (1980). Children's use of the discounting principle: A perceptual approach. *Journal of Personality and Social Psychology* **39**, 719–728

Keasey, C. B. (1977a). Children's developing awareness and usage of intentionality and motives. *In* C. B. Keasey (ed.) *Nebraska Symposium on Motivation.* Lincoln: University of Nebraska Press

Keasey, C. B. (1977b). Young children's attributions of intentionality to themselves and others. *Child Development* **48**, 261–264

Kelley, H. H. (1967). Attribution in social psychology. *Nebraska Symposium on Motivation* **15**, 192–238

Kelley, H. H. (1971). Moral evaluation. *American Psychologist* **21**, 293–300

Kelley, H. H. (1972a). Attribution in social interaction. *In* E. E. Jones, D. Kanouse, H. H. Kelley, R. E. Nisbett, S. Valins and B. Weiner (eds) *Attribution: Perceiving the causes of behavior.* Morristown, N.J.: General Learning Press

Kelley, H. H. (1972b). Causal schemata and the attribution process. *In* E. E. Jones, D. E. Kanouse, H. H. Kelley, R. E. Nisbett, S. Valins and B. Weiner (eds) *Attribution: Perceiving the causes of behavior.* Morristown, N.J.: General Learning Press

Kelley, H. H. (1973). The processes of causal attribution. *American Psychologist* **28**, 107–128

Kelley, H. H. (1980a). Antecedents of attribution. Paper presented at conference on 'New developments in attribution theory', Oxford

Kelley, H. H. (1980b). The causes of behaviour: Their perception and regulation. *In* L. Festinger (ed.) *Retrospections on social psychology.* New York: Oxford University Press

Kelley, H. H. (1980c). Magic tricks: The management of causal attribution. In D. Görlitz (ed.) *Perspectives on attribution research and theory: The Bielefeld Symposium.* Cambridge, Mass.: Ballinger

Kelley, H. H. and Michela, J. L. (1980) Attribution theory and research. *In* M. R. Rosenzweig and L. M. Porter (eds) *Annual Review of Psychology* **31**, 457–501. Palo Alto: Annual Review Inc.

Kelly, G. A. (1955). *The Psychology of personal constructs* 2 vols. New York: Norton

Kelman, H. C. and Lawrence, L. H. (1972). Assignment of responsibility in the case of Lt. Calley: Preliminary report on a national survey. *Journal of Social Issues* **28**, 177–212

Key, M. R. (1975). *Male/female language.* Methuchen, N.J.: Scarecrow Press

Kneale, W. C. and Kneale, M. (1962) *The Development of Logic.* Oxford: Oxford University Press

Koffka, K. (1935). *Principles of Gestalt psychology.* New York: Harcourt, Brace

Kohlberg, L. (1966). A cognitive developmental analysis of children's sex-role concepts and attitudes. *In* E. E. Maccoby (ed.) *The development of sex differences.* Stanford, California: Stanford University Press

Kohlberg, L. (1969). Stage and sequence: The cognitive-developmental approach to socialization. *In* D. A. Goslin (ed.) *Handbook of socialization theory and research.* Chicago: Rand McNally

Kohlberg, L. (1971). From is to ought: How to commit the naturalist fallacy and get away with it in the study of moral development. *In* T. Mischel (ed.) *Cognitive development and epistemology.* New York: Academic Press

Kohlberg, L. (1976). Moral stages and moralization: The cognitive-developmental approach. *In* T. Lickona (ed.) *Moral development and behaviour.* New York: Holt

Köhler, W. (1929). *Gestalt psychology.* New York: Liveright

Krauskopf, C. (1978). Comments on Endler and Magnusson's attempt to redefine personality. *Psychological Bulletin* **85**, 280–283

Krug, S. and Hagel, J. (1976). Motivänderung: Erprobung eines theoriegeleiteten Trainingsprogramms. *Zeitschrift für Entwicklungspsychologie und Pädagogische Psychologie* **8**, 274–287

Kruglanski, A. (1975). The endogenous-exogenous partition in attribution theory. *Psychological Review* **82**, 387–406

Kruglanski, A. (1979). Causal explanation, teleological explanation: On radical particularism in attribution theory. *Journal of Personality and Social Psychology* **37**, 1447–1457

Kruglanski, A. (1980). Lay epistemo-logic, its process and content: Another look at attribution theory. *Psychological Review* **87**, 70–87

Kuhn, D. and Phelps, H. (1976). The development of children's comprehension of causal direction. *Child Development* **47**, 248–251

Kun, A. (1977). Development of the magnitude-covariation and compensation schemata in ability and effort attributions of performance. *Child Development* **48**, 862–873

Kun, A. (1978). Evidence for preschooler's understanding of causal direction in extended causal sequences. *Child Development* **49**, 218–222

Kun, A. (1980). Perceived additivity of intrinsic and extrinsic motivation in young children: Refutation of the 'overjustification' hypothesis. (Manuscript submitted for publication)

Kun, A., Parsons, J. and Ruble, D. (1974). Development of integration processes using ability and effort information to predict outcome. *Developmental Psychology* **10**, 721–732

Lakoff, R. (1975). *Language and woman's place*. New York: Harper and Row

Lalljee, M. (1981). Attribution theory and the analysis of explanations. In C. Antaki (ed.) *The psychology of ordinary explanations of social behaviour*. London: Academic Press

Lambert, W. E. (1979). Language as a factor in intergroup relations. In H. Giles and R. St. Clair (eds) *Language and Social Psychology*. Oxford: Blackwell

Langer, E. J. (1978). Rethinking the role of thought in social interaction. In J. H. Harvey, W. J. Ickes and R. F. Kidd (eds) *New directions in attribution research* Vol. 2. Hillsdale, N.J.: Erlbaum

Latané, B. and Darley, J. M. (1968). Group inhibition of bystander intervention in emergencies. *Journal of Personality and Social Psychology* **10**, 215–221

Laurendeau, M. and Pinard, A. (1962). *Causal thinking in the child*. New York: International Universities Press

Lazzerini, A., Cox, T. and Mackay, C. (1979). Perceptions of and reaction to stressful situations: The utility of a general anxiety trait. *British Journal of Social and Clinical Psychology* **18**, 363–370

Leahy, R. L. (1976). Developmental trends in qualified inferences and descriptions of self and other. *Developmental Psychology* **12**, 546–547

Leahy, R. L. (1979a). The child's concept of mens rea: Information mitigating punishment judgements. *Journal of Genetic Psychology* **134**, 71–78

Leahy, R. L. (1979b) Developmental changes in the use of information in impression formation. *Journal of Genetic Psychology* **134**, 185–191

Lemaine, G., Desportes, J. P. and Louarn, J. P. (1969). Rôle de la cohésion et de la différenciation hiérarchique dans le processus d'influence sociale. *Bulletin du C.E.R.P.* **28**, 237–253

Lenauer, M., Sameth, L. and Shaver, P. (1976). Looking back at oneself in time: Another approach to the actor-observer phenomenon. *Perceptual and Motor Skills* **43**, 1283–1287

Lepper, M. R., Greene, D. and Nisbett, R. E. (1973). Undermining children's intrinsic interest with extrinsic reward: A test of the 'overjustification' hypothesis. *Journal of Personality and Social Psychology* **28**, 129–137

Lerner, M. J. (1970). The desire for justice and reactions to victims. In J. Macaulay and L. Berkowitz (eds) *Altruism and helping behavior*. New York: Academic Press

Lerner, M. J., Miller, D. T. and Holmes, J. G. (1976). Deserving and the emergence of forms of justice. In L. Berkowitz and E. Walster (eds) *Advances in experimental social psychology* Vol. 9. New York: Academic Press

Lesser, H. (1977). The growth of perceived causality. *Journal of Genetic Psychology* **130**, 143–152

LeVine, R. A. and Campbell, D. T. (1972). *Ethnocentrism: Theories of conflict, ethnic attitudes and group behaviour.* New York: Wiley

Lévy-Bruhl, L. (1928). *The 'soul' of the primitive.* London: George Allen and Unwin

Lewin, K. (1935). *A dynamic theory of personality.* New York: McGraw Hill

Lewin, K. (1936). *Principles of topological psychology.* New York: McGraw Hill

Lewin, K. (1948). *Resolving social conflict.* New York: Harper

Lewinsohn, P., Mischel, W., Chaplin, W. and Barton, R. (1980). Social competence and depression: The role of illusory self perception. *Journal of Abnormal Psychology* **89**, 202–212

Lickona, T. (1976). Research on Piaget's theory of moral development. *In* T. Lickona (ed) *Moral development and behaviour.* New York: Holt

Lind, E. A., Erickson, B. E., Conley, J. and O'Barr, W. M. (1978). Social attributions and conversational style in trial testimony. *Journal of Personality and Social Psychology* **36**, 1558–1567

Linden, A. M. (1977). *Canadian negligence law* (2nd edn). Toronto: Butterworth

Lippa, R. (1976). Expressive control and the leakage of dispositional introversion-extraversion during role-played teaching. *Journal of Personality* **44**, 541–559

Livesley, W. J. and Bromley, D. B. (1973). *Person perception in childhood and adolescence.* London: Wiley

Lloyd-Bostock, S. M. A. (1979a). The ordinary man and the psychology of attributing causes and responsibility. *Modern Law Review* **2**, 143–168

Lloyd-Bostock, S. M. A. (1979b). Common sense morality and accident compensation. *In* D. Farrington, K. Hawkins and S. Lloyd-Bostock (eds) *Psychology law and legal processes.* London: Macmillan

Lloyd-Bostock, S. M. A. (1983). Fault and liability for accidents: The accident victim's perspective. *In* C. Harris (ed.) *Compensation for illness and injury.* Oxford: Oxford University Press

London, H. *Personality: A new look at metatheories.* New York: Wiley 1978

Looft, W. R. and Bartz, W. H. (1969). Animism revived. *Psychological Bulletin* **71**, 1–19

Lowe, C. A. and Medway, F. J. (1976). Effects of valence, severity, and relevance on responsibility and dispositional attribution. *Journal of Personality* **44**, 518–538

Luft, J. (1969). *Of human interaction.* Palo Alto, California: National Press

Maccoby, E. E. and Jacklin, C. N. (1974). *The psychology of sex differences* Vol. 1. Stanford, California: Stanford University Press

Mackie, J. L. (1974). *The cement of the universe: A study of causation.* Oxford: Clarendon

Mackie, J. L. (1977). *Ethics: Inventing right and wrong.* New York: Penguin

MacRae, D. (1954). A test of Piaget's theory of moral development. *Journal of Abnormal and Social Psychology* **49**, 14–18

Magnusson, D. (1971). An analysis of situational dimensions. *Perceptual and Motor Skills* **32**, 851–867

Magnusson, D. (1979). On the psychological situation. Dept. Report No. 544, University of Stockholm

Magnusson, D. and Ekehammar, B. (1973). An analysis of situational dimensions: A replication. *Multivariate Behaviour Research* **8** 331–339

Magnusson, D. and Endler, N. (1977). *Personality at the crossroads.* Hillsdale, N.J.: Erlbaum

Magnusson, D. and Stattin, H. (1978). A cross-cultural comparison of anxiety responses in an interactional frame of reference. *International Journal of Psychology* **13**, 317–332

Maiman, L. A. and Becker, M. H. (1974). The Health Belief Model: Origins and correlates in psychological theory. *Health Education Monographs* **2**, 336–353

Mann, J. F. and Taylor, D. M. (1974). Attribution of causality: Role of ethnicity and social class. *Journal of Social Psychology* **94**, 3–13

Marchand, B. (1970). Auswirking einer emotional wertvollen und einer emotional neutralen Klassifikation auf die Schatzung einer Stimulus-Serie. *Zeitschrift für Sozialpsychologie* **1**, 264–274

Marsh, P., Harré, R. and Rosser, E. (1978). *The rules of disorder*. London: Routledge and Kegan Paul

McArthur, L. Z. (1972). The how and what of why: Some determinants and consequences of causal attributions. *Journal of Personality and Social Psychology* **22**, 171–193

McArthur, L. Z. (1976a). Note on sex differences in causal attribution. *Psychological Reports* **38**, 29–30

McArthur, L. Z. (1976b). The lesser influence of consensus than distinctiveness information on causal attributions: A test of the person-thing hypothesis. *Journal of Personality and Social Psychology* **33**, 733–742

McArthur, L. Z. and Post, D. (1977). Figural emphasis and person perception. *Journal of Experimental Social Psychology* **13**, 520–535

McArthur, L. Z. and Solomon, L. K. (1978). Perceptions of an aggressive encounter as a function of the victim's salience and the perceiver's arousal. *Journal of Personality and Social Psychology* **36**, 1278–1290

McCauley, C. and Jacques, S. (1979). The popularity of conspiracy theories of presidential assassination: A Bayesian analysis. *Journal of Personality and Social Psychology* **37**, 637–644

McClelland, D. C., Atkinson, J. W., Clark, R. A. and Lowell, E. L. (1953). *The achievement motive*. New York: Appleton-Century-Crofts

McGarrigle, J. and Donaldson, M. (1974). Conservation accidents. *Cognition* **3**, 341–350

McGowan, J. and Gormly, J. (1976). Validation of personality traits: A multi-criteria approach. *Journal of Personality and Social Psychology* **34**, 791–795

Mehrabian, A. (1977). A questionnaire measure of individual differences in stimulus screening and associated differences in arousability. *Environmental Psychology and Non Verbal Behaviour* **1**, 89–103

Meldon, A. I. (1961). *Free action*. London: Routledge and Kegan Paul

Mendelson, R. and Shultz, T. R. (1976). Covariation and temporal contiguity as principles of causal inference in young children. *Journal of Experimental Child Psychology* **22**, 408–412

Mervis, C. B. and Rosch, E. (1981). Categorization of natural objects. *In* M. R. Rozenzweig and L. M. Porter (eds) *Annual Review of Psychology* **32**. Palo Alto: Annual Review Inc.

Meyer, W. W. (1973). *Leistungsmotiv und Ursachenerklarung von Erfolg und Misserfolg*. Stuttgart: Ernst Klett Verlag

Michotte, A. (1946). *La perception de la causalité*. Paris: Erasme

Michotte, A. (1963). *The perception of causality*. New York: Basic Books

Miller A. G. (1974). Perceived freedom and the attribution of attitudes. *Representative Research in Social Psychology* **5**, 61–80

Miller, A. G. (1975). Constraint and target effects in the attribution of attitudes. *Journal of Experimental Social Psychology* **12**, 325–339

Miller, D. T. (1976). Ego involvement and attributions for success and failure. *Journal of Personality and Social Psychology* **34**, 901–906

Miller, D. T. and Norman, S. A. (1975). Actor-observer differences in perceptions of effective control. *Journal of Personality and Social Psychology* **31**, 503–515

Miller, D. T. and Porter, C. A. (1980). Effects of temporal perspective on the attribution process. *Journal of Personality and Social Psychology* **39**, 532–541

Miller, D. T. and Ross, M. (1975). Self-serving biases in the attribution of causality: Fact or fiction? *Psychological Bulletin* **82**, 213–225

Mischel, W. (1968). *Personality and assessment.* New York: Wiley

Mischel, W. (1973). Toward a cognitive social learning reconceptualization of personality. *Psychological Review* **80**, 252–283

Mischel, W. (1977). The interaction of person and situation. *In* D. Magnusson and N. Endler (eds) *Personality at the crossroads: Current issues in interactional psychology.* Hillsdale, N.J.: Erlbaum

Mischel, W. (1979). On the interface of cognition and personality: Beyond the person-situation debate. *American Psychologist* **34**, 740–754

Mischel, W., Jeffrey, L. and Patterson, C. (1974). The layman's use of trait and behavioural information to predict behaviour. *Journal of Research into Personality* **8**, 231–242

Monahan, L., Kuhn, D. and Shaver, P. (1974). Intrapsychic versus cultural explanations of the 'Fear of success' motive. *Journal of Personality and Social Psychology* **29**, 60–64

Monson, T. C. and Hesley, J. (1980). Causal attributions for behaviors consistent or inconsistent with an actor's personality traits: Differences between those offered by actors and observers. Unpublished manuscript, University of Texas at Arlington

Monson, T. C. and Snyder, M. (1977). Actors, observers, and the attribution process: Toward a reconceptualization. *Journal of Experimental Social Psychology* **13**, 89–111

Monson, T. C., Hesley, J. and Chernick, L. (1980a). The role of personality traits and situational constraint on the prediction of behaviour. Unpublished manuscript, University of Texas at Arlington

Monson, T. C., Tanke, E. D. and Lund, J. (1980b). Determinants of social perception in a naturalistic setting. *Journal of Research into Personality*

Montanelli, D. S. and Hill, K. T. (1969). Children's achievement expectations and performance as a function of two consecutive reinforcement experiences, sex of subject, and sex of experimenter. *Journal of Personality and Social Psychology* **13**, 115–128

Moore, B. S., Sherrod, D. R., Liu, T. J. and Underwood, B. (1979). The dispositional shift in attribution over time. *Journal of Experimental Social Psychology* **15**, 553–569

Moos, R. H. (1968). Situational analysis of a therapeutic community milieu. *Journal of Abnormal Psychology* **73**, 49–61

Moos, R. H. (1969). Sources of variance in response to questionnaires and behaviour. *Journal of Abnormal Psychology* **74**, 405–412

Moos, R. H. (1970). Differential effects of psychiatric ward settings of patient change. *Journal of Nervous and Mental Disease* **151**, 316–321

Morris, H. (ed.) (1961). *Freedom and responsibility: Readings in philosophy and law.* Stanford: Stanford University Press

Moscovici, S. (1961). *La psychanalyse, son image et son public.* Paris: P.U.F.

Moscovici, S. (1972). L'homme en interaction, machine à répondre ou machine á inférer. *In* S. Moscovici (ed.) *Introduction à la psychologie sociale* Vol. 1. Paris: Larousse

Moscovici, S. and Faucheux, C. (1972). Social influence, conformity bias and the study of active minorities. *In* L. Berkowitz (ed.) *Advances in experimental social psychology* Vol. 6. New York: Academic Press

Nagel, E. (1961). *The structure of science: Problems in the logic of scientific explanation.* New York: Harcourt, Brace

Nesdale, A. R. and Rule, B. G. (1974). The effects of an aggressor's characterisations and an observer's accountability in judgements of aggression. *Canadian Journal of Behavioural Science* **6**, 342–351

Neulinger, J. (1978). *The psychology of leisure.* Illinois: C. Thomas

Newell, A. and Simon, H. A. (1972). *Human problem solving.* Englewood Cliffs, N.J.: Prentice-Hall

Nicholls, J. G. (1975). Causal attributions and other achievement-related cognitions: Effects of task outcome, attainment, value, and sex. *Journal of Personality and Social Psychology* **31**, 379–389

Nicholls, J. G. (1978). The development of the concepts of effort and ability, perception of academic attainment, and the understanding that difficult tasks require more ability. *Child Development* **49**, 800–814

Nisbett, R. E. and Borgida, E. (1975). Attribution and the psychology of prediction. *Journal of Personality and Social Psychology* **32**, 932–943

Nisbett, R. E. and Ross, L. (1980). *Human inference: Strategies and shortcomings of social judgment.* Englewood Cliffs, N.J.: Prentice-Hall

Nisbett, R. E. and Wilson, T. D. (1977). Telling more than we can know: Verbal reports on mental processes. *Psychological Review* **84**, 231–259

Nisbett, R. E., Caputo, C., Legant, P. and Maracek, J. (1973). Behaviour as seen by the actor and as seen by the observer. *Journal of Personality and Social Psychology* **27**, 154–164

Nisbett, R. E., Borgida, E., Crandall, R. and Reed, H. (1976). Popular induction: Information is not necessarily informative. *In* J. S. Carroll and J. W. Payne (eds) *Cognition and social behaviour.* Hillsdale, N.J.: Erlbaum

Nummendal, S. G. and Bass, S. C. (1976). Effects of the salience of intention and consequence on children's moral judgements. *Developmental Psychology* **12**, 475–476

Oakley, A. (1974). *The sociology of housework.* London: Martin Robertson

Olum, V. (1956). Developmental differences in the perception of causality. *American Journal of Psychology* **69**, 417–423

Olweus, D. (1977). 'Modern' interactionism in personality psychology and the analysis of variance components approach: A critical examination. *In* D. Magnusson and N. Endler (eds) *Personality at the crossroads.* Hillsdale, N.J.: Erlbaum

Oppenheim, A. (1966). *Questionnaire design and attitude measurement.* London: Heinemann

Orne, M. T. (1962). On the social psychological experiment: With particular reference to demand characteristics and their implications. *American Psychologist* **17**, 776–782

Orvis, B. R., Cunningham, J. D. and Kelley, H. H. (1975). A closer examination of causal inference: The roles of consensus, distinctiveness and consistency information. *Journal of Personality and Social Psychology* **32**, 605–616

Orvis, B. R., Kelley, H. H. and Butler, D. (1976). Attributional conflicts in young couples. *In* J. H. Harvey, W. J. Ickes and R. F. Kidd (eds) *New directions in attribution research* Vol. 1. Hillsdale, N.J: Erlbaum

Osgood, C. E. (1966). Dimensionality of the semantic space of communication via facial expressions. *Scandinavian Journal of Psychology* **7**, 1–30

Osgood, C. E., Suci, G. J., and Tannenbaum, P. H (1957). *The measurement of meaning.* Urbana, Illinois: University of Illinois Press

Passer, M. W., Kelley, H. H. and Michela, J. L. (1978). Multidimensional scaling of the causes for negative interpersonal behaviour. *Journal of Personality and Social Psychology* **36**, 951–962

Peabody, D. (1968). Group judgements in the Philippines: Evaluative and descriptive aspects. *Journal of Personality and Social Psychology* **10**, 290–300

Peabody, D. (1970). Evaluative and descriptive aspects in personality perception: A reappraisal. *Journal of Personality and Social Psychology* **16**, 639–646

Pearson Commission (1978). Report of the Royal Commission on Civil Liability and Compensation for Personal Injury (Chairman, Lord Pearson). London: H.M.S.O.

Pendleton, D. and Wakeford, R. (1980). Training in clinical skills. An evaluation study. Unpublished paper, Oxford University

Pepitone, A. (1975). Social psychological perspectives on crime and punishment. *Journal of Social Issues* **31**, 197–216

Pervin, L. (1976). A free response description approach of person situation interaction. *Journal of Personality and Social Psychology* **34**, 567–585

Pervin, L. (1978a). *Current controversies and issues in personality.* New York: Wiley

Pervin, L. (1978b). Definitions, measurements and classifications of stimuli, situations and environments. *Human Ecology* **6**, 71–105

Peterson, C. R. and Beach, L. R. (1967). Man as an intuitive statistician. *Psychological Bulletin* **68**, 29–46

Pettigrew, T. F. (1979). The ultimate attribution error: Extending Allport's cognitive analysis of prejudice. *Personality and Social Psychology Bulletin* **5**, 461–476

Phares, E. J. and Wilson, K. G. (1972). Responsibility attribution: Role of outcome severity, situational ambiguity, and internal-external control. *Journal of Personality* **40**, 392–406

Piaget, J. (1926). *The language and thought of the child.* London: Routledge and Kegan Paul

Piaget, J. (1929). *The child's conception of the world.* New York: Harcourt, Brace. (Originally published, 1926)

Piaget, J. (1930). *The child's conception of physical causality.* London: Routledge and Kegan Paul

Piaget, J. (1932). *The moral judgement of the child.* London: Routledge and Kegan Paul

Piaget, J. (1969). *The child's conception of physical causality.* Totowa, N.J.: Littlefield Adams. (Originally published, 1927)

Piaget, J. (1973). An autobiography. *In* R. I. Evans' *Jean Piaget: The man and his ideas.* New York: Dutton

Piaget, J. (1974). *Understanding causality.* New York: Norton

Piaget, J. (1977). *The grasp of consciousness.* London: Routledge and Kegan Paul

Piaget, J. (1978). *Success and understanding.* London: Routledge and Kegan Paul

Piaget, J. and Inhelder, B. (1969). *The psychology of the child.* New York: Basic Books

Pleban, R. and Richardson, D. C. (1979). Research and publication trends in social psychology: 1973–1977. *Personality and Social Psychology Bulletin* **5**, 138–141

Pollner, M. and Wikler, L. (1981). The social construction of unreality: A case study of the practices of family sham and delusion. Unpublished manuscript, Department of Sociology, University of California, Los Angeles

Price, R. H. and Bouffard, D. L. (1974). Behavioural appropriateness and situational constraints as dimensions of social behaviour. *Journal of Personality and Social Psychology* **30**, 579–586

Prosser, W. L. (1971). *Handbook of the law of torts.* St. Paul, Minnesota: West

Pruitt, D. J. and Insko, C. A. (1980). Extension of the Kelley attribution model: The role of comparison–object consensus, target–object consensus, distinctiveness, and consistency. *Journal of Personality and Social Psychology* **39**, 39–58

Pryor, J. B. and Kriss, M. (1977). The cognitive dynamics of salience in the attribution process. *Journal of Personality and Social Psychology* **35**, 49–55

Reed, S. K. (1972). Pattern recognition and categorization. *Cognitive Psychology* **3**, 382–407

Reeder, G. D. and Brewer, M. B. (1979). A schematic model of disposition attribution in interpersonal perception. *Psychological Review* **86**, 61–79

Regan, D. T., Straus, E. and Fazio, R. (1974). Liking and the attribution process. *Journal of Experimental Social Psychology* **10**, 385–397

Robinson, W. P. (1972). *Language and social behaviour.* Harmondsworth: Penguin

Robinson, W. P. (1979). Speech markers and social class. *In* K. R. Scherer and H. Giles (eds) *Social markers in speech.* Cambridge: Cambridge University Press

Rosenkrantz, P., Vogel, S., Bee, H., Broverman, I. and Broverman, D. (1968). Sex-role stereotypes and self-concepts in college students. *Journal of Consulting and Clinical Psychology* **32**, 287–295

Ross, L. (1977). The intuitive psychologist and his shortcomings: Distortions in the attribution process. *In* L. Berkowitz (ed.) *Advances in experimental social psychology* (Vol. 10). New York: Academic Press

Ross, L., Lepper, M. R. and Hubbard, M. (1975). Perseverance in self-perception and social perception: Biased attributional processes in the de-briefing paradigm. *Journal of Personality and Social Psychology* **32**, 880–892

Ross, L., Greene, D. and House, P. (1977a). The 'false consensus effect': An egocentric bias in social perception and attribution processes. *Journal of Experimental Social Psychology* **13**, 279–301

Ross, L., Lepper, M. R., Strack, F. and Steinmetz, J. L. (1977b). Social explanation and social expectation: The effects of real and hypothetical explanations upon subjective likelihood. *Journal of Personality and Social Psychology* **35**, 817–829

Ross, M. and DiTecco, D. (1975). An attributional analysis of moral judgements. *Journal of Social Issues* **31**, 91–109

Rotter, J. (1954). *Social learning and clinical psychology.* New York: Prentice-Hall

Ruble, D. M. (1977). Premenstrual symptoms: A re-interpretation. *Science* **197**, 291–292

Ruble, D. M. and Feldman, N. S. (1976). Order of consensus, distinctiveness, and consistency information and causal attributions. *Journal of Personality and Social Psychology* **34**, 930–937

Ruble, D. M. and Rholes, W. J. (1981). The development of children's perceptions and attributions about their social world. *In* J. H. Harvey, W. J. Ickes and R. F. Kidd (eds) *New directions in attribution research* Vol. 3. Hillsdale, N.J.: Erlbaum

Ruble, D. M., Feldman, N. S., Higgins, E. T. and Karlovac, M. (1979). Locus of causality and the use of information in the development of causal attributions. *Journal of Personality* **47**, 595–614

Ryan, E. B. (1979). Why do low-prestige language varieties persist? *In* H. Giles and R. St. Clair (eds) *Language and social psychology.* Oxford: Blackwell

Ryan, E. B. and Carranza, M. A. (1975). Evaluative reactions of adolescents towards speakers of different language varieties. *Journal of Personality and Social Psychology* **31**, 855–863

Ryle, G. (1949). *The concept of mind.* London: Hutchinson

Sagatuin, I. and Knudsen, J. (1977). The interactive effect of attributor role and event on attributions. Paper presented at Pacific Sociological Association, California

Sarason, I., Smith, R. and Diener, E. (1975). Personality research: Components of variance attributable to the person and the situation. *Journal of Personality and Social Psychology* **32**, 199–204

Schanck, R. L. (1932). A study of a community and its groups and institutions conceived as behaviors of individuals. *Psychological Monographs* **43**, No. 2

Schanck, R. L. and Abelson, R. P. (1977). *Scripts, plans, goals and understanding: An inquiry into human knowledge structures.* Hillsdale, N.J.: Erlbaum

Schleifer, M. (1966). *Responsibility.* Unpublished thesis, University of Oxford

Schleifer, M. (1973). Psychological explanations and personal relations. *In* A. Montefiore (ed.) *Philosophy and personal relations.* London: Routledge

Schroeder, D. A. and Linder, D. E. (1976). Effects of actor's causal role, outcome severity, and knowledge of prior accidents upon attributions of responsibility. *Journal of Experimental Social Psychology* **12**, 340–356

Schwartz, S. (1975). The justice of need and the activation of humanitarian norms. *Journal of Social Issues* **31**, 111–135

Scott, M. B. and Lyman, S. M. (1968). Accounts. *American Sociological Review* **33**, 46–62

Secord, P. and Peevers, B. (1974). The development and attribution of person concepts. *In* T. Mischel (ed.) *Understanding other persons.* Oxford: Blackwell

Sedlak, A. J. (1979). Developmental differences in understanding plans and evaluating actors. *Child Development* **50**, 536–560

Sedlak, A. J. and Kurtz, S. T. (1981). A review of children's use of causal inference principles. *Child Development* **52**, 759–785

Sedlak, A. J., Thompson, V. D. and Sands, R. E. Effects of outcome, motive and intentionality on children's moral judgements and lie decisions. (Manuscript submitted for publication)

Selby, J. W. (1976). Inferential sets and descriptive versus evaluative aspects of behavioural inference. *Journal of Personality and Social Psychology* **33**, 13–24

Selg, H. (1971). *Einfuhrung in die experimentelle Psychologie.* Stuttgart: W. Kohlhammer

Seligman, M. E. P. (1975). *Helplessness.* San Francisco: Freeman

Shantz, C. U. (1975). The development of social cognition. *In* M. Hetherington (ed.) *Review of child development research* Vol. 3. Chicago: University of Chicago Press

Shatz, M. and Gelman, R. (1973). The development of communication skills: Modifications in the speech of young children as a function of listener. *Monographs of the Society for Research in Child Development* **38**, (No. 5) Serial No. 152

Shaver, K. G. (1970). Defensive attribution: Effects of severity and relevance on the responsibility assigned for an accident. *Journal of Personality and Social Psychology* **14**, 101–133

Shaver, K. G. (1975). *An introduction to attribution processes.* Cambridge: Mass.: Winthrop

Shaw, J. I. and McMartin, J. R. (1975). Perpetrator or victim? Effects of who suffers in an automobile accident on judgmental strictness. *Social Behavior and Personality* **3**, 5–12

Shaw, J. I. and Skolnick, P. (1971). Attribution of responsibility for a happy accident. *Journal of Personality and Social Psychology* **18**, 380–383

Shaw, M. E. (1967). Some cultural factors in sanctioning behaviour. *Psychonomic Science* **8**, 45–46

Shaw, M. E. and Iwawaki, S. (1972). Attribution of responsibility by Japanese and Americans as a function of age. *Journal of Cross-Cultural Psychology* **3**, 71–81

Shaw, M. E. and Reitan, H. T. (1969). Attribution of responsibility as a basis for sanctioning behavior. *British Journal of Social and Clinical Psychology* **8**, 217–226

Shaw, M. E. and Schneider, F. W. (1969a). Negro-white differences in attribution of responsibility as a function of age. *Psychonomic Science* **16**, 289–291

Shaw, M. E. and Schneider, F. W. (1969b). Intellectual competence as a variable in attribution of responsibility and assignment of sanctions. *Journal of Social Psychology* **78**, 31–39

Shaw, M. E. and Sulzer, J. L. (1964). An empirical test of Heider's levels in the attribution of responsibility. *Journal of Abnormal and Social Psychology* **69**, 39–46

Shaw, M. E., Briscoe, M. E. and Garcia-Esteve, J. (1968). A cross-cultural study of attribution of responsibility. *International Journal of Psychology* **3**, 51–60

Shepherd, J. W. and Bagley, A. J. (1970). Effects of biographical information and order of presentation on the judgement of an aggressive action. *British Journal of Social and Clinical Psychology* **9**, 177–179

Sherrod, D. and Farber, J. (1975). The effect of previous actor-observer role experience on attribution of responsibility for failure. *Journal of Personality* **43**, 231–247

Shrauger, S. and Altrocchi, J. (1964). Personality of the perceiver as a factor in person perception. *Psychological Bulletin* **62**, 289–308

Shultz, T. R. (1979b). Development of the concept of intention. *In* W. A. Collins (ed.) *The Minnesota symposium on child psychology* Vol. 13. Hillsdale, N.J.: Erlbaum

Shultz, T. R. (1980). Causal and logical reasoning. Paper presented at the International Congress of Psychology of the Child, Paris

Shultz, T. R. (1982). *Rules of causal attribution. Monographs of the Society for Research in Child Development* **47**, 1–51

Shultz, T. R. and Butkowsky, I. (1977). Young children's use of the scheme for multiple sufficient causes in the attribution of real and hypothetical behavior. *Child Development* **48**, 464–469

Shultz, T. R. and Mendelson, R. (1975). The use of covariation as a principle of causal analysis. *Child Development* **46**, 394–399

Shultz, T. R. and Ravinsky, R. B. (1977). Similarity as a principle of causal inference. *Child Development* **48**, 1552–1558

Shultz, T. R. and Schleifer, M. (1982). Judgements of causation, moral responsibility and reward in cases of benefit. (Manuscript in preparation)

Shultz, T. R. and Wright, K. (1982). Concepts of intention and negligence in the assignment of moral responsibility for harm and benefit. Submitted for publication

Shultz, T. R., Butkowsky, I., Pearce, J. W. and Shanfield, H. (1975). Development of schemes for the attribution of multiple psychological causes. *Developmental Psychology* **11**, 502–510

Shultz, T. R., Wells, D. and Sarda, M. (1980). Development of the ability to distinguish intended actions from mistakes, reflexes, and passive movements. *The British Journal of Social and Clinical Psychology* **19**, 301–310

Shultz, T. R., Schleifer, M. and Altman, I. (1981). Judgements of causation, responsibility, and punishment in cases of harm-doing. *Canadian Journal of Behavioural Science* **13**, 238–253

Siegel, L. S. and Brainerd, C. J. (eds). (1978). *Alternatives to Piaget: Critical essays on the theory.* New York: Academic Press

Siegel, S. (1956). *Nonparametric statistics for the behavioural sciences.* New York: McGraw Hill

Siegler, R. S. (1975). Defining the locus of developmental differences in children's causal reasoning. *Journal of Experimental Psychology* **20**, 512–525

Siegler, R. S. (1976). The effects of simple necessity and sufficiency relationships on children's causal inferences. *Child Development* **47**, 1058–1063

Siegler, R. S. and Liebert, R. M. (1974). Effects of contiguity, regularity, and age on children's causal inferences. *Developmental Psychology* **10**, 574–579

Simard, L., Taylor, D. M. and Giles, H. (1976). Attribution processes and inter-personal accommodation in a bilingual setting. *Language and speech* **19**, 374–387

Sloan, R. P. (1977). *The assignment of responsibility.* Unpublished thesis, New School for Social Research

Slovic, P. (1974). Hypothesis testing in the learning of positive and negative linear functions. *Organisational Behaviour and Human Performance* **11**, 368–376

Slovic, P. and Lichtenstein, S. (1971). Comparison of Bayesian and regression approaches to the study of information processing in judgement. *Organizational Behavior and Human Performance* **6**, 649–744

Slovic, P., Fischhoff, B. and Lichtenstein, S. (1977). Behavioral decision theory. *Annual Review of Psychology* **28**, 1–39

Small, K. H. and Peterson, J. (1980). *Actors and observers: Effects of setting context and attributional predisposition on causal perceptions.* Unpublished manuscript. Claremont Men's College

Smith, J., Monson, T. C., Hesley, J. and Graziano, W. (1979a). *Familiarity with an actor's behavioral history as a determinant of the actor-observer effect.* Paper presented at the meeting of the Midwestern Psychological Association, Chicago

Smith, J., Monson, T. C. and Graziano, W. (1979b). *Focal attention and the actor-observer effect.* Presented at the Southwestern Psychological Association Convention, San Antonio

Smith, M. C. (1975). Children's use of the multiple sufficient cause schema in social perception. *Journal of Personality and Social Psychology* **32**, 737–747

Smith, P. M., Giles, H. and Hewstone, M. (1979). Sociolinguistics: A social psychological perspective. *In* R. St. Clair and H. Giles (eds) *The social and psychological contexts of language.* Hillsdale, N.J.: Erlbaum

Snyder, M. L. (1974). The self-monitoring of expressive behavior. *Journal of Personality and Social Psychology* **30**, 526–537

Snyder, M. L. (1979). Self-monitoring processes. *In* L. Berkowitz (ed.) *Advances in experimental social psychology* Vol. 12. New York: Academic Press

Snyder, M. L. and Frankel, A. (1976). Observer bias: A stringent test of behavior engulfing the field. *Journal of Personality and Social Psychology* **34**, 857–864

Snyder, M. L. and Jones, E. E. (1974). Attitude attribution when behavior is constrained. *Journal of Experimental Social Psychology* **10**, 585–600

Snyder, M. L. and Monson, T. C. (1975). Persons, situations, and the control of social behavior. *Journal of Personality and Social Psychology* **32**, 637–644

Snyder, M. L. and Swann, W. B. (1976). When actions reflect attitudes: The politics of impression management. *Journal of Personality and Social Psychology* **34**, 1034–1042

Snyder, M. L. and Tanke, E. D. (1976). Behavior and attitude: Some people are more consistent than others. *Journal of Personality* **44**, 501–517

Snyder, M. L., Stephan, W. G. and Rosenfeld, D. (1976). Egotism and attribution. *Journal of Personality and Social Psychology* **33**, 435–441

Sohn, D. (1977). Affect-generating powers of effort and ability self attributions of academic success and failure. *Journal of Educational Psychology* **5**, 500–505

Soloman, S. (1978). Measuring dispositional and situational attributions. *Personality and Social Psychology Bulletin* **4**, 589–594

Srull, T. K. and Wyer, R. S., Jr. (1979). The role of category accessibility in the interpretation of information about persons: Some determinants and implications. *Journal of Personality and Social Psychology* **13**, 1660–1672

Steiner, I. D. (1970). Perceived freedom. *In* L. Berkowitz (ed.) *Advances in experimental social psychology* Vol. 5. New York: Academic Press

Steiner, I. D. (1980). Attribution of choice. *In* M. Fishbein (ed.) *Progress in social psychology*. Vol. 1. Hillsdale, N.J.: Erlbaum

Steiner, I. D. and Field, W. I. (1960). Role assignment and interpersonal influence. *Journal of Abnormal and Social Psychology* **61**, 239–245

Storms, M. D. (1973). Videotape and the attribution process: Reversing actors' and observers' points of view. *Journal of Personality and Social Psychology* **27**, 165–175

Storms, M. D. and McCaul, K. D. (1976). Attribution processes and emotional exacerbation of dysfunctional behavior. *In* J. H. Harvey, W. J. Ickes and R. F. Kidd (eds) *New directions in attribution research* Vol. 1. Hillsdale, N.J.: Erlbaum

Storms, M. D. and Nisbett, R. E. (1970). Insomnia and the attribution process. *Journal of Personality and Social Psychology* **16**, 319–328

Street, H. (1972). *The law of torts* (5th edn). London: Butterworth

Streufert, S. and Streufert, S. C. (1969). Effects of conceptual structure, failure and success on attribution of causality and interpersonal attitudes. *Journal of Personality and Social Psychology* **11**, 138–147

Streufert, S. and Streufert, S. C. (1978). *Behavior in the complex environment*. Washington, D.C.: Winston

Strickland, L. H. (1958). Surveillance and trust. *Journal of Personality* **26**, 200–215

Suppes, P. (1970). *A probabalistic theory of causality*. Amsterdam: North-Holland

Tajfel, H. (1959). Quantitative judgement in social perception. *British Journal of Psychology* **50**, 16–29

Tajfel, H. (1969) Cognitive aspects of prejudice. *Journal of Social Issues* **25**, 79–97

Tajfel, H. (1972). La catégorisation sociale. *In* S. Moscovici (ed.) *Introduction à la psychologie sociale*. Vol. 1. Paris: Larousse

Tajfel, H. (ed.) (1978). *Differentiation between social groups: Studies in the social psychology of intergroup relations*. London: Academic Press

Tajfel, H. (1981) *Human groups and social categories*. Cambridge: Cambridge University Press

Tajfel, H. and Turner, J. C. (1979). An integrative theory of intergroup conflict. *In* W. G. Austin and S. Worchel (eds) *The social psychology of intergroup relations*. Monterey, California: Brooks/Cole

Tajfel, H. and Wilkes, A. L. (1963). Classification and quantitative judgement. *British Journal of Psychology* **54**, 101–114

Tajfel, H., Flament, C., Billig, M. and Bundy, R. P. (1971). Social categorization and intergroup behaviour. *European Journal of Social Psychology* **1**, 149–178

Taylor. D. M. and Jaggi, V. (1974). Ethnocentrism and causal attribution in a south Indian context. *Journal of Cross-Cultural Psychology* **5**, 162–171

Taylor, S. E. and Fiske, S. (1975) Point of view and perceptions of causality. *Journal of Personality and Social Psychology* **32**, 439–445

Taylor, S. E. and Fiske, S. (1978). Salience, attention, and attribution: top of the head phenomena. *In* L. Berkowitz (ed.) *Advances in experimental social psychology*. Vol. 11. New York: Academic Press

Taylor, S. E. and Koivumaki, J. H. (1976). The perception of self and others: Acquaintanceship, affect, and actor-observer differences. *Journal of Personality and Social Psychology* **33**, 403–408

Taylor, S. E., Crocker, J., Fiske, S. T., Springen, M. and Winkler, J. D. (1979). The generalizability of salience effects. *Journal of Personality and Social Psychology* **37**, 357–368

Teglasi, H. (1977). Influence of situational factors on causal attributions of college females. *Psychological Reports* **41**, 495–502

Thibaut, J. W. and Kelley, H. H. (1959). *The social psychology of groups*. New York: Wiley

Thibaut, J. W. and Riecken, H. W. (1955). Some determinants and consequences of the perception of social causality. *Journal of Personality* **24**, 113–133

Tomkins, S. S. (1962). *Affect, imagery, consciousness: The positive affects*. New York: Springer

Tomlinson, P. (1980). Moral judgement and moral psychology: Piaget, Kohlberg and beyond. *In* S. Modgil and C. Modgil (eds) *Towards a theory of psychological development within the Piagetian framework*. Slough: NFER

Trope, Y. and Burnstein, E. (1975). Processing the information contained in another's behavior. *Journal of Experimental Social Psychology* **11**, 439–458

Trower, P., Bryant, B. and Argyle, M. (1978). *Social skills and mental health*. London: Methuen

Turner, R. G. (1978). Effects of differential request procedures and self-consciousness on trait attributions. *Journal of Research in Personality* **12**, 431–438

Tversky, A. (1967). A general theory of polynomial conjoint measurement. *Journal of Mathematical Psychology* **4**, 1–20

Tversky, A. and Kahneman, D. (1971). Belief in the law of small numbers. *Psychological Bulletin* **76**, 105–110

Tversky, A. and Kahneman, D. (1973). Availability: A heuristic for judging frequency and probability. *Cognitive Psychology* **5**, 207–232

Tversky, A. and Kahneman, D. (1974). Judgement under uncertainty: Heuristics and biases. *Science* **185**, 1124–1131

Tversky, A. and Kahneman, D. (1980). Causal schemes in judgements under uncertainty. *In* M. Fishbein (ed.) *Progress in social psychology*. Vol. 1. Hillsdale, N.J.: Erlbaum

Ullian, D. Z. (1976). The development of conceptions of masculinity and feminity. *In* B. Lloyd and J. Archer (eds) *Exploring sex differences*. London: Academic Press

Valins, S. E. (1966). Cognitive effects of false heart-rate feedback. *Journal of Personality and Social Psychology* **4**, 400–408

van Heck, G. and van der Leeuw, E. (1975). Situatie ed dispositie als variante-komponenten u zelf beoordelug en beoordelug van de ander. *Gedrag tijdshrift voor Psychologie* **4**, 202–214

van der Plight, J. (1981). Actor-observer differences: Divergent perspectives or divergent evaluations? *In* C. Antaki (ed.) *The psychology of ordinary explanations*. London: Academic Press

Veroff, J., McClelland, L. and Ruhland, D. (1975). Varieties of achievement motivation. *In* M. T. S. Mednick, S. S. Tangri and L. W. Hoffman (eds) *Women and achievement*. Washington: Hemisphere

Vidmar, N. (1972). Effects of decision alternatives on the verdicts and social perceptions of simulated jurors. *Journal of Personality* **22**, 211–218

Vidmar, N. (1977). Effects of degree of harm and retribution motives on punishment reactions. Paper presented at the meeting of the Canadian Psychological Association, Vancouver

von Wright, G. H. (1971). *Explanation and understanding*. London: Routledge and Kegan Paul

von Wright, G. H. (1974). *Causality and determinism*. New York: Columbia University Press

Wachtel, P. (1973). Psychodynamics, behavioural therapy, and the implacable experimenter: An enquiry into the consistency of personality. *Journal of Abnormal Psychology* **82**, 324–334

Wallace, W. A. (1974). *Causality and scientific explanation II: Classical and contemporary science:* Ann Arbor: University of Michigan Press

Wallace, W. P. (1965). Review of the historical, empirical, and theoretical status of the von Restorff phenomenon. *Psychological Bulletin* **63**, 410–424

Walster, E. (1966). Assignment of responsibility for an accident. *Journal of Personality and Social Psychology* **3**, 73–79

Walster, E. and Piliavin, J. (1972). Equity and the innocent bystander. *Journal of Social Issues* **28**, 165–189

Walster, E., Berscheid, E. and Walster, G. W. (1979). New directions in equity research. *Journal of Personality and Social Psychology* **25**, 151–176

Ward, C. (1979). Differential evaluation of male and female expertise: Prejudice against women? *British Journal of Social and Clinical Psychology* **18**, 65–69

Warr, P. and Knapper, C. (1966). The role of expectancy and communication context in indirect person perception. *British Journal of Social and Clinical Psychology* **5**, 244–257

Weiner, B. (1972). *Theories of motivation*: Chicago: Markham

Weiner, B. (ed.) (1974). *Achievement motivation and attribution theory*. Morristown, N.J.: General Learning Press

Weiner, B. (1977a). An attributional approach for educational psychology. *Review of Educational Research* **4**, 179–208

Weiner, B. (1977b). Attribution and affect: Comments on Sohn's critique. *Journal of Educational Psychology* **5**, 506–511

Weiner, B. (1979). A theory of motivation for some classroom experiences. *Journal of Educational Psychology* **71**, 3–25

Weiner, B. and Kukla, A. (1970). An attributional analysis of achievement motivation. *Journal of Personality and Social Psychology* **15**, 1–20

Weiner, B. and Kun, A. The development of causal attributions and the growth of achievement and social motivation. *In* S. Feldman and D. Bush (eds) *Cognitive development and social development*. Hillsdale, N.J.: Erlbaum (in press)

Weiner, B. and Peter, N. (1973). A cognitive developmental analysis of achievement and moral judgements. *Developmental Psychology* **9**, 290–309

Weiner, B., Frieze, I., Kukla, A., Reed, L., Rest, S. and Rosenbaum, R. M. (1971). *Perceiving the causes of success and failure*. Morristown, N.J.: General Learning Press

Weiner, B., Kun, A. and Benesh-Weiner, M. (1978). The development of mastery, emotions, and morality from an attributional perspective. Paper presented at the Minnesota Symposium on Child Psychology

Weinreich, H. and Chetwynd, J. (1976). *Ideology, psychology, and social change; The case of sex role stereotyping*. Unpublished manuscript

Weinreich-Haste, H. (1978). Sex differences in fear of success among British students. *British Journal of Social and Clinical Psychology* **17**, 37–42

Weinreich-Haste, H. and Kelly, A. (1978). *What sex is science?* Unpublished manuscript, University of Bath

Weir, T. (1979). *A casebook on tort* (4th edn). London: Sweet and Maxwell

Wells, G. L. and Harvey, J. H. (1977). Do people use consensus information in making causal attributions? *Journal of Personality and Social Psychology* **35**, 279–293

West, S. G., Gunn, S. P. and Chernicky, P. (1975). Ubiquitous Watergate: An attributional analysis. *Journal of Personality and Social Psychology* **32**, 55–65

Westland, G. (1978). *Current crises of psychology*. London: Heinemann

Whitehead, G. I. and Smith, S. H. (1976). The effect of expectancy on the assignment of responsibility for a misfortune. *Journal of Personality* **44**, 69–83

Wicker, A. W. (1969). Attitudes v. actions: The relationship of verbal and overt behavioral responses to attitude objects. *Journal of Social Issues* **25**, 41–78

Williams G. and Hepple, W. A. (1976). *Foundations of the law of tort.* London: Butterworth.

Wimer, S. and Kelley, H. H. (1982). An investigation of the dimensions of causal attribution. *Journal of Personality and Social Psychology* **43**, 1142–1162

Winer, B. J. (1962). *Statistical principles in experimental design.* New York: McGraw-Hill

Wish, M. and Kaplan, S. (1977). Toward an implicit theory of interpersonal communication. *Sociometry* **40**, 234–246

Wittgenstein, L. (1953). *Philosophical investigations.* Oxford: Blackwell

Woll, S. and Yopp, H. (1978). The role of context and inference in the comprehension of social action. *Journal of Experimental Social Psychology* **14**, 351–362

Wortman, C. B., Costanzo, P. R. and Witt, T. R. (1973). Effect of anticipated performance on the attributions of causality to self and other. *Journal of Personality and Social Psychology* **27**, 372–381

Wright, D. (1971). *The psychology of moral behaviour.* Harmondsworth, Middlesex: Penguin

Wyer, R. S., Jr. and Carlston, D. E. (1979). *Social cognition, inference and attribution.* Hillside, N.J.: Erlbaum

Young, G. (1979). *Selective perception in neurotics.* Unpublished doctoral dissertation, Oxford University

Zuckerman, M. (1978). Sensation seeking and psychopathy. *In* R. Harré and D. Scalling (eds) *Psychopathic behaviour.* New York: Wiley

# Author Index

# Subject Index